CASTLES
Made of
SAND

CASTLES
Made of
SAND

A Century of Anglo-American Espionage
and Intervention in the Middle East

André Gerolymatos

Thomas Dunne Books ⚏ New York
St. Martin's Press

THOMAS DUNNE BOOKS.
An imprint of St. Martin's Press.

CASTLES MADE OF SAND. Copyright © 2010 by André Gerolymatos. All rights reserved. Printed in the United States of America. For information, address St. Martin's Press, 175 Fifth Avenue, New York, N.Y. 10010.

www.thomasdunnebooks.com
www.stmartins.com

Book design by Susan Yang

ISBN 978-0-312-35569-2

First Edition: December 2010

10 9 8 7 6 5 4 3 2 1

TO BEVERLEY,

the beautiful sunsets are never ending.

○○

CONTENTS

ACKNOWLEDGMENTS

This project has been a unique journey that has afforded me the opportunity to gain insight into the complex and, at times, tragic history of Anglo-American intelligence operations and their impact on the Muslim world from the Middle East to South Asia.

If this book falls short of achieving its objectives, and for any errors, the fault is mine; however, it is my pleasant duty to thank all those who have given of their time and energy in order for me to complete this study. As always, I am grateful to my agent, Bill Hanna, whose support and guidance over the years has made it possible for me to undertake and complete several books. I also would like to acknowledge Thomas Dunne of St. Martin's Press for having faith in this project and Rob Kirkpatrick for his insightful editorial suggestions and valuable comments.

I am thankful to Graham Fuller, a former vice chairman of the National Intelligence Council of the CIA, for useful comments on parts of the manuscript. Furthermore, I am indebted to Professors Amikam Nachmani and Shlomo Shpiro at Bar Ilan University for their valuable help with research in Israel. The support of the Social Sciences and Humanities Research Council of Canada provided me with a generous grant that made the research possible.

The book would not have been realized without a group of students from Simon Fraser University who ably assisted me in the research phase. Vanessa Rockel and Julian Brooks worked with me from the beginning and later were joined by Adrian O'Sullivan, Kelly Hammond, Simon Pratt, Lucia Petersen, and Inbal Negbi. I am appreciative of the staff of the Hellenic Studies Program, Maria Hamilton and Trina Mateus, for their help with a variety of administrative tasks.

Finally, to my wife, Beverley, editor, lifelong companion, and best friend for her patience, encouragement, and faith in me, I owe the greatest debt.

PREFACE

Anglo-American intelligence operations hold a unique place in the history of Middle East and Muslim politics. Directly and indirectly, first British and later American intelligence officers served as catalysts to events that forever changed the region. During the colonial period, from the nineteenth century to the end of the Second World War, the men (and a few women) of the covert services were a critical part of the control mechanism that enabled the British Empire to rule the Middle East and South Asia with minimal military forces. The method of control adopted by the British, and followed by the Americans, was to try to exploit Islam as an ally in maintaining their hegemony over the region.

The rapid decolonization of the Middle East after the Second World War coincided with an Arab nationalism that swept aside the corrupt monarchies of the Middle East (later the new secular rulers indulged in the same corruption). The rapid change challenged how London and Washington perceived the future development of the Middle East and how they coped with the aggressive Soviets, who were ready to establish their own hegemony over the region. However, the wartime allies, notwithstanding the special Anglo-American relationship, did not share a common approach in dealing with the postcolonial Middle East. In 1956, the British, along with the French and Israelis attempted to use raw military power to impose their will on Egypt's Gamal Abdel Nasser and regain control of the Suez Canal, but the effort ended in dismal failure when the United States condemned the operation.

Although the Americans were opposed to colonialism and while President Dwight Eisenhower fumed over the Suez Crisis debacle, the CIA was trying to implement Operation Straggle to overthrow the government of Syria. Consequently, it was not that Washington was opposed to interference in the Middle East, but rather to the British mechanisms of intervention. The American preference was for the use of covert operations with a penchant for coups led by a favorite regional puppet. But the frequent exposure of failed CIA coups made a mockery of secrecy, revealing naked American intervention. A climate of pending conspiracy anticipating American machinations prevailed in the capitals of most of the Middle East countries, particularly those that followed either a policy of neutrality or maintained warm relations with the Soviet Union.

Nonalignment and failure to cater to American strategic and economic interests guaranteed U.S. intervention through the CIA.

In Syria, the American efforts (sometimes in concert with the British) at
regime change ultimately solidified the dictatorship of Hafiz al-Asad and expanded Soviet influence in Damascus as well as in Cairo. Not remarkably, the
same cycle of coups and countercoups followed American policy in Iraq and
led to the dictatorship of Saddam Hussein.

After the Second World War, and until September 11, 2001, the role of British
and American intelligence services in the Middle East remained relatively obscure. In the public imagination, spies working for the CIA and MI6 were primarily identified with operations against the Soviet Union in Europe, to a
lesser extent in South America, and only rarely with events in the Middle East
or South Asia.

Interest in the Middle East was generally limited to oil supplies and the price
of gasoline, punctuated by the highjacking of airplanes by the PLO, the Palestine
Liberation Organization, and a terrorist outrage in Israel. There were exceptions,
when the Middle East came to the forefront of events, such as during the 1980s,
when Muslim extremists in Lebanon kidnapped American diplomats and CIA
officers. The 444-day drama of the American hostages in Tehran and the cata-
strophic failure of the CIA and U.S. Special Forces to effect a rescue captured
public interest, but it dissipated after the hostages were released. The Middle East
dominated the headlines for a short period with the onset of the first Persian Gulf
War, but interest waned again after the successful end of the conflict.

Fundamentally, the Middle East, and certainly South Asia, pose the greatest challenge to Western security and a major problem for Anglo-American
secret services. Berlin and the Eastern bloc may have served as the backdrop to
the Cold War, but Cairo, Jerusalem, Beirut, Damascus, and the Northwest
Frontier command the attention of the CIA, MI6, and the successor organizations of the KGB.

The tragedy of 9/11 and the rhetoric of weapons of mass destruction that
escalated into the War on Terror that preceded the second Persian Gulf War in
March 2003 will forever filter perceptions of the Middle East. Over the course
of both conflicts, Saddam Hussein became a household demon and the central
figure in the War on Terror. Indeed, the new enemy in Iraq quickly superseded
the short-term American victory in Afghanistan.

The demonized Hussein was only one of a series of Middle East strongmen
and dictators who were, depending on the occasion, first courted, then vilified
by the British and the Americans. In fact, the first steps down the path to 9/11
were set in motion when in the 1950s the Americans began to flirt with militant

Islamic organizations to checkmate Arab nationalism. In this context the Saddam Hussein type of bogeyman mirrored U.S. attitudes toward Abdel Nasser in the 1950s. Remarkably, both men initially had been covert allies of the United States and to a considerable degree owed their achieving power to the machinations of the CIA.

But, ultimately, Hussein and Nasser were just two in a parade of characters spewed out by the upheavals of the post-Ottoman Muslim world. Indeed, the eclipse of the Ottoman Empire and the termination of the Caliphate led to the destabilization of the spiritual center of the Sunni Muslim community. Ironically, both the American intelligence services and the followers of political Islam, with divergent interests, have been trying to find a suitable replacement. What follows is a modest attempt to tell the story of the efforts of the Anglo-American intelligence community to find a credible substitute for the Caliphate in order to contain nationalist and other unwelcome leadership stirring in the Muslim world.

The focus of this book is the history of British and American intelligence establishments and the Muslim organizations they tried to exploit. Although it has not been possible to examine all the countries of the Muslim world in detail because of the lack of sources, some such as Egypt, Arabia, Israel, Syria, Iran, and the region of South Asia offer excellent historical case studies to understand the relationship between the Anglo-American intelligence communities and Islam. This study is an account of the historical events that were, to a considerable extent, catalysts to 9/11 and its aftermaths in Iraq and Afghanistan.

A NOTE ON SOURCES

Writing intelligence history on the basis of archival records can be a baffling exercise in frustration. Of course, it comes as no surprise that the U.S. government should want to conceal documents that might connect Western intelligence agencies with Islamic fundamentalist groups in the aftermath of the events of September 11, 2001. However, the scale of the reclassification of intelligence-related documents has been described as excessive.[1]

A case in point would be the experience of two of my researchers who in the spring of 2006 looked for files regarding alleged OSS and early CIA contacts with radical Islamic organizations. When informed of their project, a CIA archivist just laughed, saying that the files were classified and inaccessible. In fact, a digital archive of CIA files is available through the CIA's CREST computer database, but many of these declassified files are heavily sanitized.

For example, my search for a CIA officer who reportedly met regularly with Muslim Brotherhood founder Hassan al-Banna turned up only a few trivialities, such as an invitation to the agent's retirement party. A State Department archivist was not much more encouraging, suggesting that the best avenue would be to go through department files in relevant geographical areas, on the chance that one might find a document that was missed by the censors. While this strategy did reveal some interesting anecdotes and circumstantial evidence, it did not yield documentation that would provide concrete proof of connections between intelligence operatives and Islamic militants.

President Bill Clinton's Executive Order 12958 of 1995 required the release of all classified U.S. government historical records after twenty-five years. However, thanks to the work of former National Security Agency officer Matthew M. Aid, it became publicly known in 2006 that various American government agencies had been involved in several large-scale document reclassification projects. Because of resistance to EO 12958 by the CIA and other American intelligence agencies, only 1,400 documents were actually reclassified between 1999 and 2000. Under the administration of George W. Bush the reclassification program was endorsed and expanded. It was further intensified after the events of 9/11, which led to a revision of EO 12958. Since 2001, some 9,500 documents have been reclassified, often in a somewhat wholesale fashion. Many of these documents concern intelligence dating back to the Second World War.[2]

If the Americans cut swaths with a sword, British censors tend to operate with scalpels. There are plenty of declassified files in the British archives that concern topics of potential interest to intelligence historians. The release of such files during the 1990s can be credited to the Waldergrave Initiative, launched in 1992 to release more documents to the public. Prominent intelligence historian Richard Aldrich calls the initiative a "qualified success" in terms of the quantity of material released.[3] Aldrich points to major breakthroughs, such as the release of records concerning British intelligence operations to investigate military science in Warsaw Pact countries during the Cold War, but other areas remain less accessible. As my researchers discovered, it is often not that a file has been withheld, but that it has been "weeded" of its key documents that might yield vital evidence. According to Aldrich, weeding can be of varying quality, involving weeders who know little of the material they are working on nor the subject area in general.[4]

One weeder with plenty of experience is J. R. Green of the Prime Minister's Office. Mr. Green's treatment of the Records of the Prime Minister's Office (PREM) has touched a number of files relevant to this study. Some documents have been removed from files, while others have been removed and destroyed. For instance PREM 11/515—regarding Iran in the months prior to the 1953 Anglo-American coup—has had some twenty-nine documents removed. By the British National Archives' own admission, many of the recently released records of the security service have been heavily weeded. Most of these files contain only photocopies; some pages have words blacked out.

Notwithstanding the obstructions and the efforts of the likes of Mr. Green, the CIA, and the Bush minions, sufficient documents have survived that, combined with diaries, autobiographies, biographies, and histories of the region, have enabled this historian to piece together the history of Anglo-American intelligence in the Middle East. There are other sources; however, I would rather keep such information from the weeders in the U.S. and U.K. archives. Despite these drawbacks, I am grateful to the staff of the National Archives in Maryland and Kew for their help in wading through thousands of documents. Like many researchers, I wish that John Taylor, a pioneer in archival research and one who guided me in the initial stage of this work, had lived to see the publication of this book.

CASTLES
Made of
SAND

PROLOGUE:
STORIES FROM THE BAZAAR

The storyteller sits on a tattered rug spread across the grime and dust of the ground near the edge of the bazaar.[1] He will mesmerize his audience with stories of war, intrigue, and guile from a bygone golden age. In the modest bazaars of small towns and out-of-the-way neighborhoods in large cities, he is the connection between past and present, and a sojourn into escapism for the humble folk who can spare a coin or two. The priests and mullahs may have the souls of the faithful, but this street historian captures and holds their imagination—if only for a brief time.

A man such as our storyteller lacks the practical skills to secure employment in the cities or villages and drifts from place to place scratching out a living on the fringes of society. In the Balkans, men such as these are usually Gypsies leading a tumbleweed existence from town to town, effortlessly crossing in and out of state borders.

In the Middle East, storytellers do not belong to the nomadic tribes that have drifted across the deserts for millennia. Besides, such men would be too old and too weary to take part in punishing raids for booty or revenge. Our storyteller is equally unsuitable to the dozens of secret societies and paramilitary organizations challenging local authorities for control of the street. No, our conjurer of tales is a loner. His stories are distilled from a variety of conspiracy theories legitimized over time and by sheer repetition, as well as from historical accounts filtered through myth and legend. Yet, despite the inaccuracies and convoluted interpretations of the past, for a brief moment in time, the storyteller reigns supreme in the marketplace.

After a small crowd gathers, the storyteller is ready to begin his performance. He shifts the weight of his body and, crossing his legs, settles in a comfortable position. His theme is the Crusades, but more importantly the story that he cobbles together from parts of history, myth, and conspiracy theory will stress that the success of Western armies was a shabby victory won by subterfuge, clandestine tricks, and unspeakably brutal force. For an instant, he glances at the eager faces of the young and the expectant faces of the old who have distilled into a small crowd around him. He takes a deep gulp of the cool evening air and in a soft melodic voice begins his tale with the hindsight of nostalgia.

In the late 1950s, I came across such a storyteller in a small bazaar on the outskirts of Athens. He transfixed his audience with tragic and grisly tales spun out of the Crusades. He was a Gypsy, and the bazaar at that time was as common in Greece as it is today in some parts of the Middle East. It struck me that he drew on the Crusades for the theme of his stories and assumed that, by elaborating on the cruelty of Western Christians against the Muslims, this theme would find resonance with an Eastern Orthodox audience. He was not far off, at least with respect to the Fourth Crusade.

In the convoluted cauldron of Balkan myth and legend, the sack of Constantinople by the Fourth Crusade in 1204 remains a bitter and painful legacy. Accordingly, the sympathy of the Eastern Orthodox, insofar as the Fourth Crusade is concerned, lies with the Muslims; the Franks (the general name for the Crusaders) are depicted as the scourge of civilization.

My storyteller also touched on another important theme that appealed to his audience—the notion of waging war against a superior force by subterfuge, cunning, espionage, and intrigue. Generally the role of spy and saboteur is frowned upon by most cultures and considered beneath the martial dignity of a warrior, although in times of defeat and occupation by a foreign opponent it was, and still is, acceptable in most societies to resort to clandestine warfare.[2] In the Middle East, such stories (along with others) of deception, espionage, and subterfuge are transmitted via the unofficial culture that exists (and continues to do so) beyond the watchful eye of the authorities.

As was the case in the bazaar in Athens, which operated without official sanction, the marketplace in the Middle East is a venue for the transmission of unedited ideas and information carried by word of mouth that provide the building blocks of legend and mythology. The "Arab Street," the masses that make up the urban poor, feed on the retelling of a variety of stories, including that of the Crusades, along with ample doses of conspiracy theories. At the end of the twentieth century, the notion of the Crusades as a grand conspiracy of the West received new impetus when in 1990 President George H. W. Bush proclaimed "a new world order."

Although Bush's remarks referred to the post–Cold War era in the Middle East, writes the controversial Daniel Pipes, "the phrase was widely understood as signaling a plan for 'the United States, master of the new world' to establish hegemony over the entire globe."[3] Hence perceptions in the Middle East point to the "new world order" as further evidence of a policy of "crushing Islam and its people" and "a Jewish plan for a Greater Israel and a Christian 'spirit of the Crusades.'"[4]

Yet this conspiracy theory is a by-product of the legacy of the Crusades that has continued to resonate in the region since the end of the thirteenth century. As noted by Carole Hillenbrand, Akbar Ahmed, a prominent Islamic scholar, remarks:

> The memory of the Crusades lingers in the Middle East and colours Muslim perceptions of Europe. It is the memory of an aggressive, backward and religiously fanatic Europe. This historical memory would be reinforced in the nineteenth and twentieth centuries as imperial Europeans once again arrived to subjugate and colonize territories in the Middle East. Unfortunately this legacy of bitterness is overlooked by most Europeans when thinking of the Crusades.[5]

Another scholar, Amin Maalouf, echoes with similar sentiments:

> It is often surprising to discover the extent to which the attitude of the Arabs (and of Muslims in general) towards the West is still influenced, even today, by events that supposedly ended some seven centuries ago.
>
> Today, on the eve of the third millennium, the political and religious leaders of the Arab world constantly refer to Saladin, to the fall of Jerusalem and its recapture. In the popular mind, and in some official discourse too, Israel is regarded as a new Crusader state. . . . In his days of glory, President Nasser was regularly compared to Saladin, who, like him, had united Syria and Egypt—and even Yemen! The Arabs perceived the Suez expedition of 1956 as a Crusade by the French and the English, similar to that of 1191.[6]

More recently, Osama bin Laden has frequently used the term "Crusaders" and "Crusade" in his characterization of the West and its role in the Middle East. But it was President George W. Bush who inadvertently linked the Crusades with the clandestine war on the extremists and fanatics in the Muslim world. In a speech on the future course of American action eight days after 9/11, he cast the war against terror (what essentially would be a series of intelligence and covert operations) as "a crusade" against terrorism, thus inadvertently invoking the specter of a religious, as well as secular, conflict against Islam.

Perhaps this is not such an outlandish concept. In the Middle East, the Crusades inexplicably continue to cast a long shadow. These "holy" wars between

East and West have filtered the perceptions of the West to generations of Muslims. In the present, these notions are further reinforced by the exigencies of the war on terror waged by covert means around the world and primarily aimed against Muslims, as well as by the ground conflicts in Iraq and Afghanistan.

Like the Crusades, this conflict is waged essentially outside the rules of war. Notorious though the concept of crusading may be, however, it has always been subject, by and large, to a set of self-imposed regulations observed by warring states in the West. Their genesis originated in the medieval code of chivalry, but they only applied to fellow Christians. The twentieth-century Geneva Convention, on the other hand, was designed for conventional warfare and did not make provisions for covert operations or espionage.[7] So, in this context, both the Crusades and the murky world of covert operations are conflicts waged without recourse to any universal rules.

In the twentieth and twenty-first centuries, both the Anglo-American and the Axis intelligence organizations (followed later by the Soviets) became the point of contact between the West and the nationalists, militant Muslim groups, and any other radicals in the Middle East. Necessity in the First and Second World Wars created the momentum for a secret relationship between the intelligence services of Great Britain (and later the United States) with the emerging secular radicals in the various Arab nationalist movements and conservative religious organizations, such as the Muslim Brotherhood. The Anglo-American secret services desperately needed agents to use, first against the Ottomans and later against the Axis, and finally as a means to contain the rising Arab nationalism that British operatives such as T. E. Lawrence had helped to instigate in 1916. In most cases the relationship was, at best, qualified by expediency and mutual suspicion.

Throughout the course of this unusual association, the Middle Eastern perceptions of the British and Americans, as well as of other representatives of the Western powers, were—and still are—to a degree defined by the Crusades. Hence the Crusades are, at least for most Muslims, part of the negative cultural construct that has typified the Western presence in the region.

The Crusaders not only brought war and destruction to the Middle East; they also attempted to graft European medieval feudalism onto an entrenched culture and religion that anchored the societies of the freshly conquered territories to a different reality. For instance, the most important nobles assumed regal titles and carved out their realms as islands of Christendom within a sea of Islamic civilization.

Despite the eventual triumph of Islam in the Holy Land, the Crusades engendered a cycle of defeat for many Muslims. They also serve as stock themes for the blend of mythology, history, and romanticism with which storytellers entertain the Arab Street in the bazaar. To radical Muslim and Arab nationalists, the struggle against the European hegemony (and later the United States), as well as against those Muslims perceived to be working with the West, had to be waged underground through urban warfare, assassination, propaganda, espionage, and subversion.

One such instance is the 1979 incident that took place in the Great Mosque of Mecca.[8] In the early morning of November 20, just before the beginning of the Islamic New Year, approximately two hundred well-armed men, as well as women and children, seized the al-Masjid al-Haram Mosque in Mecca. Most of them were students at the Islamic University of Medina, and some were locals, as well as Muslims from other countries. They were led by Juhaiman al-Utaibi and Abdullah ah-Qahtani. Utaibi came from a prominent Arab family, and he, along with the other militants, were members of the puritanical Wahhabi sect, which is also the official state version of Islam in Saudi Arabia.

A number of the militants were also members of the Egyptian Muslim Brotherhood, a radical organization calling for a return to pure Islam and the overthrow of secular governments throughout the Islamic world.[9] The presence of Brotherhood adherents in Saudi Arabia was an example of regional blowback. King Faysal had invited the MB to Arabia in the 1960s as part of a scheme to undermine Nasser of Egypt. Nasser had ruthlessly suppressed the Brotherhood because of its opposition to his rule, as well as its religious militancy.[10] Many MB members accepted Faysal's asylum and became active in several of the new religious universities established by the Saudi royal family and had come into contact with Juhaiman al-Utaibi and Abdullah al-Qahtani.

The capture of the Great Mosque was not only a religious act but was also meant to stir up an Islamic uprising against the Saudi royal family. After he took over the mosque, Utaibi announced that he and his followers were condemning the House of Saud for its moral laxity, corruption, and the destruction of Saudi culture by imitating the West. According to him, the Saudi monarchy had lost its legitimacy and thus had to be removed. He also proclaimed that Abdullah al-Qahtani was the true "Mahdi"[11] and asked the imam leading the morning prayers to proclaim him as such.[12]

The seizure of one of the most sacred mosques in Islam stunned Muslims throughout the world and had considerable repercussions for the United States and its allies. A flurry of rumors, conspiracy theories, and outright fantasies carried the crisis in Mecca to every corner of the Muslim world. In Islamabad, Pakistan, a Pakistani newspaper proclaimed that an American operation was in the process of landing a task force in Arabia in order to take control of the Persian Gulf. A short while later the same newspaper revealed that Israeli paratroopers were to be dropped on Mecca or Medina, perhaps both. The theocratic regime in Tehran immediately accused the United States and Israel.

> It is not far far-fetched to assume that this act has been perpetrated by the criminal American imperialism so that it can infiltrate the solid ranks of Muslims by such intrigues. It would not be far-fetched to assume that, as it has often indicated, Zionism intends to make the House of God Vulnerable.[13]

On November 21, the day after the Grand Mosque was seized, Pakistani students and militants from Pakistan's militant Islamic organizations stormed the American embassy in Islamabad and burned down the building as Pakistani police and security forces slowly came to the rescue of the Americans. The howling mobs were driven by the conviction that the United States had seized the Grand Mosque and they had to exact vengeance.[14] Although a major Kuwaiti newspaper, *al-Siyassa,* published large extracts of the musings of the rebels in the Grand Mosque on November 29, many Muslims continued to assume that the capture of the mosque was the work of a variety of hostile foreigners. Mobs of young militant Muslims and students attacked American institutions in Turkey, India, and Bangladesh and stormed the American embassy in Tripoli, Libya.

The Saudi government sealed off Mecca and severed all communications within the kingdom and between the kingdom and the outside world, in order to rule out the possibility of a coup supported by a foreign power. At the same time, any military action to retake the mosque had to wait because of the real possibility that the building would be damaged, thus earning for the Saudi royal family the enmity of the Muslim world. The question on whether to use force was submitted to the Ulema (the religious establishment), which, after some deliberation, sanctioned government use of force to remove the militants from the mosque.[15]

Once they got the green light, the Saudis deployed the National Guard, but their assault failed with the loss of twenty-one soldiers killed. What followed remains ensnared in purposeful obscurity. According to some accounts, the recapture of the mosque was accomplished by Pakistani troops in conjunction with French paratroopers. Others have proposed that there were some foreign troops but do not name them, while some make no reference to the presence of non-Muslims.[16]

Robert Fisk provides another explanation. He argues that the Saudis deployed ten thousand troops to retake the building, but many of the militants
escaped into the labyrinth of caves and tunnels beneath the mosque. In the
process the troops flooded the tunnels with water and inserted electric cables
in order to electrocute the rebels.[17] In actual fact this did not take place. The
retaking of the Grand Mosque was accomplished by Saudi troops under the
direction of a French antiterrorist unit.

Officers from a French special unit, Groupe d'Intervention de la Gen-
darmerie Nationale (GIGN) were brought to Mecca two weeks later and trained
a select number of Saudi military. Under French supervision, from afar, the
Saudis hunted down the militants by flooding the basement of the mosque and
its tunnels with a chemical, dichlorobenzylidene-malononitrile (CB), which is
essentially an irritant that blocks respiration and inhibits aggressiveness and
nonlethal as long as the subject of the attack is removed in less than five minutes.[18] The operation was successful and a large number of the insurgents were
captured. A short while later, sixty-three of the militants were publicly beheaded on January 9, 1980.

The event, regardless of the significance it had for the Saudi royal family—as
well as for its major ally the United States and the Muslim world in general—was
quickly overtaken by the Soviet invasion of Afghanistan and the aftershocks of
the Ayatollah Khomeini's revolution in Iran. For most of the outside world, the
incident at the Great Mosque was just that: yet another episode in a series of
confrontations between radicals and state authority in the tumultuous Middle
East. However, the rebels who challenged the legitimacy of the Saudi dynasty
also signaled the rise of militant Sunni Islam in its various manifestation
throughout the Muslim world.

But in 1979–1980 it was Khomeini's brand of Shiite Islam that was of major
concern to the West and to the conservative regimes of the Middle East. Indeed, the United States was beginning to tap into the militant stream of Wahhabism in order to secure Islamic mujahidin (freedom fighters) for the covert
war against the Soviet Union in Afghanistan. The Saudis, as well as other Middle
East governments, anxious to get rid of potential troublemakers and to be of
assistance to the Americans, killed two birds with one stone and facilitated the
transportation of these new covert warriors to the Islamic jihad (holy war) in
Afghanistan, including the infamous Osama bin Laden.[19]

In that unfortunate country, under the tutelage of experts from the Central Intelligence Agency working through Pakistan's Inter-Services Intelligence
(ISI) agency, the mujahidin learned the tradecraft of espionage, sabotage, commando operations, psychological warfare, and counterintelligence, which they

later successfully employed against the West.[20] In cases where the U.S. Congress had placed restrictions on some practices, the CIA outsourced them to the British. Gus Avrakotos, a veteran CIA officer who took part in organizing the jihad against the Soviets, commented:

> The Brits were eventually to buy things that we couldn't because it infringed on murder, assassination, and indiscriminate bombings. They could issue guns with silencers. We couldn't do that because a silencer immediately implied assassination—and heaven forbid car bombs! No way I could even suggest it, but I could say to the Brits, "Fadlallah in Beirut was really effective last week. They had a car bomb that killed three hundred people." I gave MI6 stuff in good faith. What they did with it was always their business.[21]

Although Afghanistan was the culmination of covert operations by the United States, the relationship between the Muslim militants, as well as nationalists, and the intelligence organizations of the West emerged from the First World War. Part of the British intelligence community remained focused on the Northwest Frontier, while other elements focused on Egypt.

ONE

Assassination

"What's all this nonsense about isolating Nasser?
I want him destroyed, can't you understand?"
—*Anthony Eden to Anthony Nutting*[1]

At 7:31 P.M. on a pleasantly cool evening with a light breeze from the sea, Gamal Abdel Nasser stood on the podium and began to speak—slowly and quietly at first. Then he grew excited, waving his right hand in sweeping gestures, and soon the crowd responded. Torrents of applause washed over him each time he recalled the past, to highlight Egypt's struggle for independence. Close to 250,000 spectators had jammed into the Midan el Tahir (Place of Liberation) in Alexandria on Tuesday, October 26, 1954, to hear Nasser proclaim the end of British rule in Egypt. Earlier, on October 19, Nasser had signed the formal Evacuation Agreement with Britain's representatives, but Tuesday was reserved for jubilation with the people of Egypt.[2]

As Nasser progressed through his speech, in the eighth row in front of the podium, a round-faced man with a clump of black hair hanging down over his forehead stood up. His hand shook slightly as he aimed a .36 caliber Italian revolver at Nasser and began shooting. The first bullet went wild. The second hit an electric light globe near Nasser's head. The man fired six more times, but remarkably he missed the Egyptian strongman.[3] Nasser heard the deadly explosions streaming past him, blinked, and brushed pieces of the shattered light globe from his shoulders. Despite the near-death experience, he remained calm and, looking at the crowd, shouted over and over: "This is Gamel Abdel Nasser speaking to you. My blood is your blood. My life is yours. You are all Gamel Abdel Nassers. If I had been killed, it would have made no difference, for you would carry on the struggle. You are all Gamel Abdel Nassers."[4]

Initial reports on Mahmud Abd al-Latif could not agree if the would-be assassin was a tinsmith, a carpenter, or a plumber. Eventually the authorities determined that he was a thirty-two-year-old tinsmith from Cairo and had been a Muslim Brother for sixteen years. After torture, he confessed that he had not acted alone but was part of a greater conspiracy organized by the Muslim Brotherhood to kill Nasser and eventually other members of the Revolutionary

Command Council. According to Latif, the MB contacted him in early October, and he had chosen to act on October 19, the day that Nasser signed the new Anglo-Egyptian treaty, which was condemned by the Brotherhood as an act of treason because it afforded the British the opportunity to reoccupy the Suez Canal in case of war. But he could not find the appropriate opportunity to execute the plan until October 26.[5] Although the treaty infuriated the Muslim Brothers, the failure of the Free Officers, who had seized power in 1952, to transform Egypt into an Islamic state was the primary motive for the plot to kill Nasser and overthrow the government.

The Muslim Brothers were not the only ones who despised Nasser enough to kill him. Anthony Eden, Britain's last imperial prime minister, had developed an almost pathological hatred for Egypt's new hero. In a fit of fury, Eden had ordered MI6, the British intelligence service, to kill Nasser at all costs.[6] Nasser, however, was convinced that the British were in collusion with the MB and said so in a victory speech on December 21, 1965, in which he accused the Brotherhood of holding conspiratorial meetings at the British embassy in Cairo.[7]

There may have been a grain of truth in this accusation, because MI6 had never quite developed sufficient expertise to deal with assassination and often outsourced such activity. During the course of the Second World War, for example, MI6 employed third parties to eliminate problematical Axis agents, but special operations and killing were practiced with considerable skill by its wartime equivalent, the Special Operations Executive (SOE). After the war, MI6 absorbed some sections of the SOE that included individuals who had experience in assassination into its Special Operations Branch, but elimination of unwanted elements was still farmed out to third parties. Although the British government had abandoned assassination as part of clandestine warfare by 1950, it continued to receive credence within certain ranks of MI6.[8]

Overall, the British attempts to kill Nasser, with one possible exception, bordered on the ludicrous. One plan involved flooding the ventilation system in one of Nasser's headquarters with nerve gas, but Eden rescinded it in favor of a joint French-Israeli operation that failed to bear fruit.[9] Another effort relied on using a group of renegade Egyptian officers, but that too collapsed when the weapons to be used proved defective. MI6 also contemplated using a dart tipped with poison and fired from a cigarette pack, but that also was scrapped because it would have been impossible to avoid a direct link between the British and Nasser's death.[10]

In 1956, a German mercenary was hired to murder the Egyptian leader. When he arrived in Cairo, however, the Egyptian authorities received an anonymous warning about him, and he surreptitiously left the country.[11] Other comic-book-style endeavors included giving Nasser a box of spiked chocolates and finding someone willing to lace his food with strychnine.[12]

Remarkably, after almost seventy years of dominion over Egyptian affairs, by the early 1950s the British presence in that country was rapidly fading. MI6 controlled a handful of agents in place, but few in senior positions in the Egyptian military and political establishment. Operating out of the well-respected Arab News Agency (ANA), however, Britain's intelligence service did manage to establish links with radical student and religious groups, as well as with cashiered officers. Other contacts included ties to the ousted royalist groups and exiled politicians.

Unfortunately, in 1956, what was left of MI6's intelligence network collapsed. In August of that year, the Egyptian security service raided the British-controlled ANA and arrested thirty of its staff, as well as expelling two members of the British embassy. The ANA not only served as a cover for MI6 in Cairo but also for intelligence operations throughout Egypt and the Middle East. Some of its agents were Britons working in Egypt as businessmen, journalists, or teachers, while the Egyptian agents were royalists and opponents of the Nasser regime.[13]

According to the Egyptian secret police, the Mukhabarat, those arrested constituted an espionage ring that, in addition to conducting intelligence work, was also planning the overthrow of the government. Of the thirty arrested, two Britons were eventually acquitted, while James Swinburn, the business manager of the ANA, was convicted in May 1957. Some of the Egyptians were executed, and others faced long prison sentences.[14] Other Britons, such as the representative of the Prudential Assurance Company, John Stanley, along with Alexander Reynolds, George Sweet, and George Rose, had already left for Britain and were tried in absentia.[15]

Swinburn, the accused ringleader of the plot, was subjected to intensive interrogation and confessed to collecting information on military deployments, confidential political meetings, Alexandria's defenses, and coordinating missions to communist countries. The Mukhabarat also claimed that documents found in Swinburn's house included reports on the disposition of Egyptian military units, information on new Soviet-built tank transports, antitank weapons, and considerable details on a new radar station on the outskirts of Cairo. Other agents working under journalistic cover provided by the ANA reported on communist activities in the Middle East.[16] The head of the ANA, Tom Little, who was a correspondent for *The Economist* and *The Times,* was the senior MI6 officer in Cairo, but the Egyptians left him free and fed him considerable disinformation, so that he could pass it on to MI6.[17]

J. G. Gove, head of the visa section of the British embassy, and J. B. Flux, commercial first secretary, had supervised the clandestine network and were expelled by the Egyptian government.[18] Mohamed Heikal, Nasser's confidant and longtime friend, writes that the two British diplomats had also been in contact with "student elements of a religious inclination" with the purpose of instigating Islamic fundamentalist riots and thus provoking foreign military intervention to protect the Europeans.[19] There is little doubt that the student elements were members of the Muslim Brotherhood or had links to the remnants of the organization.

Although the British lost a major intelligence network in Cairo and the Middle East, they persisted in trying to destabilize Egypt's government by a coup or by the assassination of Nasser. In 1953, MI6 recruited Mahmud Khalil, after he was appointed head of the intelligence directorate of the Egyptian air force. Khalil was first approached in August by Hussein Khayri, former deputy head of Egypt's military intelligence prior to the overthrow of the monarchy in 1952. Khalil remained cautious and noncommittal.

A few weeks later, the two men met at the Riviera Hotel in Beirut, and on this occasion Khayri introduced the Egyptian officer to John Farmer of MI6. During the course of this meeting, Khalil agreed to form a secret organization of Egyptian officers, with the aim of implementing a coup against the Nasser regime. Khalil, however, set one nonnegotiable condition—that he be in charge and the go-between for the British and the conspirators. Farmer accepted and handed over to Khalil an envelope containing £1,000. However, Khalil insisted that he would require at least £100,000 to maintain his organization, so Farmer agreed that sometime in the future this sum would be made available.[20]

Meanwhile, MI6 continued to hatch a variety of means to terminate Nasser, including Operation Unfasten, an unorthodox plan to be executed by Khalil's secret organization in Cairo. This particular plot was a cross between a comic-book fantasy and a James Bond movie. In actual fact, Operation Unfasten revolved around Nasser's beard. The Egyptian strongman had a heavy beard, which forced him to shave several times a day. The MI6 plan called for giving Nasser a Remington electric shaver filled with plastic explosive that would detonate the moment he switched the shaver on.[21]

In the meantime, MI6 wove an elaborate scheme to protect Khalil as a source. In order to justify Khalil's frequent journeys (secret meetings with representatives from MI6) to foreign countries, the British passed to him valuable intelligence about Israel, as well as providing substantial funds to maintain the secret organization of Egyptian army officers. Although bilateral relations between Britain and Israel were good, as they were between

Mossad (Israel's intelligence service) and MI6, the British had few qualms about divulging material detrimental to the Israelis to Khalil, in order to make their agent look good. Later, Yaacov Caroz, deputy chief of Mossad, wrote: "Harming Israel's security by handing over secret information about her did not apparently trouble the conscience of the British."[22] However, in the murky world of espionage, to paraphrase an oft-quoted maxim, "there is no such thing as a friendly intelligence agency, only rival agencies of friendly countries."

The plan to kill Nasser was shelved temporarily, although MI6 continued to shop around for a coup. From late August to early September 1957, Julian Amery and Neil "Billy" McLean, accompanied by two MI6 officers, held several secret meetings in the south of France with exiled Egyptian royalists and members of other groups hostile to Nasser. Amery and McLean were both participants in the so-called Suez Group, a collection of backbenchers, ex-ministers, former members of Britain's intelligence community, and young and newly elected MPs opposed to any proposed changes in the Anglo-Egyptian relationship affecting the Suez Canal.[23]

Julian Amery was the son-in-law of Harold Macmillan and secretary of the Suez Group. Both McLean and Amery had been officers in the SOE during the Second World War and took part in several special operations in the postwar period. In the late 1940s, Amery had been involved with the joint MI6-CIA operation to overthrow the communist government of Albania. Amery and McLean were not the only ex-intelligence officers either; others from Britain's wartime clandestine agencies, such as Fitzroy Maclean and Lord Hankey, the father of the British modern intelligence community, were members of this imperial caucus, and they cast a long shadow over MI6.[24]

In 1958, together with John Bruce Lockhart, another former MI6 officer, Amery had helped to organize covert operations in Cyprus against the local insurgents. In particular, Amery had blackmailed Archbishop Makarios, the Greek Cypriot prelate and political leader, about his homosexuality, and had forced Makarios to make concessions to the British. In effect, the Suez Group was both a customer of MI6's intelligence product and an instigator of covert operations.

After their meetings in France, Amery and McLean traveled to Geneva to meet with representatives of the Muslim Brotherhood, although they informed MI6 that they kept this part of their trip secret from other members of the Suez Group. Their efforts resulted in the establishment in Cairo of a "shadow government" ready to seize power at the first opportunity.[25] It is not certain what took place at this encounter in Geneva between Britain's lingering imperialists and Egypt's fundamentalist Muslims, but it was not the first time that these unlikely allies had collaborated against a common enemy.

On October 29, 1956, after the Israelis, based on a prearranged secret agreement, had attacked Egypt, the British and the French seized the Suez Canal. The military attempt failed, in large measure thanks to U.S. opposition, and finally brought the curtain down on imperial Anglo-French ambitions in Egypt and the Middle East. The invasion had placed a hold on any of the covert plans, but, after the debacle, MI6 reactivated the assassination plot.

In October 1957, an MI6 courier delivered the lethal razor to Khalil, along with £166,000.[26] The Saudis may have provided part or all of the money—not the first time that Arab petrodollars would be used to finance a coup.[27] The razor failed to explode. Then, on December 23 at a massive rally in Port Said celebrating the first anniversary of the Anglo-French withdrawal from the Suez Canal, Nasser unmasked the so-called Restoration Plot and claimed Khalil was a double agent who had been working for Egypt's security service. Nasser donated the £166,000 that Khalil received to Egyptians whose property had been damaged by the British naval bombardment of Alexandria during the Suez Crisis.[28] Nasser's revelation effectively gutted what was left of Britain's intelligence capability in Egypt.

The outcome of these events demonstrated that there was little coordination between the covert activities of MI6 and the grand strategy of the British government with respect to Egypt. Insofar as the British military and Foreign Office were concerned, clandestine intervention in Egypt was reserved as a last resort. Accordingly, such last-minute attempts, hastily organized, forced MI6 to work with unreliable individuals and often double agents.

British covert efforts in Egypt failed, to a great extent, because Eden and his close partners in the cabinet preferred to bypass not only the normal process within the governmental apparatus but also the chain of command in the intelligence community. The Suez Group, with its direct links to MI6 and powerful influence over Eden and succeeding prime ministers, blurred the lines between the government and the intelligence community. For that matter, MI6 was implementing its own policy, albeit loosely based on Eden's irrational loathing of Nasser and his directive to have the Egyptian leader eliminated.

As a result, covert operations, as well as the fate of agents, were at the mercy of several masters. The use of back channels in MI6 and the propensity to employ gifted amateurs, a long tradition in the history of British special operations, fragmented any serious efforts and compromised the handful of clandestine networks in Egypt. Since MI6 did not officially exist, ultimate responsibility for failure reverted to the government, while the organization was free to continue to launch maverick operations. Scott Lucas and Alistair Morey rightly point out that "MI6 could still withhold or, worse, fabricate intelligence and neglect to pass details of operations to its Foreign Office overseers."[29]

Furthermore, the intelligence fiascos in Cairo enabled the Egyptian security service to round up most of the opposition to Nasser, thus diminishing any future opportunity to recruit Egyptian agents. Finally, the destruction of the secular opposition left the field almost exclusively to Muslim extremists. Although the Brotherhood received a serious blow in 1954 following the assassination attempt against Nasser, it survived as an organization and also took root in several countries in the Middle East. At the same time, it inspired or spawned new extremist Muslim organizations, one of which, Egyptian Islamic Jihad, succeeded in assassinating Anwar al-Sadat, Nasser's successor.[30] Two decades later, Egyptian Islamic Jihad merged with al-Qaeda into the Qaeda al-Jihad.[31]

In the future, the Anglo-American intelligence community would face the impossible task of penetrating the Muslim opposition to the nationalist governments in the region. Even when the American or British intelligence agencies managed to establish links with the Muslim opposition to the Arab secular leadership, they only did so under conditions that suited the fundamentalists and were not able to access the rank and file. For most of the twentieth century, the Muslim Brotherhood, perhaps the most significant political-religious and clandestine network, remained beyond the reach of the U.S. and British intelligence establishment.

Although the Brotherhood was shunned by more radical organizations like Egyptian Islamic Jihad and al-Qaeda, it was one step in the evolution of what is now described as "political Islam."[32] The label of "political Islam," which lacks the intensity of other descriptions such as "fundamentalist Islam," "militant Islam," or "radical Islam," is closer to defining the religious-political movement that has gripped the Muslim world. Political Islam is not, however, a phenomenon of the twentieth or twenty-first centuries, but stems in part from reaction to the European colonization of the region, as well as to the endemic corruption that has plagued the Middle East from the nineteenth century.

Colonialism, writes Adeed Dawisha, was subsumed by imperialism and became the much needed "other" for Arab nationalism. This was particularly the case at the height of Arab nationalism between 1954 and 1967, personified by the regime of Nasser. The ideological construct of anti-imperialism was based on the notion that Dawisha describes as follows: "The 'imperialist forces' were outsiders, alien to the area, had committed many injustices against the Arab people, and therefore were 'deserving' of the abuse heaped upon them."[33] When the Nasser bubble burst, following the humiliating defeat in the 1967 war with Israel, it not only underscored the failure of Arab nationalism but, along with it, secularism. For the Arabs, as well as the other Muslims of the Middle East, secular leadership and secular states became synonymous with failure and systemic corruption.

For the practitioners of political Islam, defining the historic injustices perpetrated by the West remained integral in promoting jihad against the West. One familiar theme is the Crusades. In dredging the past to explain the present, the Crusades and U.S. support of Israel (and more recently the invasion and occupation of Iraq) bracket the rhetoric that dominates the discourse of political Islam.

TWO

The Mahdi

"One is what one has the nerve to pretend to be."
—*Alan Furst*[1]

Death to the Christians!" With this cry, thousands of native Egyptians, accompanied by Bedouin, flooded into the European quarter of Alexandria on June 11, 1882.[2] The crescendo of thousands of voices, together with an army of feet pounding the streets, generated a deep roar that shattered the comfortable silence that embraces most Mediterranean cities and towns after noonday. This tidal wave of desperate humanity, roused to a murderous passion, poured into the narrow roads and alleys, crashing into the luckless Europeans found on the streets. In the initial moment of frenzy, the angry swarm greeted the foreigners with a barrage of clubs, mercilessly beating them down and trampling their victims underfoot. These clubs or *naboots,* which inflicted the most harm, were long thick pieces of wood used by the native watchmen.[3]

The instigator of the riot remained a mystery, but several developments quickly pointed to Tawfik, the Khedive of Egypt. Cartfuls of clubs had been distributed to the poor on instructions from the prefect of police, who was sympathetic to the Khedive.[4] Further evidence that the Egyptian ruler was behind the rampage that engulfed Alexandria was the presence of large numbers of armed Bedouin (also loyal to the Khedive) who had slipped into the city by the side streets and who later began to use their long rifles to shoot down Europeans.[5] Traditionally the Bedouin had little interest in constitutional reform and remained loyal to the head of state.[6] The signal for the onset of the massacre was a funeral procession accompanied by locals wearing green turbans that took place between 10:00 A.M. and noon. The dozens of warnings given to the Europeans by their Egyptian servants and tradesmen is further evidence that the pogrom unleashed in Alexandria was not spontaneous but carefully planned.

From early afternoon until sundown, mobs armed with a variety of makeshift weapons, along with some rifles and swords, attacked any foreigners on sight. Outside the Austrian post office, the frenzied horde beat to death a five-year-old boy.[7] Shortly afterward they caught a man staggering along the rue des Soeurs dripping with blood, but the sight only excited the mob, and they dispatched him with clubs. The rioters killed anyone they could get their hands on and then proceeded to strip the victims of all their belongings. That was not enough to satiate their thirst for violence; after the plunder they focused their fury on the corpses, leaving them horribly mutilated and then tossing them into the harbor.[8]

Throughout that afternoon the mob's fury gained further momentum, and more Europeans succumbed to stabbings, beatings, and gunshots. The bloodthirsty crowd poured into nearby shops, cafés, and any other establishment that was foreign-owned, to feed their anger and to fill their pockets. Members of the city's law enforcement detachments for the most part stood idly by and occasionally even joined the mob in beating to a pulp some hapless man, woman, or child who had the misfortune to seek asylum with the police. In the evening, Egyptian troops arrived, and the mob suddenly melted away. No arrests were made. However, the violent episode was merely the first act in a course of events that transferred Egyptian sovereignty from the court at Constantinople to London.

Ominously, in the harbor, Britain's Mediterranean fleet trained its guns on the city but did not fire a single shot in anger. In London, the government of William Gladstone sought a political solution in concert with the other European powers but found no takers. The French, who had initially insisted on a show of force, now backed away from any involvement, except to offer the British moral support. After a month of uneasy quiet a second riot exploded in the streets of Alexandria on July 11, leaving a longer trail of death and destruction. This time, the British fleet opened fire and began to demolish the harbor, but in the ensuing riot the looters satiated their appetite for hatred of the Europeans by consigning the city to flames. The next day, a British force of 250 sailors, along with 160 marines, established order among the burning rubble of Alexandria's European quarter. The troops came across the macabre spectacle of streets littered with mutilated corpses and of women dousing rags and mattresses with petroleum and using them to burn the remaining houses. A portent of Britain's dependency on Egypt (in addition to the Suez Canal) was the shutting down of the Egyptian post offices, which left the Eastern Telegraph Company little choice but to withdraw its staff and instruments. Communication with India stopped, and the London Stock Exchange tumbled; millions of pounds sterling evaporated.

The mobs and the violence were products of deep-seated exasperation fueled by hatred for the foreigners and encouraged, behind the scenes, by Tawfik. Egypt's wretched ruler, desperate to regain absolute power, believed that the full fury of the Great Powers would descend on the Nationalists who had diminished his power. He had tried to take advantage of a political crisis instigated by the British and French but had only succeeded in alienating the most influential sectors of Egyptian society, as well as the masses of peasants, who had to bear the brunt of the economic woes plaguing the country. Surrounded by a coterie of reactionary, landowning Turks and courtiers, Tawfik had lost touch with the realities of Egyptian society, concentrating almost exclusively on trying to out-maneuver the Nationalists and the Egyptian army. The Khedive's efforts, unfortunately, had only ushered in a series of plots and counterschemes, eventually drowning Egypt's body politic in a sea of conspiracies. Prior to the events in June and July, Tawfik's ineptitude had surrendered the political momentum for change and progress to the army, members of the Islamic establishment, and the small professional class.

The countdown to the June–July riots began in the winter of 1882, when the Chamber of Notables, whose majority was held by these groups, had proposed to give itself the right to vote on the disposition of half of Egypt's annual budget of £9 million, conceding that the other half was pledged to pay down the foreign debt. The chamber also proposed to increase military expenditures to promote native officers, as well as raising the army to eighteen thousand as decreed by the Ottoman Sultan. Unfortunately, the British and French controllers refused to relinquish their hold on Egypt's finances and rejected both recommendations.[9] Meanwhile, European bondholders, whose fortunes rested on financing the Egyptian debt, were becoming increasingly nervous at Egypt's endemic instability. The government, via the caprice of military coup, also shook the confidence of the French and British governments in Egypt's capability to pay down the enormous debts or service the interest on them.

In the late nineteenth century, financial insolvency had paved the way to gradual colonization of North Africa and the Middle East. As the rulers of the semiautonomous provinces of the Ottoman Empire foolishly fell victim to the siren call of the European moneylenders, they did not realize that with each loan they parceled out their sovereignty. Egypt's financial crisis was not unique amongst the territories of the Ottoman Sultan but part of a pattern that ushered in, in stages, European colonization of the Middle East. The Ottoman Viceroy of Tunisia, for example, had preceded the Egyptian Khedive in compiling huge debts and then declaring bankruptcy in 1869. A similar international debt commission was established, with representatives from France, Great Britain, and Italy.

However, at the Congress of Berlin in 1878, the Great Powers, not just for the sake of bond issues, but to preserve the balance of power in Europe, sacrificed the independence of Tunisia. Tunisia was the consolation prize to France for Britain's acquisition of Cyprus.[10] In April 1881, the French government took advantage of raids mounted by Tunisian tribesmen and compelled the Ottoman

Viceroy to accept a French protectorate. The Treaty of Bardo provided legal finesse to otherwise blatant annexation, but it also provoked uprisings in the south and center of the country, which were contained by the deployment of French troops. However, the rebels were joined by thousands of tribesmen, and by June the initial French success had degenerated into a protracted conflict.[11] Regardless, the French convinced themselves that rebellion in Tunisia was part of a larger Muslim uprising that would expand into a pan-Islamic movement, spilling over into Egypt and Algeria and undermining France's position in North Africa.[12]

The British, on the other hand, had little concern over the situation in Egypt and even less sympathy for the French predicament in Algeria and Tunisia. Furthermore, the liberal Gladstone was opposed to foreign interventions, and felt that, if something had to be done about the internal Egyptian crisis, it was a matter for the European Concert. Nonetheless, the Gladstone government was equally determined to maintain good relations with France and agreed to issue a Joint Note on January 8, 1882, which assured the Khedive of Anglo-French "support against the difficulties of various kinds which might interfere with the course of public affairs in Egypt." The note went on to state: "the assurance publicly given of their formal intentions in this respect will tend to avert the dangers . . . to which the Government of the Khedive might be exposed, and which would certainly find England and France united to oppose them."[13]

The Anglo-French guarantee to defend the Khedive against all enemies from within or without, reinforced by the presence of the British warships in Alexandria, set the irrevocable course that led to the riots of June and July and ultimately stifled Egypt's sovereignty. Tawfik immediately embraced the protection of the foreign powers and, at the onset of the mob violence he himself had inspired, sought refuge under the British guns in Alexandria. By so doing, Tawfik forfeited his legitimacy to rule the Egyptians almost at the same time that Islamic fundamentalism was emerging as the alternative to secular authority in the Sudan and Tunis.

Ironically, the French had urged intervention in order to check the perceived spread of a pan-Islamic movement, only to instigate it through the British bombardment of Alexandria. The leader of the Nationalists, Ahmed Arabi's, first reaction to the presence of the British warships was to communicate to Gladstone that "use will be made of the religious zeal of the Mohammedans, to preach a holy war in Syria, in Arabia and in India. . . . I repeat again and again, that the first blow struck at Egypt by England or her allies will cause blood to flow throughout the breadth of Asia and of Africa." In his letter to the British prime minister, he also threatened to confiscate all European property, cancel the Dual Control, disown the debt, destroy the canal, and cut the telegraph connecting Britain to India.[14] There was little room for compromise, and events quickly catapulted into a violent confrontation. The British government, with Gladstone at its head, became convinced that Arabi and his followers had imposed a military dictatorship and organized the riots.

When the British guns leveled Alexandria's forts, Arabi and his followers took power and prepared for war. A reluctant Gladstone ordered direct military intervention, and 18,500 British troops landed on Egyptian soil. After several weeks of skirmishes, both armies finally clashed on September 13, 1883, at Tel-el-Kebir, north of the canal. After a hard-fought battle, British forces, commanded by Sir Garnet Wolseley, defeated Arabi's Egyptian army of fifteen thousand. Egypt was restored to the incompetent Tawfik. The British then decided to rule the country through the compliant Khedive, buttressed by a small army of British soldiers and a handful of civil servants. The foreigners soon returned to a rebuilt Alexandria and also spilled over to Cairo, quickly taking over Egypt's economy and trade.

The pan-Islam feared by the French did bubble to the surface—not in Egypt, Algeria, or Tunisia, but in the Sudan[15] under the banner of Muhammad Ahmad ibn Abd Allah, who, taking advantage of the discontent of the Sudanese against the Egyptian administration, proclaimed himself the Mahdi, "the Expected One," the redeemer of Islam.[16] His purpose was to revive the Islamic faith and practice of the Prophet through the restoration of the Koran and the establishment of an Islamic republic.[17] The Mahdi preached adherence to the teachings of Mohammed based on a return to the virtue of strict devotion, prayer, and simplicity as laid down in the Koran. He also condemned the use of tobacco and alcohol, and he advocated the segregation of women from male society.[18] He attracted a large following that expanded into hundreds of thousands. Although his theology was similar in extremism and austerity to that of the Wahhabi sect in Saudi Arabia, the Mahdi was trained in the Sufi school. However, he preached a fundamentalist and virulent strain of Islam that in time appealed to many Muslims beyond the Sudan.

To accomplish these ends, the Mahdi declared a jihad against the Egyptian administration; his followers gladly sought battle to achieve martyrdom. The Mahdi's armies of what British soldiers called "fuzzy-wuzzies"—half-naked Hadendoa warriors, armed with spears and swords and drunk with religious fervor—easily smashed the ill-led and ill-prepared forces sent by Cairo, and by 1883 had overrun most of the scattered Egyptian garrisons in the Sudan. Thousands of Egyptians were stranded and faced a cruel fate at the hands of the

Mahdi and his followers. A large number had sought refuge in Khartoum, one of the last garrisons still under Egyptian control.[19] In 1864, the British government asked General Charles Gordon to lead a relief force of native troops to rescue the stranded Egyptians.[20] General Gordon succeeded in evacuating about 2,500 women and children from Khartoum before the Mahdi's army laid siege to the city.

The British government, however, was less motivated by humanitarian sentiments than by the fact that the Mahdi's rebellion had engulfed the eastern Sudan and threatened the ports that guarded the southern exit of the Suez Canal, linking the Sudan with Jeddah and Mecca. The major concern was that, if the Mahdi succeeded in spreading his rebellion to the Arabian provinces of the Ottoman Empire, it could threaten the route to India. Furthermore, if he succeeded in capturing Khartoum, the Mahdi would control the Nile Valley from the Sudan to the Mediterranean. In London and Cairo the consensus among British officials was that, to contain the Mahdi uprising in the Sudan, they had to remain in Egypt.

Gladstone continued to preach that Britain would pull out of Egypt, but it was a hollow promise. What concerned his government was that there were insufficient resources to secure Egypt and restore control over the Sudan. When the Mahdi's armies succeeded in spreading the revolt in the eastern Sudan, the British government decided to consolidate its forces in Egypt, essentially abandoning Gordon and Khartoum. There was one serious attempt to relieve the siege and rescue Gordon, but it failed. On January 26, 1885, Khartoum fell, and General Gordon was hacked to pieces and beheaded. For the next ten years, the British forgot about Gordon and Khartoum and left the Sudan to the Mahdi and his successors.

"Egypt was the graveyard of Gladstonian diplomacy," writes Paul Kennedy.[21] In vain Gladstone kept assuring the British public that it was only a matter of time before all British officials and soldiers would leave the country, but the problem of the security of the Suez Canal persisted, skewing the great liberal's plans, quickly souring relations with the French, and holding every prospect of raising the specter of the Eastern Question. Egypt was still a province of the Ottoman Empire, whose ruler held power through the beneficence of the Sultan in Constantinople.

Albeit longstanding, the goodwill of the Sultan was ceremonial, but legally Egypt remained an appendage of the Ottoman domain, and any radical aggrandizement of the Sultan's territories would certainly invoke the interests of the other European powers. The 1884 Berlin Conference had established a modicum of broad understanding over the formal European exploitation of

Africa, and any dramatic change in Egypt and the Sudan could easily unravel the agreements.[22]

The security of the Suez Canal effectively left little recourse for the British, except to stay and consolidate their hold over Egypt, as well as over the immediate region. The process was made easier when the collapse of Italy's Ethiopian colonial ambitions facilitated Britain's expansion of Egypt to include the Sudan. On March 1, 1896, the Italian army suffered a disastrous defeat at Adowa in Abyssinia, losing over half of its soldiers to the well-organized forces of Menelik II, the emperor of Ethiopia.[23] The defeat encouraged Khalifa Abdullahi, the Mahdi's successor, to lay siege to the Italian fort at Kassala in the northeastern Sudan.[24] The Italians appealed for help in order to rescue their garrison and in the process triggered a chain of events that transformed the Sudan into another British colony.

The government of Lord Salisbury decided it was preferable to conquer the Sudan on the pretext of saving the Italians, rather than allow the French to move into the region.[25] In a single stroke, Salisbury satisfied imperial security and revenge for the death of General Gordon at Khartoum. After a grueling three-year campaign (1896–1899), Horatio Herbert Kitchener conquered the Sudan and captured Khartoum, ostensibly in the name of the Khedive, but in actual fact to secure the Suez Canal for Great Britain. According to A. J. P. Taylor:

> The British expedition to the Sudan completed the revolution in Mediterranean politics. Previously the British had intended to oppose Russia at the [Bosporus] Straits and therefore sought to keep France neutral. The collapse of Italy gave the final blow to this policy. The Italian fleet was useless: the Italians would need help instead of giving it. . . . Since the British could not pass the Straits, they decided to stay in Egypt permanently and to defend the Suez Canal by the armed forces stationed there.[26]

Although the Mahdi's Islamic state survived for only twenty years after his death, his rebellion and subsequent success attracted a great deal of attention throughout the Muslim world. During this brief interlude in the otherwise insatiable European expansion in the Middle East, the Mahdi's spectacular victories had clearly demonstrated that Islam could defeat the West. The lesson he taught was that a purified Islam, unified under the leadership of a Caliph (significantly his successor was designated as Caliph), could be a potent force.[27]

However, the legacy of the Mahdi left an equally strong impression on the Europeans, particularly the British and the Germans, who convinced themselves that manipulation of Islam's power by controlling the Caliph offered a considerable edge in the race for their looming imperial confrontation. Yet neither the British and the Germans, nor any of the other European powers, appreciated that the lure of a purified Islamic state, headed by the secular-theocratic Caliph, had already become an idée fixe for a small, but steadily growing, army of Muslim intellectuals, theologians, and students. These continued to morph into a variety of Muslim organizations and militant underground forces, culminating in the radical and terrorist groups that have played a disproportionate role in shaping the discourse of political Islam in the late twentieth- and early twenty-first centuries.

From the First World War until the 1970s, the Western intelligence services sought to harness the energy of political Islam for their own purposes. In 1914, imperial Germany, quickly followed by Great Britain, tried to exploit the spiritual influence of the Caliphate, to achieve specific strategic military objectives in the Middle East. The Germans convinced the Ottoman Sultan to declare a jihad that fell on deaf ears, while the British tried to set up the Sharif of Mecca, the steward of the holy cities of Mecca and Medina, as an Arab Caliph, in contrast to the Turkish Sultan, only to discover that it barely caused a ripple of interest in the Muslim world. Both empires misjudged and misunderstood the significance of the Caliphate and the degree to which political Islam could serve the interests of the West.

THREE

The Eclipse of Imperial Islam

"I think that this pan-Islamic movement is one of our greatest
dangers in the future, and is indeed far more of a
menace than the 'Yellow Peril.'"
—*Sir Arthur Nicolson, Permanent Undersecretary, Foreign Office*[1]

On March 3, 1924, at 5:30 A.M. a small convoy of three cars followed by a truck snaked its way through the wet streets of Constantinople. Occasionally the cars got stuck in the muddy streets, and the gendarmes who escorted the party of eight had to get out and place stones under the tires to get the vehicles moving. The convoy bounced along the Bosporus, over the Galata Bridge, past the Bayezid Mosque, then through the Edirne Gate, circumventing the ancient walls to Yedikule, and finally to the Catala train station. At 11:00 A.M. the last Caliph, Abdulmecit II, stepped out of the car followed by two of his wives, his son and his daughter, and accompanied by his chief chamberlain, his personal physician, and his private secretary.[2] The station manager offered Abdulmecit every courtesy and accommodated the party in his home located next to the station. The police formed a cordon to keep away the faithful and the curious, as well as to ensure that Abdulmecit accepted the decision of the new Turkish parliament: to leave the country.[3]

At midnight and at a leisurely pace, the Orient Express puffed into the station and in a short while was ready for the new passengers. Just before Abdulmecit boarded the special coach assigned to him, the governor of Istanbul handed over to him an envelope containing £2,000 and temporary entry visas issued by the Swiss consulate. And so, with little fanfare, the Ottoman Caliph, supreme spiritual and political leader of the Sunni Muslim world, resigned his office and stepped into oblivion.[4] The half millennium of the Ottoman imperium drew to a hurried and shabby end on the platform of the Calata train station, a few steps from the Orient Express, and the continuum with the successors of Mohammed was severed forever.[5] In his memoirs, Ismet Inönü, one of the founders of the Turkish Republic and, along with Ataturk, an advocate of the abolition of the Caliphate, recalled:

We encountered the greatest resistance when we abolished the caliphate. Abolishing the sultanate had been easier, as the survival of the caliphate had satisfied the partisans of the sultanate. But the two-headed system could not go on forever. It nourished the expectation that the sovereign would return under the guise of caliph . . . and gave hope to the [Ottoman dynasty]. This is why the abolition of the caliphate . . . had deeper effects and was to become the main source of conflict.[6]

Elsewhere reaction appeared to be muted; few people took notice and fewer still seemed to care when Abdulmecit issued a statement announcing his resignation after his train crossed the Turkish-Bulgarian border. However, it was impossible to gauge the sentiments of ordinary Muslims in the Middle East and beyond. Certainly in 1924 the European powers had swallowed major tracts of the Muslim regions, leaving only a handful of countries, including the new republic of Turkey, independent of foreign rule. It is unlikely that the European masters of these Islamic communities made any effort to measure the reaction of their new Muslim subjects to the momentous event at the Calata train station. Gilles Kepel has noted, "one of the greatest traumas to affect Islam in the early twentieth century was Ataturk's abolition of the Caliphate in 1924. The caliphate was already a spent political force at the time, but it represented the ideal of spiritual unity within the Muslim world."[7]

On the eve of the First World War, with a few exceptions, a large part of the Middle East had been within the tired grip of the Ottoman Empire. The Ottomans, a disparate assortment of Turks and Muslim converts, had gravitated from Central Asia as mercenaries and in time evolved into a formidable army that swept away the remnants of the Byzantine Empire. In 1453 the Ottomans conquered the great city of Constantinople and by the next century spread out from the Balkans and Asia Minor to envelop most of the Middle East. The Ottoman armies proved unbeatable, and by the sixteenth century they had conquered most of North Africa, all of southeastern Europe, and parts of Hungary, and had twice brought their armies to the gates of Vienna.

As Caliph, the Ottoman ruler represented the secular and the religious unity of Islam that reached beyond the confines of the empire to Muslims beyond its frontiers.[8] By the eighteenth century, Ottoman supremacy had eclipsed, and the empire began a long and almost irreversible decline until its final demise at the end of the First World War.[9] However, the Great Powers, particularly Britain, could not allow the total collapse of the Ottomans and the ensuing political vacuum in the Middle East, and they therefore undertook to prop up the Ottoman state. British fears were based on the real possibility that if the Ottoman Empire vanished, large parts of its territories would fall to Russia and expose the land route to India.

British policy, as well as that of France, Austria-Hungary, and Prussia, toward the "Sick Man" of Europe (the description of the Ottoman regime in the nineteenth century) was to maintain the integrity of the empire, in order to keep the Russian battle fleet and Russian influence locked up in the Black Sea. As long as the Ottoman Empire remained more or less intact, the Sultan, with the backing of the Royal Navy, could maintain sovereignty over the Straits (the Dardanelles and Bosporus) and thus deny the Russian Black Sea fleet access to the Mediterranean. However, in periods of weakness, it suited the Russians for the Sultan to keep the Straits closed to all warships and prevent Russia's rivals from entering the Black Sea. Of course, this did not deter Britain, France, Italy, and Russia from colonizing large tracts of Ottoman territories and finalizing partition of the former empire after the First World War.

In 1914, the Ottomans chose to link their fortunes with Imperial Germany in a desperate bid to reacquire lost territories and past glories. Initially, the Ottomans had tried to ally themselves with Britain, France, and even Russia, but each one had turned them down. The decision to join Germany placed the Ottoman Empire on the side of the defeated Central Powers and instigated a feeding frenzy amongst the Entente allies for the Sultan's lands in the Middle East. Events, once again, brought the Middle East full circle, and Western powers, in the period after the First World War, controlled most of the Islamic world. Muslim fundamentalists argue this is still the case in the twenty-first century.

During the war, the allies—particularly the British—needed the Arabs to fight against the Ottomans, but they also saw in the Arabs the key to countering the influence of the Sultan as Caliph of all Muslims and his ability to declare a jihad. The notion of holy war instigating a massive uprising of Britain's Muslim subjects dominated the thinking of British officials in Whitehall and Cairo as much as in Berlin. Politicians and bureaucrats on both sides were convinced that an appeal to Islam held a strategic advantage. Ultimately, neither the Sultan's role as Caliph nor declaration of a jihad had any significant impact on the war.

The Islamic factor, however, skewed British policy toward the Middle East both during and after the First World War, as bureaucrats, politicians, and intelligence officers in London and Cairo misunderstood religion and nationalism in the Middle East, assuming that they could control the former and manufacture the latter. In the decades after 1918, the British and later the Americans alternately attempted to manipulate religion and nationalism in order to secure their interests in the region, by seeking a strongman as the focal point of either Arab nationalism or as the centerpiece of Islamic unity.

The termination of the Caliphate left a significant void in the Muslim community which engendered several disparate movements that sought to reconstruct Islamic unity. However, for many a manifestation of a new Caliph held the strongest appeal.[10] One of the fundamental goals of the Muslim Brotherhood, established four years after the resignation of the Ottoman Caliph, was the political unity of Islam through the reconstitution of a new Caliphate.[11] Subsequently, the quest for the leadership of the international or regional Islamic community has oscillated between the claims of Islamic militants and ambitious Muslim secular leaders. Meanwhile, British and American intelligence officers assumed that a single master could direct a "monolithic" Islam, and that—through him—they could guide events in the Middle East. This assumption was held dear by the British, and later by some Muslim experts in the Anglo-American intelligence services; it was based on the notion that some kind of entity such as the Caliphate was the centrifugal force that held the loyalty of the Muslims and also transcended national boundaries. This tenuous political and theological construct emerged in the late nineteenth and early twentieth centuries in response to the perceived imminent demise of the Ottoman Empire.

The wholesale defeat of the Sultan's armies by the Russians in 1878 and the loss of more territory were further evidence of the decline and inevitable collapse of the Ottoman Empire. Under the terms of the 1878 Treaty of Berlin, which ended the Russo-Turkish War, the Ottoman Empire lost 8 percent of its territory and almost 20 percent of its population, of which a substantial number were Christians. A unique by-product of this consequence, especially after further losses of non-Muslim populations in the aftermath of the Balkan Wars (1912–1913), was that the Muslims now constituted most of the empire's subjects.[12] The multiethnic and denominational diversity that had characterized Ottomanism for almost half a millennium receded, and the empire's universality now rested exclusively on Islam.

The new demographic, however, created an opportunity to counter the demands for self-determination by the empire's minorities, most of which after 1878 were Muslim, by invoking Islamic unity. The Ottoman Sultan, Abdulhamid II, was convinced that to rescue the empire from the accelerating slide into oblivion, it was necessary to bring it back to its Islamic roots. He believed that efforts at modernization, which emulated Western political, economic, and social structures, were doomed to fail and to further erode the Sultan's power and ability to guide the Ottoman state. Consequently, for Abdulhamid, the secular Ottoman identity proclaimed by the modernizers no longer had any resonance for most of the empire's people. Caroline Finkel, in a recent history of the Ottoman Empire, writes that Islam offered a new ideology that enabled Abdulhamid to take "the latent notion of the Ottoman Sultan as caliph and [refashion] it to command the allegiance, not just of his own people but of all Muslims, asserting more insistently than any Ottoman sultan before him the potency of his identity as caliph, and the appropriateness of Islam as a focus of loyalty for the state."[13]

However, the perception of pending imperial doom and the appeal of Islam as a political force created new ambitions for the empire's Arab potentates, as well as for its European rivals. Although the attempt to establish an independent Arabia and to cast the Emir of Mecca as a new Sultan-Caliph is part of the Lawrence of Arabia legend, the British took the first tentative attempts toward this goal in the late nineteenth century. After the debacle of the Russo-Turkish War, Hussein Pasha, the Emir of Mecca, began to flirt with the British over the disposition of the Caliphate. Emir Hussein, while openly exhibiting absolute loyalty to the Sultan, initiated a subtle but cautious communication with the British in order to prove his bona fide pro-British credentials, while indirectly hinting that the transfer of the Caliphate from Istanbul to Mecca would benefit Great Britain.[14] As an Arab, a member of the Qurayshi tribe and of the Hashemite clan, as well as the Awn family, Hussein had direct access to the succession of the Caliphate.[15] The Ottoman claim was based on the Hanafi school of Islamic jurisprudence, which was more flexible than the orthodox view and which held that the Caliph had to be a member of the Qurayshi tribe.[16] The British responded cautiously but favorably and maintained contact with the Emir through their consul in Arabia.[17]

Initially, Abdulhamid II assumed that Egypt's rulers would emerge as rivals, would challenge the Ottomans for control of the Arab provinces, and would take over the Caliphate, thus ending the Ottoman monopoly over Islamic unity. Even after the deposition of the Khedive Ismail and the reduction of the Egyptian army to eighteen thousand men, rumors persisted that his successor, Tawfik, was conspiring in the Hejaz (the region of Mecca and Medina). It did not help Abdulhamid's paranoia that the exiled Ismail was sponsoring newspapers openly calling for the transfer of the Caliphate to Cairo.[18]

At about this time, reports of Emir Hussein's secret negotiations reached the Sultan, further fueling his suspicions that the British were promoting an independent Arab Caliphate. However, the assassination of the Emir by an obscure Afghan in 1880 brought to an end, for the time being, the prospect of a future Arab Caliph.[19] The respite over the machinations of the Caliphate as a counterweight to the Ottoman Sultan for the "hearts and minds" of Muslims remained in abeyance for twenty-four years, but resumed with a greater urgency after the opening salvos of the First World War.

One of the primary architects of Britain's Middle East policy in the First World War was Field Marshal Lord Kitchener, consul general and British agent in Cairo—in actual fact British proconsul in Egypt and as such the power behind the Khedive's throne. During his tenure in Cairo, Kitchener became convinced that if a hostile power controlled the Ottoman Caliphate it could challenge Britain's hold over the millions of Muslim subjects of the British Empire. Muslims accounted for 70 million of India's population and a significant percentage of the Indian army; many continued to regard the Ottoman Sultan-Caliph as the supreme Islamic authority.[20] In contrast, the population of the Ottoman Empire in 1897 was 39 million, which also included non-Muslim minorities.[21]

Furthermore, in the early twentieth century, the Ottoman Empire was the last Muslim state that retained its full sovereignty and autonomy, making it a focal point for all Sunni Muslims. Accordingly, Kitchener reasoned, a call to arms from the only independent Muslim ruler would inflame the Muslim communities in the British Empire. Certainly Kitchener was witness to the powerful emotions stirred by appeals to Islam and jihad. In the Sudan he had seen firsthand how religious zealotry and fanaticism animated Islamic warriors armed with spears and swords to fling themselves against an army equipped with machine guns and artillery. Islamic militancy had also fueled mass uprisings in Egypt, and religious fervor had been the cause of the Great Indian Mutiny in 1857–1859.

Accordingly, the disintegration of the Ottoman Empire would undermine British interests in the Near and Middle East and the Eastern Mediterranean. However, the ensuing vacuum would create a scramble for its provinces, with Russia as one of the main contenders. In this context, Kitchener was less concerned about Germany than about Russia, concludes David Fromkin, and even after the outbreak of the First World War, the field marshal continued to harbor suspicions that the Ottoman Sultan-Caliph would become a creature of the Russian Czar.[22] Germany was primarily a European problem, but after the First World War, Russia would remain Britain's primary challenger in Asia. To Kitchener, the entente that ended the Great Game and brought Britain and Russia into an alliance with France was simply a temporary convenience whose usefulness would terminate after the defeat of Germany.

FOUR

Jihad for All Occasions

"As a nation we dearly love the bogy of a fanatical army of
millions of desert Arabs yelling 'Allah!' and putting infidels to the
sword and I imagine the idea must have started about the
eleventh century during the First Crusade."
—*Colonel C. S. Jarvis (Libyan Desert, 1917)*[1]

On November 13, 1914, in the hall of the Popkapi Palace, where the relics of the Prophet Mohammed were kept, a solemn ceremony was performed to invoke the power of Islam's glorious past. In the presence of Sultan-Caliph Mehmet V Reshat, and of clerical, military, and political dignitaries, the Sheikulislam invoked a series of fatwas allowing for the declaration of jihad, thus making it the binding duty of every Muslim to take part in a holy war against the Entente.[2] Unlike previous fatwas calling for jihad, this time it was not only addressed to the subjects of the Ottoman Empire, but also to Muslims under British, French, Russian, Serbian, and Montenegrin rule.[3]

The legitimacy of the proclamation of holy war was doubtful, since the Ottoman Empire was taking part in a war allied with Christian powers fighting against other Christian powers.[4] Nevertheless this resort to jihad was the culmination of German propaganda in the fervent assumption that the Ottoman Sultan-Caliph could provoke mass uprisings of Muslims in the British, French, and Russian empires. Yet, that fateful day in November evolved as a combination of theater and wishful thinking.

After several speeches, an attempt was made to link the events of 1914 with the roots of Islam and Mohammed. The call to holy war was followed by a procession on horseback, led by a band, through the streets of Istanbul, accompanied by two women representing the Prophet's wife, Aishah, and her attendant.[5] The procession stopped at the German embassy and was greeted by representatives from the Committee of Union and Progress (CUP), the ruling party, and a Turkish-speaking member of the German legation.

The theater continued as a Moroccan in French uniform gave a brief speech in Arabic praising the Germans for his liberation and condemning the treatment of Muslim soldiers in the French army. The crowd cheered the name of the German emperor as an ally of Islam. They then proceeded to the Austro-Hungarian embassy and, more or less, followed the same course. Afterward, some of the crowd became a mob and looted several Christian shops and houses.[6]

Gottfried Hagen has summarized the reactions of contemporary observers to the event as "curiosity, confusion, and some amusement. . . . An American report quotes rumors that the two women who represented Aishah and her attendant in their normal life sold roasted chickpeas on the bridge over the Golden Horn, as more respectable women had refused to participate."[7] The Moroccan Muslim patriot's motives turned out to be suspect. He had been taken prisoner on the Western Front and most likely had been coached on how to address the crowd. One German eyewitness, observing the scene from a balcony of the embassy, described the speech of the Moroccan soldier by stating: "I don't think that much of what he said was understood down there. People will hardly have understood his gibberish."[8]

Regardless of the issue of validity, on November 23, 1914, the Sultan, in his capacity as Caliph, formally issued the declaration of holy war throughout the Muslim world. Most scholars agree that the proclamation of jihad was the culmination of Germany's Ottoman policy rooted in the kaiser's Damascus promise to all Muslims of his eternal friendship.[9] Although the majority of members from the CUP (the real power in the Ottoman Empire) subscribed to a secular rather than religious outlook, they understood that harnessing Islam offered a means of sowing discontent among the Muslim subjects of the Entente.

The prospect of a mass uprising of Muslims after the Sultan-Caliph called the faithful to jihad had fixated the Germans and British, who expended considerable nervous energy and gold on stimulating or preventing a future holy war. Prior to the war, the Germans had established a pan-Islamic propaganda office in Berlin that focused on the Islamic issues in the Ottoman Empire, as well as in the territories of the Entente that included large numbers of Muslims.[10] For their part, the British concentrated their efforts on the Sharif of Mecca as a possible antidote to counter the Ottoman Sultan's proclamation of holy war.

In fact, German and British intelligence strategy in the Middle East was centered on the notion of jihad as the magic bullet with which to manipulate the 300 million Muslims around the globe to take up arms. Shiite Muslims were the exception; they did not belong to the Sunni branch of Islam with the Sultan-Caliph as its head. The Germans published millions of printed leaflets and had them distributed as far away as India, but the printed message was lost on millions of Muslims, who, for the most part, were illiterate.

Despite so much effort and determination to rouse the Muslims to war and to generate a pan-Islamic movement, the Sultan-Caliph's appeal to jihad failed. One factor was that while Abdulhamid was considered by a majority of Muslims, especially those outside the Ottoman Empire, as the legitimate Sultan and Caliph, the CUP had in fact toppled him.[11] Another consideration was that, by the end of the nineteenth century, the position of Caliph as a monopoly of the Ottoman Sultan faced legal and secular challenges.

Some authoritative Islamic scholars argued at the time that the Caliphate should be re-formed and restored to an Arab chieftain.[12] Ibn Saud, the Emir of the Nejd in Central Arabia and head of the puritanical Wahhabi sect, outright rejected the idea that the Sultan's role as Caliph gave him secular authority over the Muslim community. The British successfully countered the possible impact of the Sultan's jihad by securing legal opinions from Islamic legal experts and Muslim clerics in Egypt and India who asserted that it was the obligation of Muslims to obey the British authorities.[13]

Rudolph Peters, on the other hand, concludes that the main reason for the failure of the jihad "was that Pan-Islamism lacked any form of political mass organization. Despite the exaggerated notions with regard to its force and impact prevalent in Europe, it was no more than an idea espoused by some intellectuals as a reaction against the rapid spread of Western domination during the last quarter of the nineteenth century."[14]

Despite the collapse of the jihad, the fear of a pan-Islamic movement inflamed by religious fervor in an all-out holy war continued to haunt and intrigue the British—and later American—strategists. In early 1917, a few hundred Senussi tribesmen raided the Libyan Desert from Tripolitania,[15] although they were quickly defeated and scattered by a small number of British territorial forces. According to C. S. Jarvis, a British officer in the Western Desert, the raid reinforced the paranoia of an imminent jihad. Consequently, the British stationed thirty thousand troops on the western frontier, when they were badly needed elsewhere, in the conviction that the Senussi represented the vanguard of a much larger force. In all, about one thousand Senussi tribesmen tied up thirty thousand British troops desperately needed on other fronts. Jarvis went on to complain:

> It is very difficult to decide now who actually was to blame for this state of affairs—probably the Intelligence Department in the first place, as they imbued the soldiers with the idea that if the Senussi penetrated to the Nile Valley the whole of Egypt would rise in a holy war against us, which, to say the least, was a gross and absurd exaggeration. . . . For months our troops remained facing a perfectly empty desert, devoid

absolutely of water, in which the enemy could not move if he so desired, and they continued to do so until at last the authorities decided very regretfully that the Senussi was a myth.[16]

Two years later, Jarvis reported that the same paranoia seized British intelligence in Cairo, and they predicted another mass uprising of Arabs. Jarvis reminiscences that at the time:

> Telegrams were showering in on me to the effect that hordes of Arabs, estimated at 40,000, were marching on Cairo and Alexandria from the Libyan Desert. . . . After a two days' patrol that covered the greater part of the north-west portion of the Western Desert, I failed utterly to find anything in the nature of an organization and wired back to that effect. I was not believed, for the Powers that Be in Cairo had faithfully predicted that a rising of Arabs would be the natural sequence of events; and as a nation we have definitely a marked Arab complex.[17]

In the decades after the First World War, the fixation with a mass Arab uprising continued to color Whitehall's policies toward the Middle East. In 1946, R. H. S. Crossman, a Labour member of Parliament, remarked: "The danger of an Arab Holy War is now being used more and more intensively than ever by officials in the Colonial Service and in the various Middle East Embassies as an argument against the acceptance of the Anglo-American Report."[18] Although Crossman was a leading Zionist, his frustration with British diplomats and civil servants reflected an ingrained attitude that had less to do with the pro-Arab sentiments of some British officials than with an almost irrational fear of pan-Islam's leading to a jihad.[19]

In 1919, Indian Muslims organized to pressure the British government to preserve both the boundaries of the Ottoman Empire, as well as the spiritual and temporal authority of the Sultan-Caliph. For many of these officials, the Khilafat Movement that sprang up in India just after the end of the First World War served as further evidence of the latent power of pan-Islam. Yet, as the scholar Gail Minault demonstrates, the Khilafat movement was an attempt by Indian Muslim leaders to unite their community politically by means of religious and cultural symbols that could appeal to the entire community—in effect, a pan-Indian Islam.[20]

Although these Indian Muslim radicals were not unsympathetic to the fate of the Ottoman Caliph, British intelligence in India, as well as in Cairo and

London, did not understand the difference. Minault also adds that the leadership of the movement provided one set of arguments in English publications, whereas their message to Muslim Indians in Urdu and other local dialects was nuanced to reflect local ambitions.[21] Whether British intelligence officials in India ever considered the political propaganda aimed at the Indian Muslims remains an open question. As was the case in the Middle East, British colonial civil servants and intelligence officers focused their energies—and based their knowledge of Islamic factors—on regional elites.

Regardless of evidence to the contrary, neither the Ottoman Sultan nor the Sharif of Mecca succeeded in mobilizing a holy war or a mass uprising in 1914 or at any time during the First World War. Even in the period after the First World War, local rebellions in the Middle East, such as those by the Druze (an Islamic minority) and the Palestinians, as well as Rashid Ali's revolt in Iraq during the Second World War, failed to elicit sympathetic revolts in other Arab regions. Nevertheless, the same era served as a gestation period for far more intense and militant movements, such as the Muslim Brotherhood in Egypt, which aimed at resurrecting Islam as the binding force to unite all Muslims.

Although Muslim militancy had bubbled to the surface as early as the late nineteenth century, with the Mahdi in the Sudan, the end of the Ottoman Empire and the abolition of the Caliphate created a vacuum that a variety of movements and individuals have tried to fill. Yet Islamic militancy and pan-Islam have manifested themselves variously in different parts of the Middle East. For example, writes Gilles Kepel: "Present-day Pakistani Islam is the heir to a series of movements created in reaction to the British empire's dethronement of the last Muslim sovereign in 1897."[22]

Pakistan is but one example, followed by Saudi Arabia and Egypt, as well as Iran, which are home to strong currents of some form of pan-Islamic movement. In other regions of the Muslim world, such as Turkey, Islamic identity is quickly superseding secular nationalism. But even secular Turkey was anchored in the legacy of Mustapha Kemal Ataturk, who filled the role of a Sultan and Caliph stripped of Islamic trappings. The erosion of secularism after the 1980s has offered fertile ground for Turkish Muslims to try and reorganize Turkish society along Islamic principles.

The current term for militant pan-Islam is "political Islam," a concept that embraces the spiritual and cultural elements of Islam, as well as the notion of Islam as a political force mobilized for the purpose of creating a pan-Islamic state. Beyond certain shared tenets of Islam, it is perhaps the one common denominator found among both Sunni and Shiite Muslim militant ideologues.[23] The British and later the American intelligence organizations not only failed to notice this development, but attempted to harness Islam as a means to counter Arab and Iranian nationalism. Throughout most of the twentieth century, beginning after the First World War, Arab nationalism haunted the British and the Americans, who sought security for their interests in the Middle East by supporting Islamic militancy as a counterweight to nationalism and later communism.

Yet what the Anglo-American intelligence communities (as well as British colonial officials) failed to understand was that behind the veneer of Arab nationalism was the rise of pan-Islam. Equally significant is the fact that the manifestation of pan-Islam is a form of regional Muslim identity that is less centered on the concept of a universal Caliphate. However, the fog of militant Islam has clouded every other consideration. Ironically, Muslim militants, as well as British and American intelligence agencies, for opposite purposes and at various periods, have sought to find a variation of a new Caliphate that could unify the Islamic community to checkmate the Marxist and—regardless of the contradiction—the nationalist Middle East bogeyman. For the British, the search for a new Caliph originated in Arabia, which, in time, contributed to a ripple effect that inspired a new generation of Muslim militants.

FIVE

A New Caliph

"There is a dry wind blowing through the East, and the parched grasses
wait the spark. And the wind is blowing towards the Indian border."
—*John Buchan*[1]

Rifle fire tore through the stillness of the morning almost immediately after the faithful had finished prayers in the early dawn (June 10, 1916). The bullets crashed through the wooden shutters and drilled into the polished floor of the Hamidiya building that housed the offices of the Ottoman government representatives in Mecca. Bullets continued to rip through the windows and walls, igniting small explosions of wood slivers and raising tiny clouds of dust. Bimbashi Mehmed Zia Bey, the acting governor and commander of the Turkish forces in Mecca, had instinctively dropped to the floor after the first shots and remained low to escape the bullets whizzing just above his head.[2] He tried to reach the nearby Turkish barracks but to no avail—the rebels had cut the telephone lines, isolating the few Turkish troops within the city. Next he phoned Sharif Hussein, the only man with authority over the Bedouin, whom he suspected were behind the attack.[3]

Zia Bey assumed that, as had been the practice for centuries, local Arabs were attempting to extort money from the Ottoman government by attacking the nearby Turkish garrison. His discussion with Hussein was brief and disconcerting. Upon reaching the Emir, Zia Bey asked what all this (the firing) meant, saying: "The Bedouins have revolted against the government; find a way out." Sharif Hussein replied with cold sarcasm: "Of course we shall" and hung up immediately.[4] Zia Bey tried to hold his position, but with few troops, almost no ammunition, a lack of water, and no relief in sight, he capitulated.[5]

In the holiest city of Islam on that day, June 10, 1916, Sharif Hussein completed his break with the Ottoman Empire and threw in his lot with the British.[6] Yet the Great Arab Revolt was less of an explosion of Arab nationalism than a fizzle of local politics, backed by Bedouin opportunism. For the British, particularly the British intelligence community in Cairo, it came as a relief that a major custodian of Islam, Sharif Hussein of Mecca, could now serve as a counterbalance to the Sultan-Caliph of the Ottoman Empire—a factor that had focused Britain's imperial legates in Egypt on reshaping the dynamics of Islamic authority and harnessing the power of Islam to serve British interests. British intelligence officers, as well as officials in Cairo and London, believed that Hussein's revolt would garner support in the Arab and Muslim worlds, as well as induce at least 100,000 Arab troops to abandon their posts with the Ottoman army and join the Sharif. Hussein was convinced—or at least tried to convince—the British that the number of Arab deserters would be as high as 250,000: almost all the combat troops of the Ottoman army.[7]

Hussein's rebellion was perceived both in Cairo and London as the culmination of Britain's intelligence efforts in Arabia. In fact, the sleight-of-hand of vague promises practiced by Lord Kitchener and his lieutenants in convincing Hussein to break from the Ottomans had little to do with the Sharif's decision.[8] David Fromkin, as well as other scholars, has observed that Hussein opted to take his chances in declaring independence for Arabia, because he became convinced that the Turks were planning to depose him as Sharif of Mecca.[9] Yet the illusion persisted, and not for the first time in the Middle East, Western policies toward the region were held hostage by ephemeral notions and self-delusion.

Unfortunately, in the same week that Sharif Hussein raised the standard of revolt against the Ottoman Empire, Lord Kitchener, the prime architect of an Arab Caliphate, was lost at sea. On June 5, 1916, Kitchener had sailed on the armored cruiser HMS *Hampshire* for the Russian port of Archangel. Despite warnings from naval intelligence that a German submarine had laid mines along the proposed path of the cruiser, British naval headquarters failed to take notice. At the same time, the weather got progressively worse, but Kitchener would not be deterred—he was in a hurry to get on with his visit to Russia. The *Hampshire* had set sail at 4:45 P.M.; almost three hours later the ship struck a mine. According to the sole survivor, he last saw Kitchener standing calmly on the ship's quarterdeck, and fifteen minutes later the *Hampshire* slipped under the stormy waves.[10]

Although Kitchener did not live to see the fruits of his labors with respect to the Arab uprising, he, more than anyone else, had set in motion the series of events that ultimately helped shape the future of the Middle East. In the late nineteenth century, Kitchener had dreaded the idea of the Ottoman Sultan-Caliph proclaiming, in a future war, a jihad against the British, at the behest of a rival power such as Russia or Germany. He believed that only the establishment of an Arab Caliphate could forestall such an eventuality.[11] To that end, he turned to Arabia in order to create a new Middle East strategic construct as a means of securing British interests in the region and guaranteeing the loyalty of Britain's Muslim subjects. Kitchener was convinced that he could achieve this by harnessing the power of Islam to counter the spiritual monopoly of the Ottoman Sultan over the Muslim world.

Events in the early twentieth century soon fortified Kitchener's fears. The Ottoman Empire continued to decline, as new military defeats in North Africa and the Balkans in 1912–1913 resulted in further territorial losses, along with the death of almost one and a half million Muslims and the influx of 400,000 refugees flooding over its shrinking borders.[12] Conspiracies and coups further compounded the empire's difficulties and added to the general political, economic, and cultural malaise. Opposition to the Sultan's absolute authority increased in tandem with every fresh defeat, together with the deterioration of the empire's finances.

In 1889, resistance to Sultan Abdulhamid coalesced in the creation of the Committee of Union and Progress, a disparate collection of underground forces and groups advocating a variety of agendas, but united in their opposition to the Sultan. The CUP did not, however, represent a popular movement or even attempt to mobilize a mass following, but remained an elitist assortment of competing political and military groups.[13] To some degree, the political upheaval in the Ottoman Empire, in which decaying traditional monarchical rule was replaced by secular military-political elites, would be mirrored in other parts of the Middle East later in the twentieth century. Although some of these groups achieved a limited degree of popularity, for example the Free Officers led by Gamal Nasser in Egypt—and certainly Nasser himself—they did not seize power at the head of a mass following.

Kitchener's other fear, that the Ottoman Empire would become a vassal of one of Britain's rivals, was also quickly realized, as German influence supplanted British preeminence in the Sultan's court. After the losses suffered by the Ottomans as a result of the Berlin Treaty, Abdulhamid had turned to Germany, the one Great Power with no traditional interests in the Near East, to buttress his increasingly vulnerable empire. Although Otto von Bismarck opposed German involvement in the Near East, he agreed to offer limited assistance to the Sultan. Beginning in 1880, German civilian advisors arrived with the promise that soon military experts would follow.[14] In March 1890, Kaiser Wilhelm II removed Bismarck from the position of imperial chancellor and assumed direct control over foreign policy; consequently, German interest in the Ottoman Empire expanded dramatically. The kaiser saw great financial and strategic opportunities in the Sultan's lands and intended that Germany should take over Britain's traditional role in propping up the Ottoman Empire.[15]

German companies acquired lucrative contracts to build Ottoman railways and other major construction works, which contributed to the expansion of Germany's heavy industry. One such project was the Baghdad Railway, which was intended to expand the Ottoman Empire's reach to the Persian Gulf and Egypt, as well as strengthen the Sultan's hold over Arabia and the holy cities of Mecca and Medina. At the same time, the construction of the railway would also carry German influence and goods to the Middle East.[16]

In October 1898, Wilhelm undertook a grand tour of the Middle East, beginning with Istanbul, followed by a stop in Jerusalem, and culminating in a visit to Damascus. On November 8, carried away by the tumultuous reception he had witnessed during his tour, the kaiser challenged Britain's hegemony over the Middle East by appealing to the Muslims within and beyond the borders of the Ottoman Empire. At a banquet in his honor he proclaimed: "His Majesty the Sultan and the 300 million Muslims scattered across the globe who revere him as their Caliph, can rest assured that the German Emperor is, and will at all times remain, their friend."[17]

Thanks to German propaganda experts, along with generous gifts to Arabic and Turkish newspapers, the speech spread across the Muslim world as far as British India and Central Asia—at least for those who could read.[18] For the British, the kaiser's remarks underscored the increasing German influence in Istanbul and held the very real prospect that, in the event of war, the Ottoman Empire would side with the Central Powers. In that eventuality, the Sultan, as Caliph, would proclaim a jihad, not only provoking Britain's Muslims, but also closing their access to the annual pilgrimage to Mecca.

Kitchener surmised that the best means of counteracting the impact of a jihad proclaimed by the Ottoman Sultan-Caliph was to co-opt Muslim religious leaders in Arabia and the Sharif of Mecca in particular. From his perspective, the Arab territories adjacent to the Suez Canal were an integral part of Britain's security in the Eastern Mediterranean and belonged to Egypt, not to the Ottoman Empire.[19] The key to these regions and concurrently the means to preempt potential rivals for control of Islam was the Caliphate, and the road to that institution lay through Mecca. Hussein's power and influence stemmed from his inheritance and position. In the context of Islamic tradition and custom, his position was unique. George Antonius, a Christian Arab nationalist, has described Hussein and his status in the following terms:

> He was a descendant of the Prophet and the custodian of the holy
> places; and this dual claim to reverence placed him in a category of his
> own in which he had no rival, and on an eminence from which, on an
> issue involving the safety of the holy cities, he might challenge the

authority of the Caliph himself. He was lord of Mecca, the metropolis and focus of Islam, to whose voice no devout Moslim—least of all an Arab Moslim—could remain deaf. To him and to him alone, would it fall to endorse the Sultan's clamor that the Holy Places of Mecca and Medina were in danger. So that, on an issue like the call to *jihad*, his acquiescence was an important, if not the determining, factor; and would be eagerly canvassed by the Turks for the same reason as it was feared by the Entente.[20]

Fortunately for Kitchener's plans, the Sharif of Mecca, Hussein, had a history of warm relations with the British.[21] In late 1912 or early 1913, Kitchener had met with Abdullah, Hussein's second son, when he had visited Cairo as a guest of the Khedive. Abdullah was shopping for British support in the event that the Ottomans attempted to remove his father.[22] However, Britain was not at war with the Ottoman Empire, and Kitchener could do little except sympathize.[23] Adding to Hussein's alarm, as well as that of the Bedouin chieftains, in the face of Ottoman intentions in the Hejaz was the construction of a railway connecting Damascus with Medina, with plans to eventually reach Mecca.[24]

For centuries the Bedouin had enjoyed monopoly over the camel trade to Mecca and as guardians of the annual pilgrimage route. The railway now threatened this lucrative sideline, in which the Sultan paid the Bedouin an annual fee essentially not to attack and rob the pilgrims. The railway also ended the relative isolation of the Hejaz, enabling the central government in Istanbul to supply the four divisions of Ottoman troops in western Arabia, as well as to intervene in the politics of the Hejaz. The railway would end the desert isolation that had served to buffer the Sharif of Mecca from the intrigues of the Sultan's court and which had given him a significant degree of local autonomy.

Shortly after the outbreak of the First World War, Kitchener was recalled to London to assume the post of secretary of state for war, but, despite his new responsibilities, he maintained his interest and influence over events in the Middle East. A few months later, Gilbert Layton, the official representative of the Sudan government in Cairo (and, after the outbreak of war, head of all British, as well as Egyptian, civil and military intelligence), convinced Kitchener to resume communication with Hussein and to encourage the Sharif of Mecca to break with the Ottomans. After the exchange of correspondence between Sir Henry McMahon, the British high commissioner in Egypt, and Hussein, Britain's officials in Cairo were committed to inciting a rebellion within the frontiers of the Ottoman Empire: a rebellion that would require use of irregular forces and foster the creation of a separate intelligence establishment in Cairo.

To Britain's imperial paladins responsible for Egypt, the imminent collapse of the Ottoman Empire offered the opportunity, proposed by Ronald Storrs, then oriental secretary of the British Agency (assistant to the senior British official in Egypt), to establish a "North African or Near-Eastern viceroyalty including Egypt and the Sudan and across the way from Aden to Alexandretta [that] would compare in interest and complexity, if not in actual size, with India itself."[25] Consequently, such imperial desiderata became intertwined with the prosecution of the intelligence war against the Ottomans in Arabia, whose practitioners pursued quasi-independent foreign policy objectives as part of the covert struggle against the Ottoman Empire in Arabia.

Underlying these considerations, however, was the issue of promises intimated to Hussein. The Sharif was convinced that a future Arabian kingdom, whose territories remained undefined, was to be his reward; the British were convinced that the Keeper of the Holy Places would replace the Ottoman Sultan as Caliph. However, during the exigencies of war, these arrangements afforded the British government in London considerable flexibility in making territorial promises to current and potential clients in the region, while at the same time bargaining with allies such as France over the future division of the Ottoman spoils in the Near and Middle East.

The purveyors of the contradictory promises and the conjurers of the Great Arab Revolt, such as T. E. Lawrence, not only acted as the intermediaries between London and the Arabs, but afterward established the myths and illusions that shaped the perceptions of the war in the Middle East. The men and women who filled the ranks of the intelligence community that sprouted in Cairo, both British and later American, were interconnected through social networks, as well as with their links to the clandestine world of espionage and special operations. The social and personal ties facilitated the ad hoc approach of the loose constellation of military intelligence officers, civil servants, scholars, Arabists, journalists, archaeologists, and not a few eccentrics, who eventually coalesced into the Arab Bureau. The cast of characters who emerged from the shadows in the Arabian covert war bypassed the official chain of command (both military and civil service) and guided events in the Middle East theater of operations in directions that still reverberate with consequences.

SIX

Middle East Delusions: The Great Arab Revolt

"The whole thing was a castle in the air which would never materialize."
—*Sir Edward Grey to Austin Chamberlain*[1]

The bone-weary soldiers carelessly clustered around mud huts as the 100 degree heat beat down on them relentlessly. Hunger gnawed at the men; malaria and dysentery, as well as a host of other debilitating diseases, afflicted them. Hopelessness sapped the will of the strong and destroyed the weak. Death hunted freely in the makeshift hospitals and primitive barracks.[2] The survivors suffered constant torment from dense mists of flies that infiltrated every crevice and coated every morsel of food. Quickly all objects of nutrition vanished, and the men turned to anything remotely akin to sustenance; soon even the vile residue of unthinkable matter disappeared into empty stomachs. Men watched each other suspiciously, in case anyone held back on a moldy meal or horded a cache of bleached bones.

These unfortunates represented what was left of the British garrison of Kut, a village snuggled in a loop of the Tigris River, 350 kilometers upstream from Basra and approximately 170 kilometers from Baghdad. The soldiers of the 6th (Poona) Division of the Indian army suffered terribly from the calamities of defeat in this obscure and barren land: starvation, bad water, and disease carried by clouds of mosquitoes and flies. They had arrived in Mesopotamia (modern-day Iraq) in 1914 to preempt an attack on the oilfields of Persia, after the Ottoman Empire entered the war on the side of Germany. It was not the first time a Western army had been trapped in an Iraqi quagmire as a result of poor intelligence on the region and its inhabitants.

In the early stages of the British invasion, fighting the Turks was relatively easy, but as they advanced toward Baghdad, marshes, deserts, bad roads, and the meandering course of the Tigris, as well as constant skirmishing, had reduced the 6th Division from its original complement of 31,000 troops to only thirteen thousand officers and men by the time the division reached Kut on December 3, 1915.[3] There, in this nondescript village, they dug in, and after 146 days of siege, the commanding officer, Major General Charles Vere Ferrers Townshend, was compelled to surrender, although, before accepting the odium of defeat and capitulation, Townshend attempted to buy a reprieve for his doomed army. The British government concurred, and Aubrey Herbert and T. E. Lawrence, soon to become members of the Arab Bureau, attempted to negotiate with the Turks. They offered £2 million to free the garrison, but the Turkish commander rejected the offer.

On April 29, 1916, the 6th Indian Division passed into captivity. The attitude of the victorious Turks was varied: they were courteous with the British officers, even hospitable toward Townshend himself, merciless with the local population accused of aiding the enemy, and indifferent to the ordinary Indian troops. The Turks executed large numbers of local Arabs, even those merely suspected of collaboration with the British. The fortunate ones were hanged Turkish-style; the less fortunate were garroted.[4] The officers were separated from the men and transported in relative comfort to Baghdad. Townshend, wined and dined by Turkish generals, finally ended up in a luxurious villa on the island of Malki in the Sea of Marmara, where he sat out the war and forgot all about his men.

For the ordinary soldiers of the 6th Indian Division hell on earth began from the moment of surrender. Despite their desperate physical state, they had to march until dusk and were then fed hard biscuits tossed to the ground from the backs of camels. In addition to some meager nutrients, the biscuits contained straw and dirt, but the starving soldiers fell on them; some gnawed at the edges, while others used their boots to break them into smaller pieces. The few with patience soaked them for hours in water and noticed how dramatically the biscuits swelled in size. The next day, the men began to die, frothing at the mouth, while their bowels and stomachs disintegrated into a greenish slime. Almost all who ate the biscuits dehydrated and died moaning in agony.[5] This was the first stage of the Dante's Inferno that welcomed the soldiers of the 6th Indian Division. After endless marches, constant abuse, whippings, and almost no provisions, the survivors ended their days working on railway gangs in Anatolia. Only a few survived the ordeal, and handfuls of men returned home after the war, broken in body and spirit.[6]

This was the second humiliation heaped upon the British by the Ottomans. The defeat at Gallipoli had clearly demonstrated that the Ottomans still had resilience, and it was evident from the disaster at Kut that the empire's strength was formidable.[7] However, as long as the Western Front consumed armies on an industrial scale, the British could ill afford to divert significant forces to the Middle East. The alternative was to subvert the Ottoman Empire from within, as advocated by Kitchener's associates in Cairo and undertaken by the newly created Arab Bureau. The key to this strategy was the Arab provinces of the Ottoman Empire and the conviction that, with the appropriate leader who possessed the requisite secular and religious credentials, Arab nationalism would undermine Turkish control over the Middle East. Effectively, the defeats at Gallipoli and Kut added further momentum to the secret negotiations with Sharif Hussein that led to the rebellion in the Hejaz in the summer of 1916.

For the first time in the modern period, the intelligence service of a state undertook to wage clandestine and irregular warfare as an adjunct to military operations. However, a fundamental flaw with the strategy of the British intelligence establishment in Cairo was that it failed to understand the limited appeal of Arab nationalism. The Great Arab Revolt did achieve some relatively minor objectives: a small army of mostly paid Bedouin conducted successful raids against the Turkish railway lines in Arabia and other acts of sabotage. Sharif Hussein evaded the Sultan's declaration of jihad, but the declaration did not have the resonance in the Muslim world that the British and Germans had wrongly assumed it would have.[8] There was no mass uprising against the Ottoman Empire, and Britain's Muslim subjects remained relatively quiet.[9]

Despite the failure of the Sultan's call to jihad, most Arabs remained loyal to the Ottoman Empire, while raids against the Turkish railway in the Hejaz, if anything, soured the attitude of Muslims toward Hussein's rebellion, since the disruptions severely limited the annual pilgrimage to Mecca. Furthermore, to add insult to injury, the Hejaz railway was constructed with funds raised from Muslims throughout the world; every mile of rail blown up represented the loss of thousands of lira in contributions made up by both rich and poor Muslims.[10]

On the other hand, the British alliance with Sharif Hussein did guarantee access to Mecca for Britain's Muslims, and the refusal of Hussein to sanction the Sultan's call to jihad may have contributed to the collapse of an Islamic holy war against the British and the Entente. However, this was less a success for British intelligence than astute political manipulation on the part of the British, as well as Hussein.

T. E. Lawrence, whose exploits captured the popular imagination in Britain and America, compounded the problem by contributing to the illusion of the Great Arab Revolt. Part of it stemmed from his own account of the insurgency in Arabia, but that came later. The initial publicity that cemented the legend was spun by Lowell Thomas, an obscure American professor, who cast Lawrence as a romantic desert warrior, determined to give the Arabs a state.[11] However, history has been less kind to Lawrence, as historians over the decades have stripped each layer of the legend, exposing a complex yet politically astute charlatan. Perhaps H. V. F. Winstone offers the most fitting summary of Lawrence and the desert war in Arabia:

> . . . the story of "Lawrence of Arabia"; a story of stupefying naïveté that has fascinated generations of writers, historians, scholars, poets, and ordinary men and women. It is a myth to which men of academic distinction have devoted their working lives, scrambling endlessly through letters and diaries in search of the "truth" of this and that venture, writing volume after volume of appraisal and re-appraisal, countering every attempt to put the matter into some kind of perspective with charges of calumny, deliberate distortion, bullying, muckraking, and general vilification. . . . Even the Germans, whose concern for documentary evidence is usually such as to reduce the most adventurous tale to an indigestible recital of factual detail, have fallen victim to the unaccountable charisma that attaches to this diminutive, talkative soldier who looked like a girl in his pristine Arab dress and of whom few Arabs had ever heard until the publishing industry and the film-makers penetrated even their awareness, so that suddenly old men of the towns and villages of Syria and the Hejaz remembered.[12]

Although Lawrence was an extreme example, many of the men and one woman (Gertrude Bell) who formed the close-knit British intelligence community in the Middle East rarely had the opportunity to meet ordinary Arabs. For the archaeologists, geographers, historians, and other scholars, Arabia was a matter of topography, imperial politics, and academic curiosity. T. E. Lawrence, as was the case with most of his colleagues, was intimately familiar with the deserts and ruins of a bygone age but remarkably out of touch with the inhabitants. To the British, ordinary Arabs represented household help, camel drivers, waiters, farmers, shoeshine boys, and beggars, as well as the wandering Bedouin, but this constituency had no voice: political aspirations only reflected the opinions and convictions of their leaders.

In this respect, British intelligence analysis of the political sentiments of the mass of Muslims in the Middle East (and elsewhere) was filtered through Arabs in positions of authority. Compounding these difficulties was the fragmentation of Britain's intelligence efforts. In the Middle East, at least southwest of Mesopotamia, British individuals who gravitated to clandestine work coalesced in the Arab Bureau. Although not a centralized agency as originally proposed by Sir Mark Sykes, Kitchener's Middle East expert, the new organization was attached to the Cairo Intelligence Department.[13] Sykes had planned that the new agency would be a means of simplifying the competing layers of Britain's policymakers in London and throughout the empire.[14]

The Arab Bureau joined the other policy stakeholders in the Foreign Office, the War Office, the India Office, the government of India, the Colonial Office, the Admiralty, and the War Cabinet in attempting to guide British policy on the Middle East. At the same time, the Arab Bureau had to conduct a guerrilla war with Hussein's ragtag army of Bedouin and Arab deserters from the Turkish army, as well as coordinate intelligence operations in the Middle East. Hussein followed the British lead strictly out of self-interest, while relying on promises for his own state intimated through his exchange in the McMahon correspondence. Yet, at the beginning of February 1916, before the outbreak of the Great Arab Revolt and the establishment of the Arab Bureau, the Sykes-Picot Agreement divided the Ottoman provinces of the Middle East, including Arabia, among the Entente allies.[15] However, this arrangement was no less self-serving than the Sharif's deception that he represented anything more than himself—let alone the Arabs.

Whitehall recast Hussein's ambition for an Arab empire as a confederation of Arab states, each headed by an independent ruler, with the most viable and productive parts reserved for direct British and French administration. The officers of the Arab Bureau continued to maintain the illusion of a future Arab state with Hussein as head, while the wily Sharif pretended that he led a pan-Arab movement into rebellion against the Ottoman Empire. The Arab Bureau would have preferred indirect British and French rule through an obliging Arab prince, with Hussein as their primary candidate. Even Lawrence was skeptical about the viability of a truly independent Arab country, although he did not quite lose the duality of purpose that guided his sentiments toward the Arabs and a future Arabia. In a long report on Prince Feisal's, the son of Sharif, operations on October 30, 1916, which he published in the *Arab Bulletin*, Lawrence claimed:

> The Arab leaders have quite a number of intelligent levelheaded men among them, who if they do not do things as we would do them, are successful in their generation. Of course they lack experience—except of Turkish officialdom, which is a blind leader—and theory; for the study of practical economics has not been encouraged. However, I no longer question their capacity to form a government in the Hejaz, which is better, so far as the interests of their subjects are concerned, than the Turkish system which they have replaced.[16]

However, in a handwritten note attached to the report, he reached the opposite conclusion:

> They [the Arab leaders] are weak in material resources and always will be, for their world is agricultural and pastoral and can never be very rich or very strong. If it were otherwise we would have to weigh more deeply the advisability of creating in the Middle East a new power with such exuberant national sentiment. As it is, their military weakness which for the moment incommodes us should henceforward ensure us advantages immeasurably greater than the money, arms and ammunition we are now called upon to spare.[17]

Overall, the agreement was condemned as a postwar division of spoils that would result from the partition of the Ottoman Empire and a fraud with respect to the promises made to the Arabs. George Antonius, a well-known Arab nationalist (but a Christian) declares: "The Sykes-Picot Agreement is a shocking document. It is not only the product of greed at its worst, that is to say, of greed allied to suspicion and so leading to stupidity: it also stands out as a startling piece of double-dealing."[18] Other scholars have argued that the McMahon letters and accompanying promises to Hussein were not double-dealing but essentially proposed to create an Arab state, albeit one under British tutelage, to be ruled by the Sharif.[19] Certainly the members of the Arab Bureau, although pro-Arab, regretted the Sykes-Picot Agreement, but not its objective of a future Arab state attached as a client to the British Empire.[20]

In a recent study of the Arab Bureau, Bruce Westrate's view is that the policy of the Arab Bureau's Arab enthusiasts "was a more modern, and somehow more insidious, stratagem incorporating mechanisms of artifice and manipulation that would bestow the necessary flexibility to confront the rising tide of Arab nationalism and extend Britain's stay both in India and Egypt."[21] Toward this end, the Arab Bureau was to aid in the construction of an Arab nationalism that would be divided against itself and create a confederation of mutually hostile political and religious entities. Under this policy of divide-and-rule, control of Arabia and the accompanying new protectorates and subsequent territorial mandates in the Middle East, as well as leadership of the Muslim world, would pass to creatures of the British, including a new Caliph. Undoubtedly, the Sharif of Mecca and Keeper of the Holy Places fit the requirements of an able puppet. However, the failure of Hussein to ignite a bona fide Arab uprising or instigate mass desertions of Arabs serving in the Ottoman armies ultimately exposed the myth of a pan-Arab movement originating from Mecca.

Equally problematic is whether the Arab Bureau grossly overestimated the nationalist sentiments of the Arabs and indulged in the temptation of believing reports of secret societies in Syria or entertained the notion of a general rebellion against the Ottomans, which suited the interests of British officials in Cairo. The bureau's assessment of the potential of Arab nationalism and the prospects for engineering a revolt was based on reports from a young Arab officer in the Ottoman army. Lieutenant Muhammad Sharif al-Faruqi was a member of a secret society, al-Ahd, based in Damascus that included Arab officers in the Ottoman army, as well as Arab businessmen and political figures in Syria.[22] In the fall of 1915, Faruqi was posted to Gallipoli, where he crossed the lines and deserted to the British. He claimed to possess important information for British intelligence in Cairo and was transferred to Egypt.

Unfortunately Faruqi spoke little English; although several officers in Cairo's intelligence department were fluent in Arabic, some of what he said may have been lost in translation. However, he was able to convince particularly those who wished to be convinced that al-Ahd and al-Fatat (another secret society) were united in backing Hussein, and that the British should accept immediately the Sharif's demands for the creation of an independent Arab state.[23] In return, the societies would lead a rebellion against the Ottomans. He also emphasized that the Turks were offering the Arabs similar inducements to remain loyal to the Ottoman Empire, and that the societies were hard-pressed and had to respond to the Turkish offer. Faruqi told his interrogators that al-Ahd had the allegiance of 90 percent of the Arab officers in the Ottoman army, and that the society collected over 100,000 Turkish lira in membership dues. He also added that, after the union of the two societies, for which he claimed credit, they included a large number of civilian participants who had joined al-Ahd.[24]

Despite the fact that Faruqi was a junior officer and a deserter making bold claims about the intentions of secret Arab societies, the British accepted his information without reservation. Gilbert Clayton, the director of British military and political intelligence in Cairo, was convinced that al-Ahd and al-Fatat were legitimate, with extensive networks throughout the Arab provinces of the Ottoman Empire, and that because of their influence the Turks and Germans would not dare to destroy them.[25] As a result of Faruqi's information, the discussions with Hussein were concluded with McMahon, and the Sharif was assured of British support for an independent Arabia.[26]

Remarkably, just about everything Faruqi claimed to represent and the information he imparted was sheer fabrication. The members of al-Ahd represented not 90 percent, but less than 0.5 percent of the Arab officers in the

Ottoman army. According to Eliezer Tauber, "the entire society numbered at the outbreak of the war only about 50 activists, of whom 40 were officers; *al-Fatat* too numbered only about 40 activists at the beginning of the war."[27] At first, the goal of these societies, as well as those of similar organizations that had sprouted in Syria, Lebanon, and Mesopotamia, was to secure greater autonomy, while promoting the political and cultural standing of Arabs within the Ottoman Empire, rather than to achieve independence or sovereignty.

Equally significant was that part of the stated aims of the societies was their identification with Islam.[28] For some, Arab nationalism was local and specific to a particular region such as Syria or Iraq; for others, pan-Arabism was inexplicably linked to the Islamic religion and heritage. Even those who aspired to an Arab empire did so within an Islamic context. Faruqi omitted such references, while maintaining the fabrication of a pan-Arab movement committed to the Sharif. The appeal of a secular Arab nationalism was confined to Arab Christians, but they represented only a small minority.[29] However, the young Arab officer continued to impose his delusions and went so far as to write to Hussein, pretending to have influence with the British, while simultaneously telling them he represented Hussein.

Was Faruqi responsible for convincing the British to support Hussein, thus triggering the Arab Revolt? If so, it would have been a major failure of British intelligence. It is unlikely that those responsible for British intelligence in the Middle East accepted Faruqi's claims at their face value; it is much more likely that they used him to pursue an agenda driven by Cairo policy, first formulated by Kitchener, and then continued by Storrs, Clayton, and Sykes, the latter having become a recent convert to Arab independence. These men subscribed to the notion that Britain would not only act as a midwife to a new Arab state, but would use that state to expand the British Empire to encompass the Arab provinces of the Ottoman Empire.

Effectively, the intelligence service in Egypt, along with their patrons in London, implemented a separate foreign policy with respect to the Arab Middle East. On a tactical level, sowing sedition among Arab troops became necessary, as they had proven their worth fighting the British, as well as the other Entente forces, at Gallipoli. The Gallipoli front included most of the Arab divisions in the Ottoman army. Defeat at Gallipoli removed any hesitation in Whitehall with respect to using subversion and instigating rebellion to tie down Turkish units in Arab provinces of the Ottoman Empire. On the other hand, the fact that the Arabs fought well should have been an indication that Hussein's claim of mass desertions among Arab soldiers and officers was a hollow one.

In early 1916, the Arab Bureau became the hub of those ambitions and the driving force behind Hussein's Arab Revolt. The fact that the Sharif only represented himself and led an army of Bedouin, whose loyalty was bought with British gold, did not hinder the plans of the Arab Bureau for an Arabia under British tutelage. It suited their interests for Hussein not to lead a substantial Arab force or to head a pan-Arab mass-based movement. Under these conditions, it was far easier to control the Sharif's ambitions and divide the loyalties of the other Arab leaders in Arabia. However, the difficulty of a compartmentalized foreign policy was that it exposed regional interests to the dynamics of grand strategy for the postwar period, which was guided from London.

The Sykes-Picot Agreement complicated the relationship between Hussein and the British. Although the agreement was secret, T. E. Lawrence informed Feisal, Hussein's son, about it.[30] It mattered little that Lawrence betrayed the secret Anglo-French arrangement, because after the Russian Revolution in October 1917, the Bolsheviks published all secret treaties between Russia and the Entente, including the Sykes-Picot Agreement, in November 1917.[31] Regardless of the subsequent debate on what the agreement meant to achieve and to what degree the British betrayed or did not betray the Arab Revolt, the reaction in the Arab and Muslim world was negative and Sykes-Picot continues to be regarded as a fraud.[32] This was the second disillusionment: on November 2, 1917, the British government had issued the Balfour Declaration, committing Britain to the creation of a Jewish homeland in Palestine. Significantly, the McMahon–Hussein correspondence made no specific reference to Palestine, leaving advocates for both sides—then and later—to interpret the territorial stipulations in such a way as to support their respective points of view.

News of the Balfour Declaration caused considerable unrest and protest among the Arabs and throughout the Muslim world.[33] Together with the Sykes-Picot Agreement, it provided the building blocks for future Muslim accusations of British perfidy and betrayal by the West. Concurrently, the policy of the Arab Bureau in fostering the notion of an Arab state, regardless of its configuration and the realpolitik exercised by the political leadership in London, eventually engendered a duality in the Middle East that oscillated between the pursuit of Arab nationalism and the quest for the reestablishment of a state organized along Muslim principles and practices.

Both Arab nationalism and the rise of militant Islam gained considerable momentum after the First World War, but a contributing factor was the Arab reaction to the British and French division of the Ottoman Middle East, compounded by the consequences of the Balfour Declaration.[34] Certainly the British intelligence community in the region cultivated both nationalist and Muslim strains. The Arab Bureau lobbied for Hussein and Arab nationalism, which they assumed was secular, while promoting the Sharif as an Arab Caliph. Yet, with the exception of Christian Arabs and a small number of intellectuals, Arab nationalism was rooted in Islam. In attempting to play off one against the other, the British unknowingly succeeded in fortifying the Islamic identity of most Arabs. Secular Arab nationalism, except for a few decades after the Second World War, dissipated in a sea of corruption, poverty, and defeat. Ultimately, fanning the flames of Arab nationalism and Islam left a difficult legacy for the Middle East and complicated the role of Anglo-American intelligence in the region.

SEVEN

Spies, Adventurers, and Religious Warriors

"Generations of Pashas and Beys from Surrey and Kent had
devoted their lives to the Arab cause,
and had become emotionally identified with it."
—*Arthur Koestler*[1]

Captain William Shakespear was drawn to the desert and relished the loneliness that accompanied travelers daring to challenge its treacherous wilderness. He often slept and dined apart from his guides and servants, preferring solitude to campfire chitchat. He was born in the Punjab of a well-known British-Indian military family. Before the outbreak of war, Shakespear was serving as an Indian army officer and had originally been posted as political agent for the government of India with the Emir of Kuwait. Like Lawrence he was fluent in Arabic, as well as an avid traveler who made several long expeditions into the Arabian Desert along Kuwait's western frontier. In 1909, he met Abdul Aziz ibn Saud, when the latter came to visit the Emir of Kuwait, and formed a positive impression of the Emir of Nejd.[2]

One year later Shakespear had a formal meeting with Ibn Saud, who informed the Indian officer of his wish to establish an alliance with the British against the Turks. According to Shakespear's reports, Ibn Saud was the natural leader of an Arab uprising against the Ottomans, but Whitehall was opposed to the idea and considered it interference by the government of India.[3] In the spring of 1914, Shakespear paid a visit to Ibn Saud in Riyadh, where the Arab chieftain reaffirmed his desire for an alliance with Britain. Shakespear and the Wahhabi Emir became friends.

He would not be the last Englishman to fall under the desert chief's spell: a little later Harry St. John Philby, a noted geographer, senior British civil servant, and intelligence officer, would establish a close relationship with Ibn Saud. Meanwhile, after a series of meetings with him, Shakespear continued on foot and camelback for a journey of 1,800 miles eastward across the great Arabian Desert to the Hejaz and eventually reported to Lord Kitchener in Cairo.

Once again Shakespear tried to promote Ibn Saud as the future leader of the Arabs, but Kitchener and his associates remained committed to Hussein.[4]

When the Ottoman Empire opted to cast its future with the Germans, Whitehall became very interested in Arab chieftains and how to get them to join Britain or remain neutral. Shakespear was appointed political officer on special duty and was directed to secure Ibn Saud's allegiance to Britain; however, in the complex world of imperial British administration he would be acting in the interest of the government of India. He was instructed to stay with Ibn Saud and if necessary take up residence in Riyadh, the Emir's capital.[5] Ibn Saud had little love for the Turks, since the Ottoman Empire had traditionally supported his archenemy and rival for control of central Arabia, Ibn Rashid.

Before joining Ibn Saud in Arabia, Shakespear had behaved like a man haunted by a premonition. After so many dangerous adventures and missions, he was suddenly aware of his mortality. On December 11, 1914, he asked one of his colleagues to write to his mother in the event of his death; a few days later he wrote his last will and testament. Shakespear left Kuwait on December 12 and nineteen days later (December 31) joined Ibn Saud at his camp near Majmaa on the plain of Arma.[6] Ibn Saud was moving northward to make war on his pro-Turkish enemy, Ibn Rashid, Emir of Hail. Over campfires and along the trek, Shakespear and Ibn Saud managed to draft the outline of a treaty with Britain to the satisfaction of both, which Shakespear forwarded to Sir Percy Cox, the chief political agent in the Persian Gulf, on behalf of the government of India in Mesopotamia.[7]

On January 22, 1915, they camped near Zilfi, the largest town in the Sudair region, where Ibn Saud tried to convince Shakespear to leave, as it was not necessary for the British officer to take part in the upcoming battle. Shakespear refused. In the morning, Shakespear had a quick meal and decided to watch the battle from the dunes next to the sole field artillery gun, manned by a young Arab, supporting Ibn Saud's army. For a few moments, the two armies paused, and then with the cry of "Allahu Akbar" (God Is Great) they charged across the flat empty plain near the oasis of Jarab. Ibn Saud's forces, despite being outnumbered, fought well, and some of Ibn Rashid's units began to lose their cohesion.[8]

Shakespear, no longer a bystander, was directing the field gun, which was having a devastating affect on Ibn Rashid's soldiers, when it jammed. Ibn Saud's infantry lost heart and fell back, and—to make matters worse—the Ajman tribe, which made up a significant part of the cavalry, deserted to Ibn Rashid. Shakespear could easily see that Ibn Saud's army was falling victim to panic, so he tried to repair the gun, but by this time he was alone on the dune. Ibn Rashid's

cavalry advanced to his position, sweeping over the British officer and the useless gun. Several bullets struck Shakespear in the face and head, but he was still
alive when one of Ibn Rashid's attendants slashed at the fallen officer with his
sword and finished him off.[9]

Had Shakespear lived, he would have overshadowed the reputation of T. E.
Lawrence, at least with respect to audacity and daring. He had ventured into
the deserts of Arabia and traveled widely in Anatolia and Persia. He had earned
the trust and respect of Ibn Saud and his followers; however, both his exploits
and the policies of the government of India are examples of the fragmentation
of Britain's intelligence efforts in the region. Shakespear's actions demonstrated
just how the role of the secret services complicated postwar policies. He was
working for the India Office and the government of India, while Lawrence and
the Arab Bureau represented the interests of British officials in Cairo and like-
minded officials in London, as well as their own policies.

Meanwhile, the recently established Secret Intelligence Service (SIS as well
as MI6) was responsible for espionage in the rest of the world, but not in the
Middle East.[10] One consideration was that jurisdiction for intelligence operations in the Middle East was divided in 1906 among the India Office, the War
Office, and the Directorate of Military Intelligence in London, with the former
assuming responsibility for all regions in southern Arabia from Aqaba to Basra
(excluding Asir, Hejaz, and Yemen), while the latter took charge of the rest of
Arabia, including the Ottoman provinces of Syria and Mesopotamia.[11] In 1916,
the Arab Bureau's zone of operations in the Middle East was transferred to
those areas of Arabia that fell under the control of military intelligence in Cairo.

After the death of Captain Shakespear, London and Cairo almost forgot
about Ibn Saud and central Arabia, until the launching of the Great Arab Revolt made both the region and Ibn Saud interesting to British intelligence. At
the very least it was necessary to secure Ibn Saud's benevolent neutrality toward
Hussein—despite the fact that the Emir of Najd despised the Sharif of Mecca—
and if possible to convince the Wahhabi leader to wage war against the pro-
Turkish Ibn Rashid of Hail. In the years following Shakespear's demise, Ibn
Saud had extended his power over the tribes of central Arabia and was in a
strong position to cause considerable grief to the army of Hussein.

The man chosen for the mission was Harry St. John Philby.[12] In 1915,
Philby joined Sir Percy Cox, the political officer in charge of the territory occupied by the British army in Mesopotamia.[13] Cox chose Philby because he was
a gifted linguist and fluent in Urdu, Punjabi, Baluchi, Farsi, and a variety of
Arabic dialects. Cox charged Philby with the tasks of establishing a political
agency in Riyadh and wooing Ibn Saud to wage war against the pro-Turkish

Arab tribes, without attacking Hussein's forces in the Hejaz. In October 1917, Philby set out for central Arabia, accompanied by two other British officers, and by the end of November had reached Ibn Saud's capital. Philby undertook the journey by crossing central Arabia from east to west, which had only been accomplished once by an Englishman, and, in recognition of this feat, the Royal Geographical Society awarded him the Founder's Medal.[14]

After meeting and getting to know Ibn Saud, Philby became convinced that both British and Saudi interests would be best served by uniting the Arabian Peninsula under one government from the Red Sea to the Persian Gulf. Naturally this meant that the Saudis would assume the role of the Hashemites as Islamic Keepers of the Holy Places, while protecting shipping lanes on the Suez–Aden–Bombay route of the British Empire. Even though Ibn Saud was a legitimate Arab leader who was bringing Arabia under his control by war, fear, and faith, the British authorities in London and Cairo remained committed to Hussein. The Emir of Nejd was accomplishing what the Arab Bureau had planned for the Sharif of Mecca, while Hussein spent considerable effort on acquiring titles without the power to sustain his authority.

In 1917, Hussein had proclaimed himself King of the Arabs, but had had to modify the title to King of the Hejaz, further rankling Ibn Saud, who could not wait until he came to terms with the Sharif. In May 1919, Ibn Saud's fierce Wahhabi warriors, along with the forces of Khalid ibn Mansur ibn Luway, launched a lightning night raid on the British-trained army of Hussein's son Abdullah camped in the oasis of Kurma. Hussein's troops were taken by surprise and close to five thousand were slaughtered. Abdullah managed to escape only by running away in his nightshirt. After this disaster, which destroyed the Sharif's army, both sides agreed to a truce. Although Philby was in England on leave, he used Ibn Saud's victory to drive home the point with the British government that Ibn Saud was the only outstanding leader in Arabia.

Remarkably, the response from Whitehall was to proclaim Feisal king of Syria (and, after he was toppled by the French, the British gave him the newly constructed state of Iraq). They also awarded Transjordan (present-day Jordan) to Abdullah. In 1924, after Mustapha Kemal had abolished the Ottoman Empire and the Caliphate, the Sharif of Mecca declared himself Caliph—to the consternation of most Arabs and Muslims. Then, adding insult to injury, Hussein decided to ban all Wahhabi Muslims from taking part in the pilgrimage to Mecca.

This ill-conceived gesture only provoked Ibn Saud to launch another attack against the Hejaz, and within a short span of time he captured the holy cities of Mecca and Medina, and finally Jeddah. Ibn Saud assumed control of the holy places, as well as responsibility for the Hajj, giving him a powerful influence over Sunni Muslims. These events had little impact on Whitehall. T. E. Lawrence pronounced Ibn Saud's accomplishments in unifying Arabia as "a figment, built on sand."[15] Yet the British did not entirely abandon Ibn Saud: the Emir continued to receive a monthly stipend and military aid.

In 1929, after failing to prevent some Wahhabi tribesmen from carrying out raids and massacres, Ibn Saud attacked them. With the support of four British warplanes, and two hundred radio-equipped armored cars and troop carriers, he annihilated the entire force of Wahhabi cavalry, which was armed with old rifles, lances, and scimitars. Regardless of his overwhelming fire-power, it took Ibn Saud ten months to put down the rebels. In so doing, he effectively brought to an end the chronic tribal warfare that had plagued the region for millennia, establishing the Islamic-based nation-state of Saudi Arabia. However, the new Arabian state had few resources and even fewer links with the outside world, and it was vulnerable to British power.[16]

Philby missed out on most of these events in Arabia while on leave in England, and, after his return, the British closed down the mission in Riyadh. Shortly after, the war came to an end, but the peace did not grant the Arabs a single state. Even those new states that did not fall under the mandate system acquired only limited independence.[17] Philby was outraged and made his views known to anyone who would listen. After languishing without a posting, he was placed as advisor to the Iraqi minister of the interior in October 1920. Philby's appointment came in the aftermath of a major uprising in Mesopotamia, which was becoming known as Iraq.[18]

In this uprising, tribesmen, Shiite clergy, notables, and young intellectuals rose in rebellion, partly in response to British rule and partly from local grievances, such as high prices and taxes. The Turks, as well as the Bolsheviks, also had a hand in the revolt and had sent agents to encourage opposition to the British. It is not certain if the uprising was a national revolt or simply a coalition of disparate groups whose only common agenda was opposition to the British. Eliezer Tauber concludes, "to the local people the meaning of the national struggle was: a struggle for liberation from foreign rule, the achievement of independence, and the establishment of a local government."[19] In April 1920, at the Conference of San Remo, the League of Nations agreed to the British mandate over Iraq. This agreement left little doubt that the British would not leave Iraq and contributed to the causes of the uprising. Many intellectuals in Baghdad and other major cities in Iraq denounced the decision of the allies and called for the inhabitants of Iraq to fight against foreign rule.[20]

It was symptomatic of British attitudes toward the Middle East—and Arabs in particular—to ignore the interests of the local inhabitants. Despite promises of independence and U.S. President Woodrow Wilson's proclamation of self-determination, the British continued to rule most of the Middle East, convinced that they knew what was best for the Arabs. Captain Arnold Wilson and Gertrude Bell administered Iraq and, regardless of their differences, both believed they understood the sentiments and wishes of the locals. Wilson advocated direct rule, while Bell preferred a protectorate.[21]

However, both agreed that self-determination was not an option. Bell wrote: "the people of Mesopotamia, having witnessed the successful termination of the war, had taken it for granted that the country would remain under British control and were as a whole content to accept the decision of arms."[22] She went on to say that the notion of self-determination proposed at the Paris Peace Conference "opened up other possibilities which were regarded almost universally with anxiety, but gave opportunity for political intrigue to the less stable and more fanatical elements."[23] The British political leaders at Versailles were less concerned about what and how the new country was constituted, however, than with the problem of petroleum, which seemed to be abundant in Mesopotamia.[24]

As a result the British government decided to recast Mesopotamia as Iraq by lumping together the Ottoman provinces of Mosul, Basra, and Baghdad, regardless of the religious differences of the people inhabiting the region. The conflicting religious and national identities of the new citizens of Iraq remained with the country for the rest of the twentieth century and spilled into the twenty-first. At present, the West—particularly the United States—has yet to come to terms with the dynamics of Iraqi society and continues to apply the Western concept of nationalism to it. It does so despite the unique mix of Arabs, Kurds, and a small minority of Assyrians that underlies the delicate and often volatile relationships of the Shiite majority with the smaller Sunni and Christian minorities.

Bell wrote a lengthy report on the situation in Mesopotamia—her magnum opus in fact—which contributed to how the borders of the new country were finally delineated and which led to Sunni domination over the country, until the American intervention in 2003.[25] She held the conviction that Iraq had to be led by the Sunni minority, because the majority Shiites were "unworldly and apolitical," while the Sunnis were "educated, powerful, financially astute."[26] Like Shakespear and Wilson, Bell represented that unique combination of spy, explorer, bureaucrat, and adventurer which left its lasting imprint on the Middle East in one form or another. The Iraqi rebellion, however, terminated Wilson's tenure as chief civil administrator and, although he was sent home and given a knighthood, he could not accept the outcome and left the

British civil service.[27] Bell, on the other hand, remained and continued to play a critical role in the development of the new state. Percy Cox kept her employed in Iraq, since he shared her views about the final disposition of the new country and its relationship with Britain.

Philby also owed his new job in Iraq to Percy Cox, who had employed him in Mesopotamia during the early years of the First World War. When Cox arrived in early October 1921 and was given responsibility for Iraq, he moved quickly to establish a temporary all-Iraqi government, but one buttressed by British advisors. Although he supported the concept of Iraqi self-rule, Cox equally believed that the Arabs could govern themselves only up to a point, and beyond that he would remain the final and supreme authority.[28] The role of the British advisors was to guide the Iraqi ministers to make the correct decisions and, under these terms of reference, the first government of Iraq was established on October 25, 1920.

Philby accepted this arrangement, but his patience with the British system came to an end when Winston Churchill as colonial secretary, T. E. Lawrence, and Gertrude Bell engineered the election of Feisal as king of Iraq. Philby made his views known to anyone willing to listen, and in 1921 he was forced to leave after Feisal assumed the crown.[29] As compensation, he was sent to Transjordan as chief British representative.[30] After three years there, he had had enough, and so had the British high commissioner in Jerusalem, but Philby succeeded in tendering his resignation before he was relieved of his duties.[31] Whether this was a sudden act born of frustration or had been building up over the years, Philby decided to abandon the Indian civil service and transfer his allegiance to Ibn Saud. Although the change in loyalties did not come about that easily and quickly, the culmination of disappointments may explain Philby's motives for his ultimate metamorphosis from British civil servant and intelligence officer into advisor to King Abdul Aziz ibn Saud and convert to Islam.[32] Although most historians agree that Philby's conversion to Islam was cynical and self-serving, nonetheless his determination to curry favor with the Arab leader was such that he underwent a painful circumcision to meet all the requirements of being a Muslim.[33]

Philby was a courageous combination of explorer, adventurer, social misfit, and spy—and also an avid bird watcher.[34] Unlike T. E. Lawrence, Philby, regardless of his own selfish motives, was genuinely captivated by the austere Ibn Saud and saw him as a "great and outstanding figure."[35] Eventually he not only became the monarch's chief advocate, but also in the process betrayed his own country. In the years to come, his more famous son, Harold Adrian Russell "Kim" Philby, also deceived friends and colleagues, but Kim's "religion"

was Marxism and the Soviet Union. In his memoirs, Kim Philby addresses the
theories of certain writers:

> who have attributed the unusual course of my life to the influence
> of my father. It is possible that his eccentricities enabled me, in early
> youth, to resist some of the more outrageous prejudices of the English
> public-school system of forty years ago. But very little research would
> show that, [at] all decisive turning points in my life, he was thousands
> of miles out of reach. If he had lived a little longer to learn the truth, he
> would have been thunderstruck, but by no means disapproving.[36]

Few people who knew Kim Philby can ever be convinced of his comments
regarding his life. Yuri Modin, the KGB officer responsible for the so-called
Cambridge spies (the British moles recruited by Soviet intelligence in the
1930s), wrote in the endorsement section of Kim Philby's book:

> [Philby] never revealed his true self. Neither the British, nor the
> women he lived with, nor ourselves ever managed to pierce the ar-
> mour of mystery that clad him. His great achievement in espionage
> was his life's work, and it fully occupied him until the day he died. But
> in the end I suspect that Philby made a mockery of everyone, includ-
> ing ourselves.[37]

Perhaps John le Carré's comments ring closer to the common traits shared
by father and son:

> Philby has no home, no women, no faith. Behind the inbred
> upper-class arrogance, the taste for adventure, lies the self-hate of a
> vain misfit for whom nothing will ever be worthy of his loyalty. In the
> last instance, Philby is driven by the incurable drug of deceit itself.[38]

When the Saudi court interpreter, who knew the older Philby, read Kim's
memoirs, he remarked that Kim was "a true replica of his father."[39] Like his son,
the senior Philby remained a complex and unscrupulous individual throughout
most of his life, never hesitating to use anyone to further his own ends. During
the period between leaving the civil service and working for Ibn Saud, St. John
Philby tried his hand at making money, but with little success. He set up a trad-
ing company in Riyadh, but he achieved less success with commerce than with
exploring the deserts of Arabia. He became involved with a wealthy business-

man, Remy Fisher, in order to secure lucrative contracts for himself. When Fisher showed an interest in Philby's wife, Dora, rather than being offended, Philby urged Dora to encourage Fisher's advances. The reason was to placate Fisher, so the Philby family could vacation on his estate in France.[40]

In May 1932, Francis B. Loomis, representing Standard Oil of California (SOCAL),[41] approached Philby through the American consul-general in London with a proposal for talks aimed at securing rights for oil concessions. Philby had been encouraging Ibn Saud to consider the possibility that under the soil of Arabia ran rivers of oil that could augment the Saudi kingdom's income. The prospect of petroleum deposits offered a new and desperately needed source of revenue for the Arabian monarch. The finances of the Kingdom were in dire straits: expenditure by Ibn Saud and his court exceeded revenue, and by the early 1930s they were defaulting on payments to their creditors.

On May 31, 1935, SOCAL discovered oil in Bahrain, which convinced the company that it was worthwhile to explore for petroleum deposits in Arabia. Representatives from SOCAL resumed contact with Philby and sought his help in convincing Ibn Saud to grant them rights to explore, as well as concessions in the event oil was discovered. Philby luxuriated in his new role as advisor to the king and simultaneously as middleman for SOCAL. Although he was hired as a paid consultant by SOCAL, he also, behind the back of the American company, approached the Iraq Petroleum Company (whose major shareholder was the Anglo-Persian Oil Company), in an effort to drive the price higher and secure further commissions for himself.

After much hard bargaining, the Saudis agreed, and SOCAL secured its first oil contract with Arabia. Philby acquired a lucrative monthly consulting fee of £1,000, as well as signing bonuses and other financial advantages.[42] The agreement was signed on May 29, 1933, and eventually SOCAL and its successors obtained exclusive access to one of the world's largest petroleum deposits.[43] The representatives from the Iraq Petroleum Company had given up much earlier and did not pursue further negotiations. Their interests were not so much in acquiring new sources of oil but essentially in preempting any future competitors.[44] This proved to be a strategic blunder, which deprived the British of another source of petroleum and billions of dollars in profits, as well as leaving them dependent on Persian oil wells, with all the consequences this held for Great Britain in the future.

One critical factor in how the Americans won the Saudi oil concessions was Philby's role on their behalf; another was British shortsightedness in failing to appreciate the potential of Saudi oil: perhaps Britain's greatest intelligence failure of all time. Philby's intentions were a combination of greed, ego, and—to some degree—revenge against Britain's Middle East policies. However, the renegade British spy and civil servant was also strapped for cash to pay his son's fees at Cambridge University, so that Kim Philby could complete his education. In effect, St. John Philby and his son underwrote the decline of British intelligence until the early 1960s and helped seal a Faustian bargain between America and Saudi Arabia.

SOCAL and its successors discovered vast reserves of petroleum, which generated considerable wealth for American oil companies and enriched the Saudi royal family beyond their wildest dreams. In 1950, the lopsided arrangement, which favored American petroleum companies to the detriment of the Saudis, was modified so that the spoils were divided on a 50–50 basis, which dramatically increased the Kingdom's revenue.[45] Great wealth infected common sense, and the House of Saud then followed the siren's song of greed that left it hostage to the foreign—and especially American—addiction to fossil fuel. In order to sustain their expanding appetite for almost limitless opulence, future kings and the extended royal family of approximately one thousand members surrendered Saudi society to the Wahhabi clerics, who kept their version of extreme Islam simmering.

By the end of the Second World War, St. John Philby had become increasingly disgusted by the corruption, poor administration, and avarice and indulgence of the Saudi royal family, and he said so publicly. This proved too much for Ibn Saud's successor, and he banished Philby. Ironically, the ex-Saudi advisor chose London as his place of banishment.[46] In April 1955, Harry St. John Bridger Philby returned home from Arabia, leaving behind him a legacy of oil, money, and corruption that served as the handmaidens to fanatical Islam.

EIGHT

Absolute Faith: The Muslim Brotherhood and the Politics of Intelligence

"My word will be stronger if they kill me."
—*Sayyid Qutb*[1]

On dank mornings at the end of August, the wind carries the flavors and scents of the desert to Cairo. Overnight, the sand sucks up the cool moisture and releases the wetness a few hours before dawn. The smells of Cairo at that hour are a confluence of the sterile odors of desert dampness with hints of the delta that combine manure and pungent whiffs of stagnant irrigation water. Later in the day, Cairo becomes engulfed by the signature aroma prevalent in most cities of the Middle East: a mélange of exhaust fumes, cheap incense, manure, and animal sweat.[2] To all outward appearances, August 29, 1966, seemed like a typical early morning in Egypt's capital. Yet a few hours later, the Egyptian government set in motion a chain of events that would mark that day as a new threshold for the Middle East. Later that morning, the execution of an Islamic theologian and ideologue of jihad provided Muslim militants with a fresh and influential martyr.

The prisoner in the special cell block of Tura prison, however, seemed almost impervious to his fate: wearing the traditional red burlap pajamas of a condemned man, he waited with resignation. Two policemen came by, just after the break of dawn, and, taking one arm each, practically carried Sayyid Qutb to a waiting automobile in the prison courtyard. It was part of a small convoy of police and military vehicles that sped quickly to the place for executions. Upon arrival, Qutb was taken to a makeshift hanging post, and a rope was placed around his neck. The executioner waited patiently under a black flag for the signal to initiate the final ordeal for the condemned man. As the guards and the other men sentenced to death waited for the killing to commence, a car screeched to a halt outside, and a senior Egyptian officer burst into the death chamber.

Anwar Sadat, a former member of the Muslim Brotherhood and a close associate of Nasser, entered the place of execution and offered Qutb a simple proposition: appeal the sentence, and Nasser would grant him mercy. Nasser had realized, especially as the streets of Cairo were beginning to bulge with demonstrators, that Qutb would be more dangerous dead. Qutb refused.[3] The hangman then proceeded to pull the rope, slowly lifting Qutb above the ground. Qutb gasped and thrashed violently; in a matter of minutes he had collapsed.

In a feeble attempt to put the genie back in the bottle, the Egyptian government refused to release the body to the family, in order to prevent the gravesite from becoming a shrine, but it was too late.[4] Even as the Muslim Brotherhood appeared at the point of disintegration, Qutb's execution and martyrdom represented a line in the sand in the evolution of political Islam, and his writings became essential scriptures for the disciples of modern jihad.[5] In a moment of supreme irony, Qutb's death helped relaunch the Brotherhood during the first decade of Nasser's Egypt (1954–1965), concurrently with the peak of secular Arab nationalism.[6]

To a great extent Qutb's life and death is a metaphor for the spiritual and ideological journey that has transported many men and women in the Middle East from a commitment to secular political ideals to the absolutism of political Islam. Initially, Qutb was a mild-mannered young schoolteacher who achieved a reputation in literary criticism. His political experience in the post–Second World War nationalism that was sweeping over Egypt and his contacts with the West convinced him to seek salvation in Islam. Sayyid Qutb became the spiritual guide of the Muslim Brotherhood and preached an interpretation of Islam that bridged the beliefs of the puritanical Wahhabis and those outside Arabia, which ultimately provided an intellectual and theological framework for Osama bin Laden and his followers in al-Qaeda.[7] Qutb despised the West, especially the United States, and was equally ill-disposed toward Nasser's Arab nationalism.

The Islamic martyr was born in 1906, in Mush, a small village in Upper Egypt. In 1921, he was sent to live with an uncle in Cairo to complete his studies and graduated from Dar al-'Ulum, a teacher-training institute. After graduation, he was sent to the provinces as a teacher, eventually returning to Cairo as an inspector of schools for the Egyptian Ministry of Education. In the 1930s and 1940s, he gained some distinction as a literary critic, writer, and journalist.[8] Like most Egyptians of his generation, he dabbled in politics and resented the British domination of Egypt. At this time, Qutb was not a religious activist but confined his interests to literary criticism, poetry, and—after

1945—Egyptian nationalism. He devoted himself to the cause of Egyptian nationalism with such fervor that he irritated King Farouk, who proposed to have
him arrested. However, thanks to his political contacts, the Ministry of Education spirited him away to the United States in 1948 for further training.[9]

Qutb's experience in America was in effect his road to Damascus, trans-
forming the young Egyptian man of letters into a committed Islamic ideologue.
Almost immediately, his newfound resolve was tested on the ocean liner, as a
drunken American woman attempted to seduce him. Qutb did not succumb,
nor was he later won over by the charms of the American way of life. He was
repelled by its prejudice against Arabs and shocked by the freedom that American men allowed their women. He described the churches as "entertainment
centers and sexual playgrounds."

After two and a half years of exposure to Western civilization, Qutb realized that he despised everything about it. So, on his return to Egypt in 1951, he
resigned from the Ministry of Education and joined the militant Muslim Brotherhood.[10] In 1954, Nasser's police arrested him and many other members of the
MB. Qutb spent ten years in prison and, despite the harsh conditions, he was
able to continue writing and publishing. He was released in 1964, but was
arrested again in 1965 after members of the Brotherhood had attempted to assassinate Nasser.

Qutb became the most influential advocate of the contemporary concept
of jihad. For many militants in the Middle East, his new interpretation of holy
war legitimizes violent Muslim resistance to governments that claim to be
Muslim, but whose implementation of Islamic precepts is flawed. Qutb is especially popular in Saudi Arabia, but his extensive publications have also been
translated into most Muslim languages. In the 1960s and 1970s, when many
Afghan religious scholars came under the influence of the Muslim Brotherhood, Qutb's ideas attracted particular interest in the faculty of religious law in
Kabul, and the scholar Burhanuddin Rabbani translated his writings into the
Afghan language, Dari.

Although Qutb is studied everywhere from Malaysia to Morocco, there are
many versions of militant Islam, and his writings have been interpreted in a
variety of ways. Some Muslim radicals have even written polemics against
Qutb's version of Islam. Still, Qutb is regarded as the father of contemporary
militant Islam, and the inspiration and influence for many radical Muslims,
including Osama bin Laden.[11] Years later, Qutb's brother, Muhammad, was
teaching at King Abdul-al-Aziz University, where he indoctrinated many
young Arabs, including bin Laden. Another Muslim Brother, Abdullah Azzam, also an instructor at the Saudi university and a follower of Qutb, spent

considerable time with the future terrorist in Peshawar, Pakistan, during the war in Afghanistan.[12]

Until the appearance of al-Qaeda in the 1990s, Qutb and the Muslim Brotherhood carried the banner of radical and—to Western, as well as established Muslim regimes—fanatical Islam. The Brotherhood had burrowed deep into Egyptian society, and its tentacles had spread throughout the Arab Muslim world. Although on the surface it appeared that Arab nationalism had captivated Egypt and other Arab states in the post–Second World War period, it was the Muslim Brotherhood that had captured the soul of Egypt's poor and young intellectuals.

Equally significantly, the Muslim Brothers had acquired powerful allies: in the late 1940s, the Central Intelligence Agency supported these Egyptian radicals to counterbalance the unsettling rise of Egyptian nationalism.[13] The Dulles brothers—Allen as director of the CIA (1953–1961) and John Foster as secretary of state (1953–1959)—came to regard Nasser as a pro-Soviet communist and believed that Islam was the magic bullet with which to kill Arab nationalism, thereby depriving Moscow of potential allies in the Middle East.[14] Accordingly, they encouraged Saudi Arabia and Jordan to aid and finance the MB's struggle against Nasser. The irony was that, only a few years earlier, the CIA had covertly supported Nasser.[15]

However, the Americans were not the first to seek Islamic militants as allies in containing nationalist and secular movements in Egypt. The British had implemented the same recipe during the First World War by trying to exploit Islam against the Ottoman Empire. In the late 1920s, they had donated £500 Egyptian, through the Suez Canal Company, to Hassan al-Banna and had helped establish the MB.[16] Ten years later, the Muslim Brothers began advocating nationalization of the canal.[17] Despite the apparent contradiction, the British had few reservations over tolerating and even supporting an organization that was antithetical to their presence in Egypt. This cynical approach was motivated, in part, because, like the British, the MB was also opposed to Egyptian nationalists, left-wing organizations, independent labor institutions, and communist entities in general.

The raison d'être of the Muslim Brotherhood was—and continues to be—cleansing Islam of all foreign elements and restoring it to its pristine essence as practiced at the time of the Prophet Mohammed. To accomplish this resurrection of the true faith, the Brotherhood and its later offshoots worked with grim determination and fanaticism toward the establishment of a theocratic Islamic republic. To this end, the Muslim Brothers have consigned themselves to do battle throughout the Middle East and beyond.

The foundation of the organization in the 1920s came at a time when the Muslim world was in disarray. Ataturk (Mustapha Kemal) had dismantled the Ottoman Empire in 1924 and had supplanted it with a secular Turkish republic. The Muslim territories, with the exception of Turkey, were parceled out by the victorious European powers and recast as "mandates," in order to avoid using the label "colonies." The end of the Ottoman Empire also spelled the end of the Caliphate and the fragmentation of Islam. Gilles Kepel asserts:

> The Muslim Brothers formed their society in Egypt in order to reclaim Islam's political dimension, which had formerly resided in the person of the now-fallen caliph. Confronted by the Egyptian nationalists of the time—who demanded independence, the departure of the British, and a democratic constitution—the Brothers responded with a slogan that is still current in the Islamist movement: "The Koran is our constitution."[18]

Ever since 1924, in one form or another, various Muslim organizations and individuals have been trying to re-create the Islamic unity that they perceive as having been represented by the Ottoman Caliph. The search for an all-embracing Islamic entity, through either the leadership of a single religious-political entity or that of an individual, remains at the crux of the Muslim restlessness that has marked the twentieth and early twenty-first centuries. The strange characters spewed forth by the chaos of the post-Ottoman Middle East came at the forefront of competing ideologies and movements offering pan-Arabism or pan-Islam, but with the purpose of uniting the disparate Muslim world. Secular Arab leaders advocated either local or regional nationalism; however, although Muslim activists welcomed the notion of unifying the Arabs, they saw this only as a first step to the establishment of an Islamic state to replace the central role of the Caliphate.[19]

Al-Banna and the Brotherhood attempted to fill that void by preaching Islam as the salvation of the Arabs, and later on of all Muslims beyond the frontiers of Egypt. Until 1936, the MB concentrated on acquiring members, creating branches in Egypt, and delivering social welfare. But after 1936, the Muslim Brothers expanded their activities beyond the borders of Egypt. The outbreak of the Arab rebellion against the British mandate in Palestine offered al-Banna a unique opportunity to engage the society in a cause that was quickly capturing the hearts and minds of Arabs and Muslims throughout the world.[20] He threw the weight of the Muslim Brothers into organizing a recruiting campaign for volunteers to fight in Palestine, as well as to raise money.

The Palestinian crisis of 1936 was neither the first nor the last, but one in a series of violent rebellions that ultimately became a major stimulant to radical movements within the Muslim world in the twentieth and the beginning of the twenty-first century.[21] Arab resistance to the British provided inspiration for the rise of Arab nationalism in Egypt. It also helped to instigate pan-Arabism, which many believed would come under Egyptian leadership, thus paving the way for Nasser's revolution of 1952. The Palestinian struggle beckoned secular Arab nationalists, because it underscored the fight by Arabs in Palestine for self-determination and statehood. At the same time, the position of Jerusalem in Islam acted as a magnet for the religious militants, who could not accept the loss of the third sacred city so critical in the Islamic faith.

At the center of the Palestinian conundrum stood Hajj Amin al-Husseini, the Mufti of Jerusalem, who owed his position to the British, and who was also their most bitter enemy before and after his appointment.[22] Al-Husseini has stalked the history of Palestine since the beginning of the British mandate until the present; he has cast a long shadow over the roots of political Islam. Remarkably, in 1921 he was not the first choice for Mufti; in fact, he received the lowest number of votes from the Muslim electors appointed by the British administration of Palestine to elect the Mufti.[23] However, al-Husseini and his supporters organized a campaign to promote his candidacy and with considerable venom negated the others. Letters of support from Palestinian notables (including leaders of the Christian communities), as well as petitions with hundreds of signatures, inundated the British authorities. Although these made some impact on the mandate administration, other factors conspired to confer the position of Mufti on al-Husseini.

One recent theory advocated by David Dalin and John Rothmann is that a key player in the appointment of al-Husseini was Ernest Richmond, the assistant political secretary of the British High Commission in Jerusalem. Richmond was the high commissioner's advisor on Arab affairs, but equally significantly, according to Dalin and Rothmann, "it was rumored that Richmond and al-Husseini were involved in a passionate homosexual relationship. As a result of their relationship, Richmond enthusiastically used his political influence to persuade Sir Herbert Samuel to appoint al-Husseini as mufti."[24] Equally interesting is the claim of these authors that "Richmond, who had previously been employed as a minor British government official in Cairo, had been brought to Jerusalem from Egypt by his longtime lover and mentor, Sir Ronald Storrs, the British mandatory governor of Palestine."[25]

There is little evidence for these outrageous assertions. Dalin and Rothmann base their theory on one single reference in a study by Elie Kedourie, in which he states that Richmond and Storrs had shared a house in Jerusalem—as they had also shared a flat earlier in Cairo.[26] Beyond that, Kedourie offers no further insight into the relationship between Richmond and Storrs, and he certainly provides no comment on any possible homosexual ménage-à-trois embracing al-Husseini, Richmond, and Storrs. However, Kedourie does stipulate that Richmond's intervention with Samuel was decisive and that it practically ensured al-Husseini's appointment.[27]

Perhaps Dalin and Rothmann's claim of a homosexual connection is in response to the widespread incredulity that someone as ill-qualified as al-Husseini should have been elected. He had neither the education nor the experience of the other contenders who could have been appointed by Samuel to the post of Mufti. Equally remarkable is the fact that Samuel was Jewish and a Zionist, while al-Husseini clearly demonstrated anti-British and anti-Jewish biases. It begs the question why someone with Samuel's convictions would have even considered such a poor choice, insofar as British and Zionist interests were concerned. Kedourie speculates that the choice of al-Husseini was a product of timing and the decisive intervention by Richmond. On the other hand, Philip Mattar argues that the Husseini family had monopolized the position of Mufti since the seventeenth century, thus affording al-Husseini religious legitimacy.[28]

Another possibility is that the British disingenuously appointed al-Husseini precisely because of his shortcomings. His lack of credentials, combined with the Husseini family history, made him a perfect candidate for manipulation.[29] The history of British imperial policy is replete with the concept of ruling through compliant indigenous leaders. To contain al-Husseini, the British confirmed him simply as Mufti, not Grand Mufti, and did not give him an official letter of appointment.[30] Furthermore, Samuel appointed al-Husseini president of the Supreme Muslim Council, which controlled the religious schools, orphanages, Islamic courts, mosques, and the funds of the awqaf (charitable foundations). This gave al-Husseini considerable power over Muslim affairs in Palestine.

One additional factor that may substantiate the theory that the British believed they could manipulate al-Husseini is that, according to Rashid Khalidi, the office of Mufti was refashioned to accommodate the interests of the mandate authority. First, the British changed his title to Grand Mufti of Palestine (as opposed to Mufti of Jerusalem); although important, the new office was limited in terms of geography and influence. The Mufti of Jerusalem, prior to the appointment of al-Husseini, had no authority over the other muftis in Palestine.[31] Under the terms of this new arrangement, with the title and powers of the reconstituted office, the Grand Mufti of Palestine, combined with the position of president of the Supreme Muslim Council, afforded the officeholder consid-erable jurisdiction and power over the lives of the Palestinians. Consequently, if the British could manipulate the Mufti, they could exercise through him a greater degree of control over the Muslims throughout Palestine.

Regardless of all these theories, al-Husseini proved to be a disastrous choice for the British and caused them endless difficulties. He instigated numerous riots and revolts; eventually he collaborated with the Nazis, spending most of the Second World War in Berlin, where he had the ear and protection of the German führer himself. By the end of the war, he had come full circle, and he was once again employed by the British. In the interim, al-Husseini had be-come yet another catalyst for political Islam and, perhaps more than anyone, was responsible for making the cause of the Palestinians the ethos of both Arab nationalists and Muslim militants.

The 1936 Arab Revolt in Palestine, led by al-Husseini, was more than an uprising both with respect to its duration (1936–1939) and its impact on pan-Arabism and Egypt.[32] Furthermore, the desire of the Palestinians to free them-selves from British rule spilled outside the confines of Palestine and manifested itself as a cause espoused by Arab nationalists and Muslim militants, as well as ordinary people in the Middle East.[33] Indeed, the Palestinian struggle eventu-ally became submerged in the rhetoric of pan-Arabists and militant Muslims, but also in that of radical and revolutionary organizations in the West.[34]

The Palestinian revolt was the first opportunity for the Muslim Brother-hood to blood many of its members. The three-year crisis and the eventual de-feat of the Palestinians radicalized an entire generation of Arabs and engendered the notion of Egypt as the champion of the rights of all Arabs, eventually inspir-ing the establishment of the Arab League in Cairo on March 22, 1945. Conse-quently, the work of the Muslim Brothers in Palestine elevated the organization from the fringes of society to a rapprochement with mainstream Egyptian po-litical elites.[35]

For the Mufti, the 1936 revolt was the beginning of a lifelong journey of running and hiding, all the while waging a relentless war against the British. By October of 1936, al-Husseini and the other Arab leaders were becoming concil-iatory and came close to reaching an agreement with the British to end the re-bellion. However, when the Peel Commission, set up to examine what led to the outbreak of violence, recommended the partition of Palestine, al-Husseini con-demned it and on July 8, 1937, vowed to continue fighting the British and the Zionists.[36]

NINE

The British-Jewish Military Alliance

"Rags, wretchedness, poverty and dirt, those signs and symbols
that indicate the presence of Muslim rule
more surely than the crescent-flag itself."
—*Mark Twain*[1]

For millennia a strange and exotic assortment of characters has left its mark on the blood-drenched land of Palestine. Some were prophets, holy men, soothsayers, vagabonds, charlatans, evangelists, missionaries, zealots, pilgrims; but most were soldiers committed to wresting from history their version of the Holy Land. For others, Palestine was, and continues to remain, a land of religious imagination. During the nineteenth century, thousands of books, travel guides, histories, memoirs, and novels published in North America and Europe offered a Western-tainted version of Palestine as the land of the Bible. The notion of Palestine as the Christian Holy Land and Palestine as the home of the Jews shaped Western perceptions of the region.[2] Concurrently, millions of Muslims conceived of Palestine, particularly after 1948, as inextricably linked to their faith but lost to Islam. Regardless of religious affiliation or national identity, these unique individuals contributed to the legend that shaped the legacy of the region.

In 1938, one such character was a military pilgrim by the name of Orde Charles Wingate. Occasionally a perplexed passerby walking across the rolling fields and orchards of the Galilee would notice a bearded and pith-helmet-wearing British officer, with mismatched socks and twin revolvers slung over his hips, leading a ragged band of Jewish fighters and a handful of British soldiers.[3] According to one observer, Moshe Shertok, "He looked like a man devoured by a kind of inner fire, addicted to a single idea that had captured his imagination."[4] Basil Liddell Hart, Britain's distinguished military historian, described Wingate as a kind of Lawrence of the Jews.[5] He became such an ardent Zionist that he earned the term "Ha Yadid," or "The Friend."[6]

Yet Wingate's background should have predisposed him to be pro-Arab, as was the case with certain elements of the British army. In stark contrast to Wingate's staunch Zionist convictions, his cousin Sir Reginald, for example, was a former high commissioner who believed that the Jews had dragged the Ottoman Empire into war against the British.[7] Wingate was born in India, the son of a colonial officer, and had followed in the footsteps of his ancestors by pursuing a military career. As a young man he attended a prestigious school and early on he developed an interest in Arab affairs. In 1936 he arrived in Palestine as an intelligence officer and became obsessed with Zionism.[8]

The notoriously eccentric Wingate and his men comprised the Special Night Squads (SNS), effectively one of the first Special Forces units. The 1936 Arab uprising had expanded rapidly into full-blown rebellion and the British desperately needed reinforcements. Wingate organized his elite force of counterinsurgency troops to scatter, terrorize, and often kill the Arab guerrillas in nighttime ambushes. The SNS included four platoons comprising about two hundred soldiers, of which 150 were Jews, and operated in the Galilee. Ostensibly the task of the SNS was to guard the oil pipeline from Iraq, but its primary task was to counter terrorism with terrorism.[9]

Ultimately, Wingate's tactics laid the guidelines for the Israeli army and the basic framework for the organization and deployment of Israel's Special Forces. According to a publication issued by the Israeli Ministry of Defense, "The teaching of Orde Wingate, his character and leadership were a cornerstone for many of the Haganah's commanders, and his influence can be seen in the Israeli Defence Force's combat doctrine.[10]

British security cooperation with the Jewish fighters was not limited only to training, equipment, and logistical support but also included intelligence and espionage work. The Haganah also provided Arabic-speaking Jews who proved to be of considerable assistance to the British since the mandate authority lacked officers and men proficient in the language.[11] Committed pro-Zionists like Wingate were an exception. British-Jewish collaboration in Palestine was based on self-interest in response to the 1936 Arab rebellion, which dashed the prospect of any compromise between the Jews, Arabs, and the British over coexistence in Palestine.

Although, with some exceptions, the 1920s were comparatively peaceful, the British could not find a mechanism to balance Arab fears over Jewish immigration and increasingly extensive land purchases.[12] Both the issue of land and immigration were exacerbated in the 1930s by the anti-Semitic policies of Poland and by the mass persecution of Jews by Nazi Germany, which dramatically increased the number of Jewish refugees pressing on the shores of Palestine.

The 1936 rebellion was a multifaceted affair not necessarily driven by nationalism or religion exclusively, but it had a critical impact on the future of the

Arab Palestinians. The British had from the beginning of the mandate encouraged religion and supported traditional institutions as a means to counter nationalism. In this respect they created the precedent for the Americans, who followed the same policy in the twentieth and twenty-first centuries and also tried to use Islam to counter Egypt's Nasser and in 1979 armed and trained the mujahidin to counter the pro-Soviet secular regime in Afghanistan.

In Palestine the mandate officials tried to channel the leadership of the Palestinians away from nationalism by refashioning institutions such as the office of the Mufti and by the establishment of the Supreme Muslim Council. The British appointed Hajj Amin al-Husseini as Mufti in the belief that he would not oppose the mandate, and that this position, along with the Supreme Muslim Council, would undermine the emergence of a national and secular political leadership.[13] But the 1936 rebellion both politicized and internationalized the Palestinian issue and restructured the leadership of the Palestinian Arabs.

The 1936 rebellion trigger occurred on the evening of April 15, 1936, when a group of armed Arabs set up a roadblock near the village of Tulkarm to ambush passing Jewish and British convoys as well as extort donations from Arab drivers. On this occasion, they shot three Jewish drivers, one died immediately, another five days later, but the third survived.[14] Quickly the cyclone of vengeance and retribution sucked in Jews, Arabs, and the Arab Christians. The members of a radical Zionist organization, the Hairgun Hatzvai Haleumi Be Yisrael (National Military Organization, or IZL), killed two Arabs in a house near the city of Petah Tikva. A few days later, on April 19, mobs of Arab peasants vented their anger by rampaging through Jaffa, taking the lives of nine Jews and injuring another sixty. Muslim notables who spread rumors that the Jews had murdered an Arab woman and several Syrian workers incited the mob. From April 19–21 national strike committees sprouted in almost every Arab town from Gaza to Nablus. During the summer armed groups formed in the countryside, particularly in the rural regions of central and northern Palestine. Violence spread rapidly and labor strikes paralyzed several cities.[15]

The British were ill-prepared to deal with the rebellion since it lacked a particular center of geographic and leadership gravity. Effectively, the rebellion was driven by local and regional forces and not guided from the top. An attempt was made by the Mufti and by the existing political parties to seize control of events, but Arab leadership remained fragmented.[16] From the beginning of the mandate, Arab society was riddled with factions and local rivalries among the various notables—a condition that the British readily exploited, but it did them little good in the 1936 rebellion since the uprising was grass-roots-based.[17]

Because of cutbacks, after 1930 the mandate authority had at its disposal two infantry battalions and an RAF armored car squadron. Initially, the British response was restrained in the mistaken notion that the violence would quickly blow over. But in the first few weeks of the uprising the British forces were overwhelmed and an additional twenty thousand troops were brought from Egypt and Britain. Despite the reinforcements, by June 1936 the rural areas of Palestine came under the power of armed guerrilla bands and the British only maintained control over the cities.[18]

In September of 1937, after the intervention of the Arab leaders of Saudi Arabia, Iraq, Yemen, and Transjordan, the violence came to an end.[19] Peace was short-lived because the recommendations of the Peel Royal Commission, although tolerable to the Jews, were not acceptable to the Arabs. The Royal Commission recommended the end of the mandate and the partition of Palestine into a Jewish state and an Arab area. The Arab zone was to include 70 percent of the mandate territory, but would be merged with Transjordan; only 20 percent was allocated for a Jewish state; and 10 percent, the areas from Jaffa to Jerusalem, would be remain under a redefined British mandate.[20] The Jewish leadership responded with qualified support but the Arabs officially denounced the commission's proposals and demanded the establishment of an Arab state to include all of Palestine.

Unwittingly, the recommendations of the Peel Commission mobilized Arab opinion not only in Palestine but throughout the Arab world. The rebellion resumed with renewed ferocity. Despite the extensive and harsh British reprisals, the Arab infrastructure and capability for guerrilla warfare had remained intact. The British had failed to destroy or disarm the armed guerrilla bands during the previous year. In this case Arab lack of unity worked to the advantage of the insurgents. When the British eliminated a particular band of fighters another group quickly took its place. The absence of a central command and infrastructure did not afford the British the opportunity to strike at the core of the rebellion.

The Arabs, on the other hand, had the advantage of attacking stationary targets and targets of opportunity—police stations, the railway system, roads, telephone and telegraph lines, the pipeline of the Iraq Petroleum Company, and British convoys trying to supply isolated posts. The Arabs deployed snipers positioned in strategic locations who were able to shoot at patrols, vehicles, and civilian passersby.[21] Assassination of moderate Arabs as well as against individuals members of the mandate authority discouraged collaboration and kept the British confined in the cities and towns. For example, on September 26 Arab gunmen assassinated Lewis Y. Andrews, the acting district commissioner of the Galilee. During 1937, Arab rebels launched a total of 438 attacks, 109 against British military and police forces, 143 against Jewish settlements, and the remainder aimed at other Arabs. Ninety-seven people were killed and 149 wounded.[22]

Faced with an expanding and diffused insurgency, the British increased cooperation with the Palestinian Jews. As a result, the British received considerable intelligence on Arab activities from the far better informed Haganah intelligence service, Sherut Yediot (SHAI, or Information Service), in exchange for concessions to the Haganah's own attempts to expand militarily.[23] The British also created special military units to protect Jewish civilians and to mount joint operations against the Arab rioters. One of these, the special Jewish police force, called the Notrim, or Guards, also included an elite and mobile Settlement Police force, the Nodedot. Almost every member of the Notrim was part of the Haganah and thus the Nodedot had in addition to its official British chain of command an "illegal" Haganah commander.[24] The Haganah used the British training to evolve the Nodedot into the first unit that established a long tradition of the use of unconventional Special Forces, which have played a crucial and significant role in Israeli military history.[25] The other joint operations military unit was the Special Night Squads, formed in 1938 by Orde Wingate.

The Special Night Squads carried out their nighttime ambushes against Arab fighters from 1938 to 1939. Beginning in 1938, without authorization from his superiors, Wingate led small patrols at night of Haganah soldiers from the besieged kibbutz of Hanita in an effort to incite the Jewish fighters to go "beyond the fence" and switch their defensive mentality to an offensive one.[26] These patrols comprised the unofficial first actions of what would later become the single most effective counterinsurgency unit that the British forces ever employed against the Arab rebels in Palestine.

In spring of 1938, the British high command in Palestine approved Wingate's seventeen-page proposal for the recognition of the Special Night Squads as a joint Anglo-Jewish military unit deployed "to persuade the gangs that in their predatory raids there is every chance of running into a government gang which is determined to destroy them not by an exchange of shots in the distance but by bodily assault with bayonet and bomb."[27] Quartered in three north Jewish settlements,[28] the Anglo-Jewish squads succeeded in ambushing the majority of Arab attacks on the Haifa oil pipeline, and managed to end the siege on Kibbutz Hanita.[29]

On July 10, 1938, the Night Squads expanded its operations and advanced on Dabburiya, a small town on the slopes of Mount Tavor, approximately eight kilometers southeast of Nazareth, in response to rebel attacks against Nazareth.

Wingate's force included thirty-two British soldiers and fifty-five Jewish fighters, about half of the SNS. On July 11, he initially had moved on the town of Ein Mahil, but upon finding it free from insurgents proceeded to nearby Dabburiya. On the outskirts of Dabburiya, Wingate's men lost the element of surprise after engaging two Arab sentries and spent the next several hours exchanging fire with the rebels until the Arab guerrillas melted into the nearby hills.

Unfortunately, in the confusion—multiple squads pursuing fleeing guerrillas—one of the SNS units fired upon Wingate and several of his men, whose silhouetted figures were indistinguishable at night from those of the enemy. Wingate was hit five times in his extremities by ricocheting bullets, while a Jewish member of the unit was shot several times in the stomach and died shortly after. One of the British officers in the SNS recalled, "Though Wingate's face was white as a sheet and very taut, he was sitting there, in the hay, covered in blood and giving orders in English and in Hebrew quite calmly. . . . He was quite an extraordinary man." Zvi Brenner, a Jewish squad leader, recalled how Wingate refused to leave until all of his men were confirmed to be safe, despite his injuries: "He looked very pale and frightened and sorry for himself. He hated pain and the first thing he said to me was: 'I hope I'm not going to die because of you. I refused to leave until I made sure you were all right. Now take me to a hospital quickly.'"[30]

Further successful operations followed, with the Night Squads killing large numbers of Arab guerrillas while suffering almost no losses of their own. The most spectacular of these was possibly Wingate's fast response to the ongoing October 2 massacre of nineteen Jews (eleven of whom were children) in Tiberia. Rushing to the scene, the Night Squads managed to kill between forty and fifty of the Arab fighters with no losses. Furthermore, in a mop-up operation two days later at the port town of Dabburiya, Wingate radioed the local RAF squadron for tactical air support—unusual and innovative thinking for 1938. Emboldened by his success, Wingate intensified his training program at Ein Herod and began a school for Jewish officers there as well, though only one cohort would ever graduate, in early October 1938.[31] At the same time, however, he became more outwardly eccentric, growing a beard and donning an old pith helmet. On another occasion, he showed up to a wardroom party on a ship in Haifa in a filthy field uniform and carrying a bag of grenades over one shoulder.[32] For British officials in Palestine, the unprecedented and brutal battlefield successes of the largely Jewish-staffed SNS and its fervently Zionist commanding officer held uneasy portents for the future.

In the spring of 1939, the Arab rebellion was winding down and the mandate authorities decided to disband the SNS and to transfer Wingate out of

Palestine. The end of the crisis evaporated British interest in arming Zionists. A cascade of recriminations along with convenient hindsight followed on the heels of the British victory of the 1936 Arab rebellion. A conference of British officials voiced their opposition to "dressing Jews up as British soldiers . . . [and] to have a proportion of Jews in SNS detachments." Others held the ambush tactics of the SNS in distaste. Hugh Foot, who would later become Lord Caradon and Britain's last governor of Cyprus, complained that the SNS "forfeited our general reputation for fair fighting."[33]

On May 11, 1939, Wingate was reassigned, and though he offered to resign his commission and remain in Palestine illegally to assist the Zionist cause, on May 26 he departed Palestine, never to return. Cooperation between the British security forces and the Jewish community in Palestine came to an abrupt end but the exigencies of the Second World War forced the renewal of the relationship. Wingate was transferred to Britain and at the outbreak of the war commanded an antiaircraft gun but shortly after he secured a posting to the Sudan.

In East Africa he distinguished himself using similar Special Forces tactics he had developed in Palestine culminating in the establishment of the Gideon Force—a guerrilla group of approximately 1,700 composed of British, Sudanese, and Ethiopian soldiers in which he invited a number of veterans of the Haganah SNS to join him. During the East Africa campaign, Wingate's small force fought ferociously and at the end took the surrender of twenty thousand Italians. But victory did not result in promotion or recognition for his efforts. He was again sent home to Britain, and in February 1941 he arrived in Burma. Once again he organized mobile commando forces to strike behind enemy lines and achieved some success. Tragically, on March 24, 1944, Wingate flew to assess the situation of his commando forces in Burma, but on the return flight the American B-25 Mitchell crashed into the jungle-covered hills near Bishnupur in northwest India killing him and nine others.[34] He died at the age of forty-one.

For the Jews, the outbreak of the war in Europe offered an opportunity to aid their fellow Jews by joining the fight against the Nazis, while for the British the rapid victories of the Nazis left them vulnerable and they sought help from all quarters. However, the 1939 British Report, which had severely limited Jewish immigration to Palestine, strained relations between the Yishuv and the mandate authorities. Certainly, the British were anxious to avoid equipping and training a "Jewish army" that would eventually challenge the mandate and stir Arab dissent, despite the willingness of Palestinian Jews to fight against the Axis. David Ben-Gurion's (Zionist leader) famous declaration, "We must fight

Germany as though there were no White Paper, and fight the White Paper as though there were no war,"[35] encapsulated the Zionist policy. The British, on the other hand, officially rejected the notion of cooperating with the Jews, and instead established a clandestine relationship under the auspices of the British intelligence services.

In June 1940, the French surrendered and their colonies in Syria and Lebanon came under the control of the Vichy regime. In the same month Italy's Benito Mussolini threw in his lot with Adolf Hitler, and overnight Palestine came under threat of an Italian invasion. Underscoring the new crisis for both the British and Jews in Palestine, Italian planes bombed Haifa and Tel Aviv.[36] In September 1940, the British called for recruits of any nationality from Palestine—nearly ninety thousand men and over fifty thousand women (out of a total of 650,000 Jews living in the Yishuv) volunteered to join in various capacities.[37] Although cooperation with the British meant providing labor for constructing bases and roads throughout Palestine and industrial trade with the British army, approval for military participation or acceptance of Jewish volunteers into the British army was refused.[38] The official consensus in Whitehall was that the Jews should not be given a combat role in the war.

However, cooperation in clandestine activities between British intelligence and the Jewish Agency, which represented Jewish interests in Palestine, had begun as early as July 1940. Propaganda operations in Syria were conducted with Jewish assistance and a Free French radio transmitter was placed in the Haifa home of David Cohen, a high-ranking SHAI[39] agent. At the same time, a network of agents run by Yishuv intelligence officer Tuvya Arazi in Syria and Lebanon was distributing propaganda leaflets. These propaganda operations were carried out under the direction of Brigadier Iltyd Clayton, head of army intelligence at British headquarters in Cairo.[40]

The Special Operations Executive also initiated a secret relationship with Jewish organizations. The chief of SOE in Cairo, Sir John Pollock, worked clandestinely with the Jewish Agency to establish special units that included Jewish fighters from the Haganah who could operate undercover in Arab populations.[41] The plan was to send this "Arab Platoon" into Syria and Lebanon to collect intelligence and conduct sabotage, should the Germans occupy Syria after the surrender of the French army in June.[42] This collaboration was the first significant initiative between British intelligence and the Yishuv.

The majority of the members of the Arab Platoon (Arabic-speaking Jews) had come from Arab countries and were able to effectively blend in with native Arab populations. They received their training at the SOE school on Mount Carmel, near Haifa, and platoon members were taught Arab customs such as singing and dancing, games such as backgammon, and other similar cultural practices, alongside their military training. Even so, their training did not always keep them from being unmasked. On one occasion two of the undercover Arabs were arrested by the Vichy French security service in Damascus. Major Nick Hammond, the SOE liaison with the Arab Platoon, which involved sending two Palmach (the strike-force of the Hagana) agents disguised as British deserters, later extracted them in an elaborate scheme. C. M. Woodhouse also worked with Reuven Zaslany, a SHAI officer and the Jewish Agency but, like Hammond, was posted to the SOE mission with the Greek resistance.[43] Ultimately, as the Italians or the Germans did not invade Syria, the twelve Arab Platoon fighters in Damascus were left in place with little to do.[44]

In May 1941, when the Allies had finalized their plans to invade the Vichy-controlled Levant, SOE headquarters in Cairo employed Jewish agents from Palestine in a plan to infiltrate north into Lebanon and sabotage the oil refineries in Tripoli. On May 18, 1941, a group of twenty-three Haganah fighters embarked on the cutter *Sea Lion* in Haifa, under the command of Major Anthony Palmer, a well-connected young cavalry officer. Palmer, a twenty-six-year-old Royal Dragoon Guards officer, had left this elite unit for service with the SOE in occupied countries.[45]

An hour later the team ceased radio contact after reporting they had entered Lebanese waters. No trace was found of the boat and its crew for some time. Eventually the SOE received reports that members of a captured German radio post mentioned that an Italian submarine had intercepted a boat of Jews and British soldiers. Another report referred to a French officer who buried seven bodies washed ashore on a beach in Lebanon at the end of May 1941. Another witness reported that a Vichy judge in Tripoli had told him of a group of Palestinian prisoners transferred to Aleppo on May 22, 1939, and summarily executed—their boat having been destroyed by the explosives it had been carrying.[46]

On May 15, 1941, the Haganah created an elite military force, the Palmach (Plugot Sadeh or Storm Companies), to "carry out actions against the enemy . . . with or without the help of [British] forces." This decision was influenced by the SOE-Haganah reconnaissance patrols in Syria as well as by the Tripoli operation.[47] Nine companies of thirty volunteers each were organized and scattered throughout various kibbutzim (where they also worked part-time in the fields) in Palestine under the control of the Haganah.[48] The Palmach had two official objectives: to protect the Yishuv from Arabs and to defend Palestine in the event of a German invasion. In the latter case, the Palmach would use guerrilla tactics to disrupt German communication lines and sabotage enemy airfields.

The companies even boasted of a "German Platoon" composed of German and Austrian Jews who were familiar with all Wehrmacht arms and weapon systems.

Recruitment to the Palmach was conducted in secret, and Yitzhak Sadeh, the commander of the Palmach and the former commander of FOSH, and his company commanders personally screened each potential fighter carefully. By 1943 the Palmach consisted of more than one thousand fighters and included a naval commando unit, Palyam (Sea Companies), which trained its soldiers in amphibious landing, naval sabotage, and deep-sea operations, and an air force, Palavir (Air Companies), whose pilots flew gliders and small transport planes. Ultimately, the Palmach proved to be a training ground for Israel's ruling elite and Palmach veterans dominated the upper echelons of Israeli political and military leadership.[49]

The Palmach went into action for the Allies prior to the Anglo-American invasion of Syria and Lebanon. One hundred of the Palmach's Shachar Company, composed of Jews disguised as Arabs and influenced by the Arab Platoon of the Haganah, infiltrated into Vichy territory, where they assisted Free French agents in various clandestine operations and collected intelligence for the British.[50] Then, on the eve of the July 8 British invasion of Syria and Lebanon, the SOE sent two companies of the Palmach, commanded by Moshe Dayan and Yigal Allon, into Vichy territory to cut telephone lines, open routes for Australian army reconnaissance units, and seize and hold several bridges. Dayan lost his eye in this operation after his field glasses were struck by a French bullet and disintegrated into his face.[51] When a colonel from the Australian army's 7th Division offered to recommend the Palmach fighters for decorations for their bravery and skill in seizing a bridge spanning the Litani River in Lebanon, Allon declined and asked that he instead be permitted to keep any captured weapons. The colonel agreed, and out of gratitude even offered up an additional cache of arms seized from the French.[52]

Though Dayan was unfit for combat following the loss of his eye, Reuven Zaslany had another plan for his injured friend. As Dayan commented:

> British intelligence asked Zaslany for a proposal for the creation of an underground network that would gather military intelligence and relay it somehow to the British [in the event of a German invasion of Palestine]. I took it upon myself to organise this network . . . in August 1941 I submitted a detailed proposal . . . the British approved the plan and in September 1941 a course was held for 20 wireless operators . . . the network's official name was P.S. (for Palestine Scheme), but it was

known was "Moshe Dayan's network" . . . I suggested that if the Germans took Palestine, we would increase our intelligence gathering activities, and add to the group of wireless operators units of "Fake-Arabs" or "Fake-Germans" that we would train. As I saw it, the best way to gather information would be to enlist the help of Jews who could look, speak and behave like Arabs or Germans. . . . The idea of setting up a German unit and an Arab unit was later actually carried out in the Palmach.[53]

Zaslany was in charge of implementing the plan. He received the necessary operational details from the British officer in charge of the operation on January 12, 1942, and developed the training program for Dayan's men.[54] On March 8, 1942, the Haganah approved Zaslany's request to include Palmach companies in the scheme and by April the first training course for sharpshooting and explosives had begun at Kibbutz Mishmar Ha'Emek, with courses in reconnaissance. The first of the trainees graduated on May 30, 1942.[55]

The local mandate authorities were kept in the dark over the activities at the kibbutz, as it contravened British policy of maintaining neutrality among the Palestinian communities in order to avoid inciting political violence. Thus when the Palestine police discovered Palmach soldiers bearing arms and carrying out military exercises at the kibbutz, Captain Aubrey Eban,[56] a young South African working for army intelligence in Cairo, was dispatched to ensure that the SOE's operation and the Palmach units were left undisturbed. He was later appointed liaison between the SOE and Haganah HQ. He recalls this appointment:

> I was supposed to obtain my posting from the commander of the Special Operations Section in Cairo, Colonel Dumwill, known both for his courage and for his enormous capacity for alcohol. I therefore requested an appointment at ten in the morning, in order to be sure of finding him sober. Despite a large bottle of whiskey on the table, everything went well. I left his office with the impressive title of liaison officer between Special Operations and the Jewish Agency for Palestine.[57]

During the duration of the Mishmar Ha'Emek camp's operation, six hundred Palmach fighters were trained in groups of one hundred using the same sets of false papers in succession.[58] However, when the Axis forces faced defeat in North Africa, the cooperation between the Palmach and the SOE ended on a poor note. After the training camp at Mishmar Ha'Emek was closed, the British refused to return to the Haganah the arms that the Jewish militia had contributed and in retaliation a Palmach platoon broke into the SOE training school on Mount Carmel and stole 277 rifles and twenty-two machine guns from its arsenal.[59] That was end of SOE-Jewish cooperation for the duration of the Second World War, but not the end of the relationship between clandestine Jewish organizations with British intelligence.

Apart from the SOE, MI9, the "escape and evasion" unit of British intelligence, entered into a secret arrangement to employ the Jews of Palestine for covert operations. The officer in charge of the MI9 unit for southern Europe at the British armed forces headquarters in Cairo was Anthony Simmonds. Simmonds had served with Wingate in Palestine and Ethiopia, as well as with the SOE in Palestine.[60]

Early in 1943, Zaslany and Ze'ev Shind, a senior commander of Ha'Mossad le'Aliya Bet,[61] the illegal immigration department of the Jewish Agency's Istanbul branch, signed an agreement with Simmonds to use Jews for work behind enemy lines. The plan called for Jewish agents from Palestine to parachute into Nazi-occupied Europe and arrange the evacuation of Jews from Romania into Turkey as well as use their network to assist British soldiers who had escaped captivity. According to Shaul Avigur, of the thirty-two parachutists trained for this mission, twenty-six carried out operations, and twenty-one of them did so with MI9.[62]

The MI9 operation had some success, but also carried a heavy price. Reuven Dafni parachuted into Yugoslavia on March 13, 1944, and managed to organize the rescue of 124 British and American airmen. Unfortunately, by the end of the mission thirteen out of the original twenty-six agents were captured and seven of those were executed.

In addition to collaboration between the SOE and MI9, MI6 established a separate relationship with the Jewish clandestine organizations. In 1943, the Inter-Services Liaison Department (ISLD), the Secret Intelligence Service's code name in the Middle East, desperately needed radio operators for Romania and to maintain contact with Tito's partisans. The ISLD approached the Jewish Agency, and Zaslany of the SHAI in Haifa selected fourteen volunteers, who, once deployed, would be handled exclusively by the British. The first volunteer, Reuven Dafni, was ready to parachute into Yugoslavia in March 1943. However, the mission was delayed until May because the Jewish recruits refused to enlist in the British army contrary to the agreement between the ISLD and Zaslany. The problem was resolved and the operation continued until the summer of 1944.[63]

British contacts with clandestine Jewish organizations, although secret, were between directorates of Britain's intelligence community and organizations controlled by the Jewish Agency—the legitimate body representing Palestinian Jews. The British needed agents with fluency in a variety of languages, knowledge of European cities, and familiarity with the terrain in North Africa and the Middle East. The Jewish Agency and other Jewish organizations collaborated with the British and the Allies both to fight the common enemy and to exploit British as well as American military and intelligence expertise for the creation of an Israeli state.

However, the clandestine relationships with Jewish Palestinians extended beyond the quasi-legal departments of the Jewish Agency to much more radical groups committed to the use of terror and whose tactics would inflict considerable damage to the British in the postwar period.

TEN

Kill the Mufti:
Politics and Blowback

"The Mufti's removal is unlikely to have ill effects, since it is strength,
not weakness, which is admired in the Arab world."
—*British Chiefs of Staff, 1940*[1]

On September 26, 1937, when the Arab extremists killed Lewis Y. Andrews, district commissioner of Galilee, the British seized the opportunity to go after the Mufti and the other Arab leaders of the uprising. Over two hundred leading members of the Arab community were arrested, and the British stripped al-Husseini of his chairmanship of the Waqf (Islamic charity) Committee in Jerusalem. Fearing arrest, the Mufti slipped out of Jerusalem on the evening of October 14 and shortly after reached Lebanon. From exile, al-Husseini continued to direct the revolt, but after the collapse of the rebellion in Palestine, he made his way to Baghdad in late October 1939.

In Iraq, the Mufti helped instigate and became an integral part of the 1941 Iraqi revolt against the British. Al-Husseini attempted to orchestrate a common front of Arab leaders from Palestine, Iraq, Transjordan, and Syria. He also facilitated negotiations with the Germans to secure arms and political support from the Axis.[2] The British authorities in London believed that if Iraq reached a secret agreement with the Axis, this outcome would represent a major setback in the Middle East. Furthermore, a pro-Axis government in Baghdad would threaten Britain's supply of petroleum, as well as the overland and air routes to India.[3] In the spring of 1941, the tide of war was turning against the British, with defeats in mainland Greece, Crete, and North Africa. As such, the Iraqi revolt could not have come at a worse time for the British. Al-Husseini compounded matters by issuing a fatwa urging Arabs and Muslims to lend their support to free Iraq from the British.[4]

As early as October 1940, the British government had begun to consider several options for dealing with al-Husseini, including kidnapping. Leo Amery of the India Office speculated as follows: "Would it be possible for a few bold lads to kidnap the Mufti in Baghdad, run him south by car out to a waiting airplane, and then to Cyprus? Nashashibis[5] in Palestine, Jews, and indeed all the Middle East would laugh, and a real big danger would be averted."[6] However, the secretary of state for the colonies responded with less enthusiasm, pointing out:

> an attempt to kidnap the Mufti would not be practical politics. . . . No doubt the Nashashibis and the Palestine Jews would be pleased, but I am sure that the feelings aroused in Iraq, Egypt, and Saudi Arabia would be very different. I understand that in Baghdad the Mufti is now something of a popular hero, and any direct action against him at our instigation would be widely resented. Moreover, the Mufti has influential friends in Egypt, and we should have difficulty in explaining the position to the Egyptian Government and for that matter to Ibn Saud.[7]

He went on to caution:

> there can be no certainty that the kidnapping could be successfully carried out. I understand that the Mufti has his own private bodyguard. There would probably be resistance and one or two casualties. Perhaps the Mufti himself would be killed. Perhaps the kidnappers would be caught and imprisoned, and the whole story would come out in the Iraqi law courts. I fear that the outcome would be a severe blow to British prestige throughout the Middle East.[8]

The Chiefs of Staff, on the other hand, proposed to have al-Husseini eliminated. In a report to the War Cabinet, the chiefs stated: "There is ample evidence that [al-Husseini] is in enemy pay. The Mufti's removal is unlikely to have ill effects, since it is strength, not weakness, which is admired in the Arab world."[9] The Eastern Department of the Foreign Office was opposed to assassination and concerned over the possible repercussions, whether the event succeeded or failed since, they feared, it would undoubtedly alienate Arab public opinion. Churchill bypassed these objections by stating that the department concerned "could take action required to implement the various recommendations, which [the report of the Chiefs of Staff] contained."[10]

Effectively, Churchill's ambiguous ruling set into motion an attempt to eliminate the Mufti and thus crossed a critical threshold in clandestine operations by authorizing the use of assassination in wartime.[11] In July 1940, the British had established the Special Operations Executive with a mandate for subversion, sabotage, and propaganda. Implicit in this mandate was the use of assassination as an alternative means of achieving military and political objectives. Consequently, the policy framework was established, and the Mufti was to be the first target in what would eventually become a process, albeit clandestine, that would characterize British and American intelligence operations in the post–Second World War period.

However, there was still reluctance to link British policy with the odium of officially sanctioned murder. The response of the Foreign Office to the proposed killing of the Mufti was to caution that British personnel should not be involved in the assassination since "even if the murder was successfully carried out, it would probably not turn out to our advantage, whereas if the attempt were unsuccessful . . . the results might be disastrous . . . it would alienate Arab opinion throughout the Middle East."[12]

Ultimately, the consensus was to leave it to the Chiefs of Staff to decide on how and when to deal with the Mufti. The plan adopted by the Chiefs of Staff after April 1941 was to employ hitherto incarcerated members of the outlawed Irgun, disguised as Arabs, to undertake his assassination.[13] Consequently, General Archibald Wavell, C-in-C Middle East, ordered the release from a Palestine prison of David Raziel, head of the Irgun, along with several of his companions.[14]

On the evening of May 17, 1941, a Dakota aircraft landed at RAF Habbaniya, the British airbase in Iraq. Four armed men deplaned and proceeded to the makeshift headquarters of the British army. Ostensibly, their mission was to destroy Iraqi supplies of aviation fuel in Baghdad. However, before the commandos were to proceed with blowing up the storage tanks, the British commanding general instructed them to make contact with the officer in charge of an Indian unit and ascertain from him the number and strength of Iraqi units facing his army.

Raziel and a British major accompanied two of the Irgun men (Yaakov Meridor and a companion) to the outskirts of the city and sent them off on a small boat for a reconnaissance mission. Not long after they located the major in command of the Indian unit. Raziel, the British major, and the third member of the Irgun team returned to their car, but just as Raziel asked for a cigarette a bomb from a German airplane scored a direct hit on the automobile. The driver lost both legs, while the British officer and Raziel were killed instantly; only one man survived unscathed.[15]

The fact that the operation failed did not deter the British from adopting assassination as a means of achieving strategic or tactical objectives in the future. For example, in the course of the desert campaign in 1941–1942, the British made several efforts to assassinate Field Marshal Erwin Rommel, commander of the Afrika Korps. Middle East headquarters decided that if Rommel, a charismatic general whose continued victories against the British were proving embarrassing, were killed, it would destroy the morale of the Afrika Korps, as well as making it easier for the Eighth Army to defeat the Germans.[16]

The attempts, all of which failed, were implemented by Britain's embryonic Special Forces and took place behind enemy lines. On each occasion, the casualties were high, but the notion of assassination had taken root in British strategic thinking. In fact, the British had dabbled for some time in the use of Special Forces deployed behind enemy lines; to some degree the variety of commando-type units that emerged in North Africa during the Second World War drew inspiration from T. E. Lawrence and his use of Bedouin in raids and sabotage against the Ottoman forces in the Arabian Peninsula during the First World War.

In Europe, the first target for assassination was a senior Nazi officer in occupied Europe who posed a serious threat to the future course of European resistance. On May 27, 1942, two Free Czech agents, trained by the SOE, parachuted into German-occupied Czechoslovakia and killed one of Hitler's favorite SS officers, Reinhard Heydrich, by throwing a bomb at his automobile. Operation Daylight achieved its objectives by removing a vicious yet very competent Nazi leader who might have influenced Hitler in a way that would have prolonged the war.[17] However, the reprisals against the Czechs were extensive and cruel.[18]

As demonstrated in subsequent situations in Europe and the Middle East, the SS reprisals only served to radicalize the local population and contribute to the expansion of resistance activities. Not so remarkably, the assassination of Heydrich by the British SOE caused the Germans to overreact, taking revenge against the local population and thus swelling the ranks of the Czech resistance. Yet, in Palestine, the British would make the very same mistake as the Germans, by trying to suppress the Jewish resistance movement through the use of intimidation and other dubious counterinsurgency tactics. Although often harsh and violent, the actions of the British Palestinian authorities hardly compared with those of the Nazis; they did, however, succeed in alienating the Jews and leaving them little choice but to join radical and extreme paramilitary organizations.

Meanwhile, during the first years of the Second World War, the British, out of desperation, not only resorted to assassination but also organized an extensive program of cooperation with underground groups in occupied Europe. This involved training individuals in clandestine warfare, supplying them with weapons and explosives, and providing them with expertise in intelligence tradecraft and propaganda methods. Equally significant was the decision to permit the SOE to form covert alliances with organizations that were antithetical to prewar British interests and values.

Toward this end, the SOE and MI6, as well as an alphabet soup of Allied intelligence, propaganda, and security organizations, collaborated with communist resistance forces in occupied Europe and Asia; with republicans in countries that had royalist governments-in-exile in London; and with anarchists, Trotskyites, labor leaders, and Christian conservatives. In some cases, the SOE had contact with extreme-right-wing organizations and even groups that had also collaborated with the Axis. It was only a matter of time before the list extended to Jewish groups, such as the Irgun, which the British had outlawed and labeled as terrorist, and, not surprisingly under the circumstances, even to Muslim extremists.

By the beginning of the Second World War, the Arabs and the Jews had taken sides with respect to the belligerents. The Arabs for the most part supported the Axis and looked to the Nazis to help eliminate the Jews in Palestine.[19] The Jewish community, on the other hand, opted to support the British, despite the White Paper issued by London in May 1939 severely limiting the number of Jews who could immigrate to Palestine. Even so, the Jewish Agency, the de facto government of the Jewish community in Palestine, made every effort to assist the British. As early as 1940, Section D (forerunner of the SOE) began to recruit Jews to take part in covert operations in occupied Eastern Europe. Equally important for the British was the fact that the Jewish Agency could provide them with information on German activities in Palestine, as well as enabling them to exploit Jewish-Arab contacts in Syria.[20]

In 1940, it seemed probable, despite Nazi anti-Semitic policies, that Jewish communities in Eastern Europe could provide assistance to British clandestine operations. In June 1941, the Palmach, a Jewish commando force established with the connivance of the British, provided forty reconnaissance experts and sappers to the Allied campaign against the Vichy French forces in Lebanon and Syria.[21] During the period of 1943–1945, the Palmach and Haganah provided approximately twenty-five Palestinian Jews with facility in European languages to work as agents for MI6 Cairo who, after training in sabotage and radio communications, were parachuted into Nazi-occupied Europe.[22] After the war, some of the survivors of these missions joined the Mossad. The arrangement between the British intelligence services and the Jewish Agency was that information collected by the Palestinian agents was to be shared.[23]

Later, however, the SOE became less enthusiastic about employing Jewish agents in the Middle East. SOE headquarters in Cairo feared political problems with the Arabs and was reticent about supporting Zionist ambitions in the postwar period. The British Secret Intelligence Service and the SOE took exception to publications by the Jewish Agency advertising their collaboration with the British, and also feared that the Jews were trying to penetrate Britain's intelligence and security organizations in Palestine.[24] Their suspicions were not unfounded.

Over 26,000 Palestinian Jewish men and women joined the British armed forces and received some degree of military training, which became useful in the postwar struggle to create a state of Israel. In contrast, twelve thousand Arabs served with the British in the Second World War.[25] It is not known how many Jews or Arabs were employed by Britain's clandestine services. As early as 1942, the SIS (MI6) in the Middle East estimated that the Haganah had thirty thousand armed fighters out of a total of about fifty thousand to seventy thousand men and women in its ranks. A year later, Field Marshal Harold Alexander, C-in-C Middle East, warned that there was a probability that the Jewish community in Israel would rebel after the end of the war.[26]

This was certainly the case with one Jewish paramilitary group, known as the Stern Gang—and later as the Freedom Fighters of Israel (FFI)—which even from the beginning of the Second World War was violently opposed to the British. Breakaway members of the Irgun who were disenchanted with the truce between the British and the Jewish community established the organization in 1939–1941, and they were committed to a life-and-death struggle toward the establishment of an Israeli state that would include all the Jews from Europe and Russia. Abraham Stern, the head of the organization, was convinced that British interests in the Middle East were diametrically opposed to the establishment of a Jewish state. Furthermore, Stern and his followers shared the view that, although Arabs were the ultimate adversaries, the British were the immediate enemy.[27] The Stern Gang was not as numerous as the Irgun, but it was structured to wage a clandestine urban war through the use of assassination, sabotage, and fear: in effect a terrorist organization.

Stern believed that, since it was the British who were preventing the Jews from escaping Europe, Britain had to be defeated if the persecuted Jews of Europe were to find refuge in Palestine. To this end, the Stern Gang even went so far as to attempt an alliance with Nazi Germany. Late in 1940, Stern tried to establish contact with Otto von Hentig, the German emissary in Syria, to find common ground in the struggle against the British, but he was contemptuously rebuffed.[28] This did not deter Stern; later he sent a representative to meet a Nazi official in Beirut. The Jewish extremists offered the Germans military, political, and intelligence assistance, but the Nazis were not interested. Other attempts were foiled by the British security services, who arrested representatives of the Stern Gang before they could meet with Nazi officials in neutral countries, often thanks to tips from the Haganah.[29]

Unlike the mainstream Jewish organizations that had secure funding from supporters around the globe, the Stern Gang had to initiate a campaign of bank robberies to finance their operations. These actions resulted in the killing of British soldiers and, by mistake, Jewish policemen. At the same time, the shootings and acts of sabotage also killed innocent bystanders and earned the Stern Gang little support from the Jewish community in Palestine. Such unsavory tactics made it easy for the British security services, as well as the Palestine police, to find informers and eliminate many Stern Gang members. On February 12, 1942, the British cornered Abraham Stern at his safe house and shot him dead.[30] By this time only two of the Stern Gang's founding members remained, and they decided to end all violent activity while they rebuilt the organization from the ranks of inactive and reserve followers. Two years later, the Stern Gang reemerged, and with grim determination continued its war against the British until they left Palestine in 1947.

When the Stern Gang resumed their campaign of terror in 1944, the Irgun, now under the command of Menachem Begin, also decided to end their truce and declared war on the British.[31] Because both organizations now had a common goal, they easily reached agreement on political and military collaboration.[32] By the beginning of 1946, Irgun strength had grown to three thousand to five thousand men and women, while the Stern Gang numbered approximately 250.[33]

The ending of the war in the Middle East and the continued British insistence on limiting Jewish immigration to Palestine gave the Irgun new life. One critical factor in its comeback was the ability to expand its ranks with Polish Jews who had deserted from General Wladyslaw Anders's Polish army, which had been brought to Palestine by the British. The new volunteers had military training and a burning memory of the loss of family members in the Holocaust.[34] The Irgun carried out dozens of acts of violence and, combined with those perpetrated by the Stern Gang, turned Palestine into a battleground. Between September 1946 and May 1948, for example, the Stern Gang alone carried out over one hundred acts of sabotage against the British in Palestine.[35]

At first the mainstream Jewish community abhorred the violence and had little sympathy for the Stern Gang and the Irgun, but as news of the Holocaust reached Palestine, ordinary people became less inclined to support or cooperate with the British, who continued to bar Jewish refugees from reaching Palestine. Matters became worse as news reached Palestine that spontaneous pogroms had erupted against the survivors of the Nazi death camps in Poland, result-ing in thousands of new refugees crowding the displaced persons camps in Europe.[36]

Meanwhile the Stern Gang adopted a new strategy of sending small groups armed with concealed submachine guns and pistols into the streets and open-ing fire on any passing British troops or police. The British retaliated with a policy of intimidation that included mass arrests, curfews, and the imposition of the death penalty on anyone caught with firearms. These countermeasures were a complete failure; instead of intimidating the Jews, they quickly radical-ized almost the entire Jewish community in Palestine. British soldiers were no longer welcome in Jewish towns, and stores refused to serve them.[37]

ELEVEN

By Blood and Fire

"It is not those who can inflict the most, but those who can endure
the most who will conquer."
—*Terrence MacSwiney, Lord Mayor of Cork*[1]

Lord Moyne's house was in Sharia ibn Zanki, an exclusive residential area in Zamalek, near the Gezira Sporting Club in Cairo. The police guards who normally protected the British minister-resident worked in eight-hour shifts, from 8:00 A.M. to 4:00 P.M. However, most Egyptian police officers did not bother to adhere to the schedule and often let their men work two or three hours past the allotted time. Four men should have been on duty, but on November 6, 1944, Lord Moyne had, as usual, dismissed his guards early. Major A. W. Sansom, the officer responsible for counterintelligence and security of VIPs in Egypt, had repeatedly argued with Moyne about his safety.[2]

"There is no harder job for a security officer than trying to protect a brave man," writes Sansom.[3] Moyne had fought as a soldier and had been wounded in the South African War; in the First World War he had taken part in the Gallipoli campaign, as well as in Egypt, where he was awarded the DSO and bar, together with three mentions in dispatches. According to Sansom, Moyne hated being cooped up in an office; he was a man of action—an avid traveler to distant and dangerous places and an amateur archaeologist, who found it galling to suffer the limitations of security on personal movement. He frequently dismissed his guards, refusing to believe that he was in any danger or convinced he could handle any threat to his life.[4] There had been attempts by Jewish extremists on the lives of British officials in Palestine, but never outside the district and certainly not in Egypt.

Sometime after 12:45 P.M., despite the searing sun and exhausting heat, two young men on bicycles arrived at the minister's house and hid in the portico. A few minutes later, Lord Moyne arrived, and the two men leaped out of the portico, spraying the minister's automobile with fire from their tommy guns.[5] Lord Moyne's driver tried to grapple with one of the assassins, but he was cut down. The second man emptied his machine gun into the back seat, killing Moyne instantly. The two men dropped their weapons, retrieved their bicycles, and tried to disappear into the morass of Cairo traffic, but to no avail.[6] After a wild chase, Major Sansom and an Egyptian police officer literally smashed into the two cyclists and apprehended them. Except for a few cuts and bruises, the assassins were not hurt.

Both men belonged to the notorious Stern Gang, although their names were not on a list of fifty suspected members of the terrorist organization.[7] One of the assassins, Eliahu Hakim, was a deserter from the British army; the other, Eliahu Beit-Zuri, was a student at Hebrew University.[8] During the course of their interrogation and trial, they showed no remorse but continued to insist that they were soldiers in a war against the British Empire.[9] On March 22, 1945, the two men were executed by hanging, thus inaugurating the body count of martyrs—in the case of Beit-Zuri and Hakim, the process was delayed.

The extremists considered Lord Moyne to be an anti-Semite, a supporter of the 1939 White Paper limiting Jewish immigration, and pro-Arab; as such, the Stern Gang decided to make an example of him. However, the assassination outraged Jewish leaders in the United States and Britain, as well as Jewish communities around the world. Every effort was made to help the British capture the assassins and destroy the Stern Gang, but Britain's sudden moral ascendency was short-lived.[10] The positive British-Jewish relations and cooperation established at the outbreak of hostilities in 1939 did not survive the post–Second World War political changes in London. The election of the Labour Party in Britain and the cancellation of the new government's pledges to eliminate the White Paper and allow the victims of the Holocaust languishing in detention camps in Europe to enter Palestine eliminated any illusions about the future prospects for an Israeli state as long as the British controlled Palestine.[11] This finally extinguished the goodwill engendered by the aftershocks of Lord Moyne's assassination. The Jewish community responded to the new British government's policy with mass demonstrations and passive resistance. However, the British authorities in Palestine mishandled the situation.

Operation Agatha was intended to destroy the Haganah and severely limit the capability of the Jews to wage war against the British army. For a period of two weeks beginning on June 29, 1946, over 100,000 British troops and ten thousand police carried out extensive searches of Jewish towns and settlements, as well as mass arrests of suspected activists, but failed to apprehend the political or military leaders of the Jews. The operation damaged Britain's image in the United States—a critical consideration, given that the British economy and Britain's security needs depended on America—but more significantly it forced the Jewish Agency to change tactics.[12] Even before this, the Haganah had announced on May 12:

> Present British policy . . . is based on an erroneous assumption: Britain, in evacuating Syria, Lebanon, and Egypt [sic], intends to concentrate her military bases in Palestine and is therefore concerned to strengthen her hold over the mandate, and is using her responsibility to the Jewish people as a means to that end. . . . We would therefore warn publicly His Majesty's Government that if it does not fulfill its responsibilities under the mandate—above all with regard to the question of immigration—the Jewish Resistance Movement will make every effort to hinder the transfer of British bases to Palestine and to prevent their establishment in this country.[13]

Until June 1946, the Jewish Agency and its military wings, the Haganah and the Palmach, preferred a strategy of passive resistance and conventional military tactics. This supplemented by a public relations effort aimed at American policymakers, as well as Jewish financial donors in the United States. Furthermore, Zionist leaders like Chaim Weizmann had extensive contacts and personal relationships with the British political establishment and preferred to avoid excessive violence. However, Operation Agatha proved to be a critical milestone. In attempting to emasculate the military capability of the Jewish community, British forces killed and wounded hundreds of innocent bystanders and roughed up thousands of law-abiding Jews.

In the massive sweeps of Jewish cities, the British spared no effort in trying to hunt down anyone who was a member of the Haganah, Palmach, Irgun, or Stern Gang. In Tel Aviv, they combed the city block by block, meticulously examining basements and attics, and ransacking houses, schools, and even hospitals, often breaking the casts of patients suspected of being militants. Such thoroughness earned the British little honor, and ensured the searing hatred of ordinary Jews.[14]

The British actions proved too much for the more moderate leadership of the Jewish Agency. As an organization, it could not afford to follow the extremists; in order to maintain its leadership and coordination of Jewish resistance, it had to lead the battle against the British. Coming in the wake of the immensity of the Shoah, reports of the British interception and occasional sinking of ships carrying Holocaust survivors from Europe finally turned Jewish opinion in general—and specifically in Palestine—against Britain. Many of the immigrants heading for Palestine who were caught by the British ended up interned in camps in Cyprus. The spectacle of Jews behind barbed wire in transit camps, albeit nothing like the Nazi death camps, enraged moderate and radical Zionists alike. These tragic events, coupled with the overt betrayal of the Labour

Party in London and the actions of the British army in Palestine, ultimately radicalized an entire society and brutalized the British army.

The easy success of the British against the conventional forces of the Jewish Agency drove the Jewish military struggle underground. Although Colonial Office officials had argued against a "get tough" policy, which they claimed would only swell the ranks of the Irgun and the Stern Gang, the British army, led by CIGS Field Marshal Viscount Montgomery of Alamein, advocated the use of harsh tactics.[15] Instead of fighting relatively weak and poorly armed Haganah units, the British military now faced an unseen enemy whose hit-and-run tactics against their troops and other acts of sabotage stretched the limits of their capacity to secure Palestine. All past experience of the British in dealing with a Palestinian insurgency was confined to rural areas and derived from operations undertaken against the Arabs in the 1936 uprising. The Irgun and the Stern Gang, on the other hand, had concentrated their efforts almost entirely on an urban environment and were used to wage urban guerrilla warfare. Furthermore, the political section of the Criminal Investigation Department (CID) of the Palestinian police, the primary unit responsible for intelligence, was well staffed with Arabic speakers, but there was a dearth of personnel with facility in Hebrew or Yiddish.[16]

Previous experience in Ireland against the Irish Republican Army, had demonstrated the futility of waging a clandestine war with conventional means against an enemy who struck quickly and just as quickly disappeared into the general population. For example, during the Irish War of Independence (1919–1921), Michael Collins of the IRA organized flying columns of fifteen to thirty men who ambushed British army units and police on solitary country roads or in city alleys; attacked police barracks; and burned down courthouses, tax offices, and coast guard stations. In 1919 alone, the IRA conducted three thousand raids that resulted in the killing of two hundred police and soldiers.[17] Collins also set up a special unit known as the Squad, which included twelve handpicked volunteers who in a single day executed fourteen members of Britain's intelligence service within a half-hour period.[18] The British responded by creating two special counterinsurgency units—the Royal Irish Constabulary Reserve Force (Black and Tans) and the Royal Irish Constabulary Auxiliary Division (Auxies)—with which to terrorize the terrorists.[19]

The Black and Tans and the Auxies undertook a campaign of violence and intimidation that earned them little except odium as brutal thugs. For Collins, the excesses of these counterinsurgency troops proved to be a considerable advantage, as outraged Irishmen swelled the ranks of the IRA, while such atrocities tarnished Britain's image abroad.[20] Despite the lessons of Ireland, the

British also briefly established a special unit in Palestine to fight terrorism with counterterrorism—effectively a halfhearted attempt at torture and assassination that had the same consequences in Palestine as in Ireland. The debilitating effect of such activities on British personnel was underscored by the ending of the otherwise distinguished career of a highly decorated officer, Major Roy Farran, who was accused of killing a young Palestinian terrorist in cold blood.[21]

In February 1947, Brigadier General Bernard Fergusson,[22] deputy inspector general of the Palestine police, organized a special paramilitary unit made up of squadrons (Q Patrols) that included former soldiers of the Special Air Service (SAS) and the SOE who had experience with the use of terror during the Second World War. These Q Patrols undertook "special measures," such as infiltration, kidnapping, and ambush against the terrorists, which were beyond the scope of the regular police and army.[23] Farran himself described the thrill of being part of this new special force when he received his orders:

> In Jerusalem Police Headquarters the brief was explained to us. We would each have full power to operate as we pleased within our own specific areas. We were to advise on defence against terror and to take an active part in hunting the dissidents. . . . It was to all intents and purposes a *carte blanche* and the original conception of our part filled me with excitement. A free hand for us against terror when all others were so closely hobbled![24]

The squads of the special unit moved about in civilian delivery trucks and dressed like ordinary members of the Jewish community. Their primary missions were to set ambushes and to pick up suspected members of the Irgun and the Stern Gang. However, the Rubowitz case compromised the entire operation. In May 1947, Farran was accused of kidnapping and murdering Alexander Rubowitz, a sixteen-year-old member of the Stern Gang.[25]

The abduction of Alexander Rubowitz became linked with Farran through the discovery at the scene of a civilian felt hat with the letters FAR-AN embossed on the sweatband. Although this was the only evidential link with Farran, and witnesses to the abduction of Rubowitz failed to pick Farran out at three identification lineups, the officer remained a suspect.[26] Moreover, because of the sensitivity of public opinion in support of the Jewish situation in Palestine, particularly in the United States, the British high commissioner decided that Farran should be remanded for trial by court-martial on a charge of murder. Farran was placed under house arrest; suspecting that he might be made a scapegoat, he escaped to Syria.[27]

It is not certain whether any assurance was given, but Farran surrendered to the British consul in Damascus ten days later. The court-martial was held in Jerusalem on October 2, 1947. In the absence of any evidence that Rubowitz was actually dead—his body had not been found—together with the failure of the prosecution to link Farran directly with the alleged crime of murder, the court ruled in favor of acquittal. The disappearance of Rubowitz was never solved. Despite this, on returning to England, Farran resigned his commission, but he could not escape the reach of the Stern Gang. In 1948 a parcel arrived at his house; when his brother Rex opened it, the package exploded, killing him instantly.[28]

This was not, however, the first time that frustration, exasperation, and fear had driven the British authorities to extreme measures. The death of Abraham Stern, usually reported as being killed in a gunfight with the police while trying to escape, was in actual fact an execution. The British told representatives of the American OSS in the Middle East that, when the British burst into Stern's safe house, the place was surrounded, and he was unarmed. But when he raised his arms to surrender, the police opened fire and shot him dead. The explanation the British offered to their American counterparts was that Stern was too dangerous to be left alive.[29]

The creation of the Palestine special unit constituted the establishment of a formal means of dealing with terrorists beyond the reach of the conventional police and security services. It operated for less than a month; that was the extent of the use of guerrilla warfare experts in Palestine.

Early in the war, the British had out of necessity turned to using commando raids and combining the clandestine deployment of Special Forces with the resistance organizations fighting the Axis. After the defeat of France and the withdrawal of the British Expeditionary Force from Dunkirk, Churchill had approved the creation of the SOE, an organization that, ironically enough, adopted many IRA tactics and used them to train the resistance organizations that evolved in Axis-occupied Europe. Both Colin Gubbins and J. C. Holland, who created the conceptual and organizational framework of the SOE, had served in Ireland during "the troubles" and had studied the techniques of Michael Collins's IRA for use with the resistance forces in occupied Europe.

Part of the mandate of the SOE was, essentially, to be politically promiscuous and "ready to work with any man or institution, Roman Catholic or masonic, trotskyist or liberal, syndicalist or capitalist, rationalist or chauvinist, radical or conservative, stalinist or anarchist, gentile or Jew, that would help it beat the nazis down."[30] However, although the SOE trained thousands of Jews to prepare for a possible German occupation of Palestine, as well as hundreds of others for clandestine work behind enemy lines in occupied Europe, it was not called upon to play a role in combating Jewish resistance in Palestine. This was despite the fact that, in the spring of 1943, the SOE had anticipated problems in the postwar Middle East and had proposed to use its contacts with such underground organizations to identify and penetrate potential terrorist groups.[31]

In 1945, the SOE was dismantled and only a handful of experts found employment with the Secret Intelligence Service, also known as MI6. The British faced similar difficulties in Greece, Italy, and France in the postwar period, as left-wing resistance organizations instantly transformed themselves into political organizations antithetical to Britain's policy. In these cases as well, the corporate memory that resided with the SOE was lost when the clandestine organization was dismantled after the end of the war. In effect, MI6 took over the task of dealing with the former underground organizations with almost no knowledge, no contacts, and no understanding of the personalities or political aspirations of the resistance in those countries.[32] In Greece, for example, the British military and political authorities contributed to a chain of events that led to a major uprising in Athens, because they had little knowledge of the susceptibilities and complexities of the postwar Greek political landscape.[33]

Under the best of circumstances, urban guerrilla warfare is difficult to counter without the deployment of excessive force and an extensive network of informants and spies. In most cases, the dynamic between resistance movements and counterinsurgency forces results in the resistance's driving the occupation army into making war on the general population. In the process, the resistance achieves three critical objectives: first, it compels a conventional force to vent its frustration against ordinary, usually law-abiding citizens, which has the effect of driving many to join the underground groups out of anger or fear; second, it uses terror to demonstrate that the resistance is in control of the streets and countryside; and third, it creates martyrs. It achieves the first objective by random killing of soldiers and the assassination of senior officers and officials; the second by acts of sabotage against major targets; and the third by inducing the enemy to execute resistance fighters, who are subsequently elevated to the status of national heroes.

Between 1939 and 1946, the British security and intelligence services had successfully identified, arrested, and killed numerous Jewish militants, but after Operation Agatha they faced a new crop of unknown recruits who had joined the clandestine struggle in the interim period.[34] Prior to 1946, the Haganah and the Jewish Agency had, directly and indirectly, assisted the British in rounding up members of the Stern Gang, but this cooperation ceased as a result of British counterinsurgency actions. Another consequence of Operation Agatha was that it brought about an alliance between the Haganah, the Irgun, and the Stern Gang. The collaboration of what used to be termed "terrorists" with the official military arm of the Jewish Agency added credibility to the Irgun and to the Stern Gang. The change of tactics by the established and respected leadership of the Jewish community effectively endorsed and legitimized the clandestine war of terror initiated originally by the Irgun and the Stern Gang.[35]

Furthermore, all attempts at intimidation by the British backfired, because every act of British brutality acquired for the Jewish resistance legions of supporters and thousands of recruits. The British tried imposing long prison sentences, whippings, and executions to combat the "terrorists," but the Stern Gang and the Irgun responded in kind. In one instance, when the British condemned two young members of the Irgun to fifteen years' imprisonment and eighteen lashes, the Stern Gang threatened retaliation. In December 1946, the British had one of the boys whipped, and in response the Stern Gang kidnapped one British major and three NCOs and had them put to the lash.

The British gave in and did not whip the second boy. In April 1947, the British sent to the gallows four Irgun fighters, followed by more executions. Shortly afterward, the Irgun captured two British NCOs and strung them up on a tree.[36] A sense of frustration, helplessness, and rage afflicted the British police and soldiers in Tel Aviv after the two British NCOs were executed, triggering a rampage. By the time order was restored, six Jews had been killed, sixteen wounded, and dozens of Jewish shops burned. British soldiers drove an armored car through a funeral procession; police officers opened fire on a bus, and shot at a crowded café.[37] However, from then until the independence of Israel, the British avoided further executions.

In effect, the underground organizations had taken control of the streets and had successfully challenged the British over the security of Palestine. As every occupation army has discovered—and as subsequent armies usually forget—the battle tips in favor of the force that can guarantee security. Nothing was beyond the reach of the Jewish terrorists, and very quickly Palestine became dangerous for British personnel—death lurked in an ally or on a main street in broad daylight—and safety became an illusion.[38] Although the British could concentrate overwhelming force in a specific city or region, impose curfews, and conduct mass arrests, the Irgun and the Stern Gang cadres simply melted away and struck in another place. Both organizations had gone underground even before the outbreak of the Second World War and avoided the curfews by issuing instructions to regional members to use their own discretion in carrying out operations. The British managed to incarcerate almost 50 percent of the Palmach membership, but this merely left the field open to the more experienced Irgun and Stern Gang to wage a nonconventional battle against a frustrated conventional force.[39]

The assassination of Lord Moyne, the execution of British officers, and killing of ordinary soldiers in Palestine demonstrated that no one was immune from the reach of the urban guerrillas. The Irgun further underscored this on July 22, 1946. On that day, a small group of Irgun fighters disguised as Arabs brought explosive charges in milk churns into the hall outside the Regency Café in the basement of the King David Hotel. That particular part of the hotel, five floors of the south wing, had been appropriated by the British and was used as an administrative headquarters. After the explosives were set, an anonymous woman telephoned the hotel switchboard operator and said that there would be an explosion in a few minutes, and that everyone in the hotel should be evacuated.[40]

Unfortunately, her warning was ignored. At 12:37 P.M., the explosions went off and five floors and twenty rooms were instantly reduced to rubble. Ninety-two Britons, Jews, and Arabs lost their lives. The victims included British military and civilian officials, as well as soldiers, clerks, typists, cleaners, drivers, and messengers. The terrorists' target was the headquarters of the British military administration of Palestine as well as several departments of the Palestine government. Equally significant, the hotel was a symbol of British imperial authority—lamentably for the British it was also the center for their counterintelligence and counterinsurgency operations.[41] By contemporary standards, its devastation and the subsequent loss of life were modest, but the destruction of the hotel effectively crippled the ability of the British security services to participate in the clandestine war being waged by the Jewish resistance.

The Jewish Agency condemned the bombing as "a dastardly crime" perpetuated by a "gang of desperados" and called upon the Jews of Palestine "to rise up against these abominable outrages." This was not mere rhetoric; it was genuine revulsion against the indecent assault of terrorism perpetrated in the heart of Jerusalem. Most of the victims were ordinary men and women—soldiers, innocent Jews, and Arabs—and of those the majority of the dead and wounded were Arabs.[42] The Jewish Agency organized a memorial for the next day, and at 3:00 P.M. on July 23, all work and traffic came to a standstill as people stood for three minutes of silence to mourn the dead.

Again, for a brief moment the British gained the moral high ground, only to squander the opportunity almost immediately. The attack on the King David Hotel and its consequences proved to be a flash in the pan—an instance in which the Jewish leadership had the ability to stay the wave of terrorism that was engulfing all of Palestine.[43] But the British either misunderstood or did not care to differentiate between moderates and radicals. Eight days after the destruction of the King David Hotel, the British isolated Tel Aviv and conducted a four-day house-to-house search that resulted in the arrest of eight hundred Jews, who were subsequently sent to detention camps. None had taken part in the bombing.[44]

The hasty rounding up of Jews was more an act of desperate impotence in the face of a determined and implacable foe than a carefully thought-out operation based on reliable information. It was difficult for the security services to apprehend the terrorists, because it was not easy to penetrate the close-knit organizations of the extreme groups. For example, Eliahu Hakim, one of Moyne's assassins, had been a childhood friend of Amihai Paglin, the chief of operations for the Irgun.[45] After his arrest, despite interrogation and the prospect of death by hanging, Hakim revealed nothing about the Stern Gang or the Irgun.

British public relations suffered another major blow when, shortly after the bombing, a confidential letter written by General Sir Evelyn Barker, C-in-C Palestine, in which he proposed to punish "the Jews in a way the race dislikes—by striking at their pockets."[46] Barker proposed to ban all fraternization between British soldiers and the Jewish community. The letter, written shortly after the blast, became a public relations nightmare for the British and did considerable damage to Britain's image around the world, particularly in the United States, by giving credibility to allegations of anti-Semitism and distracting attention from the King David Hotel tragedy.[47] Although the Haganah terminated its relationship with the Irgun and the Stern Gang as a result of the bombing, the violent tactics of the latter maintained a measure of legitimacy in the Jewish community. Furthermore, the Irgun escalated the number and intensity of its attacks. In addition to new bombings, kidnappings, and retaliatory executions of British soldiers, the Irgun also attempted to assassinate British officials outside Palestine.

The British political and military establishment in London and Jerusalem assumed that they could hold on to Palestine, regardless of the new postwar geopolitical architecture and the emotional and gut-wrenching tragedy of the Holocaust. Furthermore, the British army was ill equipped to fight a war in which there were no set boundaries delineating civilians from combatants. MI6, MI5, and field intelligence failed to appreciate the differences between the conventional military represented by the Haganah, paramilitary units such as the Palmach, and the more radical Irgun and Stern Gang.

The British relied considerably on electronic intelligence (code breaking) with which to identify Jewish members of illegal organizations. One problem with this method was that just about every member of the Jewish community belonged to an underground organization. The British were thus overwhelmed with suspects. Another difficulty was that the Irgun and the Stern Gang, as well as other extreme groups, were small and not easily penetrated by double agents. For example, when splinter members of the Stern Gang known as the Homeland Front assassinated Count Folke Bernadotte on September 17, 1948,[48] British intelligence and security in Palestine had failed to uncover the plot because the splinter group was small and had recently broken off from the Stern Gang. Although the CID was able to infiltrate the Haganah and the Palmach, and had the minutes of executive committee of the Jewish Agency within hours of its meetings, it was unable to penetrate the Irgun or the Haganah.[49] Conversely, the Jewish underground had successfully placed agents in the police and in several departments of the government of Palestine. In 1947, the JIC (Joint Intelligence Committee) in London reflected on the fact that many in the Irgun and the Stern Gang had been trained by MI6 and SOE and were using this tradecraft against the British.[50]

While MI5 was responsible for dealing with the Jewish resistance, MI6 was also operating in Palestine, but it was not charged with gathering intelligence on the radical Jewish organizations. Instead, it was directed to prevent the entry of refugees from Europe. According to Tad Szulc, the Labour foreign secretary Ernest Bevin directed MI6 to implement special operations against the Jews.[51] Until this time, only the SOE had undertaken sabotage, subversion, and assassination operations, while MI6 had always confined its activities to intelligence gathering.

Not surprisingly, MI6 turned to former SOE personnel to carry out a campaign of sabotaging the transportation of refugee Jews to Palestine. In 1941, the SOE had organized special teams to undertake several sabotage missions in the planned invasion of Vichy-controlled Syria, which had included expertise in blowing up ships. The expert chosen to train with the SOE in the techniques of destroying ships and other acts of sabotage was Cathal O'Connor; after the war, MI6 incorporated O'Connor's SOE team into its organization as the Kent Corps Specials.[52]

The mission of the Kent Corps Specials was to prevent ships chartered by the Jewish Agency from reaching Palestine. Generally, the members of this force attempted to sink such ships when they were manned by skeleton crews and anchored outside harbors. In the summer of 1947, the two largest ships procured by the Jewish Agency, the *Pan York* and the *Pan Crescent*, arrived in Marseilles and Venice respectively. The Kent Corps Specials managed to set off an explosion on the *Pan Crescent*, but the Jewish organization Mossad le'Aliyah

Bet (Institute for Illegal Immigration), forerunner of Mossad, managed to have the ship repaired and, along with the *Pan York*, it left for the harbor of Constanza in Romania.[53]

The British considered using their signals intelligence (SIGINT) capability to misdirect the refugee ships by emitting false radio messages and directing them to where they could be intercepted by the Royal Navy. However, it was decided that the Jewish organizations would soon discover this tactic and alter their radio frequencies, thus making it impossible for Britain's SIGINT monitors at Government Communications Headquarters (GCHQ) to track them.[54] Instead, the British stationed four RAF photoreconnaissance squadrons in Palestine, which, in conjunction with SIGINT, led to the interception of seventeen ships in 1946. This provoked new attacks by the Irgun and the Stern Gang and further damaged Britain's image abroad. Most of the ships were not seaworthy, and many of their passengers had to be interned in British camps on Cyprus.[55] This is also what ultimately happened to those aboard the *Pan Crescent* and the *Pan York*. Though seaworthy, they were blockaded by the Royal Navy and escorted to Cyprus, where their fifteen thousand Jewish passengers were discharged and interned on January 1, 1948.[56]

During World War II, many Jewish refugees were able to leave the Balkans with the assistance of American military transport, as well as with the help of operatives dressed as U.S. personnel.[57] During the Axis occupation of the Balkans, the SOE had created escape routes than ran from the Balkans, through Greece, to several of the thousands of Greek islands in the Aegean, and finally to Palestine and Egypt. The purpose of these secret routes was to facilitate the escape of the hundreds of thousands of British soldiers who had been trapped after the withdrawal of the British Expeditionary Force from Greece in April 1941. Several of the SOE operatives were Palestinian Jews who used their wartime expertise to arrange for the smuggling of refugees into Palestine.

British protests to Washington fell on deaf ears. The administration of Harry Truman was not willing to stir public opinion in the United States by being linked to Britain's anti-Jewish policies. Beyond the odium of preventing victims of the Holocaust and the death camps from leaving the shores of a continent that had heaped upon them every imaginable indignity, culminating in mass extermination, there was the issue of the Jewish American vote. Consequently, the British changed tactics and tried to cast the Jewish underground railroad as part of a Soviet plot to flood Palestine with thousands of hard-core communists. Although the specter of an army of Soviet communist Jews arriving in the West as refugees was largely self-delusion on the part of MI6, the Soviet KGB did manage to send several handpicked agents masquerading as refugees.[58]

Overall, British intelligence efforts in Palestine were a dismal failure. Richard Aldrich, in his authoritative study of British and American intelligence during the Cold War, concludes: "Palestine was the intelligence war that Britain lost. The British security forces outnumbered their adversaries by more than twenty to one, a better ratio than Britain enjoyed later in its successful campaign against the guerrillas in Malaya (seventeen to one)."[59]

The British intelligence community, as well as the government, also underestimated the impact of the Holocaust, not just on Jewish communities around the globe, but also on wider public opinion in Europe and the United States. The British embargo preventing Jewish refugees—mostly death camp survivors—from entering Palestine outraged and kept reinvigorating the radical organizations. Meanwhile, ironically, groups such as the Irgun and the Stern Gang were using British-trained Jews against the British forces. For example, in 1941, the British had armed and trained Yaakov Meridor and David Raziel to assassinate the Mufti. Raziel was killed during the unsuccessful operation, but Meridor then became leader of the Irgun and, before the British arrested him again, he recruited the man responsible for setting the charges for the explosions that blew up the King David Hotel.[60] Ultimately, the clandestine war forced the British to withdraw from Palestine and, on May 14, 1948, Israel became a nation-state. The covert field of operations immediately shifted to the Muslim regions of the Middle East and now involved the Americans.

Although the undeclared war in Palestine lasted for only two years, it manifested a microcosm of a never-ending cycle of terrorism and counterterrorism that would bedevil policymakers in Washington and London, along with their intelligence establishments, for decades to come. In May 1948, when Israel became a republic, it subsumed all the existing radical, extremist, terrorist organizations. Some former terrorists returned to civilian life; others found employment in the new Israeli intelligence and security services. After 1948, the terrorists of yesterday were combating the terrorists of tomorrow.

Having faced defeat at the hands of the Israelis in 1948, some Arabs turned to clandestine operations with which to fight the state of Israel, and eventually the British and the Americans too. Unlike former members of the Irgun and the Stern Gang, who could begin new political or professional careers in modern, democratic Israel, their Arab Palestinian counterparts faced a lifetime as professional refugees. Each failure to reclaim Palestine compounded their sense of alienation and betrayal. The loss of Palestine stained the consciousness of generations of Arabs in the Middle East, as well as Muslims in the rest of the world. Many chafed at the inability of the Arabs to defeat Israel, which they linked to the secularism of the Arab state. To many Arabs, occupied Palestine—as they defined Israel—was part of a history of humiliation inaugurated by the demise of the Ottoman Empire and the end of the Sultan-Caliph.

The first Arab-Israeli War in 1948 attracted thousands of Muslim Brothers, who volunteered to fight in Palestine. Although embodying defeat for the Arabs, Palestine became a training ground for radicals and Islamic militants. At the same time, organizations such as the Muslim Brotherhood became the shock troops of the Egyptian government; soon, however, they turned against the secular and bankrupt monarchy of King Farouk. In the kaleidoscope of Middle East politics, secularism, pan-Arabism, and pan-Islam competed relentlessly in a life-and-death struggle for control of the Muslim states. In the period after the Second World War, Arab secularism and nationalism attained a superficial supremacy, which spawned a new set of leaders, whose policies antagonized first the British and later the Americans. The antidote to Arab nationalism was perceived to be Islam, and toward this end the Anglo-American intelligence services were attracted as moths to a flame. In the first decade after the Second World War, the Americans continued the British policy of securing the services of a Muslim strongman—either a religious or secular figure—who could hold sway over the Middle East on behalf of Washington, and at the same time deny the region to the Soviets.

TWELVE

The CIA and Nasser: A Muslim Billy Graham

"Nasser's attempt at the role of a male Cleopatra playing off the
two superpowers and British stubbornness in clinging to the remnants
of empire were bound to bring a clash, and a bad one, though not one
in which we lost, as we did, the confidence of everyone."
—*Dean Acheson*[1]

As early as 1947, the Truman administration believed that Egypt seemed primed for Soviet penetration, unless the United States replaced the decaying British colonial stranglehold on the Middle East with a benevolent American security system. The Americans were convinced that lingering British colonialism, as well as Egypt's post–Second World War slide into chaos, would eventually facilitate communist penetration of the country. These fears were underscored in January 1952, as mass demonstrations swept through the streets of Cairo and Alexandria, reminiscent of the violence in 1882. At that time, the Egyptians had taken to the streets to protest the increasing and pervasive foreign influence that had reduced their country to a client state of Britain and France. Unfortunately, the 1882 riots triggered a chain of events that gave a succession of governments in London cause to transform Egypt into a quasi-British colony.

In 1952, well-organized demonstrations wreaked violence and destruction in response to a British attack on an Egyptian police barracks on January 25. The root cause for the riots was the failure of the British to leave the country after the Egyptian government unilaterally canceled the 1936 Anglo-Egyptian Treaty.[2] The treaty was Britain's legal facade for occupying the Suez Canal Zone and, although the Egyptian government unilaterally annulled the treaty, the British refused to leave. The Suez Canal was just too important to British interests to be left in the hands of the Egyptians—at least that was the thinking in London. Suez had become synonymous with empire; a forlorn notion that still resonated in London's Tory circles, which took heart in the return of Churchill's Conservative government in 1952. The Egyptians did not agree, and they retaliated when British forces remained in place. Over sixty thousand workers left their jobs in the Canal Zone; many carried out acts of sabotage before withdrawing their services, and hundreds volunteered for guerrilla warfare training.

The British were convinced that the Egyptian auxiliary police were responsible for arming and training guerrilla groups. Tensions reached breaking point when rioters shot dead an Irish-born nun after forcing their way into a convent. In retaliation, British troops seized the town of Ismailia, just outside the Canal Zone. On January 25, 1952, British armored forces stormed a police barracks in Ismailia, leaving forty-three dead and many more wounded.[3] The news both enraged and electrified the Egyptians. The next day, Black Saturday, thousands of students in Cairo took to the streets; very quickly they were joined by thousands of cadres from the Muslim Brotherhood as well as from other radical political organizations—including the policemen dispatched to control the crowds. Many from the MB had also taken part in the guerrilla campaign against the British in the Canal Zone between 1951 and 1952. Just for this occasion, the MB had formed a temporary alliance with the Egyptian communists and socialists, and they collaborated to make the demonstrations particularly vicious.[4]

The rioters stormed the streets, focusing their anger on foreigners unlucky enough to be seized by the mobs and on buildings identified with the West. Throughout the day, frenzied demonstrators, along with cool-headed and well-organized professional agitators, torched 475 structures. According to Wesley Adams, second secretary of the American embassy, the mobs concentrated primarily on movie theaters, fashionable restaurants, every liquor store in Cairo, and any foreign establishment they came across, including the Shepheards Hotel and the Turf Club—both grand symbols of British imperialism.[5] In addition, they murdered or maimed any European who inadvertently came across their way, along with innocent Egyptians caught in the foreign establishments under attack. While Cairo burned, Farouk hesitated, hoping to exploit the crisis. After two hours, he ordered the army to restore order. Meanwhile the British had dispatched their own troops, and there was a strong probability that they would clash with Egyptian forces.

Earlier, in late 1951, American policymakers and diplomats had feared that the ongoing dispute between Egypt and Britain would give Moscow a window of opportunity for expanding Soviet influence in the Middle East; the January riot was just such an occasion. Dean Acheson at the State Department and Allen Dulles at the CIA were also convinced that Egypt and Britain were on the brink of war, and that further deterioration of the situation in Cairo would lead to an even greater crisis. Acheson assumed that, if the United States did not "damp down these fires," it "threatened to involve North Africa in bloody con-flict."[6] Acheson adopted a primarily covert approach in dealing with Egypt, to avoid offending both the British and the Israelis.

Although crypto-diplomacy was not new to international relations, it was usually conducted by individuals on behalf of states and not by intelligence services. This new diplomatic role eventually placed the CIA in a position of not just executing policy (both covert and overt) but also of becoming an insti-gator of political events—in Egypt and elsewhere. The instrument of this new policy mechanism was Kermit Roosevelt, grandson of President Theodore Roosevelt and senior officer in the CIA's Middle East division.

During the Second World War, Roosevelt had served in the OSS and had been stationed in Cairo to establish an indirect channel to Egypt's government and monarchy. In October 1951, Acheson placed Roosevelt in charge of a spe-cial ad hoc interdepartmental committee to study the situation in Egypt. The committee eventually concluded: "Our principle should be to encourage the emergence of competent leaders, relatively well-disposed toward the West, through programs designed for this purpose, including, where possible, a con-scious, though perhaps covert, effort to cultivate and aid such potential leaders, even when they are not in power."[7]

Roosevelt had come to know Farouk in 1942 as an OSS officer during the tense days when the British had occupied the palace grounds in Cairo and had forced the hapless king to purge his government of pro-Axis ministers.[8] At that time, Roosevelt had established a good relationship with the monarch, despite meeting under such difficult circumstances. Roosevelt earned Farouk's trust and became an unofficial advisor to the monarch, while establishing excellent contacts with the king's immediate entourage. Roosevelt promoted the idea with Farouk that "'after the war there could be a New Deal' for Egypt that would make the king the 'first ruler of a free Egypt in two thousand years.'"[9]

In the late 1940s, Roosevelt arranged for several individuals, mostly from the Egyptian police services, to be sent to the United States and trained in fighting communism and subversion.[10] After demobilization, Roosevelt joined the Saturday Evening Post as a correspondent and traveled extensively through-out the Middle East. However, he was brought back to intelligence work in 1950, and two years later was dispatched to Cairo in order to save Farouk and Egypt. The State Department had tried to convince the Egyptian government to take part in the defense of the Middle East through the establishment of the Middle East Command (MEC), which would also have included the British.

Like them, the Americans believed that Egypt was the natural leader of the Arab states, and that the Middle East could consequently be brought under a

U.S. security umbrella, thus safeguarding the petroleum routes to and from the Persian Gulf. American interests were focused on securing access to the petroleum-rich Gulf region, as well as on the added urgency caused by the outbreak of the Korean War on June 24, 1950. Coming on the heels of the Greek Civil War (1946–1949), which the Americans believed was caused by Soviet ambitions in the Balkans and in the Eastern Mediterranean, the Korean conflict was further evidence of encroaching communism in the world in general, and in the Middle East in particular.

Even though the plan for the creation of the Middle East Command collapsed because of Egyptian objections, Acheson believed that Egypt could be brought around, if only the country could achieve stability. The U.S. secretary of state was convinced that the volatility of Egypt was the by-product of the corrupt Wafd government, and that Farouk, with American support, could stabilize the country, bringing it to join an Anglo-American alliance. Kermit Roosevelt returned to Cairo in early 1952 and attempted to convince Farouk to reform Egypt's corrupt government.

The American agent planned to orchestrate a peaceful revolution, casting Farouk in the role of an efficient dictator, to replace the corrupt political system. Part of the scheme involved giving money to Farouk with which he was to bribe the Brotherhood into supporting the monarchy. However, in the opaque world of Middle East politics, even a consummate player such as Roosevelt was a neophyte. Farouk took the idea a step further and tried to organize his own coup, by working with the MB to create a fundamentalist Muslim state. Toward this end, the Waqf (Islamic Religious Foundation in Egypt) declared Farouk a descendent of the Prophet Mohammed, with the new name of Al Sayyid Farouk I. The Muslim Brotherhood, for their part, simply took Farouk's American money and used it to establish an alliance with the Egyptian Free Officers, a secret military organization planning to overthrow the monarchy.[11]

After about a month, having finally realized that Farouk was utterly hopeless, Roosevelt returned to Washington. Although the monarch had initially displayed interest and willingness to address the country's problems, he had just as quickly turned his attention to augmenting his own considerable wealth, pornograph collection, and predilection for sexual orgies, while Egypt continued to wallow in corruption. The alternatives were either the austere and xenophobic Muslim Brotherhood or the Free Officers. The U.S. ambassador to Cairo, Jefferson Caffery, was in favor of the Egyptian army's taking power; he argued that the military would be a stabilizing force and, although practically useless in fighting external enemies, it would be able to maintain internal security.[12]

The same rationale had been applied to other crisis-ridden countries, such as post–Second World War Greece, which had appeared to American political leaders and policymakers to be on the brink of a communist takeover.[13] In these cases, the military of the exposed countries offered the best guarantee of keeping the corrupt political establishment in check and the communists at bay. Both in Greece and Egypt, the American tactic was to exploit malleable political figureheads but establish independent channels with the military through the CIA. Eventually Washington lost control over the covert relationships, leaving the CIA to conduct an independent policy toward client states. Not so surprisingly, as events played out in the Balkans, the Middle East, and South America, a military uniform was no guarantee against greed and corruption. Certainly in the case of Egypt, and later Iran, the CIA's support of military strongmen or monarchs contributed to the erosion of the political center, thus leaving the body politic at the mercy of corrupt generals or extreme religious zealots.

By 1952, the U.S. embassy in Cairo had picked up rumors of a pending coup being organized by Egyptian officers. As far as Caffery and Roosevelt were concerned, the Egyptian army offered a better alternative to salvage Egypt from systemic corruption emanating from the palace and the political establishment. Acheson agreed, and Roosevelt set the wheels in motion to find links with the Free Officers, the secret organization committed to the overthrow of the monarchy. Roosevelt sent Miles Copeland, an intrepid irregular CIA officer, to Egypt to seek out these officers and ascertain their intentions with respect to the West, and especially toward the United States.[14] Copeland established contact with intermediaries and eventually with Nasser, the leader of the Free Officers.

In March 1952, Roosevelt paid another visit to Cairo and initiated a series of meetings with Nasser and the Free Officers. According to Copeland, Nasser confirmed for Roosevelt that there would be a coup and asked the American if the United States would abstain from interfering.[15] It was also agreed that that U.S. recognition of the new Egyptian regime would include a private understanding that the "preconditions for democratic government did not exist and wouldn't exist for many years." References to "reestablishing democratic processes" and "truly representative government" would be reserved for public consumption only.[16]

Four months later, on July 23, 1952, Nasser and his Free Officers seized power and abolished the monarchy. The army-dominated Revolutionary Command Council (RCC), headed by Nasser, controlled the new regime; General Mohamed Neguib was installed as president of the Egyptian republic. In actual fact, he remained a figurehead, and Nasser ruled the country from behind the scenes. The speed and efficiency of the coup took most embassies, including the British, by surprise.[17] According to Wilbur Eveland, the U.S. embassy, as well as the CIA, were equally astonished by the coup, and he also claims it was unlikely that Kermit Roosevelt had any role, direct or indirect, in the overthrow of Farouk.[18] Copeland, for his part, states that the CIA station chief in Cairo relied on intelligence almost exclusively from officials and politicians connected with the Farouk regime, and "in fact, the station chief believed right up to the day of the coup that Farouk was following the secret activities of the Free Officers on a day-to-day basis and would lower the boom on them when the strategic moment arrived."[19]

These conflicting claims over what the CIA and the U.S. embassy knew about the coup, and to what degree American officials were involved in the overthrow of Farouk, are not so much contradictory as by-products of the overlapping agencies that loosely constituted the CIA in the early 1950s. Roosevelt and Copeland were members of the Office of Policy Coordination (OPC), an intelligence unit established in 1948 to conduct covert operations at arm's length from the U.S. government. Although its budget and staff came from the CIA, the head of the OPC reported to the secretaries of State and Defense, bypassing the director of the CIA.[20] At best, it was an awkward situation that created serious divisions within the CIA at a time when the White House administration was not certain what direction to give the new agency.

The head of the OPC, Frank Wisner, was a naval officer and wealthy lawyer from Mississippi, well connected to the Washington political establishment. Unlike the career-minded intelligencers of the CIA, Wisner selected the personnel of the OPC from the ranks of Ivy League gentlemen of independent means, along with a handful of eccentrics and mavericks who had served in U.S. intelligence during the Second World War. These differences further expanded and exacerbated the segregation of the OPC from the other directorates of the CIA. For example, the officers of the Office of Special Operations (OSO), the counterpart to the OPC, were professionals of the wartime OSS, along with a few former members of the FBI. Unlike the well-heeled gentleman of the OPC, the rank and file of the OSO, writes Copeland, "lived on their salaries and had modest homes in nearby Virginia."[21] Copeland adds that most members of the OPC belonged to "the Metropolitan Club and/or the Chevy Chase Country Club, and had upmarket homes in Georgetown or Wesley Heights."[22]

As the grandson of a famous president, Kermit Roosevelt was also a member of Washington's privileged class, yet he also belonged to that remarkable group of wartime adventurers that Frank Wisner and Allen Dulles had brought into the OPC who were accustomed to operating on their own initiative with minimal oversight from their immediate superiors. As Evan Thomas observes: "Along with his cousins Archie and Cornelius, Kim Roosevelt formed a kind of cell-within-the cell inside the CIA."[23] While outside the agency, the Roosevelts enjoyed a social primacy that enabled them to access the political establishment on a social level, occasionally bypassing the chain of command.

Roosevelt's home in leafy northwest Washington was just one block away from that of General Walter Bedell Smith, Eisenhower's former chief of staff at SHAEF (Allied headquarters) during the Second World War; Smith was one of the first directors of the CIA and undersecretary of state in the Eisenhower administration. The Roosevelts were also close family friends of Allen and John Foster Dulles, director of the CIA and secretary of state respectively. On more than one occasion, Kermit Roosevelt reported directly to the secretary of state, defense secretary, or even the president himself, over the heads of his immediate superiors.[24] Thomas adds: "When, in those early years, Archie Roosevelt's Lebanese-American wife, Selwa, worried whether she was doing the socially 'right' thing, Archie cut her off. 'Look,' he said. 'What we do is right.'"[25]

Certainly, Kermit Roosevelt exercised considerable latitude in directing America's covert policy in Egypt. Yet his unparalleled access to the U.S. political leadership also meant that Roosevelt did not act on his own but executed the objectives of the current White House administration. In 1952, U.S. policy was to keep Nasser in power and protect him from internal and external enemies preparing to assassinate Egypt's first independent leader in almost two millennia. An integral element of American policy was to establish Nasser as the leader of the Muslim world, and particularly as a reliable American ally. Copeland's succinct description of this policy was to transform Nasser into "a Muslim Billy Graham": one who would use his pulpit to guide that world toward a defensive alliance with the West and away from the clutches of the Soviet Union.[26]

THIRTEEN

The Road to Perdition: The Gehlen Organization

"It was a visceral business of using any bastard
as long as he was anti-Communist."
—*Harry Rositzke*[1]

I n less than one year, the euphoria following the end of the Second World War turned into uncertainty that escalated into Cold War paranoia. Upheavals in Europe, Asia, and the Middle East pointed to Soviet aggression as the culprit. The allies of yesterday quickly became implacable foes and soon stared each other down across an unbridgeable ideological divide that manifested itself in a series of crises. In December 1945, the Italian Communist Party had 1.8 million members and captured 19 percent of the popular vote in Italy's elections; in 1948, the CIA's Office of Special Operations (OSO) had to intervene covertly to prevent the communists from forming a government. The French Communist Party had nearly one million members; in November 1947, at the request of the Cominform (Communist Information Bureau), two million workers went on strike in France, followed by additional strikes in Italy. Civil war broke out in Greece in 1946 and threatened to bring that country into the communist bloc. In the Far East, the Chinese Civil War had also resumed, and in less than three years it brought the communists to victory.[2]

On March 12, 1947, the Truman Doctrine declared America's intentions to checkmate the Soviet Union in Greece, Turkey, and Iran. A year later, in February 1948, the communists took over Czechoslovakia. Four months later, the Soviets blocked rail and land access to Western sectors of Berlin, and the United States undertook a massive airlift to break the Soviet blockade and supply the beleaguered city with food and fuel. In June 1950, North Korean communists overran most of South Korea and threatened to annihilate the U.S. forces trying to defend what was left of the country. To make matters worse, the Soviets had successfully tested their first atomic bomb in 1949, bringing an end to the U.S. nuclear arms monopoly.[3]

The Cold War landscape confronting the United States was, for the most part, terra incognita, with the prospect of a nuclear holocaust looming on the horizon. George F. Kennan's "Long Telegram," dispatched on February 22, 1946, while he was ambassador to the USSR, was the first attempt to provide a comprehensive analysis of Soviet intentions. Kennan's interpretation of Kremlin policy offered a picture of a formidable adversary who viewed the outside world as hostile, which provided justification for Stalin's dictatorship. Whereas the U.S. government had no other intelligence to either support or repudiate Kennan's view, the Soviet Committee for State Security (KGB) immediately provided Stalin with a copy of the telegram.[4] The Truman administration and later that of Eisenhower were desperate for information on the Soviet Union in general and Soviet intentions in particular. However, America's nascent intelligence community remained in the dark, grasping at scraps of information that promised a peek into Moscow's objectives and frantically seeking agents who could prise open the Kremlin's secrets.[5]

One alternative was to look to previous enemies who had had experience in penetrating the Soviet Union. The old and well-tried maxim, "my enemy's enemy is my friend," brought U.S. army intelligence officers, and later the CIA, into occupied Germany to employ former German military intelligence officers and then, through them, former members of the Nazi SS and Gestapo. The catalyst for the CIA's relationship with Hitler's henchmen was Reinhard Gehlen, a German army general in charge of the German armed forces' Eastern Front political and field intelligence organization, Fremde Heere Ost (Foreign Armies East [FHO]), which had focused on gathering intelligence and mounting covert operations against the Soviet Union during World War II.

Toward the end of the war, Gehlen became convinced that, although Germany was going to face defeat in its struggle against communism, that fight would continue under the leadership of the Americans. To participate in this new conflict, as well as to position himself and his organization for a new role in postwar Germany, Gehlen had buried three complete sets of secret documents, including files on Soviet agents who had spied for his organization.[6] Two weeks after the end of the war, Gehlen surrendered to Captain John Boker, an officer in the U.S. Army Counter Intelligence Corps (CIC). For months, Gehlen was treated as just another prisoner of war; only after the Soviets had expressed interest in him did the U.S. Army finally debrief the German spy chief, at the G2 (divisional intelligence) level. During his interrogation, Gehlen offered to gather tactical intelligence for the United States, as well as to reactivate his agents in the Soviet Union and place them at the disposal of the Americans.[7]

The CIC finally became convinced that Gehlen had a great deal to offer and that his organization with its espionage networks, developed in Russia during the war, could be reactivated and made to work for the United States.[8] In August 1945, they brought Gehlen and his closest associates to Washington to continue negotiations. Eventually Gehlen signed an agreement with the Americans that reinvented the remnants of the FHO as the Gehlen Organization—a private intelligence agency working for U.S. Army intelligence.[9] Gehlen and his associates were eventually installed in Pullach, near Munich, in December 1947.

From 1945 to 1947, however, when Gehlen and his associates passed temporarily to the control of the U.S. military, responsibility for dealing with the Germans was given to the OSS Secret Intelligence Branch under the direction of Frank Wisner.[10] It is not certain if Wisner ever met Gehlen in person, although some CIA accounts assert that Allen Dulles sent Wisner, who shortly afterward became head of the Office of Policy Coordination, to make contact with Gehlen.[11] Eventually Wisner, as head of the OPC, would make considerable use of the Gehlen Organization, employing it as a front to sift through the refugee camps for possible volunteers with whom to penetrate the communist bloc. The Gehlen Organization also undertook other less reputable tasks in the Middle East on behalf of the OPC.

In Germany, the Gehlen Organization began searching the displaced persons camps for information and for possible volunteers willing to return to their countries of origin behind the Iron Curtain, to fight the Soviets. At the same time, Gehlen's scouts also enrolled former members of the Nazi intelligence organizations, many of whom were wanted war criminals, although he had promised his American masters that he would not recruit such unsavory individuals. Gehlen's excuse was that the ex-Nazis were valuable intelligence assets who had considerable knowledge on the Soviets. However, the information garnered from these sources was unreliable at best, and before long it proved a useful means for the Soviet intelligence services to penetrate the Gehlen Organization and feed the CIA carefully doctored intelligence. Almost from the moment that the Gehlen Organization was back in business, the Soviet NKVD (forerunner of the KGB) had planted dozens of agents amongst the Russians in the DP camps, who easily slipped into the Gehlen Organization as trusted intelligence assets.[12]

The cost of resurrecting Hitler's FHO was high, both financially and morally. The United States spent over $200 million to maintain approximately four thousand full-time members of the Gehlen Organization, while surrendering the moral high ground by embracing Hitler's former henchmen in the name of fighting communism. The intelligence produced by Gehlen's information factory at

Pullach was fabrication sprinkled with occasional tidbits of tactical data on the Red Army in East Germany. Gehlen's information contributed to the escalating tensions between the Soviet Union and the United States by indicating that the Red Army was poised to overrun Western Europe. Naturally, the perception of a hostile Soviet Union kept Gehlen on the U.S. payroll, while his reports of pending communist aggression found a receptive audience in Washington.

The emerging Cold Warriors and rabid anticommunists found validation in Gehlen's gloomy forecasts. The Pentagon also found Gehlen's affirmation of the Kremlin's warlike posture reassuring and a useful tool in prompting Congress for higher military appropriations. The fabrication of alternative realities was not new for Gehlen; after all, in Nazi Germany he had learned how to accommodate his leader's appetite for such information—Hitler only wanted to know what he wanted to hear.[13] According to Victor Marchetti, the CIA's chief analyst on Soviet capabilities—who made these comments after retirement from the agency—little had changed for Gehlen in his new incarnation as America's spy:

> The agency [CIA] loved Gehlen because he fed us what we wanted to hear.... We used his stuff constantly, and we fed it to everybody else: the Pentagon; the White House; the newspapers. They loved it, too. But it was hyped up Russian boogeyman junk, and it did a lot of damage to this country.[14]

However, three years after the end of the war, the work of American military intelligence in Germany began to wind down, while the size and cost of the Gehlen Organization had spiraled beyond the capability of U.S. Army divisional intelligence. After much pressure from the Pentagon, Gehlen and his small of army of spies were passed on to the newly established CIA.[15] Few within the agency, however, were interested in or willing to take responsibility for Gehlen. Richard Helms, the man directly responsible for Gehlen, wrote in his memoirs that, in addition to the moral objections that many in the agency had about working with Gehlen and his less reputable associates:

> CIA officers in Germany were uniformly dismayed by the noisy and insecure activity of the RUSTY [Gehlen Organization] operatives. The intelligence, particularly on East Germany, was valuable, but as seen by our German station, it hardly offset the poor security and discipline of the RUSTY operatives.[16]

Shortly after the CIA assumed responsibility for Gehlen and his agents, the OSO and OPC merged to become the agency's clandestine service. Many in the CIA opposed working with former Nazis, arguing that, once this became known, it would give the Soviets a propaganda bonanza. Others were troubled by the moral ambiguity that filtered U.S. policy toward the ex-Nazis. Officially the Gehlen group was paid to provide the U.S. intelligence service with information about the Soviet Union, but they also worked secretly for the OPC, headed by Wisner. In this capacity, Gehlen's agents helped the OPC mount covert operations and served as the link between that agency and former members of the Sicherheitsdienst (SS Security Service, SD), the Gestapo, and other disgraced elements of the wartime German military-intelligence apparatus.

The rehabilitation of Gehlen and his associates was only a small part of a major program aimed, in the interests of national security, at recruiting German scientists, technicians, and engineers to continue working on the development of rockets and new weapons systems. In the confused and paranoid period that followed the end of the war, the U.S. government believed that the new threat from the Soviet Union outweighed any moral reservations over the employment of Nazis. The transfer of the Nazi scientists to the United States took place under the cover of Operation Paperclip, which in due course facilitated the relocation of over 1,500 Germans and their families.[17] Operation National Interest was another secret maneuver to bypass U.S. laws and acquire the services of Nazis and Nazi collaborators who could be politically useful against the Soviet Union. Among them were Nazi intelligence and security specialists, as well as Nazi collaborators, who quietly moved back into the government services of the Eastern European countries.

In this new kind of Cold War, survival consisted not just in emerging from the bomb shelters in the aftermath of an atomic exchange, but in preventing a communist onslaught from overwhelming the free world. The fear of communism and the mechanics of a Cold War that left little scope for a major military clash, unless both sides were willing to risk a nuclear holocaust, fostered the shadow war of spies and the politics of subversion. Despite the absence of industrial-scale killing, at least in the first decades of the Cold War, successive American governments and the political-military-intelligence establishment in Washington believed that the struggle with the Soviet Union was a matter of survival.

Key to victory was the continuing financial success of the West, which more than rivaled the promise of Soviet collectivist socialism and which relied on unencumbered access to the oilfields of the Gulf states; that meant that there had to be a strong, unambiguous U.S. policy for the Middle East. However, the political reality of American support for the new state of Israel clashed with the geopolitical realities of Arab nationalism, backed by petroleum. The postcolonial world of the Middle East, cluttered with vociferous nationalist movements and tugged in several directions by an ambitious leadership, offered considerable opportunity for Soviet penetration. For U.S. policymakers in the late 1940s, the region was a maze of crosscurrents: national ambitions, religious zealotry, and conflicting loyalties.

Like the British before them, the Americans attempted to find a single strongman who could create order out of chaos and preempt Soviet intrigues in the Middle East. Nasser was a likely candidate—leader of a genuine national mass movement and head of the largest Arab country, which was emerging as the leading state in the region. Yet Nasser could not wholeheartedly cast his lot with the Americans, because the Israeli factor was too great a chasm to overcome. Postwar American administrations, beginning with Truman's, had also had to tread carefully in an effort to balance support for Israel with the establishment of closer ties with the Arab world. Accordingly, contact with Nasser evolved on two levels: a formal diplomatic relationship with all its limitations, and much more substantive links carried on clandestinely through the CIA. Furthermore, when the CIA could not directly provide certain services required by Nasser, it was able to use the Gehlen Organization, which could provide the necessary expertise and personnel, offering the U.S. government the fig leaf of plausible deniability.

Despite the efforts of the Muslim Brotherhood and other groups hostile to his regime, Nasser continued to dodge the assassin's bullet. One factor was luck; however, a more tangible consideration was that Nasser had an exceptionally capable security apparatus, equipped and trained indirectly by the CIA. The agency's involvement with Nasser was a consequence of the fear of communism that swept across America after the Second World War. The Truman administration, as well as subsequent governments, became interested in Nasser because of the Suez Canal, the petroleum of the Gulf states, and the fear that British and French colonialism would pave the way for the Soviet Union to gain control of the Middle East (1945–1958). After the collapse of the Soviet Union (1991), the new threat to the Middle East would be seen to be the rapidly expanding influence of political Islam,[18] whereas after the end of the colonial era, communist penetration of the region remained a fixation with the Americans.

Another critical factor that shaped early American policy toward the Middle East was the foundation of Israel. Although the ramifications of that momentous event grew in intensity over time, it immediately skewed relations between the United States and the Muslim world. Yet one mitigating factor that elevated the United States above the former European empires was the fact that the Eisenhower administration was clearly opposed to colonialism. In the 1950s, Allen Dulles, the new CIA director, and his brother, John Foster Dulles, the secretary of state, along with numerous congressmen, believed that the Suez Canal in particular had become a symbol of Western imperialism in the Middle East.[19] Such apprehensions had brought the Truman administration, and the early CIA, to consider Nasser a potential bulwark of stability in the region and hence an obstacle to communism.

Thus the CIA's developing relationship with Nasser was part of the United States' evolving security architecture, aimed at containing Soviet expansion. In the early years of the Cold War, the dearth of information on the Soviet Union was hampering American efforts to discern Soviet intentions and to counter Russia's influence around the world. Immediately after the end of the Second World War, the fledgling postwar American intelligence units, mostly remnants of the wartime OSS and CIC, lacked intelligence networks both within and outside the Iron Curtain, and they could barely keep up with Russia's formidable KGB deployed widely across the Cold War battlefields.

Eventually, the bits and pieces of the various ad hoc intelligence units operating in Europe were amalgamated within the CIA. Initially the CIA consisted primarily of the OSO. It had emerged out of the Strategic Services Unit (SSU), which was in turn the remnant of the wartime OSS, concentrating on intelligence gathering. The OPC, on the other hand, was established to undertake clandestine and paramilitary operations. It was created to counter covert Soviet aggression, as well as that of its satellites, and to undertake these tasks with the use of propaganda, economic warfare, sabotage, and subversion, as well as to encourage and support resistance against the communist regimes.[20]

Initially the CIA was itself merely a shell that facilitated salaries, supplied space for offices, and provided other administrative support for its two branches, OSS and OPC, which retained a considerable degree of autonomy and remained distinct from the CIA for several years. Frank Wisner, the first head of the OPC, did not answer to the head of the CIA; in fact, according to Evan Thomas, Wisner had complete autonomy and nominally reported to George Kennan, then head of the State Department Policy Planning Staff. In one respect, the autonomy of the OPC was useful, in that it permitted the administration to invoke the doctrine and distance itself from the more distasteful activities of the new covert directorate. However, the early years of the CIA reflected an institution that was not only less than the sum of its parts, but also honeycombed with further subdivisions of semi-independent units. The OPC, later renamed the Directorate of Operations, branded the CIA as the agency of dirty tricks—an image that continues to dog the organization today.

At first, both the OSO and the OPC desperately needed information and agents, over which they had to compete with friends and enemies alike. Almost before the Second World War was over, the intelligence organizations of the victorious Allies, including the neutrals, began to probe and grope their way around the human wreckage of postwar Europe and Asia in search of potential agents with whom to penetrate the Soviet Union. Among the ruins, CIA officers stumbled into an exotica of strange individuals and shadowy organizations, coughed up by the death throes of old Europe.

The human flotsam of information peddlers and confidence tricksters, along with small armies of self-proclaimed revolutionaries, anticommunists, arms dealers, smugglers, displaced persons, and down-on-their-luck princes and kings, were nothing more than manufacturers of intelligence and proved to be less than useless. American intelligence officials navigating through these hucksters discovered that, no matter how much they paid for secret information, it was invariably unreliable, and with enough cash they could purchase any number of lies or conspiracy theories, almost on demand.[21] Evan Thomas identifies one such example and comments:

> The thirst for intelligence inside the Iron Curtain gave rise to a whole new industry, paper mills churning ever-more fantastic tales of revolt and intrigue in the "denied areas." One U.S.-financed émigré group, known as TsOpe by its Russian initials, even blew up its own headquarters and blamed the KGB. The idea was to show that the Russians really feared TsOpe, and thus Washington should increase its funding.[22]

Many fanciful notions were entertained by American intelligence officers, driven by an almost obsessive determination to unlock the Kremlin's secrets. No idea or plan seemed too crazy; some attempts to create anticommunist forces were downright incredible. For example, the U.S. Army enlisted forty thousand refugees (from the 700,000 in the displaced persons camps) in labor service units to assist with rubble clearance in postwar Germany. Since many of these refugees came from East Germany or countries behind the Iron Curtain, they appeared to be ideal candidates for work inside the Soviet Union.[23]

Wisner used the Gehlen Organization to comb through the labor units, eventually recruiting approximately five thousand volunteers for a "secret army" to be trained as a guerrilla force to invade the USSR after a nuclear war. Others

were formed into stay-behind units that would undertake sabotage in the aftermath of a Soviet occupation of Western Europe. Several were selected for secret
missions behind the Iron Curtain. For some years, dozens of volunteers were
parachuted into the Ukraine and other parts of the Soviet Union either to spy
on the Russians or to establish links with the resistance movements that existed
mostly in the imagination of men such as Wisner. Many of the volunteers were
Ukrainian refugees who had fought for the Nazis in the Second World War,
and Wisner deluded himself into believing that these hapless individuals would
join groups of indigenous Ukrainians to wage a shooting war in the Carpathian
Mountains.[24]

Tragically, the notion of resistance movements fighting Russians was a
mirage that consumed the lives of hundreds if not thousands of Eastern European volunteers who had been persuaded to allow themselves to be parachuted
into the communist bloc, ending in torture and death. Some of the volunteers
had blood on their hands from working with the SS during the war, and undoubtedly rough justice caught up with them. However, many others were just
desperate people trying to escape life in the camps, and some were even ideal-
ists who, seduced by Wisner's siren song, went blindly to their doom.[25]

The actions of men such as Wisner must be placed in the context of the
first decade of the Cold War. He was not a lone Cold Warrior: most of America's
political and military leadership was hostage to the notion of an expanding
communist empire that threatened to gobble up Europe, the Middle East, and
Asia. In the first years following the Second World War, Soviet actions gave
every indication to Washington's political and military establishment of aggressive expansionism. Events in Europe and in the Third World, whether
instigated by Moscow or not, only served to feed an escalating Cold War paranoia. The absence of any hard intelligence on Moscow's intentions (or spurious
information from self-serving sources such as Gehlen) made matters that much
more difficult and served to heighten the suspicion that, behind every upheaval,
every nationalist movement, and every conflict, there lurked the machinations
of monolithic communism.

FOURTEEN

A New Kind of War: Subversive Operations and the CIA

"Whenever we want to subvert a place, the
British own an island within reach."
—*Frank Wisner to Kim Philby*[1]

Almost two weeks after the end of the Second World War in Europe, a Nazi officer in full SS uniform and fully armed, along with two other Germans, walked into U.S. Army headquarters in Salzburg, Austria, to surrender. Prior to his capitulation, Lieutenant Colonel Otto Skorzeny had been on the Allied list of most wanted Nazis but, despite a desperate effort to find him, the Waffen-SS officer remained elusive. Allied-controlled Radio Luxemburg, as well as the local newspapers, had made repeated appeals for his whereabouts, but all to no avail.[2]

In the early days of May 1945, the Allied intelligence organizations were confronting a fantastic but potentially nightmarish scenario. According to fanciful rumors seeping out of the remnants of Nazi Germany, Hitler had prepared an alpine redoubt from which the most fanatical of his troops would fight to the death. In the heady days following the surrender of the German armed forces, the last thing the Allies wanted was to fight an unnecessary protracted battle that would result in needless casualties.[3]

Yet the rumors persisted and, according to speculation from self-deceiving or wishful-thinking Nazi prisoners, Hitler had indeed issued such orders and had selected Otto Skorzeny as the commander of this last hurrah. Viennese-born Skorzeny had been one of Hitler's most intrepid and skillful commandos; his exploits included the audacious rescue of Mussolini from his mountain prison in 1943. Skorzeny and an elite group of commandos swooped down on the prison by glider—an almost impossible feat—and plucked the Italian dictator from his stunned guards. A year later, Skorzeny organized the infiltration of English-speaking Germans behind American lines; during the Ardennes offensive in December 1944, the Battle of the Bulge, they posed as American officers, causing considerable confusion.

On December 19, Skorzeny's notoriety reached new heights when a German air force officer, wearing a U.S. Army uniform, surrendered to the Americans near Liège in Belgium. He informed his interrogators at U.S. First Army HQ that Lieutenant Colonel Otto Skorzeny, with sixty-four German commandos, had crossed the lines in order to assassinate General Dwight Eisenhower, the Supreme Allied Commander, at his headquarters outside Paris.[4] The plot to kill Eisenhower turned out to be a hoax, but during the investigation a joint Anglo-American counterintelligence team came across a Nazi sabotage organization created by Heinrich Himmler, and in the process became convinced of the existence of the so-called alpine redoubt, which would, combined with a guerrilla war, permit the Nazis to hold out against the Allies even after the fall of Germany. According to SHAEF counterintelligence:

> The general consensus was that, after the liberation of Germany, Skorzeny would organize a terrorist campaign to . . . cause political upheaval by assassinations, terrorism, and acts of sabotage at political meetings in a such a manner as to make the blame appear to rest with Left-wing elements and Communists . . . these operations . . . will be directed toward the perpetuation of the Nazi terror with a view to dominating the German population and preventing collaboration with the Allies. The knowledge that there is a Nazi headquarters and the possibility of a Nazi revival would keep alive Nazi doctrines and encourage the formation of autonomous movements throughout Germany.[5]

Because of his many daredevil exploits, as well as his loyalty to Hitler, the Anglo-American counterintelligence team suspected that Skorzeny had been given command of the Nazi alpine redoubt, as well as the post-occupation terror campaign. As far as U.S. Army intelligence were concerned, if they could locate Skorzeny, they could verify whether there was such a hidden Nazi fortress nestled deep in the mountains. True enough, Skorzeny could have easily told them that the idea of a last-ditch defense was only a figment in the imagination of a handful of Nazis who had sought comfort in the mad musings of Hitler's last days. Skorzeny had made a tour of the so-called redoubt and, after discovering it to be a fantasy, had decided to surrender. He made repeated attempts to contact the Americans, but to no avail. He had sent letters to the nearest U.S. headquarters, but they went unanswered. Meanwhile, other American units were searching feverishly for any sign of him.[6]

So, eleven days after the end of the war, Skorzeny, along with one of his staff officers and an interpreter, came down the mountain to present himself to the U.S. Army in Salzburg. Arriving at the first American camp on the outskirts of the city, he identified himself and offered to surrender, but the duty sergeant was not impressed. However, the American informed the Germans that if they were indeed as important as they believed they were, he would provide them with a jeep and a driver, so that they could surrender to divisional headquarters. Once in the city, Skorzeny, still armed, tried again to surrender, but the first U.S. officer he came across, a major, told him to go elsewhere.[7]

Eventually someone realized that this was the infamous Skorzeny, and the comic surrender minuet came to an abrupt end. Subsequently, Skorzeny was treated with appropriate severity, befitting a dangerous prisoner. He was disarmed and stripped to ensure he was not carrying any poison. The SS commando leader was then dispatched with his colleagues to Salzburg, with a military policeman holding a machine gun to his face and was put on display for the media. Forced to sit with his hands tied behind his back, he gave an interview to the Allied press.[8] Skorzeny faced trial on several charges, including wearing an American uniform and using poison bullets. He was acquitted, but the Americans had no intention of letting him go free.

On July 27, 1948, with the assistance of three former SS officers, Skorzeny escaped from Darmstadt Interment Camp. For several years, the ex-commando traveled from Germany to France, Spain, and Syria, setting up ratlines to facilitate the escape of war criminals from Germany, which eventually enabled many unrepentant Nazis—some influential, some not—to find their way to South America and later to the Middle East. For several years, Skorzeny found employment with the Gehlen Organization—he had occasionally worked with Reinhard Gehlen in the last years of the war—until he finally settled in Spain, where he soon established a profitable international engineering consultancy and arms dealing business.[9]

During the 1950s, Skorzeny became a key player in a complex covert operation that brought a mixed bag of former German military officers and Nazi intelligence and security specialists to Egypt. The other player in this clandestine mission was a diminutive Italian-American with a checkered past but very influential friends in the U.S. State Department. Carmel Offie had grown up in a large, poor Italian family in Sharon, Pennsylvania. His parents had immigrated from the vicinity of Naples, and his father worked as a railroad hand in Portage. At the age of seventeen, Offie traveled to Washington and found employment at the Interstate Commerce Commission as a typist and stenographer.[10]

Three years later, in 1931, Offie applied to and was accepted by the State

Department as a clerk. After a short stint in Honduras, he was posted to Moscow at the end of 1934 as confidential secretary to the American ambassador, William C. Bullitt. Offie had a natural disposition to ingratiate himself and swiftly assumed the role of courtier. He became indispensable to the ambassador and undertook all manner of tasks, from professional to personal. Offie was at Bullitt's beck and call almost twenty-four hours a day, and in return the ambassador promoted him to the rank of attaché. Over time, Offie acquired the social graces missing from his background and developed an impressive list of professional and social contacts.

In August 1936, Bullitt was transferred to Paris and brought along his protégé. Burton Hersh describes Offie as: "Bullitt's pet, his performing spaniel, whose moist-eyed deferential efficiency while scampering through his protocol niceties left international society clapping."[11] Thanks to Bullitt's efforts, Offie now became third secretary at the Paris embassy. He excelled as a social butterfly who could charm men and women for Bullitt's benefit. He cultivated a number of people—a skill he perfected over the years—who proved useful in helping him navigate the back stairs of Washington's establishment. For example, he was on excellent terms with Marguerite "Missy" LeHand, President Franklin Roosevelt's private secretary. Occasionally he would send her a variety of gifts ranging from perfume to foie gras. Thus he was able to use Missy as a back channel to Roosevelt and have her give Bullitt's reports top priority, while singing his praises to the president.[12]

After Bullitt fell from Roosevelt's favor and lost the Paris embassy in August 1940, Offie was assigned to the Navy Department, but he continued to serve Bullitt in his spare time. When Bullitt began his campaign to destroy Sumner Welles, it was Offie who distributed handbills on Capitol Hill describing Welles's propositioning of two railroad porters for sexual favors. The scam worked, and Roosevelt had to dismiss Welles, but it did Bullitt little good; the president could not forgive Bullitt for his part in wrecking the reputation of one of his friends.[13] In March 1943, Offie was transferred to the staff of the Allied Advisory Council for Italy. In Europe, he acquired a unique knowledge of the personalities of the governments-in-exile and refugees from Eastern Europe, as well as the dozens of anticommunist groups that had worked for the Nazis and were now offering their services to the Allies.

Carmel Offie's career in the foreign service came to an abrupt end. In 1947, a routine check on a diplomatic pouch in Frankfurt revealed an unauthorized $4,000 in cash from Offie. Further investigation revealed unauthorized traffic in diamonds, black-market rubles, and even three hundred lobsters flown into Frankfurt on a military aircraft. Offie had little choice but to resign from the

State Department, but his many acquaintances pitched in to find him new employment. A few months later, Chip Bohlen, one of Offie's influential patrons, arranged for him to meet Frank Wisner of the newly established Office of Policy Coordination. According to Bohlen, Offie's primary expertise was his extensive knowledge of the Eastern bloc. This was not idle praise; Offie had worked with Allen Dulles in setting up Radio Free Europe and had recruited émigrés from countries occupied by the Soviet Union to broadcast behind the Iron Curtain.[14]

As a result, Wisner took on the disgraced former State Department officer as his personal assistant with responsibility for refugee affairs. As was the case with his previous employers, Offie proceeded to ingratiate himself with Wisner. He took care of Polly, Wisner's wife, as well as his children, and was soon accepted as a trusted member of the family. In addition, Offie became Wisner's social mentor. In the words of James Angleton: "Offie was a world-class sophisticate who could put a stiletto in an opponent and offer him a treatise on the cognac he was serving at the same time."[15]

The former State Department official did indeed have a feel for intelligence work and had learned at an early age to lead a double life. Like the spies he sought, Offie was expert at being all things to all people, while maintaining a secret alter ego. Offie was a homosexual, a circumstance that was lethal to any career in government or private industry in the 1940s and 1950s.[16] This experience, as well as a lifetime of perfecting skillful manipulation, enabled Offie to undertake difficult and covert tasks. At the same time, becoming part of the OPC and working in the shadowy world of spies, double agents, and within flexible moral limits, was a liberating experience for a man who had so much to hide. In the OPC, Offie dropped all attempts to hide that he was gay and had the confidence to live openly as who he was. To a great extent, Offie's newfound freedom was exorcised by the magnitude of the secrets he had to protect.

Carmel Offie and Frank Wisner became close friends. Above and beyond the courtier-master relationship, they also shared a passion for taking on the Soviets. This new epic struggle against communism overshadowed any qualms about the kind of individuals who could be drafted to fight for the greater good. Consequently, in this global contest, Hitler's henchmen, including his handmaidens of death, had to be harnessed in the covert battle of the Cold War. The race was on among the Allies who had fought and defeated Nazi Germany to enlist the services of German scientists and engineers.

Offie became the czar of Operation Paperclip—the covert program that tracked down German rocket specialists and engineers and brought them to the United States—and the deeper Operation Bloodstone, which sought out specific Nazis and wartime collaborators who could be induced, one way or another, to work for the Americans within the Soviet empire.[17] Offie knew that the Nazi collaborators who had survived the liberation of their countries and had quietly slipped back into their former professions were particularly vulnerable to persuasion or blackmail.[18] Others, particularly the Nazis recruited under the auspices of Operation Bloodstone, were brought into the United States and employed as intelligence and covert operations experts. These men and women were not misguided or even opportunistic collaborators who in the name of anticommunism had embraced Hitler's nightmare for Europe: they were high-ranking Nazi intelligence and security specialists on several war crimes lists.

Operation Bloodstone originated primarily in the State Department. On June 10, 1948, the State, Army, Navy, Air Force Coordinating Committee (SANACC) approved the operation, and a month later the Joint Chiefs of Staff expanded the activities of Bloodstone to:

> comprise those activities against the enemy which are conducted by Allied or friendly forces behind enemy lines . . . [to] include psychological warfare, subversion, sabotage, and miscellaneous operations such as assassination, target capture, and rescue of Allied airmen.[19]

In effect, the OPC had come into existence in order to implement covert attacks against the Soviet Union and its allies. One of the OPC's first forays into clandestine paramilitary operations was a disaster. In 1949, representatives of a Polish underground organization called Freedom and Independence (WIN in its Polish acronym) had approached Polish émigrés in London and claimed that they could mobilize an army of guerrilla fighters and overthrow Poland's communist regime.[20]

Initially, the OPC was skeptical, but WIN provided photos of its attacks against military installations and police stations, and even evidence of a pitched battle against Soviet tanks. This was followed by intelligence reports from WIN agents inside the Polish Ministry of Defense that included information on the Red Army's order of battle in Eastern Europe.[21] In November 1950, the OPC signed an agreement with WIN according to which the Polish underground, in return for training, money, personnel, and air drops, would provide espionage and conduct subversive work for the Americans.[22] The Americans also involved MI6, since Britain's spy agency had control over Eastern European émigré groups in London and could activate agents behind the Iron Curtain.[23]

MI6 agreed; unfortunately, however, they sent none other than Kim Philby to Washington to coordinate the Anglo-American guerrilla warfare campaign in Poland. No one knew at the time that Philby was a longtime Russian mole and part of a Soviet deception operation against the West. His opening tactic was to offer the Americans the use of a group of former Nazi counterintelligence officers the British had secretly positioned in Canada. These Germans had employed Polish and other Eastern European informers during the war, and many who had survived had managed to conceal their treason and find employment with the new communist regimes. Consequently, they were vulnerable and could be forced to cooperate with Western agencies under the threat of exposure, which would mean torture and certain death for them. As a result, the ex-Nazi counterintelligence experts were able to provide the CIA with long lists of potential agents.[24]

For eighteen months the CIA poured money and equipment into the Polish resistance, and then things began to go wrong.[25] The intelligence from WIN on the Red Army did not match information from reconnaissance photographs and communication intercepts. Furthermore, some of the agents parachuted into Poland or those activated by the former German counterintelligence experts disappeared after coming into contact with WIN, while the radio communications from others became increasingly suspect. Philby, who had been intimately involved with the program, came under suspicion by MI6, was recalled to London, and was quietly severed from the intelligence service. Finally, in December 1951, the Polish government revealed in a two-hour radio broadcast that WIN had been a deception operation all along. All the agents had been arrested the moment they came into contact with WIN, and the Polish and Soviet intelligence services had benefited greatly from the gold, weapons, and equipment generously provided by the CIA.[26]

A similar situation had developed in Albania. As in the case of WIN, Operation Valuable was a joint OPC-MI6 effort to train expatriate Albanians and return them to Albania to instigate an uprising against the communist regime or at the very least start a long drawn-out guerrilla war. Operation Valuable had originated with the British, who believed that Albania was ripe for counterrevolution. London wanted to punish the communist regime of Enver Hoxha, the dictator of Albania, for supporting the communists in the Greek Civil War (1946–1949). The Greek conflict had cost the British dearly in financial terms and eventually invoked the Truman Doctrine that ended Britain's sphere of influence in southeastern Europe and the Eastern Mediterranean.[27]

Albania was a viable target because of its location. The country had become separated from the Eastern bloc communist territories after the Tito-Stalin split in 1948. In the event of a successful uprising, the Russians would not be able to access Albania by land. Planning for the operation took place later in 1948, and the OPC and MI6 began to scour the DP camps for volunteers. The search produced two hundred Albanian refugees, most of whom were malnourished and in poor health.[28] MI6 trained their volunteers in Malta, while the OPC readied their Albanians in southern Germany. The British proposed to deliver their freedom fighters by sea on the Albanian coast, and the Americans planned to drop theirs by parachute.[29]

The British initiated their part of the operation in October 1949 by arranging for a flotilla of privately chartered boats to land twenty-six volunteers on the Albanian coast. They were ambushed almost immediately. Four were shot, but the rest managed to escape by crossing the mountains into Greece.[30] Several more attempts also met with failure, and by 1951 the British withdrew from the operation, leaving Albania to the Americans.

Earlier, in 1950, while still cooperating with Whitehall, the OPC—on Carmel Offie's initiative—had created Company 400, which included fifty Albanian volunteers. The OPC was in contact with the exiled political wing of the Albanian freedom fighters, the Balli Kombetar (National Front), based in Rome and Athens. MI6 and the OPC, however, could not agree on who should actually lead the Albanian resistance movement. There was considerable wrangling between the Allies and, according to Kim Philby's memoirs, there was some American frustration over the initial British lead in the operations. Philby mentions Wisner complaining, "Whenever we want to subvert a place, the British own an island within reach."[31]

Some of those selected by the Americans and the British had collaborated with the Germans and Italians during the war. One of their protégés, Xhafer Deva, had been Albanian interior minister under the Nazis. He had helped to establish the militarily incompetent yet dreaded 21st Skanderbeg Mountain Division of the Waffen-SS, for which he had recruited ethnic Albanians from Kosovo. On February 4, 1944, Deva had personally supervised a massacre of Albanian resistance fighters by the Gestapo. Another American choice, Hassan Dosti, had been justice minister with the Italian occupation government.[32] When the OPC tried to bring these men to the United States, it faced considerable obstacles, because some of their "guests" were wanted war criminals, and some did not even possess a passport.[33]

Carmel Offie nevertheless managed to convince U.S. Customs and Immigration officials to look the other way, in the national interest. The Albanians traveled to the United States on September 19, 1949, and opened the New York office of the American-backed Free Albania Committee. When the head of the organization died of a heart attack in New York, Offie lobbied hard to have Hassan

Dosti, the former fascist collaborator, replace him. Shortly after he managed to install Dosti as head of the committee, Offie was forced to leave the OPC.

Meanwhile, the OPC proceeded with the infiltration of the Albanian volunteers, but all attempts at transporting them by air or sea ended in tragedy. In one such effort, in June 1951, three groups were dropped by parachute. The first group was annihilated upon landing. The second managed to hide in a house, but they were surrounded by Albanian security forces, who set fire to the place, and all the occupants were burned alive. Of the third group, two were killed, and another two taken into custody. Shortly after, they were placed on trial.[34] The one group of parachutists who managed to survive began transmitting regularly, but it soon became apparent that they were under the control of Albanian state security.[35]

The Americans did have some success in bringing volunteers into Albania using the overland routes from Greece. However, those few Albanian infiltrators who managed to survive confronted a largely hostile population. Most people were too terrified of the Albanian security service to take part in any resistance movement; they were equally afraid of cruel retribution if they did not turn in the freedom fighters.[36] In April 1954, the Hoxha regime held a week-long show trial during which captured infiltrators confessed working for the CIA and made pitiful and futile attempts to plead for mercy. After this debacle, the OPC quietly shut down the Albanian operation.[37]

By 1949, Carmel Offie had become the OPC facilitator of the undesirable leftovers from the Second World War. Thousands of men and women on the wrong side of the new order in Europe and displaced by the new frontiers made ready cannon fodder for the OPC's secret wars, and thus they came within Offie's purview. Effectively, the disparate networks of émigrés, wartime collaborators, and war criminals became the CIA's talent pool for the clandestine war, even after the OPC merged with the agency. At the same time, all covert operations involving the Gehlen Organization, as well as the general use of Nazis, German counterintelligence specialists, and former German military, were routed via Offie.[38] In effect, Offie managed to transpose his flexible morality to OPC policy, and to ameliorate any qualms that his superior, Frank Wisner, may have had about employing war criminals or sending hundreds of men to certain death behind the Iron Curtain.

Ironically, Carmel Offie fell victim to the rabid anticommunist paranoia with which he and Wisner had helped to infect the Washington establishment and the American public. On April 25, 1950, on the floor of the U.S. Senate, Senator Joe McCarthy angrily denounced the subversive activities of certain government employees, although he did not mention Offie by name, and loudly proclaimed that a certain member of the CIA, formerly of the State Department, was a homosexual who spent his time hanging around the men's room in Lafayette Park.[39] Before he was forced to leave the OPC, however, Offie had helped to establish the paradigm for harnessing the services of Nazis, fascists, collaborators, and a variety of émigré groups and desperate volunteers from the DP camps in America's fight against the specter of world communism.

The pattern remained with the CIA, as the agency continued to rely on individuals and groups of radicals and extremists of one kind or another to do its bidding. However, such individuals and organizations often had their own, different agendas. Nazis and fascists, their erstwhile collaborators, fugitive war criminals, and the handful of genuine, self-sacrificing anticommunists were relatively easy to control. Once America's spy agency moved beyond its futile attempts to wage guerrilla warfare in Eastern Europe and the Soviet Union, it encountered new obstacles and troubled waters. While it met with immediate success in Latin and South America, it faced a very different situation in the Middle East. Working with Arab nationalists and Muslim extremists in the name of anticommunism may have served the short-term interests of all the parties concerned, but it also stimulated forces that, once released, ultimately spun out of control.

FIFTEEN

Nasser's Nazis

"We were the reason [Nasser] was out of reach of would be assassins
since we had ourselves designed the security arrangements around him."
—*Miles Copeland, CIA*[1]

The thinking in Washington reflected the conviction that the chaos following in the wake of old Europe's decolonization of the Middle East made the region vulnerable to Soviet penetration. The same rationale held true later in the Korean War, and then in Vietnam. The Central Intelligence Agency's initial relationship with the up-and-coming Arab nationalists in Egypt led by Gamal Abdel Nasser and later CIA involvement with the Muslim Brotherhood—and ultimately with the mujahidin in Afghanistan—took place in the context of U.S. fears of communism. The Americans were facing a shooting war in Korea, which had broken out in 1950 and which, unlike the later Vietnam conflict, was a true battlefield confrontation between East and West. Although the Russians did not participate directly in the Korean battles, they openly bankrolled the North Koreans, and later the Chinese, to fight the United States–led United Nations forces.

To counter Moscow's plans for gobbling up the oil-rich states of the Persian Gulf, the Americans looked to embracing a pro-U.S. Middle East strongman who could manage the secular and religious aspirations of Arabs and Muslims respectively. The British had attempted to cast al-Husseini of Mecca in such a role and even Ibn Saud, but neither had found resonance in the Muslim world. Arabia was too sparsely populated and too isolated to lead the Arabs, let alone all Sunni Muslims. Neither the Sharif of Mecca nor the new king of Saudi Arabia could fill the shoes of the Sultan-Caliph—a void that had left the Islamic community rudderless. After the Second World War, Nasser, as leader of the largest Muslim and Arab country, held the promise of rallying the Middle East away from the Soviets; he was indeed the Muslim-style Billy Graham sought by the CIA.[2]

The conundrum facing the Americans was that any relationship with Nasser would not only complicate U.S. support for Israel, but would also run counter to the spirit of the historic Anglo-American alliance. Washington could neither abandon the Israelis for Egypt—a country important to a degree, but not a state with petroleum reserves; nor could they permit their support for Nasser to interfere with the transatlantic special relationship. Consequently, America's links with the Egyptian leader had to be forged in secret and therefore had to be turned over to the CIA. In effect, the Office of Policy Coordination (OPC), and more specifically its Near Eastern Division, suddenly had to assume a covert diplomatic role. And matters became considerably more complicated when Nasser asked Kermit Roosevelt to help him train his military intelligence and internal security services.[3]

The mission had to be conducted covertly, so Allen Dulles turned to the Gehlen Organization and its stable of Nazi intelligence and security specialists for the appropriate know-how. Gehlen recalls that "at the request of Allen Dulles of the CIA, we at Pullach did our best to inject life and expertise into the Egyptian secret service, supplying them with the former SS officers I have mentioned."[4] The Germans had the necessary recent experience in police and security work, as well as in intelligence and counterintelligence operations. They were willing to work cheap and, since most were on several wanted lists, they could be trusted to keep their work secret. Admittedly, most of them were also rabidly anti-Semitic, but that only made them all the more acceptable to Nasser.[5] Unlike the CIA's experiments in Poland, Ukraine, and Albania, the OPC's task in Egypt was not to destabilize the Egyptian government, but to protect Nasser and indirectly enable him to wage relatively harmless, low-intensity warfare against the British.

Gehlen, for his part, attempted to subcontract the entire training mission to Otto Skorzeny, but the former SS commando leader was reluctant to accept, because he did not believe the Egyptians could pay him what he considered himself to be worth. However, Gehlen promised Skorzeny that his salary would be augmented with CIA funds, which would be laundered through the Gehlen Organization. Skorzeny remained skeptical, but "he was approached in a routine manner," relates Miles Copeland, "then at a higher level, then through a personal visit from a certain well known Major General of the American Army, and finally through his father-in-law, Dr. Hjalmar Schacht, Hitler's former Minister of Finance."[6] Because of these entreaties—or more likely because he saw some potential profit—the ever mercenary Skorzeny agreed to help.[7]

Though it is well documented in memoirs, interviews, and autobiographies, the exact trail of the connection between the CIA and Nasser's Nazi advisors has intentionally been rendered obscure. The available CIA documents do not explicitly reveal any direct involvement of the CIA in placing former Nazi officers in Nasser's security apparatus. However, when pieced together, the cumulative evidence is convincing that the agency played a significant role in the process of setting up a new Egyptian intelligence and security service. The secondary literature, mostly by American authors, strongly indicates that a deniable Egyptian operation was launched by Dean Acheson of the State Department and Kermit Roosevelt of the CIA.

The operation was conducted with the connivance of the government of Konrad Adenauer through the agency of the Gehlen Organization (and the West German Bundesnachrichtendienst, the Federal Intelligence Service, BND, which superseded it at Pullach in 1956), and with the purpose of advising the Egyptian leaders on intelligence and security and of recruiting ex-Nazi experts for Egypt. Initially, Skorzeny was brought into the operation, probably by Allen Dulles, who is also said to have supplied the leading intelligence and security professional, Joachim Deumling, although CIA records state that it was the top Nazi boss already in Egypt, Wilhelm Voss, who actually recruited Deumling. Generally, however, it seems likely that most of the Nazis trickled into Egypt individually and in small groups from various sources and by various routes and ratlines: some from West Germany, some from East Germany, some from Spain and Italy, and more than a few from South America, particularly Argentina. Skorzeny most likely facilitated the transfer of only a hundred of these men.

The impression offered by the extant CIA files, whether deliberately or not, is that it was Wilhelm Voss, already in Egypt at the behest of King Farouk since 1951, who recruited many of the Germans; it was Voss who first involved Skorzeny; and it was Voss who was working directly for Adenauer's foreign ministry, which co-opted Reinhard Gehlen. Certainly Voss seems to have always had a direct line to Bonn, to do his own recruiting, and to circumvent Bonn's diplomatic representatives in Cairo.

In the early 1950s, CIA records begin to track the backgrounds and current activities of various former Nazis, many of whom had moved to the Middle East and were now acting as security advisors to local governments and running sidelines in the arms trade and weapons smuggling. In some cases, the CIA seems to have been testing the grounds for establishing contact with these individuals, in order to gain inside information about Middle East governments. In other cases, the CIA had reason to believe that these former Nazis were already in the pay of the Eastern bloc, and hoped to turn them into double agents.

From available American documents and secondary sources, it appears that the CIA successfully used the cover of the Gehlen Organization (and later the BND) to avoid direct involvement with the actual placement of German advisors in Egypt. Later, however, the CIA established direct links with these former Nazis, once they had arrived in Egypt. As Timothy Naftali states:

> the extent of Gehlen's recruitment of former officers of the SD [the intelligence service of the SS] and Gestapo . . . was widespread. At least one hundred of Gehlen's officers and agents had served with the SD or the Gestapo, and the number may in fact be significantly higher—some of those hired had participated in the worst atrocities committed by the Nazi regime.[8]

The CIA records show that there was consistent and close contact between the agency and the Gehlen Organization or BND.[9] Members of these organizations are frequently cited as sources for intelligence reports, and are also used as intermediaries with former Nazis whom the Americans were interested in recruiting. In these reports Zipper is the code name for the Gehlen Organization and Upswing is the code name for the BND.[10]

The CIA did not introduce all the former German military and security personnel to Egypt, for some of the Germans, like Wilhelm Voss, had arrived prior to 1953 at the invitation of King Farouk. One of the first groups to arrive, numbering about thirty officers, was led by General Wilhelm Fahrmbacher and six aides in 1950.[11] Most were overt career soldiers hired by Farouk, who had always had a soft spot for the German Afrika Korps, to replace the British military mission, which had left Egypt in 1947. Economic, industrial, and administrative experts followed shortly and were joined, in turn, by missile and aircraft engineers, and other weapons scientists.

While some of the German specialists were, like Fahrmbacher, essentially military men, there was also a hard core of odious and considerably less reputable Nazis. Skorzeny's work for the CIA expanded the number of malevolent Nazis in Egypt by recruiting a cross section of former SS, Waffen-SS, Gestapo, and Sicherheitsdienst (SS Security Service, SD) members, together with virulently anti-Semitic propagandists from Joseph Goebbels's information ministry, as well as former medical officers, administrators, and guards from the death camps of the Holocaust, who were recruited to construct and run desert concentration camps for Nasser that held the Egyptian leader's enemies.

This list of fascist misfits and malcontents included approximately one hundred "advisors" dredged from their hideouts in Germany, South America, and Spain. They made their way to Egypt along the ratlines operated by various neo-Nazi and escape organizations. Some of the recruits prominent in this rogues' gallery of war criminals included, to name but a few, SS Major General Hermann Lauterbacher, gauleiter of Hannover and former deputy leader of the Hitler Youth, tried for war crimes and discharged on a technicality, sent by Gehlen to Egypt as BND liaison officer; Professor Johannes von Leers, vicious anti-Semite and senior official in Goebbels's propaganda ministry, said to have been recommended by the Mufti, whom he knew well in Berlin; his close associate, SS Lieutenant Franz Bünsch, best known for his pornographic work, co-authored with Adolf Eichmann, *The Sexual Habits of the Jews*, who served in Eichmann's Jewish Affairs section at the Reichssicherheitshauptamt (SS headquarters, RSHA) and who proposed setting up for Nasser a grandiose global intelligence network staffed by Egyptians and ex-Nazis from all over the world; and SS Colonel Sepp Tiefenbacher, Himmler's personal chief of security and friend of the Mufti, who was to become Wilhelm Voss's faithful assistant in Cairo.[12]

Skorzeny did not spend much time in Egypt; it seems his role in the training mission was to recruit the initial group, but not to direct the program. The man who most likely took charge of the German intelligence and security advisors was a very senior Nazi indeed: SS Lieutenant General Wilhelm Voss, a close friend of both Himmler and Heydrich, and one of the bearers of the elite SS death's-head ring, worn by only a very few of Himmler's innermost circle of associates. Voss, a university-educated economist and brilliant accountant, was effectively in sole charge of the entire wartime Czechoslovak economy, while also functioning as director general of the huge Skoda plant in Pilsen, where very secret weapons (jets, rockets, nuclear bombs, and antigravitational devices) were under development in the latter stages of the war. In February 1945, Voss was relieved of his post and was in command of an SS combat unit (although he denied this) when the U.S. Army captured him and, after interrogation, turned him over to the Czechs. Although he was indicted as a war criminal and destined for execution, the Czechs mysteriously returned him to the Americans.[13]

Voss testified on behalf of the U.S. prosecution in several war crimes trials and subsequently lived, mostly under house arrest, at Rottach on the Tegernsee, conveniently near the Gehlen Organization at Pullach. According to a CIA daily log, Voss was an important contact for Gehlen and, perhaps at his behest, left for Egypt in 1951.[14] According to the British embassy in Cairo, Voss presided over all the Nazi fugitives, saboteurs, and "bad hats" in Egypt.[15] His official position in Egypt was special advisor to the Ministry of National Production. So it seems likely that Skorzeny's role in the CIA-sponsored training mission to Egypt was merely that of recruiter, whereas Wilhelm Voss was the onsite director of operations, who also recruited technical specialists himself.[16]

One key member of the Nazi training mission was SS (SD) Lieutenant Colonel Dr. Joachim Deumling, a police professional and the senior intelligence and security specialist among the Germans. Deumling had been a typical German student from a middle-class family who had found in the Nazi movement an opportunity to pursue a professional career. In 1937, while working as an SS officer in the Hannover Gestapo, he completed his education and received a law degree. Two years later, he was able to advance to the elite of the SD at SS headquarters in Berlin and was placed in charge of the Polish Desk.[17]

In July 1941, he became head of the Oppeln Gestapo, but shortly after he was transferred back to Berlin and given responsibility for the Office of Polish Affairs within Germany. Significantly, his immediate superior was SS (SD) Colonel Erwin Weinmann, a trained physician who was responsible for the mass murder of Ukrainian Jews in 1942–1943. But something went wrong for Deumling,[18] and in the spring of 1943 he was dismissed from his post in Berlin and transferred to the command of an SS death squad in northern Yugoslavia: Einsatzkommando (Operational Task Squad, EK) 10B, which was part of Einsatzgruppe (Operational Task Force, EG) E (Croatia).[19]

In December 1944, Deumling was seriously wounded, and for the remainder of the war he was confined to a military hospital. After the German surrender in May 1945, he was interned by the Americans but managed to escape and, using a false name, worked as a laborer near Braunschweig for the next couple of years. Sometime in 1948–1951, he also found employment with a British army auxiliary organization and as a legal advisor in an insurance company.[20] Most likely, Wilhelm Voss recruited him through the Gehlen Organization. To reach Egypt, Deumling, expert in such matters of course, took extraordinary security precautions to avoid detection by the British. Finally, although his departure for Egypt was delayed because of a broken leg, he arrived in Cairo with his wife and three daughters in February 1954.[21]

During his two years in Egypt, Joachim Deumling passed himself off as a Ministry of Social Affairs employee working for the Ministry of Health or as directly employed by the Ministry of Social Affairs. Meanwhile, his official title was "Intelligence Advisor to the Director of Military Intelligence, Egyptian Army," although his actual work seems to have been conducted in the Ministry of the Interior. SS (SD) Colonel Leopold Gleim, former head of the Gestapo in Poland, another police professional, served as Deumling's right hand in Egypt and helped him on the security aspects of his work. The CIA file on Deumling makes note of the fact that Deumling "was active in the collection and evaluation of information," that he "had no contact with the remaining German experts in Egypt (General Fahrmbacher Group)," and that "his activities were severed from the group and kept secret."[22]

Deumling's "real job" is described as "the organization of intelligence and a central security agency similar to his former German organization."[23] In effect, Deumling's accomplishment in Cairo was reorganizing the Egyptian intelligence service along the lines of the RSHA, although Miles Copeland claims that it was modeled after the CIA.[24] However, if the Egyptian intelligence agency used the CIA organization for a blueprint, it stands to reason that officers from the American spy service would have guided the work of Deumling.

Although the CIA's Deumling file suggests that the agency did not have contact with him during his time in Egypt, it does include sufficient details to indicate that the Americans were keen to have him work for them. One June 1958 memorandum asks its recipient to "inform UPSWING [BND also Gehlen] we have requirements which [we] would like [to] levy via UPSWING if subject [Deumling] willing to cooperate. Would appreciate UPSWING making recruitment effort soonest and advise us results." This request was passed along, and Gehlen replied that they did not intend to recruit Deumling, as he was considered "unreliable." Earlier that same month, the CIA had been informed by "Winterstein" that "the BND has had operational interest" in Deumling but that "no contact exists nor does he think intelligence exploitation possible." This turn of events left the CIA in a difficult position, as they did not feel that German intelligence was being honest about their own connection to Deumling. Gehlen had admitted that Deumling was of operational interest to them.

In early June, Gehlen requested "no further contact by AIS," but were "apparently willing to service KUBARK [CIA Headquarters] requirements." In response to this, the CIA planned to pass requests from the assistant chief of staff for intelligence [ASCI] as CIA HQ requests, in order that Upswing (Gehlen) would respond to them.[25] At the request of the ASCI, military intelligence approached Deumling on May 18, with the intent of debriefing him regarding Soviet backing of Egyptian intelligence service training and operations against the United States and NATO in Egypt. Deumling refused, and resented the contact having been made. However, it was felt that Deumling might reconsider the request if it came from CIA headquarters.[26]

Although Deumling's file does not refer to interactions between him and the CIA during his time in Egypt, it does make it clear that Deumling had done intelligence work for Gehlen and/or the CIA at some time before 1958. As of June 1958, Deumling "had rejected all proposals for continued intelligence work with UPSWING (Gehlen) or any other service."[27]

Aside from any contact the CIA may have had with Deumling in Egypt, his file indicates that they were gathering information on Deumling from a "trusted source who is an ex-German Abwehr officer in Cairo."[28] Nine years later, on June 26, 1967, Deumling's Nazi past caught up with him. Along with Bernhard Baatz, Emil Berndorff, and a few other former RSHA officers, Deumling was arrested as an alleged war criminal. All were imprisoned in Berlin and charged in the so-called RSHA Trial. According to the charges, Deumling, as former head of the Polish Desk, was guilty of having assisted in the murder of 150 people by drafting and issuing state police decrees that sanctioned the bad treatment of Polish workers and prisoners of war, as well as the carrying out of executions. Ultimately, he was implicated in the killing of 3,823 people, but he was released (because of a technicality) in December 1968. He died in February 2007 at the age of ninety-seven.[29]

One of the most contentious activities engaged in by Nazi officers who provided their services to the Egyptians was the guerilla training of Muslim Brotherhood paramilitary squads. Despite the presence of highly questionable Nazi elements in Egypt, and in defiance of evidence to the contrary, German diplomats insisted that the "nearest approach made to guerilla training is the formation and instruction of a regular Egyptian unit of paratroops by a Major Mertins."[30]

In 1953, the British saw German air force Major Gerhard Mertins, a former airborne combat engineer and sabotage expert, as the key "renegade" German officer whose presence in Egypt was detrimental to British interests. While even the British viewed the other advisors as somewhat cooperative with the West German government, which was trying to ensure that the German officers did not engage in anti-British activity in Egypt, Mertins was thought to be heavily involved in training the MB squads. Some other German advisors were also thought to be involved in similar activities, but their names were not known to the Foreign Office.[31] German advisors such as Mertins were ostensibly training the Egyptian government's legitimate Liberation Battalions; despite careful attempts to obscure the reality of the situation, the archival record reveals quite a different story.

In December 1952, General Neguib announced his intention of forming an official organization of the Arbeitsdienst (labor service) type, which would be aimed at providing discipline and employment to students, and which would include a paramilitary wing, the Liberation Battalion. As the Liberation Battalion training camps were established, a highly publicized recruitment campaign was launched.[32] Throughout 1953, varying reports reached the outside world about how these camps were being organized and run, and about who was being trained in them. Although the success of the recruitment drive was debatable, information came in that attendance at the government training camps had definitely been poor, though it was improving. "It is nevertheless very unlikely that more than about 10,000 men in all have received training in the camps." Significant, however, was the fact that "of these . . . possibly as many as 6,000 have been members of the Moslem Brotherhood who have taken advantage of the training offered in Government-organized camps without in any way transferring their allegiance to the Liberation Rally from the squads of the Moslem Brotherhood."[33]

Members of the MB were indeed participating in the government camps. After the January 1952 coup, existing guerrilla organizations were disbanded. Nevertheless, the MB, which had a wealth of experience in underground warfare, remained intact, and, by the end of 1952, it was known that these squads had resumed training.[34] Until early June 1953, the MB's paramilitary wing, the IEM Kateibas, had run their own camps and used their own instructors. After that, the training was brought, at least partially, under the control of the Egyptian government and conducted by Egyptian army officers in army camps.[35] From this point onward, MB members generally attended the Liberation Battalion camps for initial training.

The MB, however, maintained its own secret training camps for the "final preparation" of its members.[36] These camps were known to recruit within the universities and were organized into three categories: unattached men, men with dependents but no children, and men with no dependents. "The most dangerous assignments will be allotted to men in the first category, who may well act as 'suicide' squads."[37] The suicide attackers that were anticipated by the British were expected to come from the ranks of the MB.[38] The Brotherhood's squads were thought to be better staffed and trained, and of higher morale than the government units. It was estimated that, in addition to the existing squads, approximately eight thousand men had been trained in the Brotherhood's own camps, and were not yet formed into squads.[39]

The German advisors were certainly involved in training at the government camps, but their presence seems to have been much stronger in the exclusive MB camps, as well as in the Liberation camps that had been set aside for the training of MB members.[40] A British report of May 1953 notes evidence of "considerable assistance" being given the Brotherhood's paramilitary arm (IEM Kateibas) by German advisors, while the same advisors had not played a direct part in training at the government camps. It went on to state:

> In particular a great deal of attention has been paid to [training]
> in explosives, demolition, sabotage, etc. which will be a feature of IEM

operations. IEM Kateibas are being trained by expert German advisors for specialist sabotage tasks. Such targets as filtration plants, 9 BAD, armouries, Main HQs and communication centres are likely to be the object of carefully timed and planned sabotage operations for which specific training and even rehearsals have been undertaken with meticulous German thoroughness.[41]

A later report noted:

> There has certainly been considerable German influence if not assistance in training. This has given rise to increased attention being paid to and probably more effective techniques in the use of explosives, sabotage and in mobile Commando type operations. Such assistance is probably more apparent at IEM than at Liberation unit establishments.[42]

Beyond the level of simple training, there were "indications of considerable German influence and even of the possibility of German leadership in Guerilla fighting."[43] Some reports insisted that a large proportion of the Egyptian population was likely armed and trained in the use of weapons, and that "extensive and coordinated attacks by German trained Liberation units are likely" in the event of conflict. Though Egyptian army officers in plainclothes or in IEM or Liberation unit uniforms would lead most of these attacks, the British assumed that larger attacks might even be led by the Germans.[44]

The MB's squads were not only being trained separately in unique tactics; they remained ideologically separate from the government units. In Lord Hankey's view, the MB would not cooperate with the Liberation forces in a clash with foreign forces. He noted that the Brotherhood as an organization remained detached from the troubles in 1951 and stated his opinion that "it is unlikely that they would now agree to pick the chestnuts of the C.R.C. out of the fire."[45] It was noted that the Brotherhood remained a "more formidable proposition" than the regular Liberation Battalions, particularly as they had "been able to take advantage of training in Government camps without losing their identity."[46] This state of affairs had been engineered by the CIA, but it was also a portent of the very dangerous environment they were helping to build. As a result, the MB's IEM Kateibas were established as the most highly trained and powerful paramilitary force in Egypt. Their isolation from the Liberation Battalions had been encouraged.

The British were anxiously observing the German advisors in Egypt, concerned that they might be encouraging or abetting anti-British activity. In 1953, they made contact with General Fahrmbacher's deputy, General Oskar Munzel, a former panzer commander in the Western Desert under Rommel. Munzel provided the British military attaché with information about the German personnel, and, as the West German government had done, reassured the British that the advisors were not involving themselves in politics that would disadvantage the British.[47] The British, however, had information to the contrary. In June 1953, in response to a parliamentary question, the government composed a draft that stated they were aware that the German advisors in Egypt had been involved in the training of guerrillas. This draft also noted that the German government had sent a representative to Egypt, despite having no direct control over these advisors who had been recruited unofficially by the Egyptians.[48]

This representative, Helmut Allardt, a West German career diplomat, subsequently denied that the Germans were engaged in activities injurious to the British, and advised against their removal. All of this information was then deleted from the approved draft, which stated simply that the West German chancellor had promised an investigation, despite the fact that the technicians had been recruited directly by the Egyptians. In response to a specific question about the training of guerrillas, the government-approved draft stated: "I have seen many reports about their activities. I should prefer not to go into detail pending the results of the investigation." This revision was made in order to save the West German chancellor embarrassment.[49]

The British were well aware that MB squads were being trained in guerrilla tactics, that "Mertins has been doing [this] on the side," and that "he is not the only one."[50] In fact, British intelligence had a significant amount of information about guerrilla training. A note on a Foreign Office file from August 1953 refers to the training of MB sabotage squads by the German advisors. "No doubt Mertins is in charge of this. I understand we have asked the German government to get him removed," writes Sir Reginald J. Bowker. During this period, the Foreign Office had the impression that the majority of the advisors—with Mertins as one definite exception—had a British-friendly attitude in their dealings with the Egyptian government, and that for this reason were not training Egyptians in guerrilla warfare.[51] Even given the knowledge that the Foreign Office had of these activities, it remains possible that they knew little in comparison to the covert British intelligence services, such as MI6.

This was just one of the many problems spawned by resorting to war criminals as part of the U.S. covert relationship with Nasser. The actions of the CIA in Egypt certainly worked against Britain, America's closest ally, and at the same time helped Soviet intelligence. A number of the Nazis recruited to work for Nasser were certainly also double agents or had at some time been under the control of the Soviet KGB. Yet neither the CIA nor Gehlen had paid much attention to the background of the Nazi recruits for Egypt.

For example, the fact that Wilhelm Voss, after his initial surrender to the Americans in 1945, was also in Russian and Czech captivity but was never tried or sentenced by either authority, and was subsequently returned to the Americans, suggests that he may have been played back to the West by the East as a mole or a double agent. The additional fact that he first appeared in Egypt accompanied by Czech assistants, and that he subsequently recruited Czech personnel, reinforces this view, as does the fact that the first prominent personality to be recruited by Voss—the rocket scientist Rolf Engel—was a known communist.[52]

Another example was Gerhard Mertins himself. After leaving Egypt, Mertins became one of the world's most powerful dealers and shippers of surplus German arms (MEREX Corporation). The British were probably well aware in 1956 of Mertins's clandestine connections with the BND and of his possible double-dealings with Moscow, which made him even more of a destabilizing presence among the MB guerrillas, whom he may even have been supplying with weapons.[53]

Of course, the Soviets did not rely solely on the Nazis in Egypt for intelligence on Nasser and the CIA. One of the best agents of Soviet intelligence was Ze'ev Avni (born Wolf Goldstein). Avni was an economist and master of several languages. He had spent the Second World War in Switzerland, where he was recruited by Soviet military intelligence, the GRU. In 1948, he immigrated to Israel and found employment in the Israeli Foreign Ministry. In 1952, he was posted to Brussels as commercial attaché, as well as security officer. He used his new position to gain access to the Israeli embassy safe, and he photographed its contents for his Soviet masters. While in Brussels, Mossad also recruited him, and he used his fluent German to pose as a German businessman. At this time he was transferred from the GRU to the KGB. Using his cover as a German businessman, he penetrated the ranks of the Nazis working for Nasser and indirectly for the CIA. Avni also passed on to the KGB the Mossad ciphers, thus enabling the Soviet spy agency to break the codes of the Israeli secret service. In 1956, he was caught and sentenced to fourteen years in prison.[54]

Undoubtedly, Moscow used Avni's information on Nasser's Nazis to keep a wary eye on those Germans already in the service of the KGB and to acquire information on the rest, in order to enlist new agents by various means of coercion. For the Americans, the use of Nazis was the beginning of a policy that called for the deployment of anyone or any organization that could be identified as anticommunist. Nasser himself fulfilled that role for a few years; after he abandoned the covert relationship with the United States and turned to the Soviets for support, the CIA reversed gears and sought to undermine the Egyptian "Muslim Billy Graham." Once again, the old maxim, "my enemy's enemy is my friend," underwrote the CIA's war against Nasser. In this case, harnessing the forces of Islam through the MB to counter Arab nationalism led by Nasser served as the harbinger of a dangerous and futile U.S. policy toward the Middle East.

SIXTEEN

A Legacy of Coups: Anglo-American Intervention in Syria

An elderly man approached a soldier who was sitting on a tank.
"What is going on my son?"
"Hush" said the soldier, signaling the old man to silence.
"This is an Inkilab [coup d'état]!"
The puzzled man responded, "Okay . . . but, what is an Inkilab?"[1]

At half an hour before midnight on March 29, 1949, the commander-in-chief of the Syrian army, Colonel Husni Zaim, dispatched military units to arrest members of Syria's government. Army detachments swooped in to gather "marked" officials, seal off streets, cut off communications, and close the Syria-Lebanon border. At 6:00 A.M. on March 30 a curfew was implemented; by morning, the takeover was complete, and the sounds of army boots echoed through the streets of Damascus. A statement issued by radio introduced the new regime and outlined Zaim's message to the country and to the world. Resonating with affected seriousness the announcer proclaimed: "Impelled by patriotic zeal, we have been forced to overthrow the former Government. We are not driven by ambition, but only by the desire to create a really democratic state." The revolt, Zaim insisted, was "purely local and has no foreign implications."[2]

The suggestion that a change of power in Syria had no foreign implications was laughable. Syria's geography straddled a strategic zone—an ideal land route for transporting oil, the country shared borders with several key Middle East states, including Israel, the ongoing flash point for the region. As a result, Syria's allies had a vested interest in who held power in Damascus. For this reason, the coup in March 1949 had not only foreign implications, but also certainly direct foreign involvement via the CIA.

From the 1500s to 1918, Syria, as well as neighboring Lebanon, Jordan, and Palestine, did not exist as states, but were administrative units of the Ottoman Empire. During the First World War, Britain proposed the creation of an independent Arab state to secure the allegiance of the Hashemite Sharif Hussein of Mecca and by extension the loyalty of the Arabs in the Ottoman Empire. Not long after, the British also offered Palestine as a Jewish national home. The British, in effect, betrayed both Hussein and Arab nationalism. The 1916 Sykes-Picot Agreement between Britain and France called for the postwar award of Syria and Lebanon to the French and designated Palestine as an international zone under a British mandate. Despite Syrian and Palestinian appeals to Woodrow Wilson's policy of self-determination, the Americans failed to support the creation of independent Arab states, and after the war the Middle East was divided more or less according to the terms laid out in the Sykes-Picot Agreement. Lebanon emerged as a state within Syria and in 1926 France made Lebanon a separate entity, thus setting in place Syria's subsequent and relentless intervention in Lebanon, whereupon all regimes in Damascus remained committed to the notion that Lebanon was part of Greater Syria.

France had established a presence in the region before the war by forming alliances with minorities in Syria and the region, claiming the right to protect the Maronite Christians, who had established links with the French during the First Crusade. Despite this historical connection, France's mandate over Syria and Lebanon was rife with repression that provoked rebellions by the native groups. It was not until the end of the Second World War that Syria finally gained independence from France.[3] The end of the war also brought about the reluctant fulfillment of the Balfour Declaration, when the United Nations created a Jewish state in Palestine—the defining moment in Syrian history.

Syria today is a complex mix of religious, cultural, social, and political factions, many of which are embroiled in a historical struggle for dominance and even survival. Entrenched divisions in the region have deepened and warped over time, manipulated by domestic and foreign elements, in the quest for financial, political, and ideological preeminence. For decades, the struggle for oil, the conflict over Israel, and Cold War rivalry effectively drove Western foreign policy in the Middle East. During the Cold War, the states of the Middle East tried to avoid officially linking their fortunes to either the West or the Soviet Eastern bloc and many preferred to remain neutral. Neutrality, however, was not palatable to Britain and the United States or to the Soviet Union. As a result, the British, Americans, Israelis, and Soviets waged a clandestine proxy war in Syria to control the region.

The fear of a communist-dominated Middle East forged Western strategic thinking, as well as the Arab nationalist movement acting as a vehicle for Moscow's agenda. Although Arab nationalism is often associated with the Egyptian leader Nasser, its roots are in early-twentieth-century Syria. The movement originated with Syrian students influenced by Arab history in the American University of Beirut and by the efforts of the Ottoman Empire to suppress Arab culture. Gradually, the concept of Arab culturalism transformed into the demand for an independent Arab nation along with a revival of Arabism.[4] Because the Arab world is composed of a spectrum of religions and spiritual sects, Arab unity implicitly meant a unity across religious boundaries. But at the same time, the mosaic of Arab religious, cultural, and minority groups was vulnerable to manipulation and exploitation by foreign powers.

Like the British before them, the CIA and other U.S. intelligence agencies co-opted political movements and dissident factions across the Middle East who could be helpful to the West, pitting them against those who posed a threat to American interests. In response to the twin evils of communism and Arab nationalism, Western powers turned to extreme religious groups, who inherently opposed both the atheist ideology of the Soviets and the secularism of Arab nationalism. The Muslim Brotherhood was one such group, armed and funded by the West to counter Arab nationalism and Soviet influence.

In the 1930s Syrian students who had attended the Al-Azhar University in Cairo brought the Muslim Brotherhood back with them to Syria.[5] The Muslim Brotherhood's political wing operated for some time in Damascus and Aleppo as the Islamic Socialist Front. But after 1945, the organization adopted the name Muslim Brotherhood to represent themselves in their political activities. Remarkably the Muslim Brothers managed to unnerve both the British and the Syrian communists. According to one Foreign Office report, the Muslim Brothers were described as "a Marxist drink in a Moslem cup."[6] Meanwhile the Syrian Communist Party branded the Muslim Brotherhood as the "British Brethren."[7] Regardless of these sentiments, in 1950 the Foreign Office was very concerned about links between the Muslim Brotherhood in Syria and Soviet communism.[8] However, the Muslim Brothers found the United States a lesser evil than the communists, while the Americans had few compunctions working with a militant Islamic organization.

The Brotherhood was one of many overt and covert organizations that found in Syria a convenient clandestine battleground. Prior to the end of the Second World War, for example, Syria and Lebanon had become bases for rival terrorist groups, some pro-Zionist, others pursuing an anti-Zionist policy. By 1943, the Jewish Agency and Haganah had created an intelligence service in Syria and Lebanon. The American Office of Strategic Services monitored this group, gathering information on those involved and following their activities.[9]

In the postwar years, the Americans and the British took a particular interest in Polish refugee groups that were building up terrorist cells in the region. American counterintelligence and British intelligence began collecting information on these Polish refugee groups, which, in turn, had links to the

Irgun.[10] By the 1950s, Lebanon even housed neo-Nazi organizations, such as the BDO (a German nationalist organization comprised of ex-Nazis), whose members hid in Beirut and became involved in Syrian political activities.[11]

Throughout the 1950s furthermore, Damascus served as an organization center for ongoing subversive struggle against Israel. In 1955, Egyptian army officers approached Syrian military intelligence asking for names of Palestinian terrorists living in Syria the Egyptians could deploy against Israel along the Jordan border. The operation was backed by Saudi Arabia, and planned in the Saudi embassy in Damascus, under the supervision of Jamal al-Hussein, a Palestinian activist, brother of Amin al-Husayni, and the founder of the Palestine Arab Army.[12] Recruits also came from supporters of Amin al-Husayni in Jordan, and the Mufti himself acted as a major organizer from his usual base in Cairo. The Mufti was rumored to be behind an extensive terrorist network, though the organization was not currently active either due to lack of funds or because its members were waiting for the right moment. Temporarily out of favor with Nasser's government due to his links with Muslim Brotherhood, the Mufti was once again welcome in Cairo, because the Egyptians believed that they could use his network to create trouble for Israel.[13]

The Foreign Office was well aware of Egypt's use of Palestinian refugees for espionage operations against Egypt, but the British avoided cautioning the Syrian government, for fear of damaging relations with Damascus.[14] In the early 1950s, the British were treading delicately in the highly unstable world of Syrian politics. The Foreign Office representative in Damascus complained of Britain's "negative" policy toward Syria, while the Cairo office stressed the importance of maintaining good relations with the Arab world as a whole. The Foreign Office argued that current British assurances regarding the maintenance or curtailing of Israeli borders were not enough.[15] The British were trapped into placating the Syrian regime because they knew that Syria, like other "neutral" Middle Eastern states, could turn to other friends. The most obvious of these was the Soviet Union; but the British were also worried about their competitive allies, the Americans. Throughout the 1940s and 1950s, the Foreign Office frequently warned London that any policy moves that upset the Arab world would simply invite Washington to replace Britain in the region.[16]

America's relationship with the Middle East began well into the twentieth century with Syria as the primary springboard of U.S. intervention in the region. Prior to the First World War, the United States had little interest in the Middle East.[17] However, by the 1920s, with the consumption of oil dramatically increasing at home, the Americans began to challenge Britain's exclusive control over the petroleum reserves of the Middle East. American investments in the Middle East petroleum expanded throughout the 1930s and 1940s, and at the end of the Second World War the security of the region was a major strategic concern for the United States. The topography of Syria was ideal for the efficient and inexpensive transportation of petroleum. Syria is situated between the Persian Gulf and the Mediterranean, making the country an ideal route for an oil pipeline, which can replace the long sea journey around Saudi Arabia to the Suez Canal. In 1949 the Trans-Arabian Pipeline Company (Tapline) had a deal in place with the Syrian government, and the oil pipeline was operating by 1950. Tapline was a subsidiary of the Arabian-American Oil Company (Aramco), which, in turn, was a subsidiary of the California-owned Texaco.[18]

Following the end of the Second World War, the United States emerged as a major player in the Middle East. After 1945, the Americans established their own intelligence networks and the State Department began receiving regular reports on key regions of the Middle East from the Office of Strategic Services, Special Intelligence.[19] The cover for American intelligence operatives was to pass as members of the Foreign Economic Administration (FEA) and in State Department posts in capitals throughout the Middle East.[20]

As the Cold War rivalry between the West and the Eastern bloc expanded, both British and American intelligence feared that Syria would become a Soviet satellite.[21] These concerns intensified after the construction of the pipeline and the growing Syrian dependence on Soviet arms and money.[22] By the late 1940s, the situation continued to deteriorate because Syria, the Americans were convinced, housed "a surprising array of left-wing political organizations, including the Arab world's most active communist party."[23] Indeed, by the 1950s, Soviet influence expanded dramatically in Syria and the KGB was well established in Damascus.[24] The Soviets, for their part, catered to Syrian needs and during the 1948 Arab-Israeli War, for example, provided them with weapons. The Arab-Israeli War, in fact, became a major source of discord between the United States and Syria, and it did not escape Washington's notice that, the more alienated Syria became from the Americans, the closer Damascus moved toward Moscow.[25] In response, London and Washington began considering the use of a covert strategy to implement anticommunist measures in Syria, and by the end of the decade the intelligence services of both countries were planning a regime change in Damascus.[26]

Meanwhile the country itself was struggling. The Arab-Israeli War of 1948 had followed immediately on the tails of the Second World War.[27] The army blamed Syria's defeat on the government, accusing them of being ill prepared. The military was further enranged by Faysal al-'Asali, a right-wing member of

Parliament, who publicly insulted the weak performance of the army. Some historians feel that these attacks led directly to the upcoming Zaim coup.[28] Thus began a trilogy of coups, which created a tremendous degree of socio-political instability in the young state and brought about widespread corruption.

The aftershocks of Syria's losses in the Arab-Israeli War of 1948 eventually led to the resignation of the elected Nationalist/Populist government. Not long after, in March 1949, Zaim, then the Army chief of staff, overthrew the interim government.[29]

Colonel Zaim's ascent to power followed a series of meetings with CIA agent Stephen Meade. In March, Meade reported Zaim's request that "U.S. agents provoke and abet internal disturbances . . . essential for coup d'état or that U.S. funds be given him for this purpose."[30] It is not possible to confirm that this money was provided, but contact between the CIA and Zaim increased considerably leading to the coup.[31] Miles Copeland, formerly a CIA agent, has outlined how he and Stephen Meade backed Zaim, and American archival sources confirm that it was during this period that Meade established links with extremist right-wing elements of the Syrian army, who ultimately carried out the coup.[32]

The CIA was also involved with the installment of Colonel Adib Shishakli, in the final coup of 1949. Zaim had been an excellent ally of the United States. After he seized power, he outlawed the Syrian Communist Party, made peace agreements with Israel and Turkey, and offered a home to Palestinian refugees. But unfortunately his tenure as head of Syria was short-lived. Zaim was murdered in August 1949 and replaced by Colonel Sami Hinnawi. Despite American fears, there is no evidence of actual Soviet involvement; Hannawi had no particular partisan political leanings and mainly opposed Zaim's erratic and high-handed rule.[33] Hannawi was a colonel who commanded the main army units in southern Syria. There are allegations that Iraq had backed the coup partly because they did not like Zaim's pro-Egypt policy and responded to Hannawi's call for Syrian-Iraqi unity. The Iraqis certainly had contact with Hannawi along with others in the Syrian army, and one of the conspirators, Lieutenant Fadlallah Abu Mansur, later claimed that Iraq was directly involved.[34]

The new Syrian strongman restored the communists, hinted at renewed hostility with Israel, and proposed to unite Syria with Iraq. The Americans were anxious to forestall Hannawi and to act quickly before the Soviets intervened. Miles Copeland had found the aspiring leader, Shishakli, to be "a likeable rogue" and arranged for him to receive American financial and military aid.[35] Shishakli took control of the government in December 1949 and cooperated with the Americans with respect to the oil pipeline and Israel. He remained in power for four years. Despite the fact that the Americans found his efforts against communism insufficient, Shishakli's pro-West policies eventually became a source of public anger. Consequently, army officers, lead by Lieutenant Colonel Adnan Malki, overthrew him in February 1954.[36]

The interim government that followed the 1954 Syrian coup was a major threat to Washington and London. Furthermore, the pro-Western opposition faced considerable internal resistance, while the army itself was divided into left- and right-wing camps. Informants told their British contacts that there was no chance of a regime change without external help, preferably from Iraq. According to them, Iraq would have support of tribes in the north, along the Turkish border, as well as some of the tribes and army factions in the south through contacts in Saudi Arabia. British and Turkish embassy staff held several discussions over the Syrian situation, while the Foreign Office mulled over the fact that one or two possible candidates for Syrian dictator were in prison.[37]

At the same time, the CIA's Allen Dulles noted in 1955 that Syria was "ripe for a military coup d'état."[38] In 1956, the Americans toyed with Operation Straggle, a scheme to back the Syrian Social Nationalist Party (SSNP),[39] a right-wing party friendly to the United States, so that it would overthrow the Malki regime. This plan was scrapped because the CIA feared that the SSNP would fail. Another critical factor was just as Straggle was about to commence the Suez Crisis exploded, further negating the prospects for an American coup in the Middle East.

After the dust settled over the Suez Crisis, London and Washington then initiated a new joint Anglo-American operation to topple the Syrian regime. Operatives of the Near Eastern Division of the CIA led by Kermit Roosevelt and its counterpart headed by Sir George Young, the deputy director of the British Secret Intelligence Service, lobbied right-leaning members of the Syrian army to plan a coup, while the CIA provided hundreds of thousands of Syrian pounds in backing the new operation. The plan called for instability within Syria and along its borders. British and American intelligence operatives would encourage internal rebellion by the Muslim Brotherhood, while staging "Syrian" attacks in Jordan and Iraq. This seeming aggressive activity on the part of Syria would then permit the United States to invoke the Eisenhower Doctrine and provide aid for Iraq to invade Syria.[40]

It is not surprising that the Muslim Brotherhood were to be the foot soldiers in the plot. In the mid-1950s, the British and Americans were enjoying a renaissance in their relations with the Brotherhood, linked by their bitter opposition to Nasser. Egypt's Nasser had cracked down harshly on the Brotherhood in 1954, imprisoning and killing many of its members. Some fled to Syria, others found refuge and support in Saudi Arabia. In addition to direct contacts with the Muslim Brotherhood, the Americans also supported Saudi efforts that facilitated the Brotherhood's terrorist activities across the Middle East.[41]

As the coup evolved, the Brotherhood had another reason to assist the British; prior to the January 1957 elections, the Ba'ath Party (a Syrian secular and nationalist organization) and the Muslim Brotherhood parted ways and soon became implacable enemies.[42] The initial rift was almost certainly caused by the growing relationship between Syria's Ba'ath Party and Egypt's Nasser, which became official by early 1957. The Ba'athists in Syria had spearheaded a successful campaign for Syro-Egyptian union (which was to come to fruition in 1958). However, Nasser was a bitter enemy of the Muslim Brothers, who were certain that a harsh fate awaited them in the case of a united Syria and Egypt.[43]

Despite the political and public relations disaster of the Suez Crisis, or rather because of it, the Americans opted to continue to use covert operations in order to intervene in the Middle East, instead of the high-handed approach of the British-French-Israelis in Egypt. Perhaps the Eisenhower administration believed that an American-financed coup would be less abhorrent than military invasion or held the conviction that the CIA would not fail. Regardless of these or any other considerations, the January 1957 Syrian elections heightened Washington's and London's fears over Syria's progressive tilt to the Soviets and accelerated plans to overthrow the Damascus regime.

The left swept to power in Syria under the Popular Progressive Front, an alliance of Communists, Ba'athists, and nationalists. The election results underlined the abilty of the army and of the leftist groups to dominate Syria.[44] The new government excluded rightist elements in general and shut out political figures who had been friendly to the West. The level of paranoia increased rapidly and the British government in London was subjected to frantic political reports from the Foreign Office that identified several major Syrian political figures as potential threats to Britain and the United States, but these men later fell victim to assassination.[45] When the Ba'ath Party swept to power, the Brotherhood, like the Americans and the British, but with dramatically divergent motives, were anxious to be rid of the new regime.

During the 1950s Syria was rife with rumors and accusations of Western interference in Syrian politics; exploiting this atmosphere of impending coup in the early morning of August 12, 1957, government agents arrested hundreds of suspects. A few months later a trial was held in Damascus during which the accused were charged with plotting to overthrow the government with support from Iraq, the United States, and Britain. Iraq, under Nuri Said, was alleged to have instigated the coup plans, which included a plot to assassinate Khalid Bikdash, the communist leader, followed by the killing of the Ba'ath Party leader; Salah al-Bizri, the chief of the Syrian general staff; and 'Abd al-Hamid Sarraj, the head of Syrian military intelligence.

Making matters worse, Washington's old friends, the SSNP, were heavily implicated in the plot thus indirectly linking the Americans.[46] Shishakli, the charges stated, had been approached by Iraqi officials at a meeting in Geneva in early 1956 after which he made a visit to Paris. In April of 1956, Adib Shishakli and his brother, Salah, who was also involved in the coup, were transported from Paris to Lebanon on a British cargo ship. Beirut was used as a base for planning the coup and the Shishaklis held meetings at a house near the British embassy.[47]

The plot uncovered in August 1957 was a variation of Operation Wappen, devised by the CIA and the SIS in 1956. A major player was Rocky Stone of the CIA. From the time that Stone had arrived in Syria as CIA station chief in Damascus in April, he had set out to work on making contacts and cultivating officers in the Syrian army. But just as Stone finally got to the point of handing over the large funds being provided by the CIA to the Syrian officers, his contacts went on national television and denounced him as a spy.[48]

The plot was organized on three levels. The SSNP was responsible for training paramilitaries, Iraq had agreed to supply arms and money, and a political group was being groomed within the Syrian government.[49] In addition to the Muslim Brotherhood, the CIA enlisted the help of a variety of extreme and militant Islamic groups that included the Islamic Society for the Salvation of the Homeland from Russian Oppression and the [Secret] Society for the Liberation of the Usurped Land to lay the groundwork for the coup.[50] Arms were smuggled into Syria from Iraq, Jordan, and Turkey and distributed to plotters inside Syria, as well as to the Druze and Massa'id tribes.[51]

A camp near Beirut, most likely Beit Mery, was used to train members of the SSNP and many of them were treated at the American University Hospital in Beirut.[52] Once all preparations were complete and sufficient arms secured, the signal for the coup was to be given during the Voice of Britain over the Near East Broadcast station, which was operated by British intelligence. The assassinations were then to take place, and one cell was to occupy the city of Homs and another Hama to complete the overthrow of the government.[53] One of the proposed victims, Sarraj, had been targeted by the Britain. In March 1957, the Foreign Office, along with the SSNP, were pressuring Sarraj to accept the post of military attaché in Cairo. Communist and socialist factions protested against the removal of Sarraj. An assassination attempt had been made on him the previous year and Syrian intelligence had blamed the Israeli Mossad, but British Foreign Office documents openly comment on the need to eliminate Sarraj, as well as the other two high-profile alleged targets of the plot.[54]

The Syrian government accused British and American intelligence services of hatching this plan from its early stages. There was ample evidence. Many of the accused were found in possession of large amounts of money, American cigarettes, and other goods the Syrian authorities claimed were given to them by Western backers. British agents had been seen in tribal areas in the months leading up to the planned coup.[55] The allegations were reported in the Western press: the Americans had offered between $300 and $400 million, and assigned Stone to carry out the scheme. The Associated Press reported that, upon revelation of the plot, Shishakli was whisked away to Beirut in an American diplomatic car.[56] He was sentenced to death in absentia by the Syrian court. Afterward he returned to Brazil, where he had been living prior to the plot. On September 27, 1964, Nawaf Ghazaleh, a Syrian Druze, assassinated Shishakli in Brazil.[57]

The disastrous failure of the 1957 plot along with the revelations of the Syrian court shredded America's reputation and drove many local groups to seek support and protection from the Soviets.[58] A similar debacle in Iraq further eroded the influence of the United States and exposed the British and Americans as feeble coup organizers. The CIA had been in collusion with the royalist government in Iraq, and was taken by surprise when it was suddenly overthrown. Iraqi officers led by Abdul Karim Qasim toppled the Hashemite monarchy; the new regime withdrew from the Baghdad Pact, the Central Treaty Organization, and established friendly relations with the Soviet Union. Equally embarrassing, the Qasim government published documents that laid out the full extent of the CIA plot against Syria.[59]

In the fallout of the Syrian debacle, the Foreign Office reported that Rocky Stone and two other American contacts had been expelled from Syria.[60] The ensuing trial and its associated publicity further eroded the reputation of the United States as well as that of Great Britain. Subsequently, for years rumors of new plots and military interventions continued to be linked to the British and Americans. In the fall of 1957, Syrians spotted American soldiers mixed in with Turkish troops along the Syrian-Turkish border.[61] The atmosphere of suspicion and paranoia made it very easy for the Soviets to implement their schemes in the region.

In the mid-1960s, the Soviets launched Operation Pulya (Bullet). Pulya was designed to "expose" a new CIA plot against the Ba'athist regime. This, however, was a disinformation campaign, in which Soviet contacts provided names and details of "spies" and "traitors" (some information was true and some was false) to the Syrian government. A member of the Soviet embassy even placed a call to a pro-American officer in the Syrian army, pretending to be a friend, warning him that he was about to be exposed as an American contact. The officer, in a panic, asked whether he should go into hiding or seek asylum in the U.S. embassy. Naturally, his telephone was tapped; this was as good as a confession and the officer was exposed as an American agent—there are no records attesting to his ultimate fate. As a result of Operation Pulya, some CIA agents and their contacts were eliminated, further straining U.S.-Syrian relations and pushing Damascus closer to the Soviets.[62]

In the aftermath of the 1957 crises, British officials were alarmed by the breakdown of American and British covert operations, particularly with respect to countersubversion. A briefing note for Harold Macmillan's visit to Washington explained the drawbacks of American intelligence:

> On the British side there is a fairly expert staff covering the Foreign Office, M.I.6, the Information Research Department, and to an increasing degree the Ministry of Defence (and Service Departments), the Colonial Office and the Commonwealth Relations Office. . . . On the American side the organisation is not so tight and the co-ordination between the State Department and the C.I.A. is not complete. Neither side trusts the other.
>
> There is a need on both sides for better forecasting of possible trouble spots, quicker provision of the type of intelligence required to launch counter-subversive operations, and above all quicker financial and logistical provision of military and other supplies for all these operations. . . .
>
> . . . Working Groups must be attended by suitably high-level people who can speak authoritatively on policy and operational matters and they must meet at frequent intervals. In the case of the Lebanon the Working Group met but State Department representation was inadequate.[63]

However, Anglo-American machinations in Syria accomplished little except to pave the way for a strong Soviet presence in Damascus. Remarkably, the Soviets, like the Americans, decided that religious groups were the best mechanism by which to gain influence in Syria. Soviet infiltration took the form of Eastern Orthodox missions to Syria and financial support awarded to religious groups in Syria. A Soviet Eastern Orthodox mission led by the Bishop of Moscow arrived in Syria for a month-long visit in May 1957 as the guest of the Damascus Orthodox Patriarchate. A Soviet "cultural mission" of six people also visited during the same period. The Patriarch of Antioch arrived in Moscow in November 1957 and in the course of the visit Alexei, the Russian Patriarch, stressed to the Syrian cleric that the friendship of the Soviet Union helped to preserve Syrian independence. Offers of money and support were also made to the Greek Orthodox Church in Syria; in a countermove the British launched plans for the Church of England to forge ties with churches in the region.[64]

In February 1958, Shukri al-Quwatli and Gamal Abdel Nasser joined Syria and Egypt into the United Arab Republic. This union lasted until September 1961, when a fresh military coup, in which the CIA was rumored to be involved, terminated the United Arab Republic.[65] The officer behind the coup was Lieutenant Colonel 'Abd-ul-Karim an-Nahwali, who belonged to a social and religious circle that had a direct link to the Muslim Brotherhood. Following the 1961 regime change, the Brotherhood regained its legitimacy and increased its membership in Syria. This, however, did not prevent the success of the Ba'athist coup of March 1963, which was carried out by the National Council of the Revolutionary Command (NCRC), essentially made up of Syrian military officers.[66] In February 1966, however, yet another army coup removed President Amin Hafiz and other members of the NCRC, and abolished the provisional constitution that had been in effect since 1964. The new regime referred to itself as Ba'athist, but claimed to be returning to a purer Ba'athist form of government.

The 1960s were marked by riots and conspiracies instigated by the Muslim Brotherhood against the Ba'athist regime. The Brotherhood's resistance was driven by objections to the secular ideology of the Ba'ath Party, the economic policies of the government, and by fear of communism. The urban small merchants and artisans, whom the Brotherhood supported, comments Hanna Batatu, "viewed the 'socialism' of the [current regime] as a weapon by which the more conscious segments of the long neglected and long suppressed rural people sought revenge against the main cities."[67] The fear of communist infiltration increased in February 1967, when a leftist military coup brought in a Moscow-friendly regime. The new government accepted financial aid from the Soviets and in return allowed the Syrian Communist Party to rebuild. This regime, under Salah Jadid, was seriously undermined by the June 1967 Six Day War with Israel in which the Syrian army was poorly armed and suffered major losses.[68] Almost everyone blamed the government and it was not long before another coup installed a new regime in Damascus.

In November 1970, Hafiz al-Asad deposed Jadid. Unlike the traditional ruling bodies of Syria, Asad (and Jadid) came from the Alawi minority. The Alawis are an offshoot of Shiite Islam and had historically been excluded from military and political positions of prominence in Syria. Yet, for reasons that remain a matter of debate, members of the Alawi sect had not only joined the Ba'ath Party and but also flourished.[69] Unlike Jadid, who avoided Alawis while in power, Asad staffed the high command and the senior intelligence posts with Alawi officers. Regardless of his Alawi origin, Asad proceeded with extreme caution, establishing up to fifteen separate intelligence and security services, which employed thousands of staff and a small army of informants.[70]

The Muslim Brotherhood had backed Asad against Jadid, because Jadid had experimented with socialist programs, which the Brotherhood and their supporters, the urban artisans and small merchants, fiercely opposed. Some younger members of the Brotherhood objected to supporting any Ba'athist faction and moved to Jordan, where they joined the Palestinian Fatah. Those who remained in Syria faced little opposition or persecution from Asad.[71] But the Brotherhood's relationship with Asad came under considerable strain after 1973 and the Brothers soon turned against the Syrian dictator.

Asad's introduction of a secular constitution in 1973 was the first point of friction.[72] The fragile friendship came to an end when the Syrian's regime moved against the Palestinians in the Lebanese Civil War. In 1976, the Syrian army assisted the Phalange massacre of Palestinians at the Tal az-Za'tar camp in Lebanon. During the same period, the Brotherhood observed that Sunni Muslims were being deliberately excluded from positions of power in Asad's regime. Although Sunni Muslims were well represented in the more visible elements of the government, the real power, according to Batatu, was held "by Asad and the leaders of three intelligence apparatuses and of two crucial heavily armed units which underpin the whole structure."[73]

In 1976, the Brotherhood began a campaign to overthrow Asad and establish Sunni Muslim rule over Syria. An assassination campaign began to target Ba'athist military officers and Alawi politicians. In June 1979, Brotherhood members locked a building at a Syrian military school and slaughtered the imprisoned trainees with automatic weapons and firebombs, killing eighty-three. The Brotherhood then attempted to assassinate Asad in 1980 and, in November 1981, killed two hundred people with a car bomb in Damascus.[74]

The Muslim Brothers were not acting alone. In 1983, Asad signed a friendship pact with the Soviet Union, and the CIA, once again, turned to the Muslim militants for help. While there is no documented evidence that the Americans directly funded the Brotherhood throughout the 1980s, there is little doubt that Israel and Jordan backed the group from the late 1970s. The Jewish state and secular Jordan, while not obvious allies of the Brotherhood, supported them as a counterbalance to the Asad regime and the PLO, the Palestine Liberation Organization. The CIA was well aware of the Israeli and Jordanian assistance to the Brotherhood, but did not discourage it. As the Near East chief of the Bureau of Intelligence and Research explained: "We knew about the Muslim Brotherhood . . . a lot more than what was in the papers. We looked benignly upon it. We knew it was risky, but life is risky."[75] The American ambassador to Syria put it even more cynically: "I don't think it bothered us too much that they were causing problems for Asad."[76]

Once the Muslim Brotherhood became linked to Western interests, the KGB decided to eliminate the organization in Syria. The instrument of the Muslim Brothers' destruction was Rift'at al-Asad, the younger brother of the Syrian dictator. In 1971 the KGB had cultivated Rif'at because as the commander of the Syrian army's prestigious Defense Brigades he had at his disposal the most effective force in the country.[77] The KGB also made contact with two terrorist organizations in the 1970s: the Democratic Front for the Liberation of Palestine, which was under the leadership of a Greek Orthodox individual, and the Popular Front for the Liberation of Palestine—General Command. This latter was a splinter group from the PFLP, of which Carlos the Jackal was a member, to work against the Muslim Brothers and the British and Americans.

The KGB supplied the terrorist organizations with money and arms while they exploited Rift'at's love of luxury. Unlike his reclusive and austere elder brother, Rif'at had acquired a taste for foreign travel and Western luxuries and had exploited his position to accumulate a small fortune. Under his direction, the Defense Brigades held a weekly market in Damascus to sell black-market goods smuggled in from Lebanon. Rif'at was often referred to as the "King of the Oriental Carpets" due to the frequent confiscations of these items by his personal Lebanese militia, disparagingly called the Pink Panthers.[78] Not surprisingly, it was Rif'at al-Asad who led the crackdown on the Muslim Brotherhood. In February 1982, Rift'at's Defense Brigades carried out a bombardment of Hama, a city of 180,000 where Brotherhood-inspired riots had taken place. The assault lasted for three weeks, ultimately killing between ten thousand and 25,000 militants and civilians.[79]

Driven by fear of Soviet penetration of Syria, Western intelligence services strengthened extremist groups and inadvertently created a culture of conspir-

acy theories that played into the hands of the KGB. The Soviet intelligence service took advantage of the prevailing fear of Western intervention by fabricating
CIA plots aimed at overthrowing the Asad regime. This hardened the Syrian
dictator's obsession with his personal security. As a result, Asad was protected
by a presidential guard of over twelve thousand, backed by no fewer than fifteen intelligence and security services with personnel of fifty thousand along
with a greater number of informants.[80] After decades in which Syria was splin-
tered by coups and countercoups, Asad had "coup-proofed" Syria.[81]

Both the CIA and the SIS repeatedly ignored reports from Western observers and even from their own officers in the field, reassuring them that Syria
was not about to "go red." Patrick Seale challenged the assumption that Syria
had ever been at serious risk of becoming a Soviet satellite, concluding that
"the CIA messed up in the region."[82] CIA agents, such as Robert Baer, tried to
convince his superiors that supporting the Muslim Brotherhood in Syria was a
serious and dangerous policy, but were told "the Muslim Brotherhood isn't
a target for us."[83]

SEVENTEEN

America's Eyes in the Middle East: The CIA and Israeli Intelligence

"I know of no country that has given such public recognition
to a foreign intelligence officer."
—*William Hood (on Israeli honors for James Jesus Angleton)*[1]

Despite differences of opinion over policy with parts of the Middle East, Britain remained a close ally of the United States. However, Israel's secret service, Mossad, became the primary source of intelligence for the CIA on the region, as well as on Eastern bloc countries and the Soviet Union. In his history of the CIA, Tim Weiner comments: "The channel [Mossad] produced much of the agency's intelligence on the Arab world, but at a cost—a growing American dependence on Israel to explain events in the Middle East. The Israeli perspective colored American perceptions for decades to come."[2]

The architect of this relationship was James Jesus Angleton, the CIA's head of counterintelligence and the one-man liaison with Israel.[3] Angleton's relationship with Israel cannot be defined in stark black-and-white terms—pro-Israel and pro-Zionist, certainly not in the absolute conviction of someone like Orde Wingate, but in subtle shades of gray. Angleton was committed to the Israeli-American alliance but suspicious of Jewish organizations in the United States as well as of Jewish individuals both in and out of the CIA. He backed a CIA operation to buy a Washington garbage company that collected trash from the Israeli embassy and the office of B'nai B'irth, and took it to the agency for sorting and analysis.[4]

Yet for over three decades, Angleton was the closest ally of Israel in Washington; even before 1948, Angleton had close ties to clandestine Jewish organizations. Israeli sentiments for this secretive American intelligence officer are on public display. Just north of Jerusalem, along the Jerusalem—Tel Aviv highway, a series of stones has been inscribed to serve as a memorial for Israeli war heroes who have made the ultimate sacrifice for their country. One of these stones is reserved for the memory of James Angleton. Inscribed on the stone in English and Hebrew: "James Jesus Angleton. 1917–1987. In memory of a Good Friend."[5] A similarly dedicated stone is on a hill overlooking the Jaffa Gate, near the King

David Hotel in Jerusalem, bearing the inscription, in English, Hebrew, and Arabic: "In memory of a dear friend James (Jim) Angleton."[6] The latter was unveiled in a special ceremony where many former and current members of Israel's intelligence community were present to reminisce on the life of their greatest American ally.[7]

Angleton's relationship with Israeli intelligence organizations dated back to the Second World War when, as an OSS (the Office of Strategic Services—America's first clandestine service) officer, he had worked with underground Jewish networks in Italy. After the war, Angleton was the official liaison with all the Allied secret services and the exclusive conduit for information from Israel's intelligence community.[8]

One of Angleton's close friends described the importance of this position:

> That's the job that was so sensitive . . . and that's the one that you don't read about. While he was liaising with everyone, he was getting them to do favors for either the CIA—things the CIA didn't want to carry out directly; like they've never killed anyone, right?—or for his own agenda. Even on a more mundane level, he could use his contacts with Israeli intelligence, which he kept to himself, as authority for whatever line he was trying to push at the CIA. You know, "My Israeli sources tell me such and such," and no one was going to contradict him, since no one else was allowed to talk to Israeli intelligence. I always had the impression that he used the Israelis in this way, getting them to say that the Russians had not really broken with the Chinese or whatever. They would be perfectly happy to do him the favour. On top of all that he felt that he was getting the benefit of Israeli networks and connections all over the place, not just in the Communist bloc.[9]

A former colleague of Angleton explained Angleton's interest in his work:

> Jim believed that the real exercise of power in and between countries occurs through networks of leaders. This was the importance of the liaison unit. It operated outside of the normal channels, which really irritated people like the State Department at times. A lot of it went back to relationships formed during and just after World War II. He cultivated these people, whether they were in or out of government.[10]

James Jesus Angleton was the prime mover that helped forge the relationship between the CIA and Israeli intelligence. The alliance began May 1951, when Angleton arranged for Prime Minister David Ben-Gurion to meet with Walter Bedell Smith, the director of the CIA at the time, and who later that year hosted the mastermind of the Israeli intelligence community, Reuven Shiloah (formerly Zaslany), to draft the first formal U.S.-Israel intelligence sharing arrangement.[11] Contrary to popular belief, this agreement was initially only in verbal form with no written contract.[12] Angleton's first trip to Israel took place in October of that year—the beginning of an annual pilgrimage that would continue throughout his career.[13]

Angleton's attitude toward Israel had been shaped by the Holocaust and was also influenced by the success of the Jewish secret networks. After recruitment by the counterintelligence section of the OSS in 1943, he served for a short time in Britain but spent most of the war in Italy. Among his best sources were Palestinian-Jewish agents who after the end of the war in Europe managed to smuggle thousands of their persecuted European cousins to Palestine through escape networks in Italy.[14] Although later he was integral to the 1951 CIA-Mossad agreement, Angleton feared that the influx of Soviet bloc immigrants into Israel would carry with it spies seeking to penetrate the West.[15] Soviet agents did indeed join the waves of immigrants, but a great number defected, were unmasked, or proved unable to function in any significant strategic employment after arrival in Israel.

It was Soviet policy in 1947 that Israel become an ally of the Soviet Union in order to counter American attempts to use the Israeli links with the Jewish community in the United States. It became the strategy of the KGB to ensure that large numbers of its agents were among the Soviet Jews permitted to leave for Israel. The most successful of the first generation of Soviet agents infiltrated into Israel was the epidemiologist Avraham Marcus Klingberg, who in 1948 was recruited to work on chemical and biological weapons. Later, Klingberg was one of the founders of the Israeli Institute of Biological Research in Ness Ziona (southeast of Tel Aviv). Remarkably he remained a successful agent of the Soviet Union for thirty-five years. Another example was that in the period 1947–1950, thirty-six of the Jews who immigrated to Israel from Bulgaria were operatives of the KGB. In 1953, the Israeli security service, Shin Bet, caught two Israeli members of the Knesset, Yaakov Riftin and Moshe Sneh, passing information on Israel's foreign policy to the Soviet embassy.[16] Both were members of Mapam, Israel's Marxist-Zionist party, and the information passed on to the Soviets reinforced Moscow's suspicions of the special nature of the Israeli-American relationship. And in the 1950s the KGB had penetrated the Mossad itself through the services of Ze'ev Avni, an Israeli diplomat and agent of Mossad.

Just about the time of Avni's capture, the KGB recruited Yisrael Beer, a professor of military history at Tel Aviv University and a military commentator and lieutenant colonel in the Israeli Defense Forces (IDF) reserves. Beer became a close friend of Shimon Peres, then deputy minister of defense. Until Beer was unmasked as a Soviet agent, he was able to provide his masters with Peres's secret attempts in 1957 to obtain assistance from West Germany and purchase refurbished German submarines. Beer most likely leaked the information to the media and the subsequent public outcry almost caused David Ben-Gurion to resign. Shortly afterward, in 1961, he was caught and one year later sentenced to seventeen years in prison, but died after four years of incarceration.[17]

Although none of the Soviet Jews or Israelis recruited in the 1960s achieved anything as valuable as Avni and Beer, Angleton remained cautious about the vulnerability of Israel's population of immigrants whose backgrounds could not be traced behind the Iron Curtain. A report from the British embassy to the Foreign Office underscored these concerns, warning:

> the perpetual problem of security which Israel by its very nature is bound to face . . . [is that] it is a country of immigrants about whose origins and past in many cases nothing is known except for what they themselves reveal. It has been pointed out that hundreds of people in responsible positions in theory offer the same kind of risk as Beer.[18]

Despite the apparent liability, neither Angleton nor most of the senior leadership of the CIA could afford to ignore Israeli intelligence assistance. Mossad collected a great deal of intelligence on the Warsaw Pact powers from the steady stream of Jewish refugees making their way to Israel and forwarded it to Washington through Angleton.[19] When Nikita Khrushchev, the leader of the Soviet Union made his speech condemning Stalin's excesses before the Twentieth Congress of the Communist Party of the Soviet Union in February 1956, Mossad was able to deliver a copy to Angleton in April 1956, who passed it on to a grateful Allen Dulles.[20]

Victor Grayevski, a Polish Jew and journalist with a strong sense of Zionism, had managed to obtain an unofficially reproduced copy of the speech from a secretary in the office of the head of the Polish Communist Party, Edward Ochab. Rather than sell the speech to the Americans or another Western power, Grayevski chose to give the copy to Israel as a gift.[21] Grayevsky allowed an Israeli diplomat to photograph all fifty-eight pages before returning the copy. When the speech landed on the desk of Ben-Gurion a few days later, he called an emergency meeting with his top officials and made the decision to hand over the speech to the CIA, thus cementing the U.S.-Israeli alliance and forging closer ties with America's intelligence agency.[22] The Israelis had acted just in the nick of time, as Frank Wisner, the CIA's deputy director for plans, had acquired his own copy of the speech from the French.[23]

It was not a one-way street, however. According to Mohamed Heikal, Angleton passed back vital information that assisted the Israelis in developing an atomic program, and at the very least he was a strong and influential voice backing Israel in Washington.[24] Heikal was a close associate of Nasser and had little love for Angleton or Israel, but it is certain that the zealous head of the CIA's counterintelligence gave Mossad something in exchange. Michael Holzman, in a recent biography of Angleton, poses an intriguing scenario:

> One monument set up by the Israelis after Angleton's death, then, the public monument might be taken to memorialize his long operational relationship with the Israeli intelligence services. The other, the more obscurely situated monument, perhaps could be taken as memorializing, in part, a quite specific service to Israel that was performed by Angleton: his help with the Israeli atomic bomb.[25]

Holzman's assertion is not entirely implausible if taken in the context of the Cold War. Above everything else, Angleton was an implacable foe of communism and it was not unreasonable for him, or any of the administrations he served, to fear a Soviet strike against Israel. Under such circumstances passing nuclear weapons technology would have been part of America's strategy of deterrence and not necessarily the sole act of a pro-Israeli Angleton.

If Angleton did not give the Israelis vital American scientific secrets, at the very least he must have used his considerable influence inside the CIA on behalf of the Jewish state. Furthermore, the sensitivity of the Truman White House to the Jewish vote was another factor in American policy toward the Middle East. On the other hand, the Eisenhower administration, which succeeded that of Truman, initially tried to secure alliances with Arab states and was not inclined to support Israel, but this policy changed after a few years.[26]

Although Angleton emerged as Israel's chief ally in Washington, it did not prevent the Israelis from trying to manipulate the CIA's counterintelligence chief. In 1956 a dispatch from the military attaché at the American embassy in Tel Aviv reported that Israel had mobilized its reserves. Kermit Roosevelt gave similar information to Dulles. Another warning came from London and

Robert Amory, the CIA's deputy director for intelligence, predicted the attack would happen within twenty-four hours.[27]

Allen Dulles called a meeting of the CIA's Watch Committee, and it met an hour later in Dulles's office. Amory recalled:

> At that moment James Angleton suddenly burst out of a bathroom that connected Allen's office and the deputy director's office next door. We used it to keep people visiting the director from meeting each other outside. You wouldn't want the head of Pakistani intelligence to meet his Indian counterpart on the way out, for instance. Anyway, Angleton comes bursting in and says "I can discount what Amory is saying. I spent last night with our friends and they have assured me that they are just carrying out protective measures against the Jordanians." Well, I got mad at that. I said to Allen, "The taxpayer lays out $16,000 a year to me as your deputy director for me to give you the best intelligence based on the evidence available. Either you believe me or you believe this co-opted Israeli agent here," and I pointed at Angleton.[28]

It was possibly the harshest thing that Amory could have said about Angleton in the presence of the head of the CIA. Nevertheless, Dulles put his faith in Angleton and when Israel attacked Egypt, on October 29, 1956, Dulles called the invasion merely a probing action. But it soon became apparent that the Israelis were moving against Egypt, and Dulles and the CIA were caught unaware. Angleton was embarrassed when Israel proceeded to invade the Sinai and seize the Suez Canal as part of its tripartite plot with Britain and France. One of Angleton's colleagues remarked, "The Israelis could get away with lying to Jim that once. I don't think they did it again."[29] However, according to Rhodri Jeffrey-Jones, "There has been considerable speculation about this presumed intelligence failure. For example, some accuse James Angleton . . . of suppressing some indications of the attack because he sympathized with its objectives, while others report that he was furious at being kept in the dark by his Israeli friends. But there is some doubt as to whether the CIA was, in fact, caught unaware."[30]

This was not the first occasion in which the American-Israeli alliance was strained. During the period of 1952–1953 the FBI determined that Mossad and Aman (Israel's Military Intelligence Directorate) were conducting espionage activities on American soil. Elyashiv Ben-Horin, an Israeli diplomat, was discovered trying to recruit Arab diplomats to spy on their countries. Though this was standard practice for Israeli intelligence agents in Western capitals, it did not sit well with their American hosts. The Israeli operation achieved debacle-like proportions when the Jordanian military attaché pretended to accept recruitment but reported Mossad's activities to the FBI. An FBI surveillance team later saved the Jordanian from a gun-wielding Ben-Horin after the attaché provoked him into an argument at a restaurant. Ben-Horin was expelled from the country and was barred from returning to the United States until years later, despite his successful career as a diplomat, including a term as ambassador to Germany. The FBI also suspected Colonel Chaim Herzog, Israel's military attaché to Washington, of attempting to steal defense technology, but as evidence against him was weak and his term at the embassy was coming to a close, no action was taken.[31] Upon his return to Israel he was promoted to the rank of general and appointed chief of Aman.

From the beginning of the intelligence cooperation agreement, Angleton had been meeting regularly with Memi de Shalit, Israel's unofficial and only semi-involved intelligence officer in Washington in 1951. Shalit was made official liaison to the CIA, and he developed a long-lasting friendship with Angleton, with whom he shared the same birth date, December 9 (the two would exchange birthday cards for decades). "Jim impressed me," Shalit reminisced, "he seemed detached and acted with great caution and circumspection." Shalit held most of his meetings with Angleton at his house on Massachusetts Avenue, and sometimes in restaurants. He recalls his meetings: "He came, two or three times a week, to my house in the early evening, and often stayed until the early hours of the morning. It happened more than once that his wife, Cecilia, phoned at about 4:00 A.M. to find out whether the meeting was still going on."[32]

Despite its early tensions, however, by 1953 the covert alliance between the two countries had settled into a productive and reciprocal relationship, and Angleton's meetings with Shalit began to yield results. Angleton had the occasional requests and sometimes favors that the CIA was not able to secure. As Shalit recalled, "Once he asked us if we could get him gold coins. For them [the CIA], getting gold coins was not an easy affair. It was very easy for us. We got them from friends in Europe and passed them on to the Americans [with which to pay their agents behind the Iron Curtain]."[33] On another occasion, Angleton inquired if Israeli intelligence could find work for the musician wife of a Soviet defector, in order to keep the man happy and talking. He wanted Mossad to ask a favor from a well-known Jewish violinist on the international concert circuit to hire the woman, but despite Israeli efforts, the violinist found the defector's wife unskilled. In return, the CIA helped Israel by giving them intelligence equipment: bugs, radio receivers, and transmitters to be installed at the Syrian border in order to transmit false information. The CIA also hosted Israeli intelligence personnel for training at Langley.[34]

The general framework of the alliance was simple: in exchange for intelligence on the Soviet bloc, Israel's intelligence community received training and technology.[35] The intelligence that Israel provided included a range of subjects on the Soviet Union. A top secret Shabak program to debrief the constant flow of immigrants to Israel from the Soviet bloc yielded vital information on topics from military installations to economic conditions and the morale of Soviet citizens. As Teddy Kollek recalled,

> our people talked with immigrants, translated what they told us into English and passed the material on to the Americans. The CIA was interested in any crumb of information from the East Bloc, from the price of bread and train timetables, to the description of the lines of people that were waiting to get into the food shops.[36]

Kollek estimated that one quarter of all information on the Soviets that the Americans acquired throughout the 1950s was from Israel intelligence sources.[37] To show their gratitude, the CIA hosted a number of senior Israeli intelligence officers in 1952 for a training course on modern intelligence and espionage techniques.[38] The Israelis even received help from former Nazi intelligence chief Reinhard Gehlen, in his capacity as head of the BND. After the Sinai War in 1956, the BND provided training and assisted in infiltrating Israeli agents. The Germans also offered the Israelis expert advice on the organization and development of intelligence services.[39]

However, the primary relationship was with the United States and the Israelis shared the spoils with their friends in the American intelligence establishment. On August 16, 1966, Israeli intelligence managed to obtain a Soviet MiG-21 and offered it to its allies in the CIA. The Americans were surprised and delighted by the opportunity to obtain detailed insight into the capabilities of Soviet bloc air forces. The operation originated in late 1964, when an Iraqi Jewish merchant, "Yosef," informed Israeli officials that his girlfriend's sister was married to an Iraqi air force pilot named Munir Radfa, who had an interest in defecting with his MiG because he was frustrated over the discrimination he faced as a Christian. Radfa was worried for his family and he knew that they would surely face punishment or even death at the hands of Iraq's security service. With extensive planning and help from Kurdish guerrillas, the Israelis managed to smuggle Radfa's family out of Iraq. Thus Radfa took off one morning from Iraq and landed his MiG in Israel. He and his family were settled under a new name and likely still live somewhere in Israel.[40]

On another occasion, Israel supplied the United States with an entire Soviet radar station, which the Israelis had captured from the Arabs a few months following the Sinai War. Earlier, the CIA had asked their Israeli counterparts to send samples of Soviet military hardware that had been captured by the IDF.[41] In September 1969, Israeli commandos raided an Egyptian radar post across the Gulf of Suez and stole an entire radar station—the most advanced in Soviet technology. The station was airlifted by four helicopters and then flown in parts to the United States for closer examination. The radar was the same model as that which was in use by North Vietnamese forces and it provided invaluable assistance to the American forces fighting in Vietnam.[42]

There were other, lesser coups that served American as well as Canadian interests. For example, Israeli intelligence was able to unmask a Soviet mole in the Royal Canadian Mounted Police. In 1959, Roy Guidon had been posted as an intelligence officer in the Canadian embassy in Moscow. Guidon tried in vain to initiate a number of affairs with women at the embassy, which brought him to the attention of the Soviet intelligence. The KGB, consequently, concocted a honey trap in the form of a young and beautiful agent who called herself Larissa Fedorovna Dubanova. The KGB arranged for Guidon to meet Dubanova in an apparent coincidence at the Bolshoi Ballet and the two carried on an affair for several months, until she informed him that she was pregnant. After a hasty illegal wedding, arranged by the KGB, Guidon was coerced into supplying the Soviets with Canada's diplomatic codes and even bugged his embassy, all under the threat of never seeing Dubanova again. Guidon continued to spy for the Soviets after his transfer to Washington, in exchange for infrequent visits with his wife—who did not give birth to any child after allegedly having an abortion. Guidon was unmasked after being transferred to the Canadian embassy in Tel Aviv, where Shabak had tapped his telephone, as was the case with most other foreign diplomats in Israel. Israeli intelligence informed MI6 after overhearing Guidon's careless conversations with his Soviet handler, and the British, in turn, shared the information with the RCMP, who lured Guidon home on a pretext and arrested him. He avoided trial and imprisonment in exchange for his full confession and cooperation.[43]

When Israeli intelligence managed to unmask the true identity of Kim Philby, the most famous Soviet mole in Britain's Secret Intelligence Service, MI6, it eventually paved the way for improving relations between London and Tel Aviv. Kollek had met Philby at the CIA's Langley headquarters when the

Israeli intelligence officer first met Angleton and at the time had warned Angleton of Philby's left-wing sentiments, which surfaced when the two were acquainted in Austria in the 1930s (a part of his past that Philby had concealed from his MI6 employers). Israeli intelligence also received information from a British Jewish woman, whom Philby had unsuccessfully tried to recruit into Soviet intelligence during the 1940s. The woman was visiting Israel in 1961 and had let the information slip at a cocktail party. Though these warnings went unheeded, after Philby defected, the warning from Israeli intelligence nevertheless impressed Maurice Oldfield, at that time deputy chief of MI6, and Peter Wright, deputy head of MI5. This new appreciation of Israel's intelligence capabilities led to the signing of a formal British-Israeli intelligence sharing agreement similar to that of the United States.[44]

Relations with Israel's intelligence community required a particular protocol. John Hadden had been posted as the Tel Aviv CIA station chief in 1963 and acquired a degree of expertise in the counterintuitive and complex skill of what liaising with Israeli intelligence entailed. Hadden described the Israeli-American intelligence as a far cry from the "card game" of tit-for-tat exchanges between friendly intelligence services such as with those of the British or the West Germans, which would eventually conclude with everyone giving each other what they wanted. The meetings with the Israelis, according to Hadden, were "crazed." Hadden recalls being subjected to the usual forty-five-minute diatribe wherein the Israelis issued a litany of the grievous threats to Israeli security and a catalogue of the military and intelligence material that they required to overcome those threats. "Christ!" Hadden remembers in frustration, "there you were in your chair and they were shouting way over behind you! Absolutely outrageous! They were asking for the goddamned moon!"[45]

Hadden's method for dealing with the Israelis, which he advised Angleton and other American negotiators to adopt, was to listen respectfully and take careful notes, then speak for forty-five minutes on the American position without allowing any interruption. During this time the Americans would ignore everything that the Israelis had said and do their best to be equally outrageous. Then both sides could slowly relax into an agreement. While some American negotiators were left infuriated by the Israeli rants and monologues, Hadden was simply amused and advised his colleagues: "Just hold on to your hat and take the ride!"[46]

Hadden also recommended to his successor at the CIA Tel Aviv posting to "learn Hebrew. Your professional peers will be afraid of you, but ordinary Israelis will speak more freely. And that is what matters for intelligence men." He urged CIA officers not to fall into the trap of other U.S. diplomats, who adored

Israelis and their country and found themselves unable to stand up to them. Hadden added:

> No matter what you really feel, you're going to get absolutely no-where unless you're one of their friends. . . . You are going to be worth-less to the United States government if you don't reserve some part of your brain to be friendly and share their interests. When you're in Hamburg, you sail. When you're in Austria, you ski. When you're in Israel, you dig.[47]

Indeed, he would suggest to CIA officers posted in Israel to take up archaeol-ogy, noting that Israelis are obsessed with their past. But he warned that the Tel Aviv posting was a career-wrecker, because work in Israel precluded working in an Arab country. He added that that they should be prepared for a long stay, as "it's going to take you more than two years for the Israelis to realize that you're not working for Saudi intelligence." And while most Israelis are talk-ative, the same cannot be said for their intelligence agents: "The Mossad and [Aman] aren't going to treat you as an ally, even if you do get some Israelis to accept you as part of the family." Hadden described Israel as neither allied territory like Britain nor enemy territory like East Germany.[48] Finally, he la-mented that there was not much to do intelligence-wise in Tel Aviv since "Washington was only interested in fighting the Russians," and the small num-ber of Soviet spies in Israel had been "completely bottled up by Israeli counter-intelligence."[49]

The alliance between American and Israeli intelligence went far beyond the exchange of technological and tradecraft favors. Israel, on the request of the CIA, served as the "hands-off" trainer and arms dealer for supporting some of the world's most brutal, yet America-friendly, regimes. In the course of Opera-tion KK Mountain during the 1960s, the Israelis received $10 to $20 million per year of funds to carry out missions that were too sensitive for the CIA or any other intelligence agency of the United States.[50] Part of these missions included Israeli training for the military and secret police of various African and South American countries as well as to the death squads of the Medellín Cartel, which prior to its destruction was the largest drug cartel in the world.[51]

The precursor to these training operations was the training and arms that Israel and the United States provided to the armed forces and security appara-tus of the Shah of Iran. In a secret CIA review written in 1976 and captured by Iranian students during the Khomeini revolution, the CIA reported:

A formal trilateral liaison called the Trident Organization was established by Mossad with Turkey's National Security Service (TNSS) and Iran's National Organization for Intelligence and Security (SAVAK) in late 1958 ... the Trident Organization involves continuing intelligence exchange plus semi-annual meetings at the chief of service level.[52]

Prior to this alliance, which included Turkey, Israel and Iran had an ongoing relationship. In 1950, Israel essentially purchased de facto diplomatic recognition from the Shah for $400,000. A mutual exchange of services began in 1954 in which Iran traded petroleum in exchange for Israeli expertise in intelligence, defense, and domestic security.

The Shah's regime viewed Israel as a gateway to the West. According to Chaim Herzog, at the time head of Aman, the Shah believed that every Israeli was a link to Washington. David Kimche, a former high-ranking Mossad officer and former chief of the Israeli Foreign Ministry, recalls, "If there'd be any anti-Iranian article in any newspaper in the United States or even in Europe, the Shah would call us and say, 'Why did you allow this to happen?' We would in vain plead innocence, saying that we don't control the whole or world media, we don't control the banks as some people think we do."[53]

Not long afterward, the Israeli security services served as a conduit and proxy for the CIA in order to create for the Shah an effective intelligence and security service. Consequently, the CIA created SAVAK in 1957 with the active assistance of Germany and Israel.[54] SAVAK was organized in several sections: the Second Department dealt with foreign intelligence, the Seventh analyzed intelligence, the Eighth carried out counterintelligence operations, while the Third was charged with internal security. It was the Third Department, with its reputation for brutality, where the CIA made use of Israel's expert training. The CIA has denied having taught SAVAK about torture, claiming that the Israelis were the ones who worked on the "hard stuff."

The Mossad-SAVAK relationship originated in the fall of 1957 in Rome, when Isser Harel, formerly of Mossad, met the first head of SAVAK, General Taimour Bakhtiar.[55] A little later Bakhtiar met with Ya'acov Zur, Israel's ambassador to France, in September 1957. The Iranian general, speaking on behalf of the Shah, suggested cooperation and an exchange of political viewpoints between the two countries. In October, Bakhtiar and Harel met again in Rome and agreed to more in-depth strategic cooperation. Iranian and Israeli relations became more intimate after the overthrow of the Iraqi monarchy by Abdul

Karim Qasim, which led to Iraq leaving the Baghdad Pact and allying itself with Nasser.[56] Then, in 1960, the head of Aman, General Chaim Herzog, arrived for his first visit in Tehran and suggested that the two countries exchange military attachés. The Shah agreed and Ben-Gurion appointed Ya'acov Nimrodi.[57]

Nimrodi was a perfect choice for the position. The corpulent officer was a former Shai (the precursor of Israel's Military Intelligence Directorate) agent and fluent in Farsi and Arabic. Nimrodi lived in Tehran for thirteen years and has warned, "When one day we shall be permitted to talk about all that we have done in Iran, you will be horrified. . . . It is beyond your imagination." Nimrodi hardly kept a low profile, but rather loudly demonstrated his power and influence, printing visiting cards with the title "Israeli Military Attaché," and holding court with Iran's top officials.[58] Meanwhile in Israel, Iranian military and intelligence officers were often spotted throughout the 1960s and barely managed to keep a low profile as they received their training.[59]

In a 1975 interview with the Arabic-language Paris newspaper *El-Mustaqbal* the Shah personally admitted to the arrangement with Israel and complained that Nasser's hostility toward Iran left him little choice. He revealed that Iran and Israel shared intelligence evaluations and exchanged information pertaining to Palestinian terrorist activities as well as information on Iranian trainers at PLO bases in Lebanon. The two SAVAK (National Intelligence and Security Organization) officers, Generals Hashemi Manucher and Ali Parvaresh, admitted in their 1979 trial that they had disclosed the location of Palestinian bases in Lebanon to their Israeli allies. In addition to intelligence cooperation, Israel trained around four hundred Iranian pilots, paratroopers, and artillery operators, as well as supplied the Shah with large numbers of arms.

The Israel-Iran alliance ended with the 1979 Iranian Revolution, when the theocracy headed by the Ayatollah Ruhollah Khomeini replaced the monarchy and declared its implacable hostility toward Israel and the West. Despite this dramatic shift in Iranian policy, Israel and the United States would resume their military support of Iran during the mid-1980s in response to the specter of an Iraq victory in the Iran-Iraq War.

In the meantime, an extensive purge of Iran's military, political, and civil service establishment followed the revolution. The security services were not exempt, but although the higher-ranking officers of SAVAK were executed, along with those officers implicated in the torture and execution of those who had been opposed to the Shah, particularly those from SAVAK's infamous Third Department.[60] However, according to an interview with Eliezer Tsafrir, the former chief of Mossad's Iran station, those officers in the middle and lower ranks of SAVAK continued their work in VAVAK—the new ministry of intelligence in post-revolution Iran—and in SAVANA, the post-revolution intelligence service. These Mossad-trained experts were vital in maintaining a high standard of proficiency for the post-revolution Iranian intelligence community.[61] Whether out of fear for their lives or out of more casual pragmatism, the former SAVAK officers decided to work for the new regime and brought with them the skills and training they had gained from Mossad and the Israeli military. When the Islamic Revolutionary Guard Corps, Pasdaran, and Iranian intelligence helped to establish Hizbullah (Party of God) in Lebanon, following the Israeli invasion in 1982, they trained their new Lebanese proxy to use Israeli weapons and Israeli intelligence tradecraft against Israel, according to the interview with former Mossad officer Eliezer Tsafrir.[62]

Both in the cases of Egypt and Iran, America's intelligence establishment enabled successive administrations in Washington to engage in secret diplomacy and wage a clandestine war against the Soviets in the Middle East. A major partner in this effort was Israel and, ironically, a range of radical organizations motivated by political Islam. On many occasions militant Muslims employed the intelligence tradecraft that the CIA and Mossad had so carefully, and secretly, transferred to individuals and organizations committed to the destruction of the state of Israel and the defeat of the United States. Yet, in the context of the Cold War, America's primary objective in the Middle East was to stymie Arab, Iranian, and South Asian nationalism from serving the interests of the Soviet Union by exploiting the role of Islam in the Muslim world.

EIGHTEEN

The Iranian Jihad

"I owe my throne to God, my people, my army—and to you."
—*Shah Mohammad Reza Pahlavi to Kermit Roosevelt*[1]

For a short period of time, Nasser was the Arab leader who held promise for contributing to American security in the Middle East. However, in the early 1950s, communism and nationalism assumed center stage in the domestic and foreign policy of the United States. Although the McCarthy anticommunist hysteria was beginning to wane in 1953, the Eisenhower administration was predisposed to suspect and fear Moscow. In particular, John Foster Dulles, the new secretary of state, believed that radical nationalism paved the way for communist penetration of the Third World. Dulles reported to the Senate that: "Whether it is in Indo-China or in Morocco or Egypt or Arabia or Iran . . . the forces of unrest are captured by the Soviet Communists."[2]

The fact that Eisenhower had surrendered foreign affairs to Dulles, and that Dulles's brother, Allen, became director of the Central Intelligence Agency, gave these comments considerable potency, as they underscored America's foreign policy. Despite these comments and his assurances to the Senate that he would extricate the nationalist gateways of communism, at first glance it appeared that John Foster Dulles could not quite make up his mind whether the United States was to become a force of change in the Middle East or a guarantor of the colonial assets of the old regimes. On the one hand, the secretary supported Nasser's nationalization of the Suez Canal (July 1954), opposed French colonialism in North Africa (1955), and countered the Anglo-French-Israeli attempt to seize the canal in 1956. On the other, he endorsed the Anglo-American coup against the Mossadeq government in Iran to uphold British oil interests. These policies were not so much contradictory as guided by the principle of self-interest in the face of a potential communist onslaught.

Dulles's Cold War anticommunism and "with-us-or-against-us" policy placed the United States in an ideological straitjacket. Against this background, Nasser's increasing role in the Nonaligned Movement and the Egyptian leader's decision to purchase arms from the Soviet Union (via Czechoslovakia) in 1955 set the United States on a collision course with Egypt.[3] Dulles made several attempts to woo Nasser back into the American fold, and particularly to join MEDO (Middle East Defense Organization), but the Egyptian leader declined and instead recognized communist China.[4]

Nasser also snubbed Dulles's attempts to mediate between Israel and Egypt. In 1954, the State Department produced Alpha, a secret proposal whereby Israel would surrender large tracts of territory in exchange for Egyptian nonbelligerency. But Nasser's meteoric rise in the Arab world made it difficult for him to compromise on the soon-to-be intractable Palestinian-Israeli issue and, after stalling, he declined.[5] A second peace plan, Gamma, fared no better, after which the secretary lost all patience with Nasser and authorized Operation Omega, with the objective of overthrowing the Egyptian government by all means except war. The plan called for denying Egypt funding for building the Aswan Dam, and it included a provision for promoting King Saud of Saudi Arabia as an Islamic "pope."[6]

Effectively, American policymakers gave up on Nasser as a modern-day Caliph who could unite the Muslims and lead them away from communism; instead they demonized him as if he were some kind of Saddam Hussein. Only, instead of harboring weapons of mass destruction, Nasser was cast as the peddler of Soviet infiltration in the Middle East. Islam became the bulwark against the Soviets since it had no possible affinity with Marxism, and devout Muslims could be counted on to shun godless Moscow's encroachments. Accordingly, along with supporting the Saudis and other conservative regimes in the Middle East, such as Iran, Jordan, Pakistan, and Turkey, the U.S. government turned to the Muslim Brothers to fight Nasser and oppose communism throughout the region.

American political officials had first established contact with Hassan al-Banna in the late 1940s in Cairo and in Jeddah. According to Herman Eilts, at the time a young diplomat in Saudi Arabia, the U.S. embassy in Cairo:

> had regular meetings with Hassan al-Banna at the time, and found him perfectly empathetic. We kept in touch with them [the Muslim Brothers] especially for reporting purposes, because at the time the Muslim Brotherhood was one element that was viewed as potentially politically important. I don't think we were alarmed by them, though there was concern when the Brotherhood's Secret Apparatus assassinated the prime minister [Mahmud Nokrashy Pasha of Egypt]. We were concerned about stability, primarily, and our judgment was that the assassinations were worrying but they did not forecast serious political instability.[7]

Every indication from the pronouncements of the Muslim Brotherhood reinforced the organization's commitment to anticommunism, further endearing it to the United States. In an interview with *Al-Mari*, Judge Hassan al-Hudaibi, supreme guide of the Muslim Brotherhood, stated, "communism denies all religions, contradicts the fundamentals of Islam and undermines its moral and social systems." In the same interview, he underlined his conviction that "Islam is the strongest bulwark against communist ideologies."[8]

After the death of al-Banna, his son-in-law, Said Ramadan, had begun to play a prominent role in the leadership of the Brotherhood and became an important contact with the Americans. In September 1953, Ramadan attended the Colloquium on Islamic Culture co-sponsored by Princeton University and the Library of Congress. However, funding for the guests from the Middle East originated from the International Information Administration, a branch of the State Department, and was taken over shortly after by the U.S. Information Agency, which was linked to the CIA.[9]

During the nine-day conference, Ramadan slipped into Washington and had a photo opportunity with Eisenhower. Robert Dreyfuss, who has chronicled Ramadan's participation in the colloquium, makes the case that there is circumstantial evidence that the CIA had set up the event in order to cultivate Ramadan as an agent.[10] According to Sylvain Bensson's article in *Le Temps* of Geneva, in the 1960s the Swiss authorities believed that Ramadan was an intelligence agent of the British and the Americans, as well as the Swiss.[11] Certainly Ramadan's subsequent career as a roving ambassador on behalf of the MB in the cause of political Islam might have given him considerable opportunity to report on developments to his handlers, but it is not likely. It is not difficult to surmise that the CIA made an effort to recruit him, and that Ramadan went along to the degree that it suited the interests of the MB. In other words, it was a mutual exploratory endeavor, but what each side got out of it is not known.

After Nasser outlawed the MB and imprisoned thousands of its members, the survivors found refuge in Saudi Arabia. King Saud tried to exploit the Brotherhood's antipathy for Nasser in his struggle with the Egyptians over leadership of the Arab world. But the Brothers in Saudi Arabia joined up with local extremists and helped to radicalize the next generation of Muslim zealots. It is ironic that today's adherents of political Islam, whether intellectual activists, militants fighting in the mountains of Afghanistan, or urban guerrillas ratcheting up the level of terrorism in the cities, were exported to the United States via the schools of radicalism staffed in part by Muslim Brothers. Indeed, the CIA's flirtation with political Islam in their struggle against Nasser or against the Soviets in Afghanistan earned the United States little gratitude among most Muslims.

The list of grievances against the Americans in the Middle East is long and begins less with the U.S. recognition of Israel in 1948 than with the coup against Iran's Mohammad Mossadeq, followed by blanket U.S. support for virtually every corrupt and repressive regime in the region.[12] The Anglo-American coup against the secular government of Iran succeeded because Kermit Roosevelt was able to tap into the well of discontent harbored by Iran's religious establishment. A key ally of convenience for the CIA operation in Iran was Ayatollah Kashani. Although the ayatollah was initially a supporter of Mossadeq, he had turned against the premier because he resented his power, and the ayatollah became open to American approaches, in order to achieve a better advantage. Roosevelt's agents advised the CIA officer that Kashani's participation in the coup could be purchased, so he handed over to one of the ayatollah's confidants the sum of $10,000.[13]

Kashani was fiercely anti-Western and despised liberal ideas, holding the conviction that Muslims should only obey secular laws that were in harmony with the Islamic legal tradition of sharia. He supported Mossadeq only because the religious leader hated the British more and wanted Iran to achieve complete independence, so that it could eventually join a pan-Islamic federation. Kashani marshaled his religious followers, who took to the streets to support Mossadeq, just as he and other religious leaders would later inflame them against the premier.[14] Like the Americans, the ayatollahs hated communism and resented Mosaddeq's political alliance with Iran's Communist Party.

The Anglo-American coup succeeded in the short term, because Roosevelt and his agents harnessed the influence of the religious establishment, bought the media, and managed to generate large demonstrations, creating the impression that there was mass opposition to Mossadeq. A key factor in the coup was the ability of Roosevelt's Iranian agents to mobilize the bazaar, with its complex layers of businessmen, mullahs, small shopkeepers, carpet dealers, spice merchants, magicians, beggars, artists, scribes, professional rabble-rousers, and not least of all, storytellers. Remarkably, Roosevelt turned the stories of Mossadeq against the premier and in favor of the Shah. It was a Pyrrhic victory, albeit one that kept the Iranian monarch in power for a quarter of a century. Twenty-six years later, the Ayatollah Khomeini was able to harness the power of public opinion, as well as the bazaar, against the Shah and in 1979 seized power in Iran.

Ayatollah Ruhollah Musavi Khomeini, the dour cleric who led the Iranian Revolution, cast himself as the avenger of the humiliations that the West had for more than a century inflicted on the Muslims of the Middle East. Unlike Ataturk or Nasser, who embraced secularism to counter the power of the West, Khomeini looked to the past and brought about an Islamic revolution. The

Ayatollah walked through history; he brought down the Iranian monarchy, but at the same time ignited mass opposition to Western ideas and practices in the Muslim world. Khomeini's victories legitimized Islam as a source of power and reinvigorated the notion of religion as the arbiter of all aspects of life.

On November 4, 1979, around three hundred to five hundred students successfully attacked and captured the U.S. embassy in Tehran. Fifty-two American diplomats were taken hostage and held for the next 444 days. The United States appeared helpless and impotent. Khomeini gave the students his full support and reveled in President Jimmy Carter's dilemma. The hostage taking was a crisis in the United States, but a unifying factor in Iran. The militancy of the students precluded any prospect of the establishment of a moderate government. Khomeini's power was further enhanced when an American rescue attempt on April 24, 1980, ended in disaster.

Khomeini's revolution had a limited shelf life outside the bounds of the Shiite Muslim world. Yet this did not deter the new regime in Tehran from attempting to project Iran's influence in the region. In a Sunni-dominated Muslim world only Lebanon offered an ideal base for Khomeini's brand of Islam to spread in the Middle East. Lebanon was fertile ground because it has had a long history as home to a complex mix of religious sects with unique loyalties to different strains of Islam as well as Christianity.

During the Crusades, the Lebanese Christian Maronites threw in their lot with the West and when the Christian warriors were driven from Lebanon, the Maronites retreated into the northern mountains where many of the original villages remain to this day.[15] Through this experience they learned that "responsibility for their own existence," writes Robert Fisk, "lay exclusively in their own hands, that their ultimate fate depended solely upon their own determination and resources. It was a characteristic that they were to share with all the minorities of Lebanon; and later with the Israelis."[16]

From the early modern period, foreign powers realized that they could exploit the region and pursue their own goals there by manipulating particular religious groups. Traditionally and because of religious affinity, the French favored the Maronite Christians, the Russians the Orthodox Christians, and the British supported the Druze by default. Consequently, the Western powers were thus able to intervene in the country under the guise of protecting their religious allies. According to Tom Russell, "This insertion of foreign interests occurred in the course of a protracted shift of power in the Mt. Lebanon area from Druze to Maronites and contributed to the tensions among the various communities and ruling clans."[17]

In 1860, a major war between the Druze and the Christians in Lebanon

THE IRANIAN JIHAD 179

gave the French the opportunity to intervene ostensibly to protect the Maronite community. In 1920, France was given its share of the Middle East with a mandate for Lebanon and Syria. Shortly after, the French created the state of Greater Lebanon, but Lebanon became a separate entity from Syria in 1926.[18]

During the Second World War, Vichy forces held the country until the British and Free French invasion in 1941. Lebanon gained independence in 1943 and French troops finally withdrew in 1946. The 1943 "national pact" organized the Lebanese government along religious lines. Russell adds, "It gave Christians a 6–5 advantage in parliament and major government posts, including the officer corps. The president must be a Maronite, the prime minister a Sunni, the speaker of parliament a Shi'a."[19]

Despite this agreement and the attempt to create a balance of power for the three primary religious groups, Lebanon was permanently altered by the creation of Israel in 1948 and the arrival of 120,000 Palestinian refugees.[20] The presence of such a large disgruntled refugee community in Lebanon engendered the creation of militant Palestinian groups that periodically attacked Israel from across the Lebanese border.

Another factor that destabilized Lebanese society was that for most of the Cold War, Lebanon, like Syria, was neutral and contested middle ground, over which the West and the Soviets battled to control Arab nationalism. In this context, Lebanon acted as a hub and propaganda platform for the Americans and Soviets throughout the Cold War.[21] Throughout the latter half of the twentieth century, Lebanon also became home not only to major Palestinian militant groups, but a variety of rival terrorist groups, exploited as secret forces by the Cold War rivals.

Ultimately, the multiple layers of competing ideologies, rivalries, and private militias fragmented Lebanon and made it ideal for Iranian penetration. The Iranians began by providing funds and military training to radical Shiite groups in the surrounding region. A camp was established close to Khomeini's home, in which terrorists were given weapons training and prepared to conduct suicide attacks. In addition to Lebanon, Khomeini's shock troops also reached Bahrain, Kuwait dictator, Saudi Arabia, and Iraq.[22]

In early 1982, Iraq's Saddam Hussein ordered the assassination of Shlomo Argov, the Israeli ambassador to London. This act, he had hoped, would be blamed on the PLO, which would in turn cause Israel to invade Lebanon. When Israel invaded Lebanon, Iran would then divert some of the troops poised to invade Iraq. The plan did not work quite as Saddam had expected. Israel did indeed invade Lebanon, on June 6, 1982. Khomeini reacted as expected, but only dispatched one thousand Revolutionary Guards to Lebanon. The Iranians established a base in the Bekaa Valley where they already had extensive networks with extreme groups.[23]

The main Shiite militia in Lebanon at this time was AMAL (Battalions of the Lebanese Resistance), a primarily secular group, fighting for economic and social rights. Many who began their militant careers under the umbrella of AMAL later broke away to form more hard-line fundamentalist organizations. The Iranians organized training centers and intelligence networks, and supplied them with weapons and money to form the resistance against the Israeli forces. The Lebanese Hizbullah was originally created not as an independent force in and of itself, but as a coordinating body to oversee the activities of all the pro-Iranian splinter groups working in Lebanon. According to Kenneth Pollack:

> Through it all, Iran was the principal moving force behind Hizballah, providing it with an organizational structure, training, material support, moral guidance, and often direction. . . . Indeed, the Hizballahis and Iranians have always been on the same ideological page.[24]

Hizbullah did not remain a mere oversight committee, but quickly developed into a major force in Lebanon. In 1983, Iran through the Hizbullah challenged the United States in the Middle East. On October 23, 1983, Hizbullah suicide bombers killed 241 U.S. marines and fifty-eight French paratroopers in Beirut. The American investigators did not identify the two men who drove bomb-laden trucks into the U.S. Marine barracks and French battalion headquarters; but Islamic Jihad claimed credit and stressed that it had been Lebanese Muslims who carried out the act and not Iranians or Palestinians. Earlier that year, Hizbullah had gutted American intelligence in Lebanon when on March 16 the Shiite militants kidnapped William Buckley, the CIA station chief in Beirut, undermining the ability of the United States to conduct a covert war in the Middle East. Although Islamic Jihad claimed to have executed the American CIA officer on October 4, 1985, he had actually died in captivity of pneumonia-like symptoms on June 3 of that year.[25]

The mishandling of covert support for the mujahidin in Afghanistan, where the United States paid for the arms and training that made the Islamic victory possible, compounded the U.S. failure in Iran and Lebanon. The stories in the bazaar lauded the mujahidin but continued to revile the Americans. Had Khomeini been a Sunni Muslim, he could have dreamed of assuming the mantle of Caliph. He may have inspired millions of Muslims, but his Shiite faith prevented him from any claim to lead all of Islam.

And so, all America's attempts to establish the king of Saudi Arabia, the strongman of Egypt, or even the Shah of Iran as a new Caliph, like those of the British before them, amounted to nothing. Certainly any attempt at finding a new Saladin to lead Islam into the future remained a dream in the sand. This tapestry of deceit and manipulation of religion and nationalism served only to reawaken militant Islam. Across the Muslim world the concept of political Islam took hold and the contagion of extreme Islamic practices spread to the Muslims of Central and Southeast Asia. Almost overnight the crisis of the Middle East became inexplicably bound with the regional paranoia and fears of South Asia and backed by the prospect of nuclear weapons.

NINETEEN

Espionage, Religion, and War in the Northwest Frontier

"All of the nightmares of the twenty-first century
come together in Pakistan."
—*Bruce Riedel*[1]

The small dinghy gently lodged against the shore of Mumbai's fisherman's colony on that fateful Wednesday evening around 9:15 and a group of ten young men disembarked. They moved silently, mimicked by the long shadows cast by the moonlit night. Bharat Tamore, a solitary figure on the beach that night, who came across the group, recalled that when he inquired what they were doing on the beach the men claimed to be students. When Tamore inquired further, the men replied "that they were tense, and that they did not need any more tension." Afterward they made their way to Mumbai, determined to wreak havoc on India's economic capital.[2]

The plan was simple. The terrorists, in teams of two, equipped with AK-47 assault rifles and 350 rounds of ammunition, descended to the center of the city and began to kill as many people as possible. At the targeted hotels, restaurants, and other public places, when circumstances permitted, they checked the identity of the prospective victims and summarily executed anyone with an American or British passport. For three days (November 26–29, 2008), the terrorists held the center of Mumbai hostage and indulged in an orgy of death that resulted in the murder of 164 civilians and Indian military personnel and left 293 wounded. By the third day, India's security forces had killed nine and captured one of the terrorists.

For a few days, Indian government officials threatened hostilities against Pakistan, which they alleged to be the source of the terrorists. Gradually, grudgingly, New Delhi accepted that Pakistan's government was not behind the attack. However, an even darker truth soon unfolded: the killers were the foot soldiers of an Islamic terrorist organization, Lashkar-e-Taiba, that was, in turn, a creature of Pakistan's Inter-Services Intelligence (ISI). Despite the shock of the Mumbai killings, the Indian government allowed itself to be convinced that the regime in Islamabad was not directly accountable for the terrorists—at least not on this occasion.

The bloody journey to Mumbai began in 1947 with the partition of India and the creation of Pakistan and was egged along with fear, hatred, and war that has dogged the relations of the two states for over half a century. This strife was, in turn, a legacy of the British Raj. For decades, the British kept control of their colony in South Asia by deliberately stoking religious rivalry that pitted Hindus, Muslims, and Sikhs against each other in a classic policy of divide-and-rule. This cynical colonial policy was particularly useful in the Northwest Frontier of the empire, where the British had to defend the most direct invasion route to India and safeguard against foreign intrigue among the unruly tribes of the region.

The Northwest Frontier in particular has a unique place in the history of British intelligence, and intelligence activities in the region have contributed greatly to the evolution of extremist political Islam. During the course of the nineteenth century, the Northwest Frontier became a training ground for the British, where they conducted special operations and espionage against the Russian empire during the course of the Great Game. Although individual British officers undertook a variety of covert missions in the region, formal intelligence organizations did not begin to operate in the Northwest Frontier until the middle of the nineteenth century.

In 1846, Colonel Sir Henry Lawrence, Britain's political agent in the Northwest Frontier, recommended the formation of a special force that was established as the Indian Corps of Guides. Lawrence required such a unit to help him maintain British control over the Punjab, and he insisted that the Guides be recruited from the local tribes. An 1852 report noted: "The Corps has been composed of the most varied elements; there is scarcely a wild or warlike tribe in Upper India, which is not represented in its ranks.... It is calculated to be of the utmost assistance to the Quarter-Master-General's Department as intelligencers, and most especially in the escort of reconnoitering officers."[3] British liking for Northwest Frontier recruits eventually influenced the organization and development of the Indian and Pakistani armed forces.

From the late nineteenth century onward, it became British policy to enlist Indian soldiers from the so-called martial races of the Northwest Frontier. Lord Roberts, who became commander-in-chief of the British Indian army in 1885, was one of the primary architects of the mythology of the "martial races." According to Roberts, the northern region of India was populated by "warlike and hardy races," while the south was composed of "effeminate peoples."[4] After the British conquered India, they deliberately kept the northern areas un-industrialized and under-educated, to protect their recruiting base and keep the "martial races" from engaging in peaceful pursuits and occupations. Even within the region itself, the British sought recruits in the most rural parts, avoiding the larger villages and towns.[5] In addition to the notion of traditional warriors, the British deliberately kept the Indian army segmented, isolating groups from particular regions within the larger military formations, and keeping them moving around the country to prevent them from forming "local" ties.[6]

As a result of the "martial races" recruitment policy, a disproportionate number of South Asian soldiers and officers were recruited among Muslims and Sikhs. Because these groups were kept together, the soldiers established strong bonds of loyalty based on religious lines. After Pakistan's creation in 1947, successive Pakistani governments, closely linked with the military, continued to recruit from the same geographical regions, following the British strategic policy of cultivating the "martial races."

During the 1980s, for example, three quarters of the Pakistani army was recruited from three districts in the Punjab and two in the Northwest Frontier Province—areas that collectively represent only 9 percent of the population.[7] Some of these army recruits also served in Pakistan's intelligence service, and the fact that they had family and tribal ties in the troubled northwest region of Pakistan created a unique relationship for Pakistan's intelligence establishment with the Northwest Frontier. In the early 1980s, for example, General Akhtar Abdur Rahman was the director of ISI and, like many Pakistani officers, was a Pashtun from Peshawar on the Afghan frontier. In 1987, General Hamid Gul, a devout Muslim from the Punjab with close ties to the Saudis, replaced Rahman as head of the ISI. Both men owed their appointments to Muhammad Zia-ul-Haq, Pakistan's dictator after 1977, who also came from the Punjab.[8]

In the 1990s, General Naseerullah Babar, the guiding hand for Prime Minister Benazir Bhutto's Afghanistan policy—some argue that he was the mastermind behind the creation of the Taliban—was also a native Pashtun from the Northwest Frontier region.[9] After he retired from the army, Babar served as minister of the interior between 1994 and 1997, during Bhutto's second term as prime minister. Indeed, the Indian subcontinent has a unique place in the history of the British and Pakistani intelligence services. Certainly, today the region is a critical battleground between political Islam and the West, while Pakistan's ISI remains a covert ally of the Muslim extremists in order to further Pakistani strategic and security interests in South Asia.

The Great Game, the competition for control over Central Asia, between the British and Russian empires, was waged almost exclusively in the shadows.[10] Spies, double agents, subversion, terror, psychological warfare, sabotage, and assassination became essential elements of the Russo-British conflict in the region. The stakes were high, and the clandestine war consumed the lives of British and Russian officers who undertook secret and dangerous missions in the name of emperor or czar. Rudyard Kipling's tales were not only good yarns, but also offered romanticized vignettes of the Anglo-Russian rivalry that inspired generations of young men.

Although Arthur Conolly, an intelligence officer in the East India Company's 6th Bengal Light Cavalry, coined the term "Great Game" it was Kipling who made the phrase popular with the publication of his novel *Kim* in 1901.[11] The novel also served as source of inspiration for Harold Adrian Russell Philby, whose father gave him the nickname "Kim" because of his affinity for the boy-spy in the novel.[12] Kim Philby was born in India and became one of the most notorious and successful moles of the twentieth century, spying on behalf of the Soviet KGB while rising through the ranks of Britain's secret service.[13]

To some degree, the use of intelligence and covert operations in Central Asia and northern India was the result of necessity, topography, and opportunity. The great distances and the long border with the Russian empire (depending on the period, from one thousand to two thousand miles in length), as well as the rugged Northwest Frontier of India and Central Asia, forced the British and Russian authorities to undertake exploration of the uncharted areas, organizing surveys, reconnaissance, and mapmaking in order to establish control over the region. In addition, the territories of a variety of tribal chiefs, emirs, and a host of petty kings lay across strategic lines of communication, spurring an Anglo-Russian race for the allegiance of these local potentates.

British officers and civilian adventurers, as well as natives in the employ of the government of India or the army, served as soldiers in the undeclared war. Both sides had to tread carefully because even simple diplomatic missions, intended to secure the allegiance of a local ruler, could result in charges of espionage, with deadly consequences. One such example was the cruel fate of Lieutenant Colonel Charles Stoddart, who like other unfortunate officers became a casualty of the Great Game.

In 1838 Stoddart traveled to Bokhara on a mission to secure the freedom of a number of Russian slaves and to offer the ruler of the place Britain's protection. The British feared that the Russians would exploit the slaves as a pretext to annex Bokhara. Unfortunately the local emir, Nasrullah Khan, suspected that espionage was the officer's real intention; equally the emir took offense at

Stoddart's failure to show appropriate respect. The British officer was oblivious to the etiquette of the place by failing to dismount from his horse before entering the city, as well as ignoring the traditional niceties of flattery and gift exchange.[14]

After a couple of days Stoddart was arrested, shackled, and thrown into Bokhara's prison. Perhaps prison is too generous a designation for the facility: it was basically a twenty-one-foot hole lined with the bones and flesh of previous inmates, as well as a home to armies of rodents and several varieties of insect. To add insult to injury, the emir compelled Stoddart to convert to Islam or face execution.[15]

For the next four years, the emir took pleasure toying with Stoddart. On some occasions the hapless English officer was removed from the hole to more pleasant confinement in the city and then, on the whim of the emir, tossed back. The emir's mood—and Stoddart's situation—fluctuated depending on the victories or defeats of the British army in Central Asia. A second British officer, Arthur Conolly (the first to use the term "Great Game"), made his way to Bokhara in 1841 to rescue Stoddart, but he too was apprehended, and both men spent a few months in the filthy hole before they were beheaded in a public execution sometime in June of 1842.[16]

A year later, the Reverend Joseph Wolff, appalled at the indifference of the British government to the plight of the two officers, decided to mount his own rescue operation. After many misadventures, which included being abandoned by his guides, Dr. Wolff eventually stumbled into Bokhara, only to find that the emir still harbored suspicions about British visitors. The poor man was also accused of espionage and tossed into the infamous prison. Fortunately the Shah of Persia intervened, and Wolff was set free.[17] Wolff was fortunate, unlike Stoddart and Conolly, because neither the British army nor the civilian leadership in India or London had had the foresight to establish a professional intelligence service with appropriately trained personnel.

In 1879, the Indian army finally got around to organizing its own intelligence department with a complement of five officers (two were assigned only part-time duties) and several native clerks and cartographers. The tasks of the new unit were military intelligence on the order of battle of the Russian army and the potential threat to India in a future conflict; but also to spy on nationalists and religious movements. As well, frontier officers continued to collect political intelligence and lead covert forays in enemy and neutral regions for the Political Department of the Indian Government.[18] In Britain, as well as in India, the British continued to reject the notion of combining the intelligence work of military units with an agency committed to espionage.

During the nineteenth century, the Indian civil service, the Foreign Department, the Survey Department, and—most importantly—the British-staffed Indian army were primarily charged with intelligence duties. By the 1870s, British authorities in London were convinced that the Russians were planning an invasion of South Asia, and that they did not have the means of gaining intelligence on Afghanistan—the traditional invasion route to India. Thomas Fergusson, a specialist in the early history of British military intelligence, writes: "Although the Indian Army was still without its own intelligence branch in the summer of 1878 . . . the War Office Intelligence Branch was not attempting to collect information inside India on its own. Practically all of the intelligence about India reached the War Office and the Branch via the India Office."[19] Not long afterward, in 1878, an Intelligence Branch was added to the Indian army that, adds Fergusson, "could pull together and report on vast quantities of information acquired not only by the Indian Army units throughout the subcontinent, but also by other branches of the Indian government, sources to which the Intelligence Branch in London had at best only indirect access."[20]

In 1904, in response to increased terrorist activities in South Asia, the British created the Department of Central Intelligence (DCI) to monitor the movements of extremists. The new intelligence establishment included religious sections organized to penetrate and influence the various religious communities in the Raj. The primary task of the religious sections was to undermine the rise of Hindu, Sikh, and Muslim independence movements. In order to implement this policy of divide-and-rule, the Indian Intelligence Bureau recruited native officers from the respective religious communities, who developed skills at manipulating religion to suit British colonial interests.[21]

In time, the British realized that Muslim groups throughout South Asia identified with Islam rather than with secular nationalist movements. The British concluded that Islam could be used to counterbalance the much larger Hindu community and stem the accompanying tide of Indian nationalism. As long as the Hindus, Sikhs, and Muslims of South Asia remained antagonistic, the British could rule the Indian subcontinent with only limited forces. Winston Churchill on February 2, 1940, described the Hindu-Muslim feud as the "bulwark of British rule in India" and added that, were it to be resolved, the peaceful coexistence of these groups would result in "the united communities joining in showing us the door."[22]

In addition to fostering Hindu-Muslim rivalry to undermine the development of a powerful nationalist movement, the British also tried to use Islam to counter the spread of communism. One of the early British intelligence agents to focus on Islamist movements in India was Norman Napier Evelyn Bray. Bray had a remarkable career as an Indian army officer, special intelligence operative, SIS officer, multilinguist, and critic of T. E. Lawrence. He was also the author of several biographical and historical works and later served in the Royal Air Force. In the 1930s, he fell on hard times: he was suspected of fascist sympathies and accused of arms smuggling.

Bray's career in intelligence work began in the early 1900s, when he was recruited by Sir Charles Cleveland, director of Criminal Intelligence in India, to trace the roots of Muslim unrest in South Asia. During the course of his investigations, Bray became familiar with the pan-Islamic movement in the Middle East, as well as with various influential Muslims in the region and in South Asia.[23]

In 1916, the colonial authorities in India became aware of an organization named the Army of God or *Al Junad Al Rabbania*, which called for a united Islamic front against the British. Instead of confronting these Muslim radicals, Bray launched his own campaign, fronted by key Muslim leaders, and attempted to undermine the Islamic movement from within the Muslim community. Bray also visited Ali bin Hussein, King of Hejaz and Sharif of Mecca, with the intention of uniting Muslims in India, Persia, and Afghanistan under the banner of the Arab Revolt.[24] A year later, Bray submitted a report to the Foreign Office on the "Muhammedan Question," in which he warned that Germany, Turkey, Japan, and Russia were actively involved in attempts to use pan-Islamic movements as a means of destabilizing the British Empire's large Muslim population.[25] Bray added, "it wasn't simply a matter of 'sincere Mohammedans' wanting independence but of 'thousands of . . . fanatics running before they can walk.' Otherwise, unless measures were taken to sever its membranes, it would become 'a real and pressing danger . . . as a weapon in the hands of a future enemy'."[26]

The strategy that would work, Bray insisted, was not suppression of Muslim radicals or of the pan-Islamic movement itself, but rather the implementation of Britain's own propaganda campaign, legitimized by Sharif Hussein, who was already a British ally and the recipient of generous military assistance. Bray felt that Hussein's Arab Revolt provided an alternative outlet for the holy war that he saw brewing in Arabia, Persia, Afghanistan, and the northwest.[27] For the duration of the war, the British continued to fear German, Ottoman, and—after 1917—Soviet manipulation and intrigue aimed at the pan-Islamists, while overlooking the rise of Arab nationalism.[28]

In the 1920s, Britain's Interdepartmental Committee on Bolshevism, led by Bray, continued warning of "Bolshevik" interference in India via the Northwest Frontier.[29] Regardless to what degree these suspicions were true, his superiors, including Churchill, were easily convinced, because the historic rivalry with Russia made such threats credible and because they were convinced that nationalism and religion provided the most serious challenge to the British Empire. Looming large in the context of these fears was the emergence of the Soviet Union—a potential ally to the dozens of nationalist and pan-Islamic movements stirring in the British Empire after the First World War.

In this climate of imperial paranoia, exploiting pan-Islamist movements offered a method of countering the perceived twin evils of communism and nationalism. To some degree, this was the legacy of men such as Bray, who saw Bolsheviks lurking at the frontiers of the British Empire and who had promoted the notion that Islam was the antidote to those evils. Such concepts not only influenced British policy in the interwar period, but also guided the British intelligence community in South Asia during the Second World War. The idea that Islam could be co-opted to serve state interests would eventually leave a dangerous legacy, not only to the Pakistani government, army, and intelligence establishment, but also to the United States.

The stakes were high in South Asia, because Britain's economic and strategic stature relied on the Raj. In the nineteenth century and the first half of the twentieth, the Middle East and Eastern Mediterranean were vital to British interests, insofar as these regions could be used to secure the sea and land routes to India. British strategic priorities in the interwar period (1919–1939) envisaged the Middle East as a staging area for military resources that would be rushed to South Asia in the event of war with the Soviet Union or Japan.

Yet British intelligence in South Asia was for, the most part, organized to deal with the internal threats of nationalism and religious movements rather than with threats from outside the empire. In India, according to one expert, Richard Aldrich, the British Secret Intelligence Service (SIS) was "effective, if narrowly focused . . . designed to address internal threats from nationalists, communists or other types of 'agitators.' "[30]

It was the outbreak of the Second World War that forced the British to shift their intelligence priorities in South and Central Asia and co-opt Islam as an ally in the new global conflict. During the war, British intelligence in India was the responsibility of the SIS (under its cover name of Interservice Liaison Department [ISLD]) and of the Special Operations Executive (SOE), in addition to local intelligence units, including the Indian Intelligence Bureau.[31] Unlike the traditional intelligence services, the SOE was a secret organization created in July 1940, specifically in response to the war and to the German occupation of Europe (and later parts of Asia). In this respect, the SOE was established with a single purpose—to fight the Axis—and did not share the SIS's anticommunist and antinationalist legacy. The long-standing colonial tilt of British intelligence in India came to an end, as the SOE concentrated on defeating the Axis, rather than the long-term preservation of the empire. Consequently, the SOE worked covertly with communist and extreme Muslim groups, to check the efforts of the Japanese in South Asia.[32]

As early as 1939, Japan had implemented an intensive propaganda effort aimed at instigating rebellion among the officers and men of the Indian army. The campaign targeted nationalists in India, and it tried to cultivate a pan-Asian nationalist movement to challenge British and Western colonialism.[33] In December 1941, the Japanese, with the collaboration of radical Indian nationalists, created the Indian National Army (INA). This force was recruited from Indian civilians in Malaya and from Indian soldiers who had been taken prisoner after the fall of Singapore in 1942. Some of these recruits joined the INA to escape the terrible conditions of the prisoner of war camps, but many more took up arms with the Japanese in reaction to the perceived racism of the British colonialists in Asia.[34]

In addition to trying to exploit Indian nationalism, the Japanese also launched a pro-Islamic propaganda campaign in Malaya, in order to persuade local Muslims to raise Islamic armies against the British, but did not achieve any significant results.[35] In response to the potentially serious threat posed by the defection of Indian soldiers to Japan, a dedicated department was formed by British intelligence. The new organization was placed under the British India Command's Psychological Warfare Section and was overseen in part by Major General Walter J. Cawthorn, who was later to establish the ISI in Pakistan.[36] By 1943, this unit had overtaken all the activities of the Indian Psychological Warfare Section, which broadcast anti-Japanese propaganda through the Far Eastern Bureau.[37] Picking up the threads of Bray's legacy, Cawthorn and British officers in the Indian army expanded contacts with Islamists as part of the ongoing British strategy to exploit Muslim groups against Japanese-supported Indian nationalists, as well as against the Indian National Congress.

The efforts of British intelligence were not the predominant reason for Japan's failure to sway the direction of the war. The Muslim League in India, in contrast to the predominantly Hindu Indian National Congress, steadfastly supported the British war effort. Mohammed Ali Jinnah, leader of the Muslim League and future father of the Pakistani state, felt it was not in the interests of the Muslims for the British to leave India until the creation of Pakistan, because Indian Muslims would be left in a hostile Hindu state.[38] Yet the creation of Pakistan was not considered by many Islamic leaders to be in the interests of the Muslim community. Regardless of how India would be partitioned, large numbers of Muslims would be left to languish in a predominantly Hindu state.

In the meantime, the Congress Party was refusing to cooperate with Britain's war effort unless independence was immediately granted. Indian leaders were encouraging resistance within India aimed at draining resources the British badly needed to fight the war. Dharmindra Gaur, who had served with the SOE during the Second World War, recalled how Britain's SOE used both Jinnah and the Muslim League to create a buffer against Indian nationalists. Gaur alleges that Churchill was greatly concerned about the formation of a national government in India and that the British armed the Muslim League for this purpose.[39]

In August 1942, riots engulfed several cities and villages in India, partly as a result of Gandhi's call for civil disobedience and partly in reaction to the defeat of Britain's armies in Asia at the hands of the Japanese. Confounding the British authorities was the fact that at the root of the unrest was an unorganized popular movement beyond the control of any particular organization or individual.[40] By imprisoning India's leaders in June 1942, the British had created a leadership vacuum that, for a period of time, had left the nationalist movement without direction and control.

The Second World War not only changed the British relationship with South Asia, but it also ushered the Americans into the complex layers of religion and nationalism in the region. Following in the steps of the British, the Office of Strategic Services (OSS), roughly the American equivalent to the SOE, pursued a long-term policy of cultivating Islam.[41] By June 1944, General William Donovan, head of the OSS, was prepared to implement a pro-Islam policy and. According to Richard Aldrich, his plan was triggered by interest in the Arab Gulf states and his desire to build up "some very much undercover 'intelligence' in Saudi Arabia, perhaps under the pretense of some large archaeological mission."[42] Donovan assigned Major Carlton S. Coon—an anthropologist, Arabist, and specialist in North Africa and the Middle East—to plan this project. Later in 1944, after an extensive tour of the region, Coon concluded that intelligence gathering should not only be limited to Saudi Arabia but had to encompass the Muslim world as a whole, with Saudi Arabia acting as a gateway to the Muslim Middle East and Muslim South Asia.[43] Even before the end of the war, the Americans had reached the same conclusion as the British that the Middle East was inextricably tied to South Asia with respect to Islam. Unfortunately, this lesson was forgotten before and after the Soviet invasion of Afghanistan.

With the creation of the Muslim state of Pakistan in 1947, the British had to reinvent their policy toward South Asia.The special relationship formed be-tween Jinnah and the British during the Second World War extended into the postwar period. The British government and its intelligence establishment felt more comfortable forming close connections with Pakistan than with India, which was still believed to be anti-British and to harbor communist connec-tions. While the British were keen to have Pakistan on their side, they were not interested in establishing an equal relationship. Two issues arose immediately between Britain and Pakistan: how much intelligence the British should share with Pakistan and what assistance London was willing to provide in the estab-lishment of Pakistan's intelligence infrastructure. Although there was exten-sive representation of British staff in senior positions in the Pakistan civil and military services, concerns lingered over security in Pakistan, specifically about the risk of intelligence leaks and communist infiltration.

During 1947 and 1948, the British Joint Intelligence Committee deter-mined that British information was safer in Pakistani hands than it would have been with India. This faith in Pakistan was, for the most part, the legacy of India's Muslims—Jinnah's Muslim League in particular—with the British during the Second World War. In London, Pakistan was also considered more reliable, in part because of the extensive presence of British officers in senior positions. The majority of officers in senior posts in Pakistan—particularly in the Minis-try of Defense and the military—were still British. For the British, this ar-rangement was essential (the Pakistani prime minister also agreed that it was beneficial for the country) in order to share confidential and sensitive infor-mation with Pakistan.[44] Pakistanis, as a whole, were also believed to be not as antagonistic toward Britain than was the case with Indian nationals.

Although Pakistan was generally seen as less problematic than India, many observers felt that security measures in Pakistan's institutions were inadequate and that the "oriental mind" would not lend itself to "view the problem [of secu-rity] as seriously as is done elsewhere."[45] Concerns about communist elements in India and Pakistan also remained. For example, in 1946–1947 certain infor-mation had been leaked to communist groups in India, and the leak was be-lieved to have been through a communist cell in the Indian military, which was assumed still to exist.[46]

After April 1948, the British treated Pakistan as nominally a Category A country; thus it could receive information up to "Top Secret," but with restric-tions placed on American-source information. In reality, Pakistan was being provided with very little information. This was a strategic practice that had been applied in India before the creation of Pakistan and was carried over to

Pakistan. By the spring of 1948, however, Pakistan had a large number of liaison officers in London, so it was no longer possible to maintain this deception.

Shortly afterward, the British reassessed Pakistan's position and shifted their policy with respect to intelligence sharing. Pakistan was to be downgraded to Category B, which meant it could receive information up to the level of "Confidential": in effect, this adjustment matched policy with actual practice. The Pakistanis were informed that this downgrade was due to the fact that their security arrangements were not adequate and that Pakistan's "political associations" were still undecided. But they were not told that American-source information could not be shared without American approval, which was unlikely in the case of Pakistan.[47]

Not everyone in the British camp had such reservations about Pakistan's reliability. Cawthorn, who was later to participate in the establishment of the ISI, defended the Pakistani military and governmental institutional security measures, insisting that the individual Pakistani was every bit as patriotic and security-minded as an Englishman. Security, he argued, was excellent in Pakistan, because of the potential threat of an Indian invasion.[48] Cawthorn also commented on "the political solidarity resulting from practically one hundred percent adherence to a common religious faith."[49] However, he was concerned that, while Pakistan had a benevolent attitude toward Britain, this was endangered by Britain's unwillingness to share intelligence openly, especially on India, and by restrictions on the training of Pakistani intelligence officers. Cawthorn and others argued that Pakistan was vital to Britain strategically, since it offered the British a base for defending the Indian Ocean. In addition, Pakistan offered special opportunities for the collection of intelligence. Particularly, as Cawthorn pointed out in a report to the Chiefs of Staff, "Pakistan as a Moslem state on the flank of the Middle East Moslem block and of Afghanistan and Persia obviously possesses considerable political potential in relation to British interests in the Middle East."[50]

Eventually, the intelligence apparatus that the British helped to establish in Pakistan was extracted from the British intelligence structure in India. An Intelligence Bureau that paralleled MI5[51] was set up in Pakistan in 1948, partly staffed by British personnel. The Intelligence Bureau was modeled on the Muslim section of the former Intelligence Bureau in India (formerly based in Delhi) and incorporated the intelligence body that had responsibility for the Northwest Frontier, Afghanistan, and Persia. A Frontier Bureau was also created to cover East Pakistan and similar organizations set up in Peshawar and Quetta.[52]

TWENTY

Pakistan's Inter-Services Intelligence and Organized Terror in South Asia

"They are our people: they are not our enemies."
—*ISI officer referring to the Taliban in the Northwest Frontier region*[1]

The Pakistani Intelligence Bureau remains in existence to this day and is now charged with overseeing politicians, political activists, and foreign intelligence agents.[2] The bureau now monitors certain international situations: in particular, nationals of countries that are considered "hostile" to Pakistan. However, in 1948, the Inter-Services Intelligence Directorate was established for the purpose of addressing foreign threats.[3] Quickly the ISI emerged as Pakistan's predominant intelligence organization and not long afterward became covertly involved in religious and political affairs.

Its first director was Brigadier Saiyid S. Hamid, formerly military secretary in India, who upon the creation of Pakistan became the director of the Pakistan National Guard.[4] Cawthorn, deputy chief of staff of the Pakistan army, as well as secretary of the Pakistan Joint Services Commanders' Committee, oversaw the organization and early operations of the ISI.[5] It was not uncommon for British officers to have served with both the Indian and Pakistani armed forces. Cawthorn had been with the Indian army for thirty years, receiving his commission during the First World War.[6] In the 1920s, he was attached to the 16th Punjab Regiment and between 1930 and 1935 saw active and covert service in the Northwest Frontier, subsequently being posted to the War Office in London.[7] However, it was Cawthorn's experience in the Northwest Frontier that prepared him for intelligence work.

In the 1930s, British intelligence was active in the Northwest Frontier; intelligence officers had been working with tribal groups in that area to counter communist influence and infiltration in the region.[8] Cawthorn's own service in the Northwest Frontier gave him considerable experience in intelligence work that he would later put to good use in the newly formed Pakistan. Undoubtedly he brought to the Pakistan intelligence service his contacts in the Northwest Frontier and forged new links for the ISI with the tribal groups of the region.

The ISI included all the Pakistani military intelligence organizations, which became part of an interservices body headed by a single director, who was advised and overseen by the Joint Service Commanders' Committee and by its secretary, Cawthorn, in particular.[9] However, each of the armed services continued to maintain separate intelligence directorates, while working closely with the ISI.[10] In April 1949, in a somewhat less restrictive environment than had existed the year before, the Joint Intelligence Committee of the British Chiefs of Staff arranged for British departments to forward relevant intelligence and information to the ISI.[11]

More than in any other issue, Pakistan was interested in British intelligence with regard to India. In the postwar period, Pakistan had to confront the considerably larger and more powerful Indian state. The 1947 war between Pakistan and India over Kashmir further underscored the fact that conventional warfare ultimately gave India the military advantage. Furthermore, the frontiers of the Pakistani state provided narrow strategic depth—effectively Pakistan's forces had limited space to fall back on if an invasion by the Indian army could not be stopped at the frontier. In response to this strategic limitation, Pakistan adopted covert and unconventional warfare operations in both Kashmir and India. Covert tactics and the use of nonattributable clandestine organizations freed the Pakistani state from any commitment to treaty obligations, but relied on the establishment and maintenance of a large intelligence service.

This was the beginning of a perfect arrangement: although a cease-fire had been agreed to by Pakistan and India in 1948, individual militants were neither party to it nor officially under the control of the Pakistani government.[12] For half a decade, the ISI assisted Islamic terrorist groups and supported a variety of radical religious organizations, as part of the grand design to further Pakistan's interests in Kashmir and bleed the Indian army through an endless guerrilla war.[13] The dispute over the Kashmir region has not only remained one of the most pervasively contentious and destructive issues plaguing India and Pakistan, but has also acted as a key ingredient in Pakistan's becoming a breeding ground for political Islam and Muslim militancy.

In the period following the creation of Pakistan in 1947, the British Dominion Office paid close attention to the role of religion and reported that Islam was the most powerful political mechanism for unity in the region. Pakistan lacked a cohesive national identity, and the British concluded that religion could form the binding ties for the new state, particularly since Islam was what distinguished Pakistan from India, a powerful and significantly larger neighbor. To this end, the British government encouraged Pakistani politicians to use religious rhetoric and appeal to Islam, yet reports filed by the Dominion Office in 1948 sound slightly alarmed, describing a "fanatical" populace, inflamed by Islam above all other social or political concerns.

All the same, while the Dominion Office described the general population as mindless fanatics, they felt assured by the leadership they had helped bring to power—primarily by Jinnah and Liaquat Ali Khan—that Pakistan would remain under secular control. These leaders, British officials assumed, would merely feign religiosity in order to enlist Islam for political ends.[14] As one report observed: "Religion has proved its worth as a potent political weapon, and it is one which may be required again."[15] Not for the first time, the British perceived a situation in which religion could be used as a vehicle for secular agendas.

As early as the 1950s, Pakistan's military had become the most powerful force in the country, and when they seized political control they adopted an Islamic facade and used it as a manipulative device. In 1958, Ayub Khan instituted a military dictatorship in Pakistan. Although it is not entirely clear what information or involvement the British had about his coup, they believed that the United States had backed Ayub Khan in overthrowing the government.[16] Officials at the British Dominion Office appeared to be satisfied with Ayub and his attitude toward Islam; some of them felt "it was primarily political—he saw it as a counterbalance to Indian challenges, but did not hold 'narrow orthodox views.'"[17]

Ayub was given conditional praise for his speeches that stressed the threat of communism to Islam in the spring of 1959. This focus on Islam was acceptable to the British and the Americans because Ayub's rhetoric also included a general criticism of dogmatism. "The miracle of Islam," said Ayub, "was that it destroyed idolatry, and the tragedy of the Muslims is that they rendered religion into the form of an idol." Ayub was lauded, of course, because his speeches denigrated communism, holding it up as the enemy of Islam. Civilian groups were also felt to be espousing a satisfactory vision of the role of Islam; Maulana Perwez, director of the Quranic Research Centre in Lahore, was said to express an "American style" democratic understanding of Islam.[18]

Throughout the late 1950s, the British continued to gather intelligence on the influence of Islam in Pakistan as a "research" interest. In the period leading up to the 1958 coup by Ayub Khan, British agents in Pakistan watched and established contacts with religious groups, which they thought could provide useful information or influence amidst the prevailing political uncertainty. One group under observation by the British Dominion Office in the mid-1950s was Jamaat-e-Islami (JI), an Islamist group characterized by its British onlookers as extremely right-wing and anticommunist. Abul Ala Maududi created the JI in

India in 1941. It was an Islamic orthodox organization and was established in part as an opponent to the Muslim League, which was seen as both pro-British and pro-secular. The JI was against the formation of an Islamic state in the 1940s, although it became the most outspoken agitator for a strict Islamic legal and political system after Pakistan achieved independence.[19] Maududi himself had been influenced by Saudi theologians and had close contact with the Saudis before the creation of Pakistan.[20]

The JI had been outlawed in 1954 after being accused of planning a coup, leading student unrest in Lahore, and receiving funds from foreign groups hostile to the Pakistani government. In 1958, the Dominion Office reported that the JI had considerable influence, but not enough to overthrow the regime. Reports compared the JI to the Egyptian Muslim Brotherhood, although no link was established between the two organizations beyond the JI's criticism of the Egyptian government's persecution of the Brotherhood.[21] The JI came to attention of the British again in 1964, when they regained legal status after the Supreme Court ruled against the Pakistani government. At this time, the JI was reported to be extremely anticommunist and to oppose the Kashmiri independence movement.[22]

By this time the British were mere observers of events in Pakistan. In the 1950s, the Americans had joined the British and had become involved with both Pakistani politics and the Pakistani army. After the arrival of the Americans, British influence in the country declined quickly, and Washington replaced London as Pakistan's patron and ally. Pakistani leaders made the adjustment easily and exploited Pakistan's geopolitical and religious credentials to maintain the relationship with the Americans and pursue a forward policy in Afghanistan.

Pakistan was seen as being in the unique position of having an ostensibly Islamic government, which in fact was sympathetic to the West, and "whose Islamic faith was . . . often not more than skin deep," while being populated by devout Muslims who could be recruited to combat communism with Islam.[23] By 1952–1953, the rise of Arab nationalism and the threat of Iran nationalizing its oil industry increased American interest in Pakistan. In 1952, Secretary of State John Foster Dulles floated the idea of a "Northern Tier" of linked Islamic states, including Iran, Pakistan, and Turkey, as a defense zone against Soviet encroachment.[24] The United States also launched various economic assistance programs in Pakistan during the 1950s, which were seen by some as fronts for political and social intervention.[25]

In effect, Pakistan became a strategic necessity for the United States, because it occupied a key geographical position, situated between the Middle East and South Asia. Furthermore, the Soviet relationship with India drastically limited Soviet influence in Pakistan. Andrei Gromyko, the Soviet foreign minister, complained of the "insidious [Western] web into which Pakistan fell almost at the onset of her existence as an independent state."[26] The new Pakistan emerged as a frontline state in the Cold War and a strategic partner of the United States from 1947 to 1989.

By the middle of the 1950s, the Pakistani army had entered into a closer relationship with the United States, primarily because of Pakistan's membership in the Baghdad Pact, which later became the Central Treaty Organization (CENTO).[27] Despite the upheaval that followed the partition of India, the creation of Pakistan in 1947 offered the British and later the Americans a unique advantage in the region. The new country was located in a critically vital zone, controlled by cooperative leaders and administered along ostensibly Islamic grounds. Unlike India, whose nonaligned policy and friendship with the Soviet Union annoyed and alarmed Washington, Pakistan remained a steadfast ally of the United States. In addition, the Americans had a poor impression of India and Hinduism. Politically, India was undesirable because the Soviets were well embedded in the Congress.[28] The Americans also viewed Hinduism as backward-looking and passive. In contrast, monotheistic Islam seemed much closer to Christianity, and Pakistan's leaders appeared "much more vigorous, energetic, forthright, and warlike, in short more manly."[29]

During this period, the Pakistani military began to shift from its British roots, as a new generation of Pakistani officers was trained in Pakistan within the framework of American military doctrine.[30] This change was also accompanied by the attitudes of some officers, who adopted an inflated estimate of their own and Pakistan's martial qualities and assumed that one Pakistani soldier equaled ten or more Indians. This perception was, of course, related to the "martial races" ideology employed by the British in India.[31] The emphasis on the unique qualities of the Pakistani army resulted in equal emphasis on the Islamic quality of the armed forces.

Religion became a critical element in the identity of the Pakistani army, since, as member of the various "martial races," the military was ethnically diverse and, except for Islam, indistinguishable from the Indian army. Although the Pakistani army is not thought to have taken a broad turn toward political Islam prior to the 1970s, the focus on Islam in connection with militarism laid the ground for later developments in the relationship between political Islam and the Pakistani army. The officers of the ISI were no exception. Domestic and international events in the 1970s expanded the organization's contacts with political Islam and to radical Muslim groups in Afghanistan.

Although Muhammad Zia-ul-Haq is the Pakistani leader primarily responsible for increasing the power of the ISI, Zia's predecessor, Zulfikar Ali Bhutto, also played an important role in bolstering the ISI and militant Islam. Bhutto made alcohol illegal and Friday a holiday. He also declared that the Ahmediyya sect, which most Muslims considered heretical, was non-Muslim. This action was most helpful to the monopoly of extremist groups in Pakistan and a concession that the JI had long demanded, but which no other leader had been willing to grant.[32] Bhutto was motivated to take such actions, at least in part, by security concerns about Afghanistan. From 1947 onward, Pakistan's military had adopted the strategy that Afghanistan was the key to redressing Pakistan's lack of strategic depth. Some believed that since invaders of India historically came through Afghanistan, Pakistan's defense could only be guaranteed by the integration of the two states, but for many a friendly and pro-Pakistan Afghanistan was far more realistic.

This notion of unification held little appeal for some Afghans, who had a sense of distinct ethnic and racial identity, but was attractive to the Pashtuns, whose tribe straddles Pakistan's northwest and Afghanistan. On the other hand, the prospect of a merger with Pakistan did appeal to Afghans committed to Islam—Almost from the inception of Pakistan, Pakistani politicians and generals remained fixated on the threat of Indian intervention in Afghanistan and the possibility that India could exploit Afghanistan to attack Pakistan. Accordingly, by the 1960s, the ISI was encouraging militant Islamic Pakistani groups to cultivate similarly minded organizations in Afghanistan.[33] Under Bhutto, Pakistani intelligence began providing arms to Afghan exiles and instigating tribal uprisings, with the aim of keeping India out of Afghanistan and from eventually absorbing the Afghan state.[34]

The use of covert operations and instigating insurgencies in Kashmir reinforced this strategy, particularly after the 1965 Pakistan-India War, when Islamabad discovered the limits of the alliance with the United States. After the outbreak of hostilities, the Americans decided to impose an embargo against both Pakistan and India. Pakistan relied almost exclusively on weapons and other military supplies from the United States, and the embargo undermined the ability of the Pakistani army to defeat India—at least that was the conclusion drawn in Islamabad. Three years earlier, the administration of John F. Kennedy had tried to improve relations with India, a move that had incited considerable outrage; and, although little was achieved, the Pakistanis opened discussions with China and Russia. The Russians did supply Pakistan with some weapons, but not enough to replace those provided by the United States. Although there had been no large-scale uprisings to coincide with the outbreak of hostilities in 1965, the ISI continued to encourage the organization of an anti-India guerrilla movement.[35]

In 1970, civil war broke out in Pakistan, with the eastern segment fighting to break away from Pakistan.[36] One outcome of this conflict, in which India aided the separatists, was that Bhutto greatly increased the ISI's budget. Significantly, some of the funding came from the United States, because the Americans had a particular interest in aiding Pakistan during the subsequent India-Pakistan confrontation of 1971. Richard Nixon and his administration believed that it was vital to show the international community—and China in particular (a staunch supporter of Pakistan)—that the United States supported its strategic partners in times of crisis. The White House assumed that India was determined to humiliate Pakistan over Bangladesh and that, toward this end, they had concluded a de facto alliance with the Soviets.

Thus the administration, over the strong objections of the State Department, ordered a diplomatic tilt toward Pakistan, to prevent the dismemberment of Pakistan and to demonstrate to China that the Americans would resist any Soviet-backed military intervention.[37] The Saudis also backed Muslim Pakistan. Although covert warfare had been used in the 1947–1948 and 1965 conflicts with India, the ISI promoted full-scale insurgency in the 1970–1971 Pakistani Civil War.[38] Islamist guerrilla armies were recruited to carry out operations in Bangladesh—a fully Islamic country. Most of these men came from carefully selected Bengali militant religious groups.[39] Increased support from Pakistan, as well as from the United States and Saudi Arabia, during the 1970–1971 war gave the ISI greater domestic authority and an enlarged network of contacts in militant Islamic guerrilla groups. As a result, the ISI was in a position to intervene covertly in Pakistani politics, religion, and society.[40]

In July 1977, Zia deposed Bhutto and instituted a military dictatorship in Pakistan that lasted for eleven years. This coup had the support of the White House, which wanted a stable Pakistan, regardless of the cost and consequences. The Americans felt that Zia was in a position to stabilize not only Pakistan, but also the entire region, including Afghanistan.[41] Despite Bhutto's earlier use of religious extremists to control Pakistan, it was Zia's regime that completed the transformation of the ISI into a political weapon and enhanced its relationship with militant Islamists. The ISI and its Islamist colleagues established a strong hold over Pakistani politics and over large segments of society. They infiltrated universities and the media and assisted in organizing terrorist groups for action abroad and at home. Through the ISI, the JI established links with the United States and the Saudis.[42] However, both the Saudis and Americans remained uneasy with the Pakistani Islamic organization.

Through the ISI, Zia used Islamic parties like the JI to counter opposition to the military dictatorship and to undermine political opponents. Zia increased support to the JI and helped to spread the influence of the organization into Afghanistan. Thanks to Zia's patronage, the JI, which had previously received less than 5 percent of the vote in free elections, grew in power and influence throughout the 1970s.

Any qualms in Washington over the legitimacy of Zia's regime evaporated with the Soviet invasion of neighboring Afghanistan in 1979. The ensuing jihad against the Soviets created the ideal circumstances for Pakistan to intervene directly in Afghanistan—only this time with the connivance of the United States. The ISI promoted the Afghan War as a battle against heathen communists and recruited fighters from across the Arab states, South Asia, and the Middle East. The ISI helped the JI form connections in Afghanistan, where they assisted the ISI in building up Islamist militant movements.[43]

The director of the ISI, General Akhtar Abdur Rahman established the Afghan Bureau of the ISI, which collaborated with American intelligence agencies and was, in turn, supplied with American and Saudi arms and funding. Zia did not want to openly oppose the Soviets, so the "secretive and aloof" ISI covertly channeled the U.S. and Saudi funds to the fighters.[44] Under the scheme, funding went through the ISI to the mujahidin, while the government denied involvement.[45] Aid was concentrated on Islamist resistance groups similar to the JI.[46] While the CIA wanted to provide aid directly to field commanders among the mujahidin, the ISI insisted on working through religious parties.[47] This arrangement worked well for Zia and the ISI, who used the American largesse to fund groups in Afghanistan that were ideologically suited to Pakistan's interests. In the long run, the Afghan War experience solidified Pakistan's—specifically the ISI's—links with Islamic militants both in Afghanistan and Pakistan, and underscored the value of covert warfare as the primary means of fighting India.[48]

The power and influence of the ISI within Pakistan has continued to grow in recent years, as their connections to radical Islam have increased. The triangular link between the Pakistan government, the ISI, and the radical mujahidin continued under Benazir Bhutto, who came to power in December 1988. General Hamid Gul, who was director general of the ISI under Bhutto, spoke openly in a 2008 interview of her ties to—and support of—"jihadis."[49] Bhutto's government was directly involved in infiltrating Taliban members into Afghanistan in the 1990s, while Bhutto claimed that Pakistan was merely returning Afghan refugees to their homeland. Without ISI support, the Taliban could not have made the gains they did in Afghanistan during the early 1990s.[50]

Meanwhile, after the defeat of the Soviet Union in Afghanistan, Washington essentially turned a blind eye to the region until the events of 9/11, when Pakistan once again became an integral part of the Anglo-American relationship with Islam.

During this period, several key members of General Pervez Musharraf's military regime who came to power in 1999, including Musharraf himself, had served in the ISI.[51] In fact, Musharraf succeeded in taking over Pakistan with the assistance of Mahmood Ahmed, the director of the ISI, who was able to bring over to Musharraf key senior officers of the Pakistani army.[52] Significantly, the Pakistani officer corps has become increasingly linked to Islamic groups. Ahmad himself, almost immediately after the coup, rediscovered his Islamic roots and became a devout Muslim, as well as an enthusiastic supporter of the Taliban and the fundamentalist Islamic groups fighting in Kashmir.

As head of the ISI and a key member of the ruling junta, Ahmad not only had control over clandestine operations but also of Pakistan's foreign policy, in effect making a sham of Musharraf's antiterrorist protestations.[53] George Tenet, director of the CIA, recalls that at a luncheon meeting with Ahmad, the Pakistani intelligence chief, "the guy was immovable when it came to the Taliban and al-Qaida."[54] Ahmad also met with congressmen on Capitol Hill just as reports were reaching Washington that aircraft had struck the Twin Towers in New York and the Pentagon. Not long afterward, Musharraf replaced Ahmad as head of the ISI as a sop to the Americans and to show that Pakistan was ready to join America's war against terrorism; little actually changed. The fact that Washington believed Musharraf is indicative of the difficulties that confronted the Americans when dealing with South Asia. Musharraf had to balance considerable pressure from the administration of George W. Bush with the trend in the Pakistani officer corps toward Islam.

Almost a decade earlier, increasing numbers of senior Pakistani officers had begun to turn to Islam and Islamic organizations. Nineteen retired Pakistani army officers were present at a 1991 JI convention, and it became common for ISI officers to take part in JI politics after retirement, including joining militant Islamic groups.[55] Furthermore, the ISI itself has been accused of wide-ranging terrorist activities in recent years, including the Daniel Pearl murder, scores of assassinations within Pakistan, the bombing of a church in Islamabad, and recently the attacks in Mumbai. According to one expert, Tariq Ali, many of these actions were intended to punish Pakistani leaders for "betraying" the Taliban after 9/11 and as a warning to the Pakistan government not to bow too far to Washington's demands.[56] Despite the accusations, it is unlikely that the SIS orchestrated these attacks—most likely it was radical groups over which the ISI has limited control.

The ISI has also been directly involved with the reorganization and ongoing support of the Taliban. The ISI provided the Taliban with access to food, medical supplies, the ability to raise funds (through private sources), and with intelligence information and strategic advice in their key battles. It even helped them negotiate deals with local commanders and warlords. Although many organizations had sprouted in Afghanistan to fight the Soviets and vie for control of the country in the aftermath of the Soviet defeat, the Taliban emerged as the most successful. As a result, the ISI abandoned the other mujahidin groups in Afghanistan in favor of the Taliban. The ISI could not have undertaken such a significant policy without the connivance of the Pakistani government. Remarkably, Pakistan's commitment to the Taliban was not expanded by a pro-Islamist such as Zia, but came about after the election of Benazir Bhutto, a woman with ostensibly liberal credentials, from a cosmopolitan family, and with a Western education. But as Rasul Bakhsh Rais comments, "she had no control over Pakistan's policy toward Afghanistan."[57]

The pro-Taliban policy of various Pakistani regimes is driven by a combination of factors: the sentiments of Pakistani Pashtuns, the influence of the militant Islamic establishment, and the ISI. The strongest backing for the Taliban comes from ethnic Pashtun tribal and regional leaders. After 2001, the bonds with the local tribal leaders became even closer when the U.S. Army forced the Taliban out of Afghanistan. As part of their campaign to ingratiate themselves with the Pashtuns of Pakistan, both the Taliban and al-Qaeda encouraged their commanders to marry into the families of the local tribal heads. In the words of Graham Fuller, former CIA station chief in Kabul:

> The Taliban represent zealous and largely ignorant mountain Islamists. They are also all ethnic Pashtuns. Most Pashtuns see the Taliban—like them or not—as the primary vehicle for restoration of Pashtun power in Afghanistan, lost in 2001. Pashtuns are also among the most fiercely nationalist, tribalized and xenophobic peoples of the world, united only against the foreign invader. In the end, the Taliban are probably more Pashtun than they are Islamist.[58]

Religion is a considerable factor and a critical part of the Taliban's survival. The Deobandis of the Jamiat Ulema-e -Islam (JUI),[59] as well as most of the other organizations that make up the Deobandi movement and the madrassa (religious schools) network, are closely bound to the Taliban.[60] Like the JI, the JUI accepts the notion of ethnicity and devotion to Islam and gets involved in Pakistani politics. It has taken part in Pakistan's election process, and in 1993–1996 had been part of Benazir Bhutto's coalition government. But, regardless of religious affinity, according to a war office report, "deep down there was a common ethnic factor binding all these elements."[61] Certainly the Pakistani officer corps, as well as the ISI, includes Pashtuns from Pakistan's northwest provinces—a legacy of the "martial races" concept that continues to dominate the Pakistani armed forces.

Ostensibly, the ringmaster of Pakistan's covert and overt policies toward Afghanistan and India is the ISI. Yet the ISI is not a rogue element, but rather represents the cream of Pakistan's officer corps, and has a thorough understanding of the Northwest Frontier better than any other organization locally or abroad. Rasul Bakhsh Rais argues that it is unlikely that the ISI could advance a separate agenda outside the political and military Pakistani leadership. Whenever circumstances in Afghanistan—or elsewhere in the region—threaten Pakistan's interests, the ISI has carried the burden of using clandestine means to meet the challenge.

In the heady months and years following the defeat of the Soviet Union in Afghanistan, America's interest in Pakistan began to wane, and eventually the region simply dropped out of Washington's field of vision. Occasionally, Pakistan and India came into sharp focus, particularly when both countries achieved nuclear weapons capability. But beyond imposing economic sanctions on both countries in retaliation, America's political leadership remained uninterested in South Asia. The Pakistani officer corps felt betrayed and abandoned by the Americans; Washington's lack of interest in Pakistan's security problems in the region compounded the deteriorating relationship between the former allies. Following the defeat of the Soviet Union in Afghanistan, the Pakistanis had even tried to establish a friendly government in Kabul, or at the very least one that would keep India out of Afghanistan.[62]

But by 1992, the interim government in Kabul had become hostile to Pakistan and thus might potentially deny Pakistan's access, through Afghanistan, to the new Islamic republics of Central Asia. Making matters worse, the Pakistani government feared that the new administration in Afghanistan might be open to overtures from India and might ultimately compromise Pakistan's influence in the region. There was also—however remote—the possibility that the Afghanistan regime might even lay claim to Pakhtunistan in northwestern Pakistan. These fears were realized as India's presence (especially the Indian intelligence service) in Afghanistan has expanded dramatically. Moreover, Pakistan had become increasingly isolated since the administration of Bill

Clinton continued to impose harsh economic sanctions on the country, while establishing friendly relations with India.[63] Under these circumstances, it became critical for Pakistan to control the political situation in Afghanistan. According to Lawrence Ziring:

> The ISI therefore developed a strategy that not only undermined the secular Afghan government, but also nourished the Afghan Islamist movement. The key ISI decision . . . was the formation of the Taliban and its recruitment of Pakistanis as well as Afghans. By 1993 the Tehrik-i-Taliban was a formidable force with direct ties to the Pakistan army.[64]

In 1995, when the Taliban called for support from Pakistan's religious schools, they received an enthusiastic response, but it was the ISI that continued to control the ongoing recruitment and training of militants and their subsequent dispatch to Afghanistan.[65] Ultimately, the Taliban fulfilled Pakistan's requirements for Afghanistan. Fuller emphasizes that "Pakistan will therefore never rupture ties or abandon the Pashtuns, in either country, whether radical Islamist or not. Pakistan can never afford to have Pashtuns hostile to Islamabad in control of Kabul, or at home."[66]

The ISI's support of the Taliban and other extremist groups like Lashkar-e-Taiba has enhanced the reach of political Islam which has emerged as a major sociopolitical factor in Pakistan. In fact, the ISI—created by the British and nurtured by the Americans and the Saudis—has become, for better or for worse, part of Pakistan's social and political evolution. The Mumbai massacre in 2008 has demonstrated that extreme Islamic organizations and terrorist groups easily slip beyond the control of the ISI. Although militant Muslim groups have not penetrated the ISI, it is clear that the Pakistani intelligence establishment has become a fellow traveler of political Islam.

NOTES

A Note on Sources

1. Matthew M. Aid, "The Secret Reclassification Program," *Organization of American Historians Newsletter* 34 (May 2006), http://www.oah.org/pubs/nl/2006may/aid.html (accessed December 2, 2009).

2. Ibid.

3. Richard J. Aldrich, "Did Waldegrave Work? The Impact of Open Government upon British History," *Twentieth Century British History* 9, no. 1 (1998), http://tcbh.oxfordjournals.org/cgi/reprint/9/1/111 (accessed December 2, 2009).

4. Ibid.

PROLOGUE: • *Stories from the Bazaar*

1. The bazaar (or *souk* in Arabic) is a marketplace that also accommodates social, cultural, religious, and political centers of activity. In this respect the bazaar is reminiscent of the ancient Athenian *agora*, which served as the hub for Greek society and remained as a meeting place until the middle of the twentieth century. However, in the Middle East the bazaar also fulfills the role of political forum. According to Mahmoud Abdullahzadeh, "The Political Significance of the Bazaar in Iran," in *Technology, Tradition and Survival: Aspects of Material Culture in the Middle East and Central Asia*, ed. Richard Tapper and Keith McLachlan (London: Frank Cass, 2002), 234–35, the bazaar has also served as an effective vehicle for communication and social mobilization.

2. In a broad sense the principle of *taqiyah* (a form of deception, secrecy, caution, and precaution), particularly in Shiite Islam, was acceptable historically in times of duress. Specifically, *taqiyah* was applied in the precautionary denial of religious belief in the face of potential persecution. Although not exclusive to them, it was originally practiced by Shiite Muslims who had been subjected to persecution by Sunnis. See "Taqiyah," *The Oxford Dictionary of Islam*, ed. John L. Esposito (Oxford: Oxford University Press, 2003), 314. According to Bernard Lewis, *The Assassins: A Radical Sect in Islam* (London: Weidenfeld & Nicolson, 2001), 25, *taqiyah* denotes an Islamic doctrine of dispensation that absolves the believer from fulfilling certain obligations of religion.

3. Daniel Pipes, *The Hidden Hand: Middle East Fears of Conspiracy* (New York: St. Martin's Press, 1996), 110.

4. Ibid.

5. Akbar S. Ahmed, *Living Islam: From Samarkand to Stornoway* (London: Penguin, 1995), 76); quoted in Carole Hillenbrand, *The Crusades: Islamic Perspectives* (Edinburgh: Edinburgh University Press, 1999), 590.

6. Amin Maalouf, *The Crusades Through Arab Eyes*, trans. Jon Rothschild (London: Al Saqi, 1984), 265.

7. Spies or any combatants out of uniform have few or no rights and were often executed or tortured with impunity.

8. The mosque is one of the sacred focal points for pilgrims to the annual Hajj and can accommodate close to 300,000 people. At the center of its courtyard, which is forty acres in size, is the Kaba, a cube-shaped structure always covered by a black cloth embroidered in gold. Muslims believe that Abraham built this to honor God and that Mohammad in A.D. 630 cleansed it of idols. Over 2 million pilgrims each year conduct their prayers and rituals at this site.

9. Madawi al-Rasheed, *A History of Saudi Arabia* (Cambridge: Cambridge University Press, 2002), 144.

10. Ibid.

11. The Mahdi is the Islamic messiah who is supposed to appear at the end of the new century.

12. Peter W. Wilson and Douglas F. Graham, *Saudi Arabia: The Coming Storm* (New York: M. E. Sharpe, 1994), 58, add that it is still debatable whether Qahtani was actually proclaimed Mahdi by Utaibi.

13. "Khomeini on Mecca Attack," *FBIS Middle East Report*, 21 November 1979, in Yaroslav Trofimov, *The Siege of Mecca: The Forgotten Uprising in Islam's Holiest Shrine and the Birth of Al-Qaeda* (New York: Doubleday, 2007), 275.

14. One hundred thirty-seven American diplomats and marines were trapped in the embassy. Two marines were killed, as well as an American pilot and two Pakistani embassy staff.

15. According to Wilson and Graham, *Saudi Arabia*, 58, the Ulema took one day and a half to formulate a judgment. One report in *Time* magazine ("Sacrilege in Mecca," *Time*, 3 December 1979) claimed it took the Ulema eight hours, while a second report filed one week later (*Time*, 10 December 1979) said the ruling was issued on the third day of the siege.

16. Stephen Schwartz, "Is Saudi Arabia Holy Soil?," *Think Israel* (September–October 2004), http://www.think-israel.org/schwartz.saudiarabia.html. The Wikipedia entry "Juhayman al-Otaibi" (http://en.wikipedia.org/wiki/Juhayman_al-Otaibi) claims that General Zia-ul-Haq, at the time directing the Pakistani army, captured the

mosque with the assistance of French paratroopers, while another *Wikipedia* entry, "Grand Mosque Seizure" (http://en.wikipedia.org/wiki/Grand_Mosque_Seizure), states that it was French GIGN counterterrorist commandos who took part in the fighting.

17. Robert Fisk, *The Great War for Civilization: The Conquest of the Middle East* (London: Fourth Estate, 2005), 1046–1047. Fisk comments that the rebels were electrocuted "Saddam style."

18. Trofimov, *Siege*, 192.

19. Although some writers, like John K. Cooley, *Unholy Wars: Afghanistan, America and International Terrorism* (Sterling, VA: Pluto, 2000), 83, 85–86, 195, 204, have claimed there have been assertions that the CIA and/or other agencies of the U.S. government directly trained Arab mujahidin, including Osama bin Laden, there is little evidence to support this, according to Peter L. Bergen, *Holy War, Inc.: Inside the Secret World of Osama bin Laden* (New York: Free Press, 2001), 64–67. Instead, America's contact with Arab mujahidin was indirect. U.S. aid in the form of training, weapons, and funding was funneled through Pakistan's ISI agency.

20. Saudi Arabia agreed to match U.S. funding for the mujahidin, and Egypt permitted the U.S. Air Force to use Egypt as a base from which it shipped to Pakistan tons of weapons and equipment. Even the Chinese contributed $600 million to the cause. Furthermore, Egypt's government of Anwar al-Sadat trained members of the Muslim Brotherhood for the jihad in Afghanistan. In the first years, in order to avoid any links with the United States, the CIA secured weapons from the First and Second World Wars, stockpiled in countries such as Egypt, India, and China. By 1985, sixty thousand tons of equipment was made available in Pakistan. See John Prados, *Safe for Democracy: The Secret Wars of the CIA* (Chicago: Ivan R. Dee, 2006), 471–72, 488; and Robert Dreyfuss, *Devil's Game: How the United States Helped Unleash Fundamentalist Islam* (New York: Metropolitan, 2005), 274–75.

21. George Crile, *Charlie Wilson's War: The Extraordinary Story of the Largest Covert Operation in History* (New York: Atlantic Monthly Press, 2003), 201. The British Secret Intelligence Service (SIS) and Special Air Service (SAS) were also able to send teams into Afghanistan. This direct contact was invaluable to the United States, because neither the CIA nor any other American agency was permitted to send men into Afghan territory.

ONE · *Assassination*

1. Anthony Nutting, *No End of a Lesson: The Story of Suez* (London: Constable, 1967), 34–35.

2.   Robert St. John, *The Boss: The Story of Gamel Abdel Nasser* (New York: McGraw-Hill, 1960), 179–80.

3.   The only casualties were a Sudanese minister and a lawyer from Alexandria, who were cut by the shattered glass.

4.   St. John, *The Boss*, 181. Cf. Richard P. Mitchell, *The Society of Muslim Brothers* (Oxford: Oxford University Press, 1969), 151.

5.   Mitchell, *Muslim Brothers*, 150.

6.   Beyond Eden's general antipathy to Nasser, certain events, such as the nationalization of the Suez Canal, would send him off in a murderous frenzy. Even unrelated and smaller instances that underlined the decline of British influence in the Middle East would convince Eden that Nasser was the culprit. On March 1, 1956, King Hussein of Jordan dismissed Sir John Glubb, the commander of the Arab Legion, a Jordanian unit commanded by British officers. Eden took this as an insult to Britain and vowed to punish Nasser, although the latter had nothing to do with the affair. It was at this time that Eden blasted his deputy foreign minister Anthony Nutting about Nasser, screaming over the phone to him, "I want him destroyed, can't you understand?" See Stephen Dorril, *MI6: Inside the Covert World of Her Majesty's Secret Intelligence Service* (New York: Free Press, 2000), 612.

7.   Certainly the British embassy emphasized Nasser's stipulation that, despite the purges of the Muslim organization, there were still many Brothers free in Egypt (Cairo to Foreign Office, VG 1015/45, FO 371/183884, The National Archives of the United Kingdom [TNA]).

8.   Dorril, *MI6*, 613–14.

9.   One French plan involved sending a commando team on rubber boats from the French embassy to destroy the Egyptian Revolutionary Command building on the northern tip of Gezira Island, but the attempt was aborted. See Mohamed H. Heikal, *Cutting the Lion's Tail: Suez Through Egyptian Eyes* (New York: Arbor House, 1987), 154n1.

10.   Peter Wright, *Spy Catcher: The Candid Autobiography of a Senior Intelligence Officer* (Toronto: Stoddart, 1987), 160–62.

11.   According to Heikal, *Lion's Tail*, 215n1, the Egyptian security service also received information about three British subjects who had been sent to Cairo to make another assassination attempt, but the mission was aborted, or they got cold feet.

12.   John Keay, *Sowing the Wind: The Seeds of Conflict in the Middle East* (New York: Norton, 2003), 436. The Israelis also tried poison to eliminate the Egyptian leader. About this time they recruited a Greek waiter employed by Groppi, the presidential catering service, to sprinkle poison in Nasser's coffee. Fortunately for the Egyptian leader, the would-be assassin became so nervous that his hand shook uncontrollably, and he broke down and confessed (Heikal, *Lion's Tail*, 215n1).

13. Dorril, *MI6*, 631; Eric Downton, *Wars Without End* (Toronto: Stoddart, 1987), 229, 341.

14. Keith Kyle, *Suez* (London: Weidenfeld & Nicholson, 1991), 218–91. Swinburn and James Zarb, an employee of Marconi in Cairo and a British subject, were released under a general amnesty in 1959 (Dorril, *MI6*, 631n84).

15. Dorril, *MI6*, 631; Yaacov Caroz, *The Arab Secret Service* (London: Corgi, 1978), 23.

16. Kyle, *Suez*, 218; Dorril, *MI6*, 631–32.

17. Dorril, *MI6*, 631.

18. Scott Lucas and Alistair Morey, "The Hidden 'Alliance': The CIA and MI6 Before and After Suez," in *American-British-Canadian Intelligence Relations, 1939–2000*, ed. Maurizio Ferrera and Martin Rhodes (London: Frank Cass, 2000), 108.

19. Heikal, *Lion's Tail*, 151n3. Heikal suggests that the intent was to re-create the conditions of 1882, during which Egyptian riots in Alexandria that resulted in the killing of Europeans and the destruction of property gave the British an excuse to land troops and eventually dominate Egypt (see also Chapter 4).

20. Caroz, *Arab Secret Service*, 21–22; Richard Deacon, *"C": A Biography of Sir Maurice Oldfield, Head of MI6* (London: Futura, 1984), 110–11.

21. Dorril, *MI6*, 653.

22. Caroz, *Arab Secret Service*, 22n.

23. Dorril, *MI6*, 603.

24. Tom Bower, *The Perfect English Spy: The Unknown Man in Charge During the Most Tumultuous Scandal-Ridden Era in Espionage History* (New York: St. Martin's Press, 1995), 231; Dorril, *MI6*, 603.

25. Xan Fielding, *One Man in His Time: The Life of Lieutenant-Colonel N. L. D. ("Billy") McLean, DSO* (London: Macmillan, 1990), 104–5.

26. Caroz, *Arab Secret Service*, 24.

27. According to Kyle, *Suez*, 149, Khalil revealed that Saudi money was involved, but few details or the exact amount.

28. Kyle, *Suez*, 149; Dorril, *MI6*, 659.

29. Lucas and Morey, "Hidden 'Alliance,'" 101.

30. Like with Nasser, an unpopular treaty, in this case the Sinai Treaty between Israel and Egypt (March 26, 1979), triggered the assassination of Sadat on October 6, 1981. As early as February 1981, Egyptian security became aware of the plot to kill Sadat after arresting a member of Egyptian Islamic Jihad, and in September Sadat had ordered the round-up of over 1,500 suspected Islamic radicals, including Jihad members, along with feminists, Coptic Christian clergy, university professors, journalists, and members of various student groups. The arrests were a part of a major crackdown on all radical Islamic organizations, including student movements. Another factor was Sadat's role in the aftermath of the assassination

attempt against Nasser. Sadat had presided as a judge and had helped to convict Muslim Brothers, who were sentenced to death or imprisonment. According to Gilles Kepel, *Muslim Extremism in Egypt: The Prophet and the Pharaoh*, trans. Jon Rothschild (Los Angeles: University of California Press, 1984), 192, the assassin, Khalid al-Islambuli, killed Sadat at the peak of the president's unpopularity.

31. "The Man Behind Bin Laden," *The New Yorker*, 16 September 2002.

32. Kepel, *Muslim Extremism*, 192–93.

33. Adeed Dawisha, *Arab Nationalism in the Twentieth Century: From Triumph to Despair* (Princeton: Princeton University Press, 2003), 284.

TWO · *The Mahdi*

1. Alan Furst, *The World at Night* (New York: Random House, 1996), 9.

2. Charles Royle, *The Egyptian Campaigns, 1882–1885: And the Events Which Led to Them*, 2 vols. (London: Hurst & Blackett, 1886), 89. Royle estimates the mob to have reached approximately 2,000–2,500.

3. The more malicious of the rioters studded them with nails for greater effect.

4. Ibid.

5. Royle, *Egyptian Campaigns*, vol. 2, 88, states that on June 8, Bedouin were observed storing their rifles in various locations throughout the city.

6. During the course of the riot, about one hundred Bedouin proclaimed their loyalty to Tawfik the Dervish Pasha, the sultan's representative. See "The Crisis in Egypt: Serious Riots in Alexandria," *The Times*, 11 June 1882; Royle, *Egyptian Campaigns*, vol. 2, 182.

7. Royle, *Egyptian Campaigns*, vol. 1, 94.

8. Ibid., 97

9. Ibid., 54–55.

10. A. J. P. Taylor, *The Struggle for Mastery in Europe, 1848–1918* (Oxford: Clarendon Press, 1965), 272–73. Taylor argues that initially the French were not interested, but they were equally determined to deny the territory to the Italians. According to Luigi Albertini, *The Origins of the War of 1914*, trans. and ed. Isabella M. Massey, vol. 1 (London: Oxford University Press, 1952), 29, a major political and cultural figure in Italy in the early twentieth century, the prime mover behind the annexation of Tunisia, was Otto von Bismarck, who believed that French hostility toward the German empire could be diverted to North Africa.

11. Thomas Pakenham, *The Scramble for Africa: The White Man's Conquest of the Dark Continent from 1876 to 1912* (New York: Random House, 1991), 121.

12. Christina P. Harris, *Nationalism and Revolution in Egypt: The Role of the Muslim Brotherhood* (The Hague: Mouton, 1964), 45.

13. Harris, *Nationalism*, 44–45; the note was delivered to the Egyptian government on January 8, 1882.

14. The letter reached Gladstone via Blunt, who had received a translated version from Jean Sabunji. on 2 July 1882 in W. S. Blunt, *Secret History of the British Occupation of Egypt: Being a Personal Narrative of Events* (London: Unwin, 1907), 371–74.

15. Nineteenth-century Sudan also included the present-day Sudan, Somalia, Eritrea, and Ethiopia.

16. The "Expected One" (or the "Guided One") is the prophesied redeemer of Islam, who will remain on earth for seven, nine, or nineteen years (depending on the interpretation) before the Day of Judgment. Sufi and Shiite Islam accept the concept, but for Sunnis it never became a formal doctrine, and it is neither endorsed nor condemned. However, according to Edward Mortimer, *Faith and Power: The Politics of Islam* (New York: Vintage, 1982), 54, it has gained a strong hold on the imagination of many ordinary, self-described "orthodox" Sunni, thanks to Sufi preaching.

17. William L. Cleveland, *A History of the Modern Middle East* (San Francisco: Westview, 1994), 117–18.

18. Rudolf C. Slatin, *Fire and Sword in the Sudan: A Personal Narrative of Fighting and Serving the Dervishes, 1879–1895*, trans. F. R. Wingate (London: Arnold, 1896), 126, 132, 141.

19. Khartoum held sixty thousand inhabitants and was defended by a garrison of two thousand men. See Dominic Green, *Three Empires on the Nile: The Victorian Jihad, 1869–1899* (New York: Free Press, 2007), 150.

20. Gordon had to arrange transportation for approximately fifteen thousand civil servants, soldiers, and their families by boat to Egypt (Green, *Three Empires*, 152).

21. Paul Kennedy, *The Realities Behind Diplomacy: Background Influences on British External Policy, 1865–1980* (Glasgow: Collins, 1981), 88.

22. The scramble for Africa, inaugurated by the conference, delineated the spheres of influence that apportioned the region to the European powers.

23. Menelik II, ruler of Shewa, an independent kingdom of Ethiopia, made himself emperor of Ethiopia with the support of the Italians. On May 2, 1889, the Italians forced him to sign a treaty that effectively turned Ethiopia into an Italian protectorate, with the establishment of a colony in Eritrea. In 1893, Menelik repudiated the treaty, and the Italians attempted to reestablish control, only to face a humiliating defeat at the battle of Adowa on March 1, 1896, which resulted in the death of seven thousand Italian soldiers and the capture of another three thousand.

24. Kassala was captured by the Mahdi army in 1885 and then by the Italians in 1897.

25. Robert Gascoyne-Cecil, Marquess of Salisbury, became leader of the Conservatives in 1881, following the death of Benjamin Disraeli, and prime minister in

1886. Except for three years (1892–1895), he remained head of the government until 1902.

26. Taylor, *Struggle for Mastery*, 367.

27. Cleveland, *Modern Middle East*, 102.

THREE · *The Eclipse of Imperial Islam*

1. Joseph Heller, *British Policy Towards the Ottoman Empire, 1909–1914* (London: Frank Cass, 1983), 39.

2. The Caliph was head of a governing institution that was both state and church. As Bernard Lewis explains in *What Went Wrong?: Western Impact and Middle Eastern Response* (Oxford: Oxford University Press, 2002), 114, the Caliph "was himself neither a jurist nor a theologian, but a practitioner of the arts of politics and sometimes of war."

3. Philip Mansel, *Constantinople: City of the World's Desire, 1453–1924* (London: John Murray, 1995), 414.

4. From Mehmed II until the resignation of Mehmed VI in 1924, the Ottoman Sultans had claimed the title of Caliph. However, according to Caroline Finkel, *Osman's Dream: The Story of the Ottoman Empire, 1300–1923* (New York: Basic, 2006), 111, until Selim I, the Ottoman Sultans used the title in a rhetorical sense rather than in a political-legal assertion of sovereignty over the Muslim community. Finkel adds that by the eighteenth century stories emerged, although there is no credence to them, that there was an actual transfer of power to Selim from the last Mamluk Caliph. In the Shiite interpretation of Islam, descent from Mohammed originates from his son-in-law Ali, who is regarded as the first imam. In the Shiite doctrine, the imams have a special religious role, divine inspiration passed on from Mohammed, that the Sunni Caliphs did not possess. See Cleveland, *Modern Middle East*, 34–35.

5. Andrew Mango, Ataturk: *The Biography of the Founder of Modern Turkey* (New York: Overlook, 2000), 403. The sultanate was abolished two years earlier on November 1, 1922.

6. From the Turkish-language memoirs of Ismet Inönü, quoted in Mango, *Ataturk*, 403.

7. Gilles Kepel, *Jihad: The Trail of Political Islam*, trans. Anthony F. Roberts (Cambridge: Harvard University Press, 2002), 43.

8. Shiite Muslims, however, did not acknowledge any Sunni Caliph. Indeed the succession of the Caliphate is at the heart of the Shiite-Sunni schism. See also Vali Nasr, *The Shia Revival: How Conflicts Within Islam Will Shape the Future* (New York: Norton, 2006), 40–43.

9.   The Turkish parliament under the direction of Mustapha Kema (Ataturk) formally ended the Caliphate on March 3, 1924. The day after the law was passed, the governor and police chief of Istanbul informed the last Caliph, Abdulmecit, that he had to leave immediately. The Ottoman Empire had officially come to an end on November 1, 1922, when the Turkish Grand Assembly in Ankara abolished the sultanate. The last Ottoman sovereign, Mehmed VI Vahdettin, departed Istanbul on November 17, 1922, with the assistance of the British. In a less than dignified manner the last Sultan escaped from his palace smuggled in an ambulance for transport to Malta on the British battleship *Malaya*. He finally settled on the Italian Riviera. For further details, see Mango, *Ataturk*, 364–65.

10. In the 1920s the Khilafat Movement sprang up throughout the British colonial territories in Asia to defend the Ottoman Caliphate. It was particularly effective in British India, where it formed a rallying point for Indian Muslims and was one of the many anti-British political movements to secure widespread support. For a few years it worked in alliance with Hindu communities and was supported by Gandhi, who was a member of the Central Khilafat Committee. The movement came to an end in 1924, after the British incarcerated most of the leadership, and several parts broke off to establish their own organizations. See Ali Rahnema, ed., *Pioneers of Islamic Revival* (London: Zed, 2005), 100–102.

11. Brynjar Lia, *The Society of the Muslim Brothers in Egypt: The Rise of an Islamic Mass Movement, 1928–1942* (Reading: Ithaca, 1998), 80.

12. According to Finkel, *Osman's Dream*, 492, after the losses from the Treaty of Berlin, three-quarters of the empire's population was Muslim.

13. Ibid.

14. S. Tufan Buzpinar, "The Hijaz, Abdulhamid II and Amir Hussein's Secret Dealings with the British, 1877–1880," *Middle East Studies* 31, no. 1 (January 1995): 99–123, 105–6, 110–16.

15. The Hashemite clan traces its ancestry to Hashim ibn Abd al-Manaf, the great-grandfather of the Prophet Mohammed.

16. Although the other three schools of Sunni Islam—Shafi'i, Hanbali, and Maliki—had maintained the Arab prerequisite of the Caliphate, they had not opposed the Ottoman claim. See Finkel, *Osman's Dream*, 494.

17. Buzpinar, "Secret Dealings," passim.

18. F. A. K. Yasamee, *Ottoman Diplomacy: Abdulhamid II and the Great Powers* (Istanbul: Isis, 1996), 89.

19. According to Yasamee, Hussein's death was not a coincidence. The assassin, despite torture, did not reveal his motives for killing the Emir, nor if he was acting on behalf of anyone else. Buzpinar, "Secret Dealings," 118–19, comments that the evidence is inconclusive whether Abdulhamid was behind the assassination. The

Sultan, though, was fully aware of the Emir's secret dealings with the British. Furthermore, Buzpinar adds, Abdulhamid's fears over conspiracies with respect to the Arab provinces breaking away had been raised by warnings from Layard, the British ambassador to Istanbul. Layard informed Abdulhamid that there was a secret society in Arabia dedicated to this end, as well as to the overthrow of the Sultan himself.

20. David Fromkin, *A Peace to End All Peace: The Fall of the Ottoman Empire and the Creation of the Modern Middle East* (New York: Avon, 1989), 97.

21. Hew Strachen, *The First World War*, vol. 1, *To Arms* (Oxford: Oxford University Press, 2001), 651.

22. Fromkin, *Peace*, 97.

FOUR · *Jihad for All Occasions*

1. C. S. Jarvis, *Three Deserts* (London: John Murray, 1941), 5. At the time, Jarvis was a major in the British army and posted to the Libyan Desert during the First World War. Later he served as governor of the Sinai Peninsula.

2. Urguplu Hayri Bey, the Sheikulislam, was Mufti of Istanbul, but in 1540 Suleyman elevated the Mufti to the role of head of the Ottoman religious establishment and supreme cleric of the empire.

3. Accordingly it was translated into Arabic, Farsi, Urdu, and Yaaric. The fatwa was a legal opinion; in this case, five fatwas were presented in the form of elaborate questions with a simple affirmative or negative answer. See Rudolph Peters, *Islam and Colonialism: The Doctrine of Jihad in Modern History* (The Hague: Mouton, 1979), 90–91.

4. Mango, *Ataturk*, 136.

5. Ulrich Trumpener, *Germany and the Ottoman Empire, 1914–1918* (Princeton: Princeton University Press, 1968), 117.

6. The details, as well as a cogent argument with respect to the failure of the jihad, are to be found in Gottfried Hagen, "German Heralds of Holy War: Orientalists and Applied Oriental Studies," *Comparative Studies of South Asia, Africa and the Middle East* 24, no. 2 (2004): 145. Mango, *Ataturk*, 136, also cites Eshref Kushchubashi, a leading member of Enver Pasha's Special Organization, who commented that the proclamation of jihad was received coolly in Istanbul and added that there would be even less enthusiasm in other parts of the Muslim world.

7. Hagen, "German Heralds," 145.

8. Ibid.

9. Trumpener, *Germany*, 112.

10. Tilman Lüdke, *Jihad Made in Germany: Ottoman and German Propaganda and Intelligence Operations in the First World War* (Münster: LIT, 2005), 48.

11. Ibid., 50. Abdulhamid was the last Sultan to rule with absolute power. He was exiled to Salonica, but after the city fell to the Greek army in 1912, Abdulhamid was brought back to Istanbul and held under house arrest at the Beylerbeyi Palace. He spent the last few years of his life studying, carpentering, and writing his memoirs, until his death on February 10, 1918.

12. Albert Hourani, *Arabic Thought in the Liberal Age, 1798–1939* (London: Oxford University Press, 1962), 51. Hagen, "German Heralds," 51, points out that, in addition to Sharif Hussein's making claims on the Caliphate, Abbas Hilmi, the Khedive of Egypt, attempted to have himself proclaimed Caliph before the outbreak of the First World War.

13. Peters, *Islam*, 90–94.

14. Ibid., 94.

15. Tripolitania, Cyrenaica, and Fessan are modern Libya.

16. Jarvis, *Three Deserts*, 4–5.

17. Ibid., 24.

18. R. H. S. Crossman and Michael Foot, *A Palestine Munich* (London: Victor Gollancz, 1946): quoted in Arthur Koestler, *Promise and Fulfilment: Palestine, 1917–1949* (London: Macmillan, 1949), 50. The Anglo-American Report was issued by the Anglo-American Committee of Inquiry established by the U.S. and British governments to look into the plight of post–Second World War Jewish refugees in Europe. The committee recommended that 100,000 of these refugees be admitted to Palestine.

19. Crossman's experience with the British civil service is chronicled in *The Diaries of a Cabinet Minister: Richard Crossman* (New York: Henry Holt, 1976), upon which the popular BBC comedy series *Yes, Minister* was based; not surprisingly, every effort was made by the Whitehall establishment to stop its publication.

20. Gail Minault, *The Khilafat Movement: Religious Symbolism and Political Mobilization in India* (New York: Columbia University Press, 1982), 2 and passim.

21. Ibid., 2.

22. Kepel, *Jihad*, 57.

23. Sayyid Qutb (1906–1966) and Mawlana Mawdudi (1903–1979), both Sunnis and major figures in the pan-Islamic movement, and Ruhollah Khomeini (1902–1989), a Shiite cleric, also subscribed to the concept of Islam as a political force. See Kepel, *Jihad*, 23.

FIVE · *A New Caliph*

1. John Buchan, *Greenmantle* (London: Nelson, 1916), 16.

2. Mecca was occupied by only 1,400 Turkish soldiers, the bulk of the garrison having

been withdrawn to Taif, the summer station of the Hejaz, to spare them from the summer heat that reached 45 degrees Celsius.

3. R. L. Bidwell, ed., *The Arab Bulletin: Bulletin of the Arab Bureau in Cairo* (Gerrards Cross: Archive Editions, 1986), vol. 1, bulletin 21, 258.

4. *Ibid.* According to George Antonius, one report claimed that Zia Bey said: "The Arabs are in revolt, and it is said that they have declared their complete independence." To which Hussein replied: "I have also heard that they want their independence. I shall certainly do all I can about it." See George Antonius, *The Arab Awakening: The Story of the Arab National Movement* (Safety Harbor, FL: Simon, 2001), 196n2. Originally published in 1939 by J. B. Lippincott.

5. The Arabs simultaneously laid siege to all the Turkish garrisons and barracks but only with rifle fire, since they lacked artillery. The fighting lasted for three days, after which the smaller Turkish posts surrendered, but the main barracks and the fort of Jiad held out for three weeks and only capitulated when the British brought up Egyptian artillery units from the Sudan (Antonius, *Arab Awakening*, 195).

6. Hussein's sons Feisal and Ali, supported by a couple of tribes, raised the revolt on June 5, 1916.

7. Fromkin, *Peace*, 219.

8. After several informal contacts through go-betweens, Hussein entered into formal negotiation in the summer of 1917. The outcome of these discussions came after an exchange of letters, four from each side, between the Sharif and Sir Henry McMahon, Kitchener's successor as high commissioner in Cairo. The letters reveal that deception colored all aspects of the agreements, and after the war both sides repudiated the hollow promises and commitments engendered by expediency. For the text of the letter, see J. C. Hurewitz, *Diplomacy in the Near and Middle East: A Documentary Record*, vol. 2 (Princeton: Van Nostrand, 1956), 13–17.

9. Fromkin, *Peace*, 218–19. According to Bruce Westrate, *The Arab Bureau: British Policy in the Middle East, 1916–1920* (University Park: Pennsylvania State University Press, 1992), 15, in January 1915, Hussein's son Ali had discovered a plot outlining a Turkish plan to depose him.

10. Fromkin, *Peace*, 217.

11. Joshua Teitelbaum, *The Rise and Fall of the Hashimite Kingdom of Arabia* (London: Hurst, 2001), 47.

12. Dennis P. Hupchick, *The Balkans: From Constantinople to Communism* (New York: Palgrave, 2002), 321. In the first Balkan War, the empire lost Western Thrace, Macedonia, and Albania; in the war with Italy, the Sultan was forced to surrender Libya.

13. The CUP also merged with the secret military society based in Thessalonica,

whose officers would eventually dominate the empire (Finkel, *Osman's Dream*, 504–5).

14. Bismarck was not indifferent to the outcome of the Eastern Question—the consequence following the disintegration of the Ottoman Empire—on several occasions he had encouraged France and Austria-Hungary to seek colonies among the Sultan's provinces and advised the British to annex Egypt. However, the imperial chancellor was equally reluctant for the Ottomans to become too dependent on Russia. See Yasamee, *Ottoman Diplomacy*, 73–75.

15. Peter Hopkirk, *On Secret Service East of Constantinople: The Great Game and the Great War* (London: John Murray, 1994) 17.

16. The Baghdad Railway included the newly built Orient Express line and was intended to run from Koyna in Turkey to Baghdad, and then on to Basra. Although the British government welcomed the proposed railway, British financiers were against it and organized public opinion to oppose the project. Because of this, the Baghdad Railway became a source of friction not only between Britain and Germany but also with Russia, since it would challenge Russia's influence in the Caucasus and in northern Persia. In 1911 and 1913, Russia and Britain reached separate settlements with Germany. The Baghdad Railway Company relinquished operations in southern Mesopotamia to the British and gave the Russians a monopoly over railways in northern Persia. French financial investment in the project also helped the achievement of a compromise (Strachan, *First World War*, vol. 1, 33).

17. Hopkirk, *Secret Service*, 23–24; Taylor, *Struggle for Mastery*, 383.

18. Hopkirk, *Secret Service*, 24.

19. Mohs, *Military Intelligence*, 14–15.

20. Antonius, *Arab Awakening*, 140.

21. Teitelbaum, *Hashimite Kingdom*, 41, states that the British ambassador to the court of the Sultan was instrumental in getting Hussein appointed as Sharif of Mecca.

22. According to Teitelbaum, *Hashimite Kingdom*, 68–69, before Abdullah left for Cairo, he confided to the French consul that he was disgusted with the Ottomans, and that he planned to give up his seat in the Ottoman parliament.

23. Abdullah used the pretext of going to Cairo in order to improve the traveling conditions of the annual pilgrimage to Mecca and in order to sound out the British. See Westrate, *Arab Bureau*, 14.

24. The Hejaz Railway was a narrow-gauge railway built mostly by the Ottomans with German advice and support; it ran from Damascus to Medina. The railway reached Medina on September 1, 1908, the Sultan's anniversary.

25. Cited in Mohs, *Military Intelligence*, 15.

SIX • *Middle East Delusions: The Great Arab Revolt*

1.   Elie Kedourie, *In the Anglo-Arab Labyrinth: The McMahon-Husayn Correspon-dence and Its Interpretations, 1914–1939* (Cambridge: Cambridge University Press, 1976), 108.

2.   The description of the surrender of the British forces at Kut is based on Russell Braddon, *The Siege* (New York: Viking, 1969), passim.

3.   This is only an approximate number; according to Kitchener's speech in the House of Lords, the total of those who surrendered was six thousand Indian and 2,970 British troops.

4.   Unlike the Western practice of hanging a person by snapping the neck, the Otto-man mode of execution relied on choking the victim at the end of a rope.

5.   The British Army doctors suspected enteritis, cholera, or even poisoning.

6.   Around thirteen thousand Allied troops survived at the time of surrender, of these, 70 percent of the British and 50 percent of the Indian troops died of disease or were killed by the Ottomans.

7.   The battle of Gallipoli took place at the Gallipoli Peninsula in present-day Turkey, west of the Dardanelles, from April 25, 1915, to January 9, 1916. The British lost 21,255 killed and 52,230 wounded. In addition, 145,000 British troops became ill from enteric fever, dysentery, and diarrhea. Other Commonwealth casualties (Aus-tralian, New Zealand, Newfoundland, and Indian troops) included 11,702 killed and 28,060 wounded. The French suffered ten thousand killed and seventeen thousand wounded.

8.   Hussein explained to the Turkish authorities was that a jihad supported by Mecca would result in the British blockading the Red Sea and causing great hard-ship to its inhabitants.

9.   Islamic juridical opinion in Egypt and India declared that it was incumbent upon Muslims to obey the British (Finkel, *Osman's Dream*, 529).

10.   Despite British efforts to discourage the practice, Indian Muslims made consider-able donations to the railway project, regardless of the fact that most of them reached Mecca after a voyage by sea. In 1990, contributions amounted to 417,000 Turkish lira; between 1903 and 1908 they climbed from 651,184 to 1,127,894 lira. The railway carried approximately thirty thousand pilgrims per year. See Kemal H. Karpat, *The Politicization of Islam: Reconstructing Identity, State, Faith and Com-munity in the Late Ottoman State* (Oxford: Oxford University Press, 2001), 255.

11.   Lowell Thomas produced a show, *The Last Crusade*, part documentary and part lore, that played to large audiences in New York and London. In 1924, *The Last Crusade* was published as a book entitled *With Lawrence in Arabia* (New York: Century, 1924).

12. H. V. F. Winstone, *The Illicit Adventure: The Story of Political and Military Intelligence in the Middle East from 1898 to 1926* (London: Jonathan Cape, 1982), 247–48.

13. The creation of the Arab Bureau in 1916 came after Sir Mark Sykes returned from a major tour of almost six months in 1915 to the Balkans, the Persian Gulf, Egypt, and India to discuss the future of the Near and Middle East with British officials in the regions. Part of his soundings included the idea of establishing a bureau to take over the administration of Arab affairs. Sykes came under considerable opposition from various quarters, including the viceroy of India, who believed that the new organization would encroach on his areas of jurisdiction. See also Fromkin, *Peace*, 170–71, and Westrate, *Arab Bureau*, 27–32.

14. But the compromise to establish the Arab Bureau was necessary, not only to appease the fears of the viceroy of India, but more importantly those of the India Office, the Foreign Office, and other agencies of British foreign policy.

15. In early February 1916, both the French and British cabinets approved the Sykes-Picot Agreement, which was then brought to Moscow in April, and the process was completed on May 1916. The region was divided into areas of direct British and French rule, and others defined as zones of influence. The Syrian littoral, as well as southeastern Turkey and Lebanon, came under direct French administration, while the interior of Syria, together with northern Mesopotamia around Mosul, was decreed a zone of influence. Britain was allocated control of areas roughly comprising today's Jordan, southern Mesopotamia (including Basra and Baghdad), and a small area around Haifa, to allow access to a Mediterranean port. Jerusalem and the holy places came under an international administration, but Britain would retain the ports of Haifa and Acre. The rest, including most of Arabia, was to be placed under an international administration that would include representatives of the Sharif of Mecca. In exchange for agreeing to the Anglo-French partition of the Middle East, Russia was to acquire Constantinople, the Straits, and the Ottoman Armenian provinces.

16. "Extracts from a Report on Feisal's Operations, 30 October 1916," *Arab Bulletin*, vol. 1, bulletin 31, 465.

17. Malcolm Brown, ed., *T. E. Lawrence in War and Peace: An Anthology of the Military Writings of Lawrence of Arabia* (London: Greenhill, 2005), 61. Originally published in Arnold W. Lawrence, ed., *Secret Despatches from Arabia* (London: Golden Cockerel Press, 1939).

18. Antonius, *Arab Awakening*, 248.

19. Efraim Karsh and Inari Karsh, *Empires of the Sand: The Struggle for Mastery in the Middle East, 1789–1923* (Cambridge: Harvard University Press, 1999), 231, argue that the Sykes-Picot Agreement constituted recognition, by the Entente powers, of the Arabs' right to self-determination. Alan Palmer, *The Decline and Fall of the*

Ottoman Empire (New York: Barnes & Noble, 1992), 236, writes that the agreement amplified, clarified, and complemented McMahon's proposals rather than invalidated them.

20. Regardless of his other recorded comments, T. E. Lawrence described the Sykes-Picot Agreement in *Seven Pillars of Wisdom: A Triumph* (New York: Penguin, 1962), 282–83, as a fraud and claimed that he "vowed to make the Arab revolt the engine of its own success . . . and vowed to lead it so madly in the final victory that expediency should counsel to the Powers a fair settlement of the Arab's moral claims." Elie Kedourie, *The Chatham House Version and Other Middle Eastern Studies* (London: Weidenfeld & Nicolson, 1970), 24, cites Gilbert Clayton, expressing his disquiet and dissatisfaction at the outcome of the Sykes-Picot Agreement.

21. Westrate, *Arab Bureau*, 205.

22. In 1909, Arab officers in the Ottoman army in Istanbul founded al-Ahd (The Covenant). A year earlier, two Arab students in Istanbul established another secret society, al-Fatat. The full name was Jamiyyat al-Umma al-Arabiyya al-Fatat (The Society of the Young Arab Nation). The program of both societies was to enhance the status of Arabs in the Ottoman Empire, but after the outbreak of war they decided to seek independence. See Eliezer Tauber, *The Arab Movements in World War I* (London: Frank Cass, 1993), 2–3.

23. Initially, the societies had approached Ibn Saud, but he declined. See Tauber, *Arab Movements*, 61.

24. "Statement by Captain X," Cairo, 12 September 1915, FO 882/15, TNA.

25. Tauber, *Arab Movements*, 73.

26. The McMahon letter of October 24, 1915, was most significant in that it promised British support for Arab independence and accepted Hussein's delineation of the borders of the proposed state. This letter and the rest of the McMahon correspondence remain controversial, as the British commitments are in dispute. In the letter, McMahon writes: "Subject to the above modifications [referring to parts of Syria that would be excluded from the new Arab state] Great Britain is prepared to recognize and support the independence of the Arabs in all the regions within the limits demanded by the Sharif of Mecca." McMahon's language was generally evasive. Although he conceded Arab independence, he stressed that British officials would be needed to organize the administration of Arab countries. See Hurewitz, *Diplomacy*, vol. 2, 14–15. Fromkin, *Peace*, 183, rightly points out that, under those circumstances, the Arab states would be British protectorates.

27. Tauber, *Arab Movements*, 76. Tauber provides a complete breakdown of the membership of the societies, as well as their participation in the revolt. He indicates that al-Fatat had a membership of thirty-seven before the war, with another seventy-eight during the conflict; al-Ahd included fifty-four before 1914, while an

additional fifty-seven signed up during the course of World War I. Only forty-six of them took part in the fighting (twenty-nine from al-Fatat and seventeen from al-Ahd). See also Tauber, *Arab Movements*, 113.

28. Tauber, *Arab Movements*, 221–22.

29. On the various scholarly interpretations of Arab nationalism and its relationship to the Great Arab Revolt, see Dawisha, *Arab Nationalism*, 30–40. Also, on the Islamic character of Arab nationalism, see Efraim Karsh, *Islamic Imperialism: A History* (New Haven: Yale University Press, 2006).

30. Jeremy Wilson, *Lawrence of Arabia: The Authorised Biography of T. E. Lawrence* (New York: Atheneum, 1990), 404.

31. The Bolsheviks published the Sykes-Picot Agreement in *Izvestia* and *Pravda* on November 23, 1917. Three days later, on November 26, the *Manchester Guardian* published it in English.

32. On these debates, see Karsh, *Islamic Imperialism*, 127–30, 130n10.

33. Antonius, *Arab Awakening*, 267.

34. Regardless of the small number of activists in the Arab secret societies, those Arabs who joined the British leaders in the war had the opportunity to take part in the debates over the future of the Middle East, and a few had the opportunity of gaining experience in the government within the British mandate administrations (Dawisha, *Arab Nationalism*, 41).

SEVEN • *Spies, Adventurers, and Religious Warriors*

1. Koestler, *Promise and Fulfilment*, 50.

2. Charles Allen, *God's Terrorists: The Wahhabi Cult and the Hidden Roots of Modern Jihad* (London: Little, Brown, 2006), 244–45.

3. Ibid., 245.

4. Ibid., 246.

5. Winstone, *Illicit Adventure*, 143.

6. Ibid., 149.

7. Ibid., 151.

8. Ibid., 152.

9. Ibid., 153. According to Allen, *God's Terrorists*, 247–48, Shakespear was observing the battle when Ibn Saud's infantrymen near him ran away, leaving him to face a party of Ibn Rashid's cavalry. Shakespear, however, was not manning the gun but held his ground on the summit of the dune and defended himself with his revolver.

10. The Secret Service Bureau was created in 1909 "to take charge of all matters relating to intelligence gathering." In 1916, the bureau was renamed the Directorate of

Military Intelligence and was divided into two sections: MI5 dealt with internal security and counterintelligence, while MI6 was responsible for overseas espionage and eventually became the SIS. In popular literature the current SIS is still referred to as MI6. See Nigel West, *MI5: British Security Service Operations, 1909–1945* (London: Triad Granada, 1983), 38.

11. Winstone, *Illicit Adventure*, 9.

12. Philby had also been an officer in the countersedition section of the Indian Police Special Branch.

13. From 1904 to 1913, Cox had been the political resident in the Persian Gulf of the government of India. Cox appointed Philby head of the financial department of the British administration in Mesopotamia.

14. The other Englishman was Captain Forster Sadler of the 47th Regiment. In 1819, Sadler was sent from India to secure the assistance of Ibrahim Pasha to put down piracy in the Persian Gulf. At that time Ibrahim was busy, on behalf of the Ottoman Sultan, destroying the Wahhabi rebellion led by Ibn Saud's forefathers. See Elizabeth Monroe, *Philby of Arabia* (Reading: Ithaca, 1973), 53.

15. Quoted in Allen, *God's Terrorists*, 254.

16. Albert Hourani, *A History of the Arab Peoples* (New York: Warner, 1991), 319. This was a factor in Ibn Saud's decision to destroy the more radical Wahhabi tribesmen, since he was afraid that the British would intervene to stop the Wahhabis from raiding Iraq and Syria. See Allen, *God's Terrorists*, 255.

17. On November 7, 1918, four days before the Armistice, Britain and France had issued the Anglo-French Declaration to the Arabs, essentially granting them self-determination but no single sovereign state. Philby viewed this as another betrayal that, along with the Balfour Declaration and the Sykes-Picot Agreement, negated the British promise of a single unified Arab nation as the reward for the Arabs having fought for the Allies.

18. Iraq, carved out of the region of Mesopotamia by Winston Churchill when he was Colonial Secretary, with advice from T. E. Lawrence, was essentially the three former Ottoman provinces of Basra, Baghdad, and Mosul.

19. Eliezer Tauber, *The Formation of Modern Syria and Iraq* (London: Frank Cass, 1995), 315.

20. Ibid., 207.

21. Fromkin, *Peace*, 449.

22. H. V. F. Winstone, *Gertrude Bell* (London: Jonathan Cape, 1978), 207.

23. Ibid.

24. Margret MacMillan, *Paris 1919: Six Months That Changed the World* (New York: Random House, 2003), 397. According to MacMillan, between 1909 and 1919, British petroleum imports quadrupled, and most of the increase came from out-

side the British Empire (from the United States, Mexico, Russia, and Persia). MacMillan adds that the British navy was arguing, without further evidence, that the Iraqi oilfields were the largest in the world. See MacMillan, *Paris 1919*, 395–96.

25. Gertrude Bell, *Review of the Civil Administration of Mesopotamia* (London: HMSO, 1920): quoted in Georgina Howell, *Gertrude Bell: Queen of the Desert, Shaper of Nations* (New York: Farrar, Straus & Giroux, 2006), 329.

26. Howell, *Gertrude Bell*, 320. The population of Iraq in 1920 was approximately 50 percent Shiite, 25 percent Sunni, and the rest included smaller minorities of Jews and Christians. A further complication was that half of the population was Arab; the rest included Kurds, Assyrians, and Persians. MacMillan, *Paris 1919*, 398.

27. As was the case with Philby, the government of India employed Wilson. During the interwar years he maintained his colorful career. He worked in business, and in 1933 he was elected a member of Parliament. At the outbreak of war in 1939, he volunteered for the Royal Air Force as an air gunner; he was shot down over France on May 31, 1940.

28. Tauber, *Formation*, 317

29. Monroe, *Philby of Arabia*, 99–100.

30. Ibid., 105.

31. Ibid., 125.

32. Philby converted to Islam in 1930.

33. He began as an ardent Christian, became an atheist and socialist at Cambridge University, and after his conversion to Islam he was named Abdullah by Saud. See Monroe, *Philby of Arabia*, 152–53; Daniel Yergin, *The Prize: The Epic Quest for Oil, Money, and Power* (New York: Free Press, 1991), 287.

34. Philby provided the scientific name for the Arabian woodpecker (*Desertipicus* [now *Dendrocopos*] *dorae*), as well as naming a subspecies of owl (*Otus scops pamelae*). He named most of his birds after women he admired.

35. Monroe, *Philby of Arabia*, 127; Allen, *God's Terrorists*, 249.

36. Kim Philby, *My Silent War: The Autobiography of a Spy* (New York: Modern Library, 2002), 131–32; originally published in 1968.

37. Yuri Modin, "On Kim Philby," in ibid., i.

38. John le Carré, "On Kim Philby," in ibid., i.

39. Cited in Yergin, *Prize*, 286.

40. Monroe, *Philby of Arabia*, 133.

41. SOCAL was owned by John D. Rockefeller, which made him one of the richest men in the world. In 1911 the United States ruled that SOCAL was a monopoly and had to be broken up into thirty-four companies. Today ExxonMobil represents a major part of the original company.

42. Thanks to Philby's intervention and Ibn Saud's need for funds, SOCAL acquired the rights to excavate for oil.

43. In return for the concessions, SOCAL agreed to pay the Saudis £35,000 in gold as a down payment, £30,000 in the form of a loan, and £5,000 as an advance royalty. Eighteen months later, SOCAL would provide a second loan of £20,000. The loans were to be repaid out of future petroleum royalties. See Yergin, *Prize*, 291.

44. Ibid., 290–91.

45. In 1949, the Saudi share of oil revenue was $39 million. See ibid., 446–47.

46. Monroe, *Philby of Arabia*, 269–71.

EIGHT · *Absolute Faith: The Muslim Brotherhood and the Politics of Intelligence*

1. Spoken in response to his sister's pleas to appeal his death sentence and accept Nasser's proposed mercy shortly before his execution. See Lawrence Wright, *The Looming Tower: Al-Qaeda and the Road to 9/11* (New York: Vintage, 2006), 31.

2. Artemis Cooper, *Cairo in the War, 1939–1945* (London: Hamish Hamilton, 1989), 4.

3. Wright, *Looming Tower*, 36

4. Ibid., 37.

5. Qutb's brother, Muhammad, has tried to claim that the jihad espoused in the writings of Sayyid emphasized the intellectual and moral efforts of Muslims to defend their faith rather than violence. See Charles Tripp, "Sayyid Qutb: The Political Vision," in Rahnema, *Pioneers*, 177.

6. Kepel, *Muslim Extremism*, 34.

7. Gilles Kepel, *The War for Muslim Minds: Islam and the West*, trans. Pascale Ghazaleh (Cambridge: Harvard University Press, 2004), 78–83, 174–75.

8. Kepel, *Muslim Extremism*, 39.

9. Ibid., 40. Qutb enrolled at the Colorado State College of Education and earned a master's degree.

10. Ibid., 40–44; Tripp, "Sayyid Qutb," 158.

11. Robert Irwin, "Is This the Man Who Inspired Bin Laden?," *The Guardian*, 1 November 2001.

12. Robert Baer, *Sleeping with the Devil: How Washington Sold Our Soul for Saudi Crude* (New York: Three Rivers, 2003), 127.

13. Rashid Khalidi, *The Iron Cage: The Story of the Palestinian Struggle for Statehood* (Boston: Beacon, 2006), xxii; Dreyfuss, *Devil's Game*, 79.

14. Baer, *Sleeping*, 99.

15. See Chapter 12.

16. Banna founded the MB in the city of Ismailia with six workers of the Suez Canal Company.

17. Lia, *Society*, 41; Mitchell, *Muslim Brothers*, 9.

18. Kepel, *Jihad*, 27.

19. Dawisha, *Arab Nationalism*, 102.

20. The mandate for Palestine was awarded by the League of Nations to the British in July 1922. The actual document was internationally recognized by the Great Powers of the day. The mandate for Palestine included the entire text of the Balfour Declaration and, like the Balfour Declaration, did not make any references to the Arabs in Palestine. For details of the establishment of the mandate, see Khalidi, *Iron Cage*, 32.

21. Benny Morris, *1948: A History of the First Arab-Israeli War* (New Haven: Yale University Press, 2008), 12, writes that the outbreaks of 1920, 1929, and 1936–1939 grew progressively more lethal and more extensive.

22. Al-Husseini came from a prominent and influential Jerusalem family. After the First World War, he found employment as a clerk with Gabriel Haddad, a Christian-Arab advisor to Ronald Storrs, the military governor of Jerusalem. In 1919, when Haddad was transferred to Damascus and assumed the position of commissioner of public safety, al-Husseini followed along and soon became involved with the Arab nationalists supporting Feisal's claim to the crown of Syria. After Haddad was transferred to London, al-Husseini returned to Palestine and helped organize demonstrations in Jerusalem in support of Feisal and shortly after against the Jews. The demonstration of April 4, 1920, led to a wave of violence with both Jewish and Arab fatalities. The British were taken by surprise by the intensity of the Arab protests and tried to arrest the ringleaders, including al-Husseini. See Philip Mattar, *The Mufti of Jerusalem: Al-Hajj Amin al-Husayni and the Palestinian National Movement* (New York: Columbia University Press, 1988), 15–17.

23. The British administration in Palestine appointed a Muslim committee of notables to elect the Mufti of Jerusalem. Four candidates were selected and the committee had to choose three with the largest number of votes. Al-Husseini was effectively eliminated (Mattar, *Mufti*, 25).

24. David G. Dalin and John F. Rothmann, *Icon of Evil: Hitler's Mufti and the Rise of Radical Islam* (New York: Random House, 2008), 21.

25. Ibid. In 1918, according to Kedourie, *Chatham House*, 63, Richmond was languishing in the Imperial War Graves Commission when he was transferred to Jerusalem, thanks to Storrs.

26. Dalin and Rothmann, *Icon of Evil*, 21.

27. Kedourie, *Chatham House*, 65.

28. Mattar, *Mufti*, 24–26, points out that there is no documentary evidence to support Kedourie's assertion that Richmond's intervention influenced Samuel.

29. The Husseini family claimed descent from Arab aristocracy back to the time of Mohammed and, with few interruptions, had held the position of Mufti since the seventeenth century (Mattar, *Mufti*, 24).

30. Mattar, *Mufti*, 27.

31. Khalidi, *Iron Cage*, 56.

32. Harris, *Nationalism*, 178–79; Mitchell, *Society*, 16.

33. Dawisha, *Arab Nationalism*, 108.

34. On one occasion Western and Middle East radicals even collaborated on a joint operation. On June 27, 1976, two Palestinians from the Popular Front for the Liberation of Palestine—External Operations (PFLP—EO) hijacked Air France Flight 139 with two Germans, Wilfried Böse and Brigitte Kuhlmann, of the German Revolutionäre Zellen (RZ).

35. Harris, *Nationalism*, 179.

36. The proposal called for the division of Palestine into three parts: the British would retain the religious section, including Jerusalem and Bethlehem; there would be a Jewish state in Galilee; and the rest of Palestine was to be united with Transjordan in a single state ruled by Britain's protégé Abdullah bin al-Hussein.

NINE · *The British-Jewish Military Alliance*

1. Mark Twain, *The Innocents Abroad* (Mineola, NY: Dover, 2003), 559.

2. Kathleen Christison, *Perceptions of Palestine* (Berkeley: University of California Press, 1999), 17.

3. Wingate had a reputation as an eccentric. He often wore an alarm clock around his wrist, which would go off, and he walked around with a raw onion hung around his neck, which he would bite into for a snack. Occasionally, he strolled around without any clothing. In Palestine, for example, recruits were used to seeing him step out of the shower wearing nothing but a shower cap and while continuing to scrub himself with a shower brush barking orders. See Charles McMoran Wilson, *Churchill: Taken from the Diaries of Lord Moran* (Boston: Houghton Mifflin, 1966).

4. Tom Segev, *One Palestine Complete: Jews and Arabs Under the British Mandate* (New York: Henry Holt, 1999), 429.

5. Liddell Hart to Churchill, 11 November 1938, 80/69/5, Haganah Archive.

6. John Bierman, *Fire in the Night: Wingate of Burma, Ethiopia, and Zion* (New York: Random House, 1999), 64–66.

7. Trevor Royle, *Orde Wingate: Irregular Soldier* (London: Weidenfeld & Nicolson, 1995), 98.

8. Ibid.

9. The pipeline was completed in 1935 by the British Iraq Petroleum Company.

10. Mordecai Naor, *Lexicon of the Haganah Defence Force* (Tel Aviv: Ministry of Defence, 1992), 140.

11. Gudrun Kramer, *A History of Palestine: From the Ottoman Conquest to the Founding of the State of Israel* (Princeton: Princeton University Press, 2002), 291.

12. In 1929, major clashes between Jews and Arabs over the use of a gender partition and the presence of tables and chairs by the Wailing Wall shattered the temporary peace of the 1920s. Tensions were further fueled by a variety of conspiracy theories claiming that the Jews were planning to rebuild the Temple of Solomon. During one week of fighting, over 250 people were killed, including 133 Jews and 116 Arabs, as well as 580 injured. See Kramer, *Palestine*, 232.

13. Khalidi, *Iron Cage*, 57–58, argues that the British had only recognized the Jews as a political or national entity and thus intended to divide, distract, and divert Palestinian Arabs so they would not unite as a national entity against the mandate.

14. Benny Morris, *Righteous Victims: A History of the Zionist-Arab Conflict, 1881–2001* (New York: Vintage, 1999), 128.

15. Kramer, *Palestine*, 271.

16. On April 25 members of the political parties formed the Arab Higher Committee, chaired by the Mufti.

17. Khalidi, *Iron Cage*, 65–73.

18. Morris, *Righteous Victims*, 131–32; Kramer, *Palestine*, 274.

19. However, the primary motive of these Arab leaders was economic. The outbreak of the Spanish Civil War had eliminated the competition for Palestinian citrus fruits, and the harvest was approaching. Under the new circumstances, prices had soared. See Kramer, *Palestine*, 278.

20. Ibid., 280–81.

21. Ibid., 276.

22. Morris, *Righteous Victims*, 144–45.

23. Haggai Eshed, *Reuven Shiloah—The Man Behind the Mossad: Secret Diplomacy in the Creation of Israel*, trans. David and Leah Zinder (Portland: Frank Cass, 1997), 32.

24. One such commander was Yitzhak Sadeh, who later became commander of the Palmach; others were Moshe Dayan and Yigal Allon. See Samuel Katz, *Israeli Elite Units Since 1948* (Oxford: Osprey, 1988), 3.

25. Yitzhak Sadeh also selected the best fighters of the Nodedot and other combat units at the Haganah's disposal to create the Haganah's first commando unit, its Plugot Sadeh, or FOSH. As *sadeh* is also the Hebrew word for field, this unit could be named "field companies," as well as "Sadeh's companies." It comprised a semiautonomous strike force that would, by 1938, command over 1,500 well-trained fighters, who conducted lightning raids against hostile Arab targets. See Katz, *Elite*, 3.

26. Bierman, *Fire*, 83.

27. Ibid., 86.

28. Ibid., 90.

29. Ibid., 98.

30. Despite this friendly-fire debacle, the action was a major success. At least nine Arab rebels were killed with two of the dead and five of the wounded attributed to the SNS. Wingate's own estimates put the numbers at fifteen killed and at least twenty wounded. Wingate was awarded the DSO for his actions. See: Bierman, *Fire,* 98–103.

31. Ibid., 107, 115–17.

32. Ibid., 108.

33. Ibid., 125.

34. John Masters, *The Road Past Mandalay* (New York: Bantam, 1979), 217–29.

35. Eshed, *Shiloah*, 42–43.

36. Ian Black and Benny Morris, *Israel's Secret Wars: The Untold History of Israeli Intelligence* (London: Hamish Hamilton, 1991), 35.

37. Jacques Derogy and Hesi Carmel, *The Untold History of Israel* (New York: Random House, 1979), 50.

38. Eshed, *Shiloah*, 45.

39. Sherut Yediot (SHAI), Information Service, was the primary intelligence-gathering apparatus of the Jewish community from the mid-1930s until the establishment of the Israel state in 1948, at which point it was assimilated into the Israeli intelligence community.

40. Eshed, *Shiloah*, 48.

41. The Hebrew term for such undercover soldiers is *mista'aravim*, based on the verb "to become" and *aravim* (Arabs). The term was revived during the Intifada to refer to undercover Special Forces units operating in the occupied Palestinian territories. Those units have been active until today, and the term remains in use.

42. Eshed, *Shiloah*, 47.

43. Black and Morris, *Secret Wars*, 32–33. Reuven Zaslany (later Reuven Shiloah, after he Hebraized his name post-1948) was an intelligence expert for the Jewish Agency's Political Department and their chief liaison officer with British security. He also organized the Yishuv's first intelligence network, SHAI.

44. Eshed, *Shiloah*, 48.

45. Hermione Ranfurly, *To War with Whitaker: Wartime Diaries of Countess Ranfurly, 1939–45* (London: Heinemann, 1994), 76.

46. Black and Morris, *Secret Wars*, 52.

47. Eshed, *Shiloah*, 52.

48. Derogy and Carmel, *Untold History*, 53.

49. Katz, *Elite*, 5.

50. Ibid.

51. Derogy and Carmel, *Untold History*, 57.

52. Katz, *Elite*, 5.

53. Moshe Dayan in Eshed, *Shiloah*, 53.

54. Eshed, *Shiloah*, 54.

55. Ibid., 55.

56. A Jew and a Zionist, he would later change his name to Abba Eban and immigrate to Israel, where he would become Israel's ambassador to the United Nations and eventually foreign minister.

57. Derogy and Carmel, *Untold History*, 52–53.

58. Ibid., 57.

59. Eshed, *Shiloah*, 56.

60. At Cairo MI9 there was, besides Simmons, another veteran of Palestine from the days of the Arab Revolt: Brigadier Dudley Clark.

61. Ha'Mossad le'Aliya Bet (Institute for Immigration B) was a special clandestine organization within the Haganah, formed in 1939 to facilitate illegal immigration in violation of the 1939 White Paper quotas on the permissible number of Jewish immigrants to Palestine. Though its networks were largely inactive during the war, they remained in place and went into operation again at the war's end.

62. Originally 250 Palestinian Jews had volunteered, and 170 received training for the mission. See Eshed, *Shiloah*, 59–68.

63. Ibid., 54–55.

TEN • *Kill the Mufti: Politics and Blowback*

1. 7 October 1940, 367/31, FO 371/32900, TNA.

2. Mattar, *Mufti*, 95. According to an intelligence report from the British military attaché, based on information received from the Turkish general staff on May 3, 1940, the Mufti's organization in Baghdad had received a large sum of money, presumably from the Germans, with instructions to begin the rebellion by assassinating British, French, and friendly Arab officials (Military Attaché Ankara to C-in-C Middle East, 3 May 1940, E1940, FO 371/24568, TNA).

3. C-in-C Middle East to War Office, 1 October 1940, E2802/448/93, FO 371/24558, TNA; Martin Gilbert, *Finest Hour*, vol. 6 of *Winston S. Churchill* (London: Heinemann, 1983), 1079, 1124.

4. Mattar, *Mufti*, 95.

5. Specifically the Mufti's chief political opponent, Raghib al-Nashashibi. The Nashashibi family were historical rivals of the Husseinis for the leadership of the Arabs in Palestine.

6. Leo Amery to Secretary of State, 5 October 1940, E2762/367/31, FO 371/24568, TNA.

7. Secretary of State to Leo Amery, 10 October 1940, E2762/367/31, FO 371/24568, TNA.

8. 10 October 1941, E2762/367/31, FO 371/24568, TNA.

9. 17 October 1940, E2900/367/31, FO 371/24568, TNA.

10. 18 November 1940, E2900/367/31, FO 371/24568, TNA.

11. Foreign Office minutes, 18 November 1940, E2900/367/31, FO 371/24568, TNA.

12. Ibid.

13. Yitshaq Ben-Ami, *Years of Wrath, Days of Glory: Memoirs from the Irgun* (New York: Speller, 1982), 245–46, claims that it was David Raziel's idea to kidnap or eliminate the Mufti. The word used in his memoirs was to "acquire" the Mufti. He also adds that the British in Habbaniya had difficulty in obtaining Arab dress for the Irgun commandos. The Irgun (Hairgun HaTzva'i HaLe'umi BeEretz Yisra'el or National Military Organization in the Land of Israel) was one of three paramilitary organizations, along with the Stern Gang and the Palmach, that originated out of the Haganah (Jewish Defense Organization). The members of the Irgun broke away from the Haganah because they decided to retaliate against the Arab revolt of 1936–1939, whereas the Haganah had adopted a policy of defense. See Y. S. Brenner, "The Stern Gang, 1940–1948," in *Palestine and Israel in the 19th and 20th Centuries*, ed. Elie Kedourie and Sylvia G. Haim (London: Frank Cass, 1982), 114.

14. Wavell was confronted by multiple threats: the German Afrika Korps in the Western Desert, the British withdrawal from mainland Greece, and the immediate threat to Crete, as well as the real possibility that a hostile government in Iraq could cut off oil supplies and expose his eastern flank to German infiltration from Vichy-controlled Syria. He tried to transfer the Iraq problem to India Command, but Churchill insisted that Wavell undertake the relief of the British forces in Iraq, because it was quicker and closer to bring reinforcements from Palestine. See Victoria Schofield, *Wavell: Soldier and Statesman* (London: John Murray, 2007), 183–84.

15. Ben-Ami, *Years of Wrath*, 246–46; J. Bowyer-Bell, *Terror out of Zion* (London: Avon, 1997), 70.

16. William Seymour, *British Special Forces: The Story of Britain's Undercover Soldiers* (Toronto: Grafton, 1985), 152.

17. As reich protector (governor) of Bohemia and Moravia, Heydrich suppressed the black market, increased food rations and pensions, and introduced unemployment insurance. On the other hand, anyone linked with the resistance movement or the black market faced torture and execution. Under Heydrich's administration, Czechoslovakia was pacified and industrial output went up. Because of his success in Prague, Hitler was considering making him governor of Paris. When

British intelligence became aware of this, they decided that Heydrich had to be stopped before he had a similar impact on France and eventually all occupied Europe.

18. Heydrich died of his wounds one week later on June 4, 1942. As a consequence, approximately thirteen thousand people were arrested, deported, imprisoned, or killed by the SS. On June 10, 1942, all males over the age of sixteen in the village of Lidice, twenty-two kilometers northwest of Prague, and another village, Ležáky, were executed. All houses and buildings in the two villages were burned and the ruins leveled. For a detailed account of the Heydrich assassination and its consequences, see Callum MacDonald, *The Killing of SS Obergruppenführer Reinhard Heydrich* (New York: Free Press, 1989).

19. According to a poll commissioned by the American consulate in Jerusalem at the beginning of the war, 88 percent of Palestinian Arabs favored Germany and only 9 percent Great Britain. See Morris, *1948*, 21.

20. 21 March 1940, 28 March 1940, 29 May 1940, and 11 September 1940, HS 3/201, TNA.

21. Morris, *1948*, 28.

22. Morris, *1948*, 28; Franklin Lindsay, *Beacons in the Night: With the OSS and Tito's Partisans in Wartime Yugoslavia* (Stanford: Stanford University Press, 1993), 361n.

23. Lindsay, *Beacons*, 361n.

24. C. M. Keble to Lord Moyne, 16 January 1943, 89637/537/1817, HS 3/209, TNA.

25. Morris, *1948*, 29.

26. Ronald W. Zweig, *Britain and Palestine During the Second World* War (London: Royal Historical Society, 1986), 165n68.

27. Howard M. Sachar, *A History of Israel: From the Rise of Zionism to Our Time* (New York: Knopf, 2007), 247; Brenner, "Stern Gang," 115.

28. Sachar, *History of Israel*, 247.

29. Morris, *1948*, 29.

30. Ben-Ami, *Years of Wrath*, 295.

31. Brenner, "Stern Gang," 121. According to a report from MI6, passed on to Washington (21 February 1944, HNO 867108, NARA), the Irgun would destroy property but not resort to assassination, whereas the Stern Gang would easily resort to murder.

32. 28 March 1946, KV 5/30, TNA.

33. During the same period, the Haganah had a field army of sixteen thousand, while the Palmach included approximately six thousand men and women. Both organizations could draw on more recruits from a static force of forty thousand based in rural and urban areas (Colonial Office, "Palestine: Statement of Information Relating to Acts of Violence," KV 5/30, TNA).

34. Sachar, *History of Israel*, 266.

35. Brenner, "Stern Gang," 134; Colonial Office, "Palestine: Statement of Information Relating to Acts of Violence," KV 5/30, TNA.

36. In 1946, over ninety thousand Jews left Poland; along with 25,000 from the Balkans, they increased the number of refugees in the West German DP camps to 250,000. See Sachar, *History of Israel*, 264.

37. Brenner, "Stern Gang," 123.

ELEVEN • *By Blood and Fire*

1. MacSwiney said this during the course of his hunger strike following his imprisonment as a member of the IRA. MacSwiney died in Brixton Prison of malnutrition as a result of a seventy-three-day hunger strike on October 24, 1920.

2. A. W. Sansom, *I Spied Spies* (London: Harrap, 1965), 168–70.

3. Ibid., 167.

4. Ibid.

5. In another account, Moyne and his driver were killed with three bullets, each fired in rapid succession. See Thurston Clarke, *By Blood and Fire: The Attack on the King David Hotel* (New York: Putnam, 1981), 44–45.

6. Sansom, *Spies*, 180.

7. Ibid., 177.

8. Brenner, "Stern Gang," 124.

9. According to a report from the Special Investigation Branch dated November 13, 1944, the British authorities in Egypt feared that indigenous troops would see the assassins as heroes and possibly emulate their actions (CO 732/88/32, TNA).

10. The Jewish Agency ordered the Haganah to track down the members of the Stern Gang and also to help the British authorities apprehend them. As a result, 279 members of both the Stern Gang and the Irgun were apprehended by the British, with the help of the Haganah. See Christopher Sykes, *Crossroads to Israel* (Cleveland: World, 1965), 257.

11. Brenner, "Stern Gang," 131. In Israeli accounts.

12. Ben-Ami, *Years of Wrath*, 376; Morris, *1948*, 35; Brenner, "Stern Gang," 132.

13. Quoted in Sachar, *History of Israel*, 264–65.

14. Sachar, *History of Israel*, 265.

15. Richard J. Aldrich, *The Hidden Hand: Britain, America and Cold War Secret Intelligence* (New York: Overlook, 2002), 261.

16. Ibid., 259.

17. Mathew Carr, *The Infernal Machine: A History of Terrorism* (New York: New Press, 2007), 60.

18. Peter Taylor, *Provos: The IRA and Sinn Fein* (London: Bloomsbury, 1997), 21.

19. Ibid., 20. The Black and Tans earned their curious nickname from their hastily assembled uniforms, consisting of surplus dark police tunics and surplus British army khaki trousers, resembling the colors of a famous pack of Irish foxhounds: the Scarteen Black and Tans.

20. In one such operation, a unit of Black and Tans captured several IRA at Kerry Pike near Cork and proceeded to cut off the nose of one man, the tongue of another, smashed the skull of a third, and cut out the heart of the fourth unfortunate victim. (Ibid).

21. Sykes, *Crossroads*, 308. Farran, whose decorations included the DSO and the MC with two bars, subsequently emigrated to Canada, where he became a successful provincial politician and cabinet minister.

22. Fergusson, formerly Wavell's ADC in Palestine, was no stranger to special operations: he had commanded a Chindit unit (16th Infantry Brigade) in the Burmese jungle and had ended the war as director of combined operations, in operational command of Britain's commandos and other Special Forces.

23. "Roy Farran (Obituary)," *Daily Telegraph*, 5 June 2006.

24. Roy Farran, *Winged Dagger: Adventures on Special Service* (London: Collins, 1970), 348.

25. Aldrich, *Hidden Hand*, 263.

26. Ibid. Farran confessed, but his written account of the events was ruled inadmissible.

27. "Major Roy Farran (Obituary)," *The Times*, 6 June 2006.

28. Ibid.

29. Robert Kumamoto, *International Terrorism and American Foreign Relations* (Boston: Northeastern University Press, 1999), 17.

30. M. R. D. Foot, *S.O.E. in France: An Account of the Work of the British Special Operations Executive in France, 1940–1944* (London: HMSO, 1966), 13–14. The curious use of lowercase letters is to be found in the original text.

31. 89846, HS 7/269, TNA.

32. André Gerolymatos, *Guerrilla Warfare and Espionage in Greece, 1940–1944* (New York: Pella, 1992), 335–36.

33. André Gerolymatos, *Red Acropolis, Black Terror: The Greek Civil War and the Origins of Soviet-American Rivalry* (New York: Basic, 2004), passim.

34. In 1946, British code breakers successfully monitored communications between the Jewish Agency in Palestine and their representatives in London and Paris. As a result, the British security services were able to arrest 2,650 men and fifty-nine women. See Ben-Ami, *Years of Wrath*, 375–76.

35. Brenner, "Stern Gang," 132.

36. The Irgun also booby-trapped the bodies, resulting in further British casualties. See ibid., 137–38.

37. Aldrich, *Hidden Hand*, 262.

38. As early as 1946, British military security in Palestine correctly surmised that the Stern Gang had adopted new tactics of terror by indiscriminately ambushing and killing British personnel as part of the organization's plan of assassinations ([1] 1282, KV 5/30, TNA).

39. In January 1947, the British security services estimated that the Irgun and Stern Gang included approximately 474 members (or suspected members) and were able to identify the country of origin for only 129 of them. The majority came from Russia (13), Poland (51), and Palestine (24); the rest originated from Czechoslovakia (9), Austria (8), Romania (7), Germany (7), Lithuania (4), Bulgaria (2), Hungary (1), Egypt (1), Turkey (1), and Iran (1). However, they were not able to identify the origin of the other 345 members (H. J. Seager to S. H. E. Burley, 6 November 1947, KV 5/38, TNA).

40. Clarke, *Blood and Fire*, 211.

41. Aldrich, *Hidden Hand*, 261.

42. Clarke, *Blood and Fire*, 250.

43. The Haganah had approved the attack but later requested a postponement. See Clarke, *Blood and Fire*, 45, 144.

44. Ibid., 251.

45. Ibid., 40.

46. Sykes, *Crossroads*, 301.

47. Clarke, *Blood and Fire*, 251–52.

48. Bernadotte was killed because he was perceived to favor the Arabs. See Brenner, "Stern Gang," 137.

49. One difficulty was that both the Irgun and Stern Gang were organized in small, self-contained cells. The members of the cells did not use their real names or address so if one were arrested he could do little to help the authorities. See Aldrich, *Hidden Hand*, 258.

50. Final, Possible Future of Palestine, 9 September 1947, JIC(47)5(0), IOR/L/WS/1/1162, India Office Records (IOR), British Library (BL).

51. Tad Szulc, *The Secret Alliance: The Extraordinary Story of the Rescue of the Jews Since World War II* (London: Macmillan, 1991), 48–50.

52. Dorril, *MI6*, 547.

53. Jon Kimche and David Kimche, *The Secret Roads: The "Illegal" Migration of a People, 1938–1948* (London: Secker & Warburg, 1954), 161.

54. Illegal Immigration to Palestine, 9 September 1947, LCS (47) 5, CAB 81/80.

55. Roy C. Nesbit, *Eyes of the RAF: A History of Photo-Reconnaissance* (Kettering: Sutton, 1996), 267–68.

56. Dorril, *MI6*, 549.

57. Ibid., 548.

58. The British intelligence and security services generated several reports indicating that the Stern Gang, the Irgun, and even the Haganah were in contact with the Soviets or were receiving funds from them (KV 5/39, TNA).

59. Aldrich, *Hidden Hand*, 257.

60. Clarke, *Blood and Fire*, 43.

TWELVE · *The CIA and Nasser: A Muslim Billy Graham*

1. Dean Acheson, *Present at the Creation: My Years in the State Department* (New York: Norton, 1969), 567.

2. Under the terms of that arrangement the British had the right to maintain military bases and collect tolls from ships, which, in turn, were guided by English and French pilots, all constant reminders of Egypt's subservient status.

3. Heikal, *Lion's Tail*, 25.

4. Harris, *Nationalism*, 187, 192, also comments that some observers claim the communists were primarily responsible for the organized violence.

5. Matthew F. Holland, *America and Egypt: From Roosevelt to Eisenhower* (London: Praeger, 1996), 24.

6. Acheson, *Creation*, 565–66.

7. Holland, *America and Egypt*, 23; Lucas and Morey, "Hidden 'Alliance,'" 97.

8. At 9:00 P.M. on February 4, 1942, the British high commissioner, Sir Miles Lampson, flanked by a detachment of British officers and a column of tanks and armored personnel carriers, compelled Farouk to accede to their wishes.

9. Holland, *America and Egypt*, 24.

10. Heikal, *Lion's Tail*, 50n2.

11. Holland, *America and Egypt*, 26.

12. Ibid., 25.

13. Ibid. On the U.S. role in the Greek Civil War, see Gerolymatos, *Red Acropolis*.

14. The primary source for the CIA's role in Egypt, as well as in Syria, is much maligned former CIA officer Miles Copeland. His three memoirs, *Game of Nations: The Amorality of Power Politics* (New York: Simon & Schuster, 1969); *The Real Spy World* (London: Weidenfeld & Nicolson, 1974); and *The Game Player: Confessions of the CIA's Original Political Operative* (London: Arium, 1989), offer an intriguing and detailed insight into CIA operations. I agree with Lucas and Morey, "Hidden 'Alliance,'" 118n44, that documentary evidence, including archival records in Washington and London, verify most of Copeland's version of events. Scott and Morey comment that his works have been "treated with skepticism by some historians," in

part "because of his tendency to exaggerate his role in events" and by "the campaign of the Agency to discredit Copeland through 'information' to trusted contacts." Clearly, a major obstacle in intelligence history is the ability of the intelligence organizations to practice deception against historians, as well as against their enemies.

15. Copeland, *Game Player*, 153–54.

16. Ibid., 154.

17. Michael Holzman, *James Jesus Angleton, the CIA, and the Craft of Counterintelligence* (Amherst: University of Massachusetts Press, 2008), 161, suggests that Roosevelt's directorate had backed the Free Officers and later organized Nasser's security forces.

18. Wilbur Crane Eveland, *Ropes of Sand: America's Failure in the Middle East* (New York: Norton, 1980), 97n.

19. Copeland, *Game Player*, 156.

20. Initially, the CIA was established in 1947 to collect and analyze information gathered through espionage, as well as from open sources, and report to the National Security Council (NSC). Its operational arm was the OSO, a remnant of the Strategic Services Unit (SSU), which, in turn, was a leftover from the OSS. However, the secretaries of state, defense, or, for that matter, the NSC did not want the CIA to be engaged in covert action, and even though the OSO was designed for this purpose, the OPC was established to undertake clandestine operations. See Evan Thomas, *The Very Best Men: The Daring Early Years of the CIA* (New York: Simon & Schuster, 1995), 29.

21. Copeland, *Game Player*, 112–13.

22. Ibid.

23. Thomas, *Very Best*, 108.

24. Kermit Roosevelt, *Countercoup: The Struggle for the Control of Iran* (New York: McGraw-Hill, 1979), 3–4.

25. Thomas, *Very Best*, 108–9.

26. Copeland, *Game of Nations*, 198.

THIRTEEN • *The Road to Perdition: The Gehlen Organization*

1. Harry Rositzke, fomer head of CIA secret operations inside the Soviet Union, quoted in Christopher Simpson, *Blowback: The First Full Account of America's Recruitment of Nazis and Its Disastrous Effect on the Cold War, Our Domestic and Foreign Policy* (New York: Macmillan, 1988), 159.

2. Mao Zedong proclaimed the establishment of the People's Republic of China in May 1949.

3. In 1950, the United States had 369 operational bombs, and the Soviet Union, five. See Niall Ferguson, *The War of the World: Twentieth-Century Conflict and the Descent of the West* (New York: Penguin, 2006), 597.

4. John Lewis Gaddis, *The Cold War: A New History* (New York: Penguin, 2005), 29–30.

5. In October 1944, Churchill and Stalin worked out the so-called Percentages Agreement that divided the Balkans into British and Soviet spheres of influence. President Franklin D. Roosevelt was not pleased with the notion of spheres of influence dividing parts of Europe. However, in December 1944, when the Greek communists attempted to take over the country and fought the British, only the Soviet press did not condemn Churchill's actions. Stalin kept his part of the bargain. Yet, after the death of Roosevelt in April 1945 and the defeat of Churchill at the polls in July of that year, Stalin's ability to keep a bargain was lost on the new political leadership in London and Washington. Indeed, a certain degree of opportunism and territorial security guided the Soviet dictator's policies after 1946, rather than a commitment to world communism. On the Percentages Agreement, see Gerolymatos, *Red Acropolis*, 125–28, 206–7; on Stalin's foreign policy, see Vladislav Zubok and Constantine Pleshakov, *Inside the Kremlin's Cold War: From Stalin to Khrushchev* (Cambridge: Harvard University Press, 1996), chapter 2.

6. Reinhard Gehlen, *The Service: The Memoirs of General Reinhard Gehlen*, trans. David Irving (New York: World, 1972), 111.

7. Richard Helms, *A Look over My Shoulder: A Life in the Central Intelligence Agency* (New York: Ballantine, 2003), 84.

8. Gehlen, *Service*, 107–8; Joseph J. Trento, *The Secret History of the CIA* (New York: Prima, 2001), 22–23.

9. According to Trento, *Secret History*, 29, Gehlen and his group remained on an army base near Washington, D.C., for ten months; according to Richard Helms, *Look*, 88–89, Gehlen and his associates stayed only a few weeks.

10. R. Harris Smith, *OSS: The Secret History of America's First Central Intelligence Agency* (Guilford, CT: Lyons, 2005), 220.

11. Gehlen, *Service*, 116; Trento, *Secret History*, 23.

12. Simpson, *Blowback*, 52–56.

13. Ibid., 60–65.

14. Marchetti interview in Simpson, *Blowback*, 65.

15. A formal agreement of cooperation took effect in June 1949. See Prados, *Safe*, 51.

16. Helms, *Look*, 88.

17. Details concerning Operation Paperclip can be found in the Records of the Office of the Secretary of Defense, RG 330, U.S. National Archives and Records Administration (NARA).

18. "Political Islam" describes the role of a wide rage of moderate to radical religious

organizations and institutions that have emerged in the twentieth and twenty-first centuries, sometimes in opposition to colonialism, secular regimes, and outright dictatorships.

19. Yergin, *Prize*, 481

20. Thomas, *Very Best*, 29–30.

21. Tim Weiner, *Legacy of Ashes: The History of the CIA* (New York: Doubleday, 2007), 17, writes that Richard Helms, head of the OSO and later CIA director, determined that at least half the information on the Soviet Union and its Eastern European satellites was useless.

22. Thomas, *Very Best*, 36. The acronym stands for Tsentralnogo Obedineniia Politicheskikh Emigrantov iz SSSR (Central Association of Political Emigrants from the Soviet Union); it was based in Munich.

23. Ibid., 25, 36. They included Ukrainians, Czechs, Poles, Hungarians, and Russians; most had fought against the Red Army in German uniform and had sought refuge in the West.

24. Ibid., 36.

25. On the Nazi collaboration of the volunteers, see Burton Hersh, *The Old Boys: The American Elite and the Origins of the CIA* (New York: Scribner's, 1992), 274–77.

FOURTEEN • *A New Kind of War: Subversive Operations and the CIA*

1. Philby, *Silent War*, 154.

2. Charles Whiting, *Skorzeny: The Most Dangerous Man in Europe* (Conshohocken, PA: Combined, 1972), 96–97.

3. Glenn B. Infield, *Skorzeny: Hitler's Commando* (New York: Military Heritage Press, 1981), 78.

4. Heron [Stuyvesant Wainwright, Jr.] to Berding, SCI Headquarters, 12 AG, 20 December 1944, Box 89, Entry 139, RG 226, NARA.

5. SHAEF, Counter Intelligence War Room London, "The German Intelligence Service," April 1945, William J. Donovan Collection, Military History Institute, Carlisle, PA.

6. Infield, *Skorzeny*, 122.

7. Whiting, *Skorzeny*, 97; Infield, *Skorzeny*, 123.

8. Whiting, *Skorzeny*, 97, claims Skorzeny's hands were manacled behind his back, but Infield, *Skorzeny*, 126, insists that he could not have appeared before the media with his hands tied.

9. According to Infield, *Skorzeny*, 155–56, Gehlen organized Skorzeny's escape.

10. Hersh, *Old Boys*, 42.

11.   Ibid., 62.

12.   Ibid., 66.

13.   Ibid., 151–52.

14.   Trento, *Secret History*, 47.

15.   Ibid., 47–48.

16.   Ibid., 47.

17.   Operation Paperclip was also sponsored by the Joint Intelligence Objective Agency, established as a subcommittee of the Joint Intelligence Committee of the Joint Chiefs of Staff in 1945. Approximately 1,500 German scientists, engineers, technicians, and their families were recruited. For complete details, see the Records of the Office of the Security of Defense, RG 330, NARA.

18.   Trento, *Secret History*, 51–52.

19.   2 August 1948, JSPC 862/3, NARS, RG 319, NARA.

20.   The information about WIN's existence comes from Joseph Sienko, a former member of the Polish resistance; see Thomas Powers, *The Man Who Kept the Secrets* (New York: Knopf, 1979), 41. Sienko brought the news to Lieutenant General Wladyslaw Anders, the commander of the Polish army-in-exile, and claimed that WIN had five hundred members, along with twenty thousand sympathizers and another 100,000 ready to fight the communists; see Harry Rositzke, *The CIA's Secret Operations: Espionage, Counterespionage, and Covert Action* (Boulder, CO: Westview, 1988), 168–71.

21.   Edward J. Epstein, *Deception: The Invisible War Between the KGB and the CIA* (New York: Simon & Schuster, 1989), 34.

22.   Hersh, *Old Boys*, 279.

23.   Epstein, *Deception*, 34.

24.   Ibid., 34–35.

25.   Over a period of almost two years, the CIA supplied $1 million in gold sovereigns, as well as radios and other equipment. See Hersh, *Old Boys*, 279.

26.   Epstein, *Deception*, 39.

27.   Aldrich, *Hidden Hand*, 160–61.

28.   Ibid., 161–62.

29.   Ibid., 162.

30.   Ibid., 163; Hersh, *Old Boys*, 270.

31.   Philby, *Silent War*, 154.

32.   The British choice to be head of the Albanian government-in-exile, Major Abas Kupi, had also resorted to collaboration with the Axis in order to protect himself against the communist partisans. See Aldrich, *Hidden Hand*, 162.

33.   Prados, *Safe*, 61.

34.   Ibid.

35. Aldrich, *Hidden Hand*, 164.

36. Ibid.; Philby, *Silent War*, 156.

37. Prados, *Safe*, 64.

38. Hersh, *Old Boys*, 269.

39. U.S. Congress, Congressional Record, 25 April 1950.

FIFTEEN • *Nasser's Nazis*

1. Copeland, *Game Player*, 165.

2. See Chapter 12.

3. Copeland, *Game of Nations*, 103.

4. Gehlen, *Service*, 260.

5. Simpson, *Blowback*, 249.

6. Copeland, *Game of Nations*, 104.

7. Ibid.

8. Timothy Naftali, "Reinhard Gehlen and the United States," in *U.S. Intelligence and the Nazis*, ed. Richard Breitman et al. (Cambridge: Cambridge University Press, 2005), 377.

9. Naftali's review of the CIA files pertaining to some of the Nazi advisors in Egypt leaves him with the view that there was no direct link between the advisors and the CIA. This view, however, is based on the fact that the CIA files do not explicitly acknowledge such a connection. It is quite possible, however, that the absence of this information demonstrates nothing more than the CIA's censorship of its own files. Naftali does not present any evidence from the files that constitutes a denial of CIA involvement, and he notes that requests for access to further CIA documents regarding Skorzeny have been denied. See Naftali, "Gehlen," 417n166.

10. See various documents regarding the attempted recruitment of Deumling in Box 13, Entry ZZ-18, RG 263, NARA.

11. Cairo Embassy to African Department, 6 February 1953, V6703174, FO 371/102869, TNA.

12. See CIA Name Files Issue 1:32-2000/06/07 and Issue 2:45-2002/A/11/2, RG263, NARA (Lauterbacher); Issue 1:32-2000/06/07, RG263, NARA (Leers); Issue 1:51-2000/07/04 and Issue 2:52-2002/A/11/3 RG263, NARA (Tiefenbacher). For more about Bünsch, see Copeland, *Game of Nations*, 154–56.

13. The most informative British archival records regarding Voss are FO 371/102869, FO 371/108489, and FO 371/118975, TNA; the relevant U.S. records are CIA Name Files Issue 1:53-2000/07/04, and Issue 2:53-2002A/11/3, RG263, NARA.

14. It is equally likely that he was invited to Egypt by King Farouk. According to Lewis A. Frank, "Nasser's Missile Program," *Orbis* 11, no. 3 (Fall 1967): 746–57, "In 1951 a

small team headed by the World War II German armaments expert, Dr Wilhelm Voss, was asked by King Farouk's government to develop a small-caliber rocket and an arms industry for modern warfare."

15. Copeland, *Game of Nations*, 87–88; Aide-memoire from Belgian counselor, JE1202/13, FO 371/102869, TNA; African Department to Cairo Embassy, 1 April 1954, JE1203/4, FO 371/108489, TNA.

16. Voss unilaterally obtained the services of some important German technical and scientific experts, who seem to have constituted his recruiting priority. See JIC Summary, Ministry of State to Prime Minister, 30 April 1953, PM/MS/53/93, PREM 11/391, TNA.

17. The British records on Deumling are flimsy; for instance, see P. A. Wilkinson, Bonn Embassy to T. W. Garvey, Cairo Embassy, 20 March 1956, JE1194/4, FO 371/118975, TNA, which notes that "the Americans here . . . expressed particular interest in Daimling [sic]." By contrast, the relevant U.S. records are relatively extensive; see CIA Name Files Issue 1:10-2000/06/04, and Issue 2:13-2002/A/10/3, RG263, NARA.

18. A former subordinate states that Deumling may have been removed from office and transferred to the death squad because he entered into some kind of unauthorized negotiations with Polish leaders. The same source also describes Deumling as "only a lukewarm Nazi." See CIA Name Files Issue 1:10-2000/06/04, RG263, NARA.

19. Michael Wildt, *Generation des Unbedingten: Das Führungskorps des Reichssicherheitshauptamtes* (Hamburg: Hamburger Edition, 2003), 934.

20. P. A. Wilkinson, Bonn Embassy to T. W. Garvey, Cairo Embassy, 6 April 1956, JE1194/6, FO 371/118975, TNA.

21. According to an unidentified source dated July 7, 1954, Deumling "was recruited by Wilhelm Voss in November or December of 1953." See CIA Name Files Issue 1:10-2000/06/04, RG263, NARA.

22. Memo, ca. 1954, Box 13, Entry ZZ-18, RG 263, NARA.

23. Report on "Activities of German Experts in Egypt," 21 October 1954, Box 13, Entry ZZ-18, RG 263, NARA.

24. Copeland, *Game of Nations*, 81.

25. Munich to Director, 29 May 1958, Box 13, Entry ZZ-18, RG 263, NARA.

26. Frankfurt to Director, 27 May 1958, Box 13, Entry ZZ-18, RG 263, NARA.

27. Memorandum, June 1958, Box 13, Entry ZZ-18, RG 263, NARA.

28. Report on "The German Advisory Group in Egypt," ca. 1954, Box 13, Entry ZZ-18, RG 263, NARA.

29. Wildt, *Generation*, 738–39, 828–30, 934–35.

30. "Egyptian Soldiers Learn the German Way," *Daily Telegraph*, 17 July 1953, JE1202/16, FO 371/102869, TNA.

31. Minutes, August 1953, JE1202/15, FO 371/102869, TNA.

32. Hankey to Salisbury, 20 July 1953, JE1202/15, FO 371/102869, TNA.

33. Ibid.

34. Ibid.

35. JE1202/15, FO 371/102869, TNA.

36. "Egyptian Para-Military Forces," HQBTE Report, August 1953, JE1202/24, FO 371/102869, TNA.

37. HQBTE Report, May 1953, JE1202/15, FO 371/102869, TNA.

38. Hankey to Salisbury, 20 July 1953, JE1202/15, FO 371/102869, TNA.

39. Ibid.

40. "Egyptian Para-Military Forces," HQBTE Report, August 1953, JE1202/24, FO 371/102869, TNA.

41. HQBTE Report, May 1953, JE1202/15, FO 371/102869, TNA. "9 BAD" was 9th Base Ammunition Depot, Royal Army Ordnance Corps (RAOC), which was permanently situated near the village of Abu Sultan.

42. "Egyptian Para-Military Forces," HQBTE Report, 24 August 1953, JE1202/24, FO 371/102869, TNA.

43. Ibid.

44. Hankey to Salisbury, 20 July 1953, JE1202/15, FO 371/102869, TNA.

45. Ibid.

46. Ibid.

47. Cairo Chancery to African Department, 6 February 1953, JE1202/2, FO 371/102869, TNA.

48. Draft response to parliamentary question, 17 June 1953, JE1202/12, FO 371/102869, TNA.

49. Ibid.

50. Minutes, August 1953, JE1202/15, FO 371/102869, TNA.

51. Ibid.

52. According to Ambassador Caffery's dispatch, Voss himself brought up the fact that there were rumors circulating to the effect that he was a communist. Voss remarked that this was obviously impossible since the Russians were responsible for the loss of his wife and sons during the war. He mentioned the terrible conditions prevailing in east Germany as compared to the favorable situation in western Germany; in this respect Voss seemed to be under no illusions about the Russian regime in the Eastern Zone. But perhaps sensing McCarthyist American suspicions, Voss may simply have been issuing preemptive denials. See Memorandum of Conversation with Dr. Wilhelm Voss, 24 June 1953, 2905, Attachment to Embassy Despatch 2276, 28 April 1953, CIA Name File, Issue 2: 53-2002A/11/3, RG263, NARA.

53. See Heinz Vielain, *Waffenschmuggel im Staatsauftrag: Was lange in Bonn geheim bleiben musste* (Herford: Busse Seewald, 1986), passim; Martin A. Lee, *The Beast Reawakens* (New York: Routledge, 2000), 184.

54. Christopher Andrew and Vasili Mitrokhin, *The World Was Going Our Way: The KGB and the Battle for the Third World* (New York: Basic, 2005), pp. 226–27.

SIXTEEN • *A Legacy of Coups: Anglo-American Intervention in Syria*

1. A commonly repeated anecdote about the dawn of March 29, 1949, when Colonel Zaim seized control of Syria. Sami Moubayed, "Keeping an Eye on Syria: March 29, 1949," *Mideastviews: Middle East Analysis by Sami Moubayed*, 29 May 2009, http://www.mideastviews.com/articleview.php?art=387.

2. "Army Coup in Syria: Government Overthrown," *Sunday Morning Herald*, 31 March 1949; "Syria Army Takes Over Government: Leaders Ousted in Bloodless Coup d'Etat," *Evening Independent*, 30 March 1949.

3. Bonnie F. Saunders, *The United States and Arab Nationalism* (Wesport, CT: Praeger, 1996), 4; Patrick Seale, *The Struggle for Syria* (London: I. B. Tauris, 1985), 15.

4. Dreyfuss, *Devil's Game*, 47; Saunders, *Nationalism*, 2.

5. Hanna Batatu, "Syria's Muslim Brethren," *MERIP Reports*, no. 110 (November–December 1982): 12–20, 34, 36; Dreyfuss, *Devil's Game*, 47–48, 199.

6. FO 370/2719, TNA.

7. FO 371/82792, TNA.

8. Ibid.

9. Indices to Series 16, 36433C, Box 351, Entry 14, RG 226, NARA.

10. Folder 8, Box 125, Entry 99, RG 226, NARA.

11. KV 2/1970, TNA.

12. The British Foreign Office was in contact with Jamal al-Hussein in 1957. At that time, the Mufti was providing them with reports on the internal situation in Syria. See FO 371/128226, TNA.

13. VR1092/120-121, VR1092/123-124, VR1092/129-130, FO 371/115899, TNA.

14. VR1092/144, VR1092/149, FO 371/115900, TNA.

15. FO 371/82800, TNA.

16. E1284, FO 371/45542, TNA.

17. Saunders, *Nationalism*.

18. Ibid., 5–7.

19. Folder 8, Box 125, Entry 99, RG 226, NARA.

20. Folders 09271-6, 09290, 09302, Box 195, Entry 210, RG 226, NARA.

21. The British Foreign Office, however, saw the Syrian Kurds as a far smaller problem than the Iraqi and Iranian Kurds.

22. Saunders, *Nationalism*, 7.

23. Douglas Little, "Cold War and Covert Action: The United States and Syria, 1945–1958," *Middle East Journal* 44, no. 1 (Winter 1990): 52.

24. FO 371/128226, TNA.

25. Little, "Cold War," 54.

26. FO 371/82792, TNA.

27. The army ultimately failed in its assault on Israel, although Syria did gain some territory beyond its original borders, which was to become an ongoing source of tension between Syria and Israel. This newly acquired territory was converted into a demilitarized zone by the United Nations, but was gradually acquired by Israel over the coming years.

28. Seale, *Struggle*, 41–43.

29. Saunders, *Nationalism*, 10–11.

30. Meade to G-2, 18 March 1949, 350 Syria, Damascus Post Files, Box 49, RG 84, NARA, quoted in Little, "Cold War," 56.

31. Little, "Cold War"; Saunders, *Nationalism*, 11–12; 27.

32. Miles Copeland, *Game of Nations*; Stephen Meade to G-2 (Intelligence), 3 December 1948, 350 Syria, Damascus Post Files, Box 49, RG 84, NARA.

33. Saunders, *Nationalism*, 11.

34. However, there is no known documented evidence that the Iraqis were involved. See Seale, *Struggle*, 73–74.

35. Weiner, *Legacy*, 159.

36. Little, "Cold War"; Saunders, *Nationalism*, 11–12; 27.

37. FO 371/128222, TNA.

38. Weiner, *Legacy*, 159.

39. Also referred to as the Parti Populaire Syrien (PPS) or Parti Sociale Nationaliste Syrien (PSNS).

40. Weiner, *Legacy*, 159–60; Saunders, *Nationalism*, 48–51.

41. Dreyfuss, *Devil's Game*, 126–27.

42. FO 371/128222, TNA.

43. Seale, *Struggle*, 310–12.

44. FO 371/128224, TNA.

45. FO 371/128220, TNA.

46. Saunders, *Nationalism*, 41.

47. FO 371/128220, TNA.

48. Matthew Jones, "The 'Preferred Plan': The Anglo-American Working Group Report on Covert Action in Syria, 1957," *Intelligence and National Security* 19, no. 3

(Autumn 2004): 401–15; Andrew Rathmell, *Secret War in the Middle East: The Covert Struggle for Syria, 1949–1961* (London: I. B. Tauris, 1995); and Weiner, *Legacy*, 159–60.

49. FO 371/128221, TNA.

50. FO 371/128221, FO 371/128231, TNA.

51. Atrash, minister of state, investigated these activities and allegedly ignored General Sir John Glubb's smuggling of arms from Jordan to Druze tribes.

52. FO 371/128220, FO 371/128221, TNA.

53. FO 371/128220, TNA.

54. FO 371/128222, TNA.

55. FO 371/128220, TNA.

56. "U.S. Accused of Syrian Coup Attempt," *The Age*, 14 August 1957.

57. Ghazaleh sought revenge for the bombardments of Jabal Druze in 1954. While in power, Shishakli had cracked down on all opposition, including on the Druze minority on Jabal Druze mountain, who had been planning a coup in coordination with Jordan. Shishakli had ordered the shelling of the Druze areas.

58. Weiner, *Legacy*, 161–63.

59. Ibid., 162.

60. FO 371/128226, TNA.

61. FO 371/128233, TNA.

62. Andrew and Mitrokhin, *World*, 196.

63. PREM 11/2324, TNA, quoted in Richard J. Aldrich, *Espionage, Security and Intelligence in Britain, 1945–1970* (Manchester: Manchester University Press, 1998), 212–13. The "working groups" referred to were responsible for coups. See Dorril, *MI6*, 656–58.

64. FO 371/128268, TNA.

65. Ibid.

66. Batatu, "Brethren," 18.

67. Ibid.

68. The Six Day War, between the Israeli army and Syria, Egypt, and Jordan, ended with the Israelis gaining control of the Sinai Peninsula, the Gaza Strip, the West Bank, East Jerusalem, and the Golan Heights.

69. Daniel Pipes has surveyed some of the scholarship on this issue. The core debate focuses on whether the Alawis made a sectarian and strategic effort to infiltrate the ranks of the Ba'ath Party. See Daniel Pipes, "The Alawi Capture of Power in Syria," *Middle Eastern Studies* 25, no. 4 (October 1989): 429–50.

70. Andrew and Mitrokhin, *World*, 197–99.

71. Batatu, "Brethren," 19.

72. Dreyfuss, *Devil's Game*, 199–205.

73. Batatu, "Brethren," 12–20, 34–36.

74. Dreyfuss, *Devil's Game*, 199–205.

75. David Long, interview with Robert Dreyfuss, April 2004, in Dreyfuss, *Devil's Game*, 202.

76. Talcott Seelye, interview with Robert Dreyfuss, June 2004, in Dreyfuss, *Devil's Game*, 203.

77. Andrew and Mitrokhin, *World*, 198–200.

78. Ibid., 200.

79. James Kelly and William Stewart, "Syria: The Proud Lion and His Den," *Time*, September 5, 1983. The CIA is alleged to have backed Muslim Brotherhood activity during this time. See Dreyfuss, *Devil's Game*, 202–5.

80. Andrew and Mitrokhin, *World*, 199.

81. Baer, *Sleeping*, 93.

82. FO 371/170603, TNA.

83. Baer, *Sleeping*, 95–97.

SEVENTEEN • *America's Eyes in the Middle East:
The CIA and Israeli Intelligence*

1. William Hood, "Angleton's World," in *Myths Surrounding James Angleton: Lessons for American Counterintelligence*, ed. William Hood et al. (Washington, D.C.: Consortium for the Study of Intelligence, 1994), 10.

2. Weiner, *Legacy*, 123.

3. Eveland, *Ropes*, 95; William Colby and Peter Forbath, *Honorable Men: My Life in the CIA* (New York: Simon & Schuster, 1978), 365, 367.

4. Holzman, *Angleton*, 154.

5. Andrew Cockburn and Leslie Cockburn, *Dangerous Liaison: The Inside Story of the U.S.-Israeli Covert Relationship* (Toronto: Stoddart, 1991), 15.

6. Appendix 21 of Eshed, *Shiloah*.

7. Dan Raviv and Yossi Melman, *Every Spy a Prince* (Boston: Houghton Mifflin, 1990), 91.

8. Gordon Thomas, *Gideon's Spies: The Secret History of the Mossad* (New York: St. Martin's Press, 2007), 37. William Colby, the CIA director who eventually forced Angleton to retire, wrote that Angleton had been one of the CIA's earliest contacts with Israeli intelligence, but this was a highly personal and special relationship. See Colby and Forbath, *Honorable Men*, 365.

9. Cockburn and Cockburn *Dangerous*, 42–43.

10. Ibid., 43.

11. Black and Morris, *Secret Wars*, 169.

12. Yossi Melman and Dan Raviv, *Friends in Deed: Inside the U.S.-Israeli Alliance* (New York: Hyperion, 1994), 61.

13. Cockburn and Cockburn, *Dangerous*, 41; Melman and Raviv, *Friends*, 63.

14. Raviv and Melman, *Spy*, 78.

15. Ibid.

16. Riftin served on the Knesset Foreign Affairs and Security Committee. See Andrew and Mitrokhin, *World*, 225.

17. Ibid., 229.

18. Tel Aviv Embassy to Foreign Office, 17 April 1961, FO 371/1546, TNA.

19. John Ranelagh, *The Agency: The Rise and Decline of the CIA* (New York: Simon & Schuster, 1978), 286; Hersh, *Old Boys*, 359.

20. The Israelis acquired a copy from one of their agents in Poland. See Hersh, *Old Boys*, 381.

21. Melman and Raviv, *Friends*, 67.

22. Ibid., 68.

23. Cockburn and Cockburn, *Dangerous*, 63.

24. Heikal, *Lion's Tail*, 86.

25. Holzman, *Angleton*, 163–64.

26. Sachar, *History of Israel*, 312, 460–61; Christison, *Perceptions of Palestine*, 67, 96–99. Eisenhower was not so much pro-Arab and later pro-Israel as anticommunist. The fear of Soviet influence in the region colored his administration's policy toward the Middle East. See Christison, *Perceptions*, 98–99.

27. Holzman, *Angleton*, 162.

28. Cockburn and Cockburn, *Dangerous*, 65.

29. Ibid., 67.

30. Rhodri Jeffrey-Jones, *The CIA and American Diplomacy* (New Haven Yale University Press, 1989), 108–9.

31. Melman and Raviv, *Friends*, 64.

32. Ibid., 62–63.

33. Ibid., *Friends*, 65.

34. Ibid., 66.

35. Eshed, *Shiloah*, 167.

36. Melman and Raviv, *Friends*, 62, 169.

37. Ibid., 62.

38. Black and Morris, *Secret Wars*, 169.

39. Ibid., 162.

40. Ibid., 207–9.

41. Melman and Raviv, *Friends*, 89.

42. Ibid., 154.

43. Raviv and Melman, *Spy*, 93–94.

44. Ibid., 91–92.

45. Interview with Hadden, in Melman and Raviv, *Friends*, 127–29.

46. Ibid.

47. Ibid.

48. Ibid., 126.

49. Ibid., 123–25.

50. Cockburn and Cockburn, *Dangerous*, 100–101.

51. Ibid., 212–15.

52. Ibid., 100.

53. Ibid., 100–102.

54. Samuel Segev, *The Iranian Triangle* (New York: Free Press, 1988), 31. The entire Iranian security apparatus had significant foreign organizers. In their trial in 1979 following the revolution, two senior SAVAK officers, Generals Manucher Vajdi and Reza Parvaresh, revealed that the United States, Britain, Israel, and Germany had helped establish SAVAK and the Iranian army. See Segev, *Triangle*, 43.

55. Cockburn and Cockburn, *Dangerous*, 103–4.

56. Segev, *Triangle*, 32–35.

57. Ibid., 39.

58. Ibid., 104–6.

59. Raviv and Melman, *Spy*, 82.

60. Cockburn and Cockburn, *Dangerous*, 103.

61. Shay Shaul, *The Axis of Evil: Iran, Hizballah and the Palestinian Terror* (New Brunswick, NJ: Transaction, 2005).

62. Interview with Eliezer Tsafrir on November 26, 2009, Ramat Ha Sharon, Israel. Tsafrir is a former Shabak and Mossad senior officer, and the prime minister's advisor on Arab affairs. He served as head of Mossad stations in Iraqi Kurdistan, Iran, and Lebanon. He was head of the Mossad station in Iran between 1987 and 1979. He has published two books on his experiences: *Satan gadol, satan katan* [Big Satan, Small Satan: Revolution and Escape in Iran] (Tel Aviv: Maariv 2002) and *Plonter* [Labyrinth in Lebanon] (Tel Aviv: Yediot, 2006).

EIGHTEEN · *The Iranian Jihad*

1. Roosevelt, *Countercoup*, 199.

2. Cited in Michael B. Oren, *Power, Faith, and Fantasy: America in the Middle East, 1776 to the Present* (New York: Norton, 2007), 510–11.

3. Hersh, *Old Boys*, 395.

4.   The U.S. foreign policy establishment considered plans to replace Britain as the preeminent power in the Middle East. Paul Nitze, then head of the U.S. Policy Planning Staff, proposed the creation of a Middle East Defense Organization that would protect the Suez Canal and provide military security to the petroleum-producing regions and the Northern Tier countries of Iran, Pakistan, and Turkey.

5.   Nasser refused to sign on to MEDO until the United States could convince the Israelis to stop raiding Egyptian territory (Oren, *Power*, 513–14).

6.   Ibid., 514

7.   Dreyfuss, *Devil's Game*, 66.

8.   Foreign Service Dispatch, *Al Misri*, 18 August 1953.

9.   Dreyfuss, *Devil's Game*, 76.

10.   Ibid., 76–77.

11.   Sylvain Besson, "When the Swiss Protected Radical Islam in the Name of Reasons of State," *Le Temps*, 26 October 2004, quoted in Dreyfuss, *Devil's Game*, 79.

12.   A great deal has been written about the coup in Iran, including publication of the actual operation: Donald Wilber, *Overthrow of Premier Mossadeq of Iran, November 1952–August 1953* (Nottingham: Spokesman, 2006). See also Roosevelt, *Countercoup*, passim. For the British perspective, see C. M. Woodhouse, *Something Ventured: The Autobiography of C. M. Woodhouse* (London: Granada, 1982), passim. Woodhouse was Roosevelt's MI6 counterpart.

13.   Mark J. Gasiorowski, "The 1953 Coup d' Etat Against Mosaddeq" in *Mohammad Mosaddeq and the 1953 Coup in Iran*, ed. Mark J. Gasiorowski and Malcolm Byrne (Syracuse: Syracuse University Press, 2004), 254, argues that it is not certain whether Kashani received the money or, if he did receive it, whether he proceeded to organize demonstrations. Ayatollah Behbahani, however, played a key role in organizing the demonstrations against Mossadeq on August 19, 1953.

14.   Stephen Kinzer, *All the Shah's Men: An American Coup and the Roots of Middle East Terror* (Hoboken, NJ: John Wiley, 2003), 75–76.

15.   Robert Fisk, *Pity the Nation: The Abduction of Lebanon* (New York: Thunder Mouth, 2002), 55

16.   Ibid.

17.   Tom Russell, "A Lebanon Primer," *MERIP Reports,* no. 133 (June 1985), 17–19.

18.   Fisk, *Pity*, 55–57.

19.   Russell, "Primer," 17.

20.   Ibid.

21.   FO 371/142062, TNA.

22.   Dilip Hiro, *The Iranian Labyrinth: Journeys Through Theocratic Iran and Its Furies*

(New York: Nation, 2005), 346; Kenneth M. Pollack, *The Persian Puzzle: The Conflict Between Iran and America* (New York: Random House, 2004) 198–205.

23. Pollack, *Puzzle*, 199–200.

24. Ibid., 201.

25. U.S. Security Council, "U.S./Iranian Contacts and the American Hostages," NSC Chronology of Events, 17 November 1986.

NINETEEN • *Espionage, Religion, and War in Northwest Frontier*

1. Bruce Riedel, "Pakistan and Terror: The Eye of the Storm," *The ANNALS of the American Academy of Political and Social Science* 618, no. 1 (2008): 31.

2. "Mumbai Terror Attacks: Nightmare in the Lap of Luxury," *The Observer*, 30 November 2008.

3. Thomas G. Fergusson, "Army Annual Inspection Report, 1852" in *British Military Intelligence, 1870–1914: The Development of a Modern Intelligence Organization* (Frederick, MD: University Publications of America, 1984), 135–36; WO 4/171, WO 6/138, WO 40/10, TNA.

4. Shuja Nawaz, *Crossed Swords: Pakistan, Its Army, and the Wars Within* (Oxford: Oxford University Press, 2008), 11, quoting Frederick Sleigh Roberts, *Forty-one Years in India: From Subaltern to Commander-in-Chief*, vol. 2 (London: Bentley, 1897), 442.

5. Nawaz, *Swords*, 11–13.

6. WO 33/36, TNA.

7. At present there are more Sikhs in the Indian army than Muslims, although the Sikhs represent 4 percent of the population and Muslims 12 percent. See Stephen P. Rosen, *Societies and Military Power: India and Its Armies* (Ithaca: Cornell University Press, 1996), 217.

8. Steve Coll, *Ghost Wars: The Secret History of the CIA, Afghanistan and Bin Laden, from the Soviet Invasion to September 10, 2001* (New York: Penguin, 2004), 64, 174–75.

9. Rasul Bakhsh Rais, *Recovering the Frontier State: War, Ethnicity, and State in Afghanistan* (New York: Lexington, 2008), 71.

10. The traditional period of Anglo-Russian rivalry in Central Asia dates from the Russo-Persian Treaty of 1813 to the Anglo-Russian Convention of 1907. After the Bolshevik Revolution of 1917, the competition between the two powers declined. During the Soviet occupation of Afghanistan and the U.S. support of the mujahidin, a new Great Game emerged that has continued between the Russian Federation and the United States.

11. Conolly had made reference in a letter to a friend of taking part in "a great game, a noble game" in Central Asia. After his death, the letters passed to the historian Sir John Kaye, who introduced the term "Great Game." See Karl E. Mayer and Shareen B. Brysac, *Tournament of Shadows: The Great Game and the Race for Empire in Central Asia* (Washington, D.C.: Counterpoint, 1999), xxiii; and Peter Hopkirk, *The Great Game: The Struggle for Empire in Central Asia* (New York: Kodansha International, 1992).

12. Philip Knightley, *The Master Spy: The Story of Kim Philby* (New York: Knopf, 1989), 24.

13. In 1949, Philby was British liaison officer in Washington with the CIA and the FBI, part of a career path that was preparing him to become head of the British Secret Service (Knightley, *Master Spy*, 1). For more about Kim Philby's father, Harry St. John Philby, see Chapter 7.

14. Robert Johnson, *Spying for Empire: The Great Game in Central and South Asia, 1757–1947* (London: Greenhill, 2006), 84.

15. Johnson, *Spying*, 85.

16. Conolly believed he would check the Russian annexation of Central Asia by uniting all the Khanates (local rulers), and when that mission failed, he went on to rescue Stoddart (Johnson, *Spying*, 86).

17. Mayer and Brysac, *Tournament*, 122–32. Hopkirk, *Great Game*, 1, begins his study of the Great Game with the execution of the two British officers and remarks that today tourists arrive at a bus stop located in a square that was once the place of execution. The remains of the two men lie in unmarked graves under the square. Hopkirk also adds that Captain Arthur Conolly coined the phrase the "Great Game."

18. The Intelligence Bureau was established in 1885. See Hopkirk, *Great Game*, 422–23.

19. Fergusson, "Report," 63. India was officially assigned to Section D during this time.

20. Ibid., 85.

21. Husain Haqqani, *Pakistan: Between Mosque and Military* (Washington, D.C.: Carnegie Endowment for International Peace, 2005), 20; Johnson, *Spying*, 127.

22. Piers Brendon, *The Decline and Fall of the British Empire, 1781–1997* (London: Jonathan Cape, 2007), 382.

23. John Fisher, *Gentleman Spies: Intelligence Agents in the British Empire and Beyond* (Stroud: Sutton, 2002), 107–8.

24. Ibid., 108–10.

25. Ibid., 112.

26. Ibid.

27. Later Bray recommended the centralization of intelligence collection, counterintelligence, and the foundation of a religious school by Sharif Hussein in Mecca. See Ibid., 112–13.

28. In the immediate postwar period and through most of the 1920s, British intelligence officials could not agree on the extent or significance of pan-Islam, either in the Middle East or in South Asia. See Martine Thomas, *Empires of Intelligence: Security Services and Colonial Disorder After 1914* (Berkeley: University of California Press, 2008), 75.

29. Fisher, *Spies*, 125.

30. Richard J. Aldrich, "Britain's Secret Intelligence Service in Asia During the Second World War," *Modern Asian Studies* 32, no. 1 (February 1998): 184.

31. Both SIS and SOE had been based elsewhere in Asia prior to the fall of Singapore in 1942, at which time they were moved to India. The SIS had maintained a base in Asia before the war, but it had been neglected. The SOE, which was not established until during the war, established a strong presence in the region and in some cases overtook the SIS in efficiency and achievement.

32. The SOE in South Asia was designated as the "Oriental Mission" and later became the "India Mission," or Force 136.

33. Japanese intelligence officers established direct links with Pritam Singh's Indian Independence League, with Captain Mohan Singh, and later with the well-known nationalist Subha Chandra Bose.

34. Christopher Bayly and Tim Harper, *Forgotten Wars: The End of Britain's Asian Empire* (London: Penguin, 2007), 19.

35. Louis Allen, "Japanese Intelligence Systems," *Journal of Contemporary History* 22, no. 4 (October 1987): 547–62. Muslim officers who joined the INA did so less out of any nationalist or religious conviction than to protect their men from the horrors of the Japanese prisoner of war camps. Others joined in order to restrict Japanese involvement or to sabotage the INA from within. See also Christopher Bayly and Tim Harper, *Forgotten Armies: The Fall of British Asia, 1941–1945* (New York: Allen Lane, 2004), 256.

36. Richard J. Aldrich, *Intelligence and the War Against Japan* (Cambridge: Cambridge University Press, 2000), 159.

37. Ibid., 163.

38. Akbar Ahmed, *Jinnah, Pakistan and Islamic Identity: The Search for Saladin* (London: Routledge, 1997), 82.

39. Dharmendra Gaur, *Behind the Enemy Lines* (New Delhi: Sterling, 1975).

40. Bayly and Harper, *Armies*, 247.

41. Aldrich, *Intelligence*, 134.

42. Ibid., 307.

43. Ibid.

44. DEFE 11/31, TNA.

45. CAB 159/6, Part 2, TNA.

46. CAB 158/3, TNA.

47. Ibid.

48. DEFE 11/31, TNA.

49. Ibid.

50. Ibid.

51. Britain's security and counterintelligence service.

52. DEFE 11/31, TNA.

TWENTY • *Pakistan's Inter-Services Intelligence and Organized Terror in South Asia*

1. Graham Usher, "Taliban v. Taliban," *London Review of Books* 31, no. 7 (9 April 2009).

2. According to PakistaniDefence.com, a news media Web site committed to independent research on the social, economic, environmental, political, and military components of global security, http://www.pakistanidefence.com/Info/Intelligence .html (accessed 7 May 2009).

3. A Joint Counter-Intelligence Bureau was also formed in late 1948/early 1949, tasked with ensuring service security; it was headed by the British officer. See Political Intelligence, India: Disclosure of Information, 3 parts, WS 17079/3-5, IOR/L/WS/1/1074, BL.

4. During Hamid's visit to London in December 1949, he stated that the ISI had been in existence for ten months, which would mean its establishment in February 1949 (see CAB 159/6, Part 2, TNA); however, Brigadier J. F. Walter, DSO, visited Hamid at ISI headquarters in Karachi in October 1948, reporting that the ISI was then in the early stages of development (see WO 208/4961; CAB 159/6 Part 2; and WO 208/4961, TNA). Hamid's full name is found in the July 1948 Strategic Intelligence Digest report on Pakistan, which lists Hamid as the director of the Pakistan National Guard (see WO 208/4960 and WO 208/4961, TNA).

5. CAB 159/6, Part 2, TNA.

6. WO 208/4960, TNA.

7. Peter Hohnen, "Cawthorn, Sir Walter Joseph (1896–1970)," *Australian Dictionary of Biography*, vol. 13 (Melbourne: Melbourne University Press, 1993), 392–93.

8. See weekly reports of the India Office Political and Secret Department, IOR, BL.

9. When a Joint Counter-Intelligence Bureau was planned, to be placed within the ISI, it was felt that a British officer should be put in charge of creating and controlling it. The head of this unit would "have full access to the Civil Intelligence Bureau and its activities." It is not clear from the documents summarized here whether or not a British officer was put in charge of this position (DEFE 11/31,

TNA). Until the division of Pakistan from India, counterintelligence was organized under the Intelligence Bureau in New Delhi and under Provincial CIDs; it
was assumed by the Joint Intelligence Committee that this system was still in
place in both India and Pakistan in the spring of 1948. At that time, the JIC had no
security liaison officer in place in Karachi as they did in New Delhi. See CAB
158/3, TNA.

10. WO 208/4961, TNA.

11. CAB 159/5, Part 1, TNA.

12. Jessica Stern, "Pakistan's Jihad Culture," *Foreign Affairs* 79, no. 6 (November–
December 2000): 117–18.

13. After the creation of Pakistan in 1947, the Muslim states of the British Raj had the
choice of joining Pakistan or India. Although the majority of the Kashmir and
Jammu population followed the Islamic faith, the maharaja, the historic ruler of
the state, preferred India. His decision, as well as the borders established for the
two new states, has never been accepted by Pakistan.

14. DO 142/345, TNA.

15. Ibid.

16. Tariq Ali, *The Duel: Pakistan on the Flight Path of American Power* (New York:
Scribner, 2008), 50. Most records currently accessible from this period derive from
the Dominion Office, and as always it is entirely possible that the "right arm" of
the British government was blissfully unaware of what the "left arm" of intelligence was up to in Pakistan.

17. Outside the—at least nominally—religious realm, the president held the "right"
attitude toward dangerous figures like Nasser; he personally disliked him and approached him with caution. See DO 35/8962, TNA.

18. Ibid.

19. Pooja Joshi, *Jamaat-i-Islami: The Catalyst of Islamization in Pakistan* (New Delhi:
Kalinga, 2003), 15–21; Ali, *Duel*, 23.

20. The Jamaat-Ulema-e-Islam (JUI) has also become a powerful player in Pakistan
and Afghanistan. They too have a Wahhabi background and basis, and fall within
the Deobandi tradition, which was seen as the "home of Sunni orthodoxy in pre-
partition India." See Ali, *Duel*, 23.

21. DO 35/5154, TNA.

22. DO 196/418, TNA.

23. See Rizwan Hussain, *Pakistan and the Emergence of Islamic Militancy in Afghanistan* (Farnham: Ashgate, 2005), 69, who also cites Miles Copeland, *Game of Nations*, 58.

24. Hussain, *Emergence*, 59.

25. Hamza Alavi describes U.S. involvement in an allegedly bogus food crisis in Pakistan in the early 1950s, which led to a change in power that favored the U.S. government. See Hamza Alavi, "Pakistan-US Military Alliance," *Economic and Political Weekly* 33, no. 25 (20–26 June 1998): 1554.

26. Andrei Gromyko, *Memories* (London: Hutchinson, 1989), 246–47. Gromyko's frustration with Pakistan is underlined by the revelations of Soviet intelligence operations in the Third World included in the documents smuggled to the West by the former KGB archivist Vasili Mitrokhin. Except for some minor intelligence activities and subversive operations, Soviet intelligence made few inroads in Pakistan, See Andrew and Mitrokhin, *World*, 341–68.

27. The Central Treaty Organization, originally known as the Middle East Treaty Organization or the Baghdad Pact, was adopted by Iran, Iraq, Pakistan, Turkey, and Britain in 1955. The pact was a cooperative and noninterventionist agreement, designed to protect the Middle East's Northern Tier from a Soviet invasion.

28. Andrew and Mitrokhin, *World*, 341.

29. George C. Herring, *From Colony to Superpower: US Foreign Relations Since 1776* (Oxford: Oxford University Press, 2008), 680–81.

30. Stephen P. Cohen, *The Idea of Pakistan* (Washington, D.C.: Brookings Institution, 2004), 102.

31. Ibid., 103.

32. Ali, *Duel*, 107. Under Bhutto, the ISI also established an "election cell," which menaced voters and rigged results. Bhutto's religious posturing deeply altered Pakistan's political integrity.

33. Haqqani, *Pakistan*, 165–67.

34. Ali, *Duel*, 119.

35. Haqqani, *Pakistan*, 265; Victoria Schofield, *Kashmir in Conflict: India, Pakistan and the Unfinished War* (London: I. B. Tauris, 2000), 113; Herring, *Colony*, 712–13. According to Arif Jamal, *Shadow War: The Untold Story of Jihad in Kashmir* (Brooklyn, NY: Melville House, 2009), 86–87, between 1965 and 1971 there were eighty underground cells established in the valley of Kashmir, some of which were working with the ISI.

36. The separatist movement was successful, and the country now known as Bangladesh was formed in 1971 from what had been East Pakistan.

37. Henry Kissinger, *Years of Renewal*, vol. 3 (New York: Simon & Schuster, 1999), 82.

38. Cohen, *Idea*, 100.

39. Ibid., 105.

40. Ibid., 100.

41. Ali, *Duel*, 113–19.

42. Ibid., 23, 123.

43. Cohen, *Idea*, 195; Hussain, *Emergence*, 249.

44. Ali, *Duel*, 119; Lawrence Ziring, *Pakistan at the Crosscurrent of History* (Oxford: Oneworld, 2003), 180.

45. Stephen Tanner, *Afghanistan: A Military History from Alexander the Great to the Fall of the Taliban* (Cambridge: Da Capo, 2002), 250.

46. Ziring, *Crosscurrent*, 177.

47. Tanner, *Afghanistan*, 254. After Zia's death in 1988, the CIA managed to gain the right to distribute arms into the field. However, the ISI and Saudi Arabia continued to manipulate the scene by providing their own aid selectively. See Tanner, *Afghanistan*, 274.

48. Even prominent U.S. politicians have been willing to concede the damage done by U.S. policies during the Afghan War. In a 2008 panel discussion, Richard Armitage, former deputy secretary of state, openly said that the United States knew what the impact of their actions during the war would be in Pakistan. "In other words they knew perfectly well that they had handed the country to religious groups and the ISI." See Ali, *Duel*, 251.

49. Ibid., 137, quoting from "Get America Out of the Way and We'll Be Okay," interview with Harinder Baweja, *Tehelka Magazine*, 2 February 2008.

50. Ali, *Duel*, 136–37, 142.

51. Hussain, *Emergence*, 249.

52. George Tenet, *At the Center of the Storm: My Years at the CIA* (New York: Harper-Collins, 2007), 142.

53. Ahmed Rashid, *Descent into Chaos* (New York: Viking, 2008), 24.

54. Tenet, *Center*, 141.

55. Cohen, *Idea*, 112.

56. Ali, *Duel*, 149–50.

57. Rais, *Recovering*, 71.

58. Graham E. Fuller, "Obama's Policies Making Situation Worse in Afghanistan and Pakistan," *Huffington Post*, 6 September 2009, http://www.huffingtonpost.com/graham-e<->fuller/global-viewpoint-obamas-p_b_201355.html.

59. Assembly of Islamic Clergy.

60. Most of the Taliban rank and file have passed through the Deobandi madrasas in the Northwest Frontier province and Balochistan. See "Pakistan: Madrasas, Extremism and the Military," *ICG Asia Report*, no. 36 (29 July 2002); "Pakistan: Karachi's Madrasas and Violent Extremism," *ICG Asia Report*, no. 130 (29 March 2007); and Rais, *Recovering*, 72.

61. Rais, *Recovering*, 71.

62. Another critical consideration was that Islamabad had to be seen to support Afghan Pashtuns for the benefit of the Pakistani Pashtuns, and also because the non-Pashtuns had found support from India, Iran, and Russia. See Rashid, *Descent*, 25.

63. Ibid., 26.

64. Ziring, *Crosscurrent*, 283.

65. Tanner, *Afghanistan*, 282.

66. Fuller, *"Policies."*

BIBLIOGRAPHY
UNPUBLISHED SOURCES

British Library (BL), London

INDIA OFFICE RECORDS

IOR/L/WS/1/1074; IOR/L/WS/1/1162.

The Haganah Archives, Tel Aviv

80/69/5.

The National Archives of the UK, Kew, Surrey (TNA)

RECORDS OF THE CABINET OFFICE

CAB 81/80; CAB 158/3; CAB 159/5; CAB 159/6.

RECORDS OF THE COLONIAL OFFICE

CO 732/88/32.

RECORDS OF THE DOMINIONS OFFICE

DO 35/5154; DO 35/8962; DO 142/345; DO 196/418.

FO 370/2719; FO 370/82792; FO 371/1546; FO 371/24558; FO 371/24568;

FO 371/32900; FO 371/45542; FO 371/82800; FO 371/102869;

FO 371/108489; FO 371/115899; FO 371/115900; FO 371/118975;

FO 371/128220; FO 371/128221; FO 371/128222; FO 371/128224;

FO 371/128226; FO 371/128233; FO 371/128268; FO 371/170603;

FO 371/183884.

RECORDS OF THE MINISTRY OF DEFENCE

DEFE 11/31.

RECORDS OF THE PRIME MINISTER'S OFFICE

PREM 11/391.

RECORDS OF THE SPECIAL OPERATIONS EXECUTIVE (SOE)

HS 3/201; HS 3/209; Hs 7/269.

RECORDS OF THE SECURITY SERVICE (MI5)

KV 2/1970; KV 5/30; KV 5/38; KV 5/39.

RECORDS OF THE WAR OFFICE

WO 4/171; WO 6/138; WO 33/36; WO 40/10; WO 208/4960; WO 208/4961.

*US National Archives and Records Administration,
College Park, Maryland (NARA)*

RECORDS OF THE CENTRAL INTELLIGENCE AGENCY (RG 263).

RECORDS OF THE FOREIGN SERVICE POSTS OF THE
DEPARTMENT OF STATE (RG 84).

RECORDS OF THE OFFICE OF THE ARMY STAFF GROUP (RG 319).

RECORDS OF THE OFFICE OF THE SECRETARY OF DEFENSE (RG 330).

RECORDS OF THE OFFICE OF STRATEGIC SERVICES (RG 226).

PUBLISHED SOURCES

Abdullahzadeh, Mahmoud. "The Political Significance of the Bazaar in Iran." In *Technology, Tradition and Survival: Aspects of Material Culture in the Middle East and Central Asia*. Edited by Richard Tapper and Keith McLachlan. London: Frank Cass, 2002.

Acheson, Dean. *Present at the Creation: My Years in the State Department*. New York: Norton, 1969.

Ahmed, Akbar S. *Jinnah, Pakistan and Islamic Identity: The Search for Saladin*. London: Routledge, 1997.

———. *Living Islam: From Samarkand to Stornoway*. London: Penguin, 1995.

Aid, Matthew M. "The Secret reclassification Program." Organization of American Historians Newsletter 34 (May 2006).

Alavi, Hamza. "Pakistan-US Military Alliance." *Economic and Political Weekly* 33, no. 25 (20–26 June 1998).

Albertini, Luigi. *The Origins of the War of 1914*. Translated and edited by Isabella M. Massey. 3 vols. London: Oxford University Press, 1952–1957.

Aldrich, Richard J. "Britain's Secret Intelligence Service in Asia During the Second World War." *Modern Asian Studies* 32, no. 1 (February 1998).

———. "Did Waldegrave Work? The Impact of Open Government upon British History." *Twentieth Century British History* 9, no. 1 (1998).

———. *Espionage, Security and Intelligence in Britain, 1945–1970.* Manchester: Manchester University Press, 1998.

———. *The Hidden Hand: Britain, America and Cold War Secret Intelligence.* New York: Overlook, 2002.

———. *Intelligence and the War Against Japan.* Cambridge: Cambridge University Press, 2000.

Ali, Tariq. *The Duel: Pakistan on the Flight Path of American Power.* New York: Scribner, 2008.

Allen, Charles. *God's Terrorists: The Wahhabi Cult and the Hidden Roots of Modern Jihad.* London: Little, Brown, 2006.

Allen, Louis. "Japanese Intelligence Systems." *Journal of Contemporary History* 22, no. 4 (October 1987): 547–62.

al-Qalanisi, Ibn. *The Damascus Chronicle of the Crusades.* Translated by H. A. R. Gibb. London: Luzac, 1967.

al-Rasheed, Madawi. *A History of Saudi Arabia.* Cambridge: Cambridge University Press, 2002.

Andrew, Christopher M. *Secret Service: The Making of the British Intelligence Community.* London: Heinemann, 1985.

Andrew, Christopher, and Vasili Mitrokhin. *The World Was Going Our Way: The KGB and the Battle for the Third World.* New York: Basic, 2005.

Antonius, George. *The Arab Awakening: The Story of the Arab National Movement.* Safety Harbor, FL: Simon, 2001.

"Army Coup in Syria: Government Overthrown." *Sunday Morning Herald*, 31 March 1949.

Baer, Robert. *Sleeping with the Devil: How Washington Sold Our Soul for Saudi Crude.* New York: Three Rivers, 2003.

Batatu, Hanna. "Syria's Muslim Brethren." *MERIP Reports*, no. 110 (November–December 1982).

Bayley, Christopher, and Tim Harper. *Forgotten Armies: The Fall of British Asia, 1941–1945.* New York: Allen Lane, 2004.

———. *Forgotten Wars: The End of Britain's Asian Empire.* London: Penguin, 2007.

Bell, Gertrude. *Review of the Civil Administration of Mesopotamia*. London: HMSO, 1920.

Ben-Ami, Yitshaq. *Years of Wrath, Days of Glory: Memoirs from the Irgun*. New York: Speller, 1982.

Bergen, Peter L. *Holy War, Inc.: Inside the Secret World of Osama bin Laden*. New York: Free Press, 2001.

Bidwell, R. L., ed. *The Arab Bulletin: Bulletin of the Arab Bureau in Cairo*. 4 vols. Gerrards Cross: Archive Editions, 1986.

Bierman, John. *Fire in the Night: Wingate of Burma, Ethiopia, and Zion*. New York: Random House, 1999.

Black, Ian, and Benny Morris. *Israel's Secret Wars: The Untold History of Israeli Intelligence*. London: Hamish Hamilton, 1991.

Blunt, W. S. *Secret History of the British Occupation of Egypt: Being a Personal Narrative of Events*. London: Unwin, 1907.

Bower, Tom. *The Perfect English Spy: The Unknown Man in Charge During the Most Tumultuous Scandal-Ridden Era in Espionage History*. New York: St. Martin's Press, 1995.

Braddon, Russell. *The Siege*. New York: Viking, 1969.

Brendon, Piers. *The Decline and Fall of the British Empire, 1781–1997*. London: Jonathan Cape, 2007.

Brenner, Y. S. "The Stern Gang, 1940–1948." In *Palestine and Israel in the 19th and 20th Centuries*. Edited by Elie Kedourie and Sylvia G. Haim. London: Frank Cass, 1982.

Brown, Malcolm, ed. *T. E. Lawrence in War and Peace: An Anthology of the Military Writings of Lawrence of Arabia*. London: Greenhill, 2005.

Buchan, John. *Greenmantle*. London: Nelson, 1916.

Buzpinar, S. Tufan. "The Hijaz, Abdulhamid II and Amir Hussein's Secret Dealings with the British, 1877–1880." *Middle East Studies* 31, no. 1 (January 1995).

Caroz, Yaacov. *The Arab Secret Service*. London: Corgi, 1978.

Carr, Matthew. *The Infernal Machine: A History of Terrorism*. New York: New Press, 2007.

Christison, Kathleen. *Perceptions of Palestine: Their Influence on U.S. Middle East Policy*. Berkeley: University of California Press, 1999.

Clarke, Thurston. *By Blood and Fire: The Attack on the King David Hotel*. New York: Putnam, 1981.

Cleveland, William L. *A History of the Modern Middle East*. San Francisco: Westview, 1994.

Cockburn, Andrew, and Leslie Cockburn. *Dangerous Liaison: The Inside Story of the U.S.-Israeli Covert Relationship*. Toronto: Stoddart, 1991.

Cohen, Stephen P. *The Idea of Pakistan*. Washington, D.C.: Brookings Institution, 2004.

Colby, William, and Peter Forbath. *Honorable Men: My Life in the CIA*. New York: Simon & Schuster, 1978.

Coll, Steve. *Ghost Wars: The Secret History of the CIA, Afghanistan and Bin Laden, from the Soviet Invasion to September 10, 2001*. New York: Penguin, 2004.

Cooley, John K. *Unholy Wars: Afghanistan, America and International Terrorism*. Sterling, VA: Pluto, 2000.

Cooper, Artemis. *Cairo in the War, 1939–1945*. London: Hamish Hamilton, 1989.

Copeland, Miles. *Game of Nations: The Amorality of Power Politics*. New York: Simon & Schuster, 1969.

——. *The Game Player: Confessions of the CIA's Original Political Operative*. London: Arium, 1989.

——. *The Real Spy World*. London: Weidenfeld & Nicolson, 1974.

Crile, George. *Charlie Wilson's War: The Extraordinary Story of the Largest Covert Operation in History*. New York: Atlantic Monthly Press, 2003.

"The Crisis in Egypt: Serious Riots in Alexandria." *The Times*, 11 June 1882.

Crossman, R. H. S. *The Diaries of a Cabinet Minister: Richard Crossman*. New York: Henry Holt, 1976.

Crossman, R. H. S., and Michael Foot. *A Palestine Munich*. London: Victor Gollancz, 1946.

Dalin, David G., and John F. Rothmann. *Icon of Evil: Hitler's Mufti and the Rise of Radical Islam*. New York: Random House, 2008.

Dawisha, Adeed. *Arab Nationalism in the Twentieth Century: From Triumph to Despair*. Princeton: Princeton University Press, 2003.

Deacon, Richard. *"C": A Biography of Sir Maurice Oldfield, Head of MI6*. London: Futura, 1984.

Derogy, Jacques, and Hesi Carmel. *The Untold History of Israel*. New York: Random House, 1979.

Disraeli, Benjamin. *Contarini Fleming: A Psychological Romance.* London: John Lane, 1927.

Dorril, Stephen. *MI6: Inside the Covert World of Her Majesty's Secret Intelligence Service.* New York: Free Press, 2000.

Downton, Eric. *Wars Without End.* Toronto: Stoddart, 1987.

Dreyfuss, Robert. *Devil's Game: How the United States Helped Unleash Fundamentalist Islam.* New York: Metropolitan, 2005.

Epstein, Edward J. *Deception: The Invisible War Between the KGB and the CIA.* New York: Simon & Schuster, 1989.

Eshed, Haggai. *Reuven Shiloah—The Man Behind the Mossad: Secret Diplomacy in the Creation of Israel.* Portland: Frank Cass, 1997.

Esposito, John L., ed. *The Oxford Dictionary of Islam.* Oxford: Oxford University Press, 2003.

Eveland, William Crane. *Ropes of Sand: America's Failure in the Middle East.* New York: Norton, 1980.

Fairlie, J. A. "The Economic Effects of Ship Canals." *Annals of the American Academy of Political and Social Science* 11 (January 1898).

Farran, Roy. *Winged Dagger: Adventures on Special Service.* London: Collins, 1970.

Ferguson, Niall. *The War of the World: Twentieth-Century Conflict and the Descent of the West.* New York: Penguin, 2006.

Fergusson, Thomas G. "Army Annual Inspection Report, 1852." In *British Military Intelligence, 1870–1914: The Development of a Modern Intelligence Organization* (Frederick, MD: University Publications of America, 1984).

Fielding, Xan. *One Man in His Time: The Life of Lieutenant-Colonel N. L. D. ("Billy") McLean, DSO.* London: Macmillan, 1990.

Finkel, Caroline. *Osman's Dream: The Story of the Ottoman Empire, 1300–1923.* New York: Basic, 2006.

Fisher, John. *Gentleman Spies: Intelligence Agents in the British Empire and Beyond.* Stroud: Sutton, 2002.

Fisk, Robert. *The Great War for Civilization: The Conquest of the Middle East.* London: Fourth Estate, 2005.

———. *Pity the Nation: The Abduction of Lebanon.* New York: Thunder Mouth, 2002.

Foot, M. R. D. *S.O.E. in France: An Account of the Work of the British Special Operations Executive in France, 1940–1944.* London: HMSO, 1966.

Frank, Lewis A. "Nasser's Missile Program." *Orbis* 11, no. 3 (Fall 1967): 746–57.

Fromkin, David. *A Peace to End All Peace: The Fall of the Ottoman Empire and the Creation of the Modern Middle East.* New York: Avon, 1989.

Fuller, Graham E. "Obama's Policies Making Situation Worse in Afghanistan and Pakistan." *Huffington Post*, 6 September 2009, http://www.huffingtonpost.com/graham -e-fuller/global-viewpoint-obamas-p_b_201355.html.

Furst, Alan. *The World at Night.* New York: Random House, 1996.

Gabrieli, Francesco. *Arab Historians of the Crusades.* Translated by E. J. Costello. Berkeley: University of California Press, 1969.

Gaddis, John Lewis. *The Cold War: A New History.* New York: Penguin, 2005.

Gasiorowski, Mark J. "The 1953 Coup d' Etat Against Mosaddeq." In *Mohammad Mosaddeq and the 1953 Coup in Iran.* Edited by Mark J. Gasiorowski and Malcolm Byrne. Syracuse: Syracuse University Press, 2004.

Gaur, Dharmendra. *Behind the Enemy Lines.* New Delhi: Sterling, 1975.

Gehlen, Reinhard. *The Service: The Memoirs of General Reinhard Gehlen.* Translated by David Irving. New York: World, 1972.

Gerolymatos, André. *Espionage and Treason: A Study of the Proxenia in Political and Military Intelligence Gathering in Classical Greece.* Amsterdam: J. C. Gieben, 1986.

———. *Guerrilla Warfare and Espionage in Greece, 1940–1944.* New York: Pella, 1992.

———. *Red Acropolis, Black Terror: The Greek Civil War and the Origins of Soviet-American Rivalry.* New York: Basic, 2004.

Gilbert, Martin. *Finest Hour.* Vol. 6 of *Winston S. Churchill.* London: Heinemann, 1983.

Green, Dominic. *Three Empires on the Nile: The Victorian Jihad, 1869–1899.* New York: Free Press, 2007.

Gromyko, Andrei. *Memories.* London: Hutchinson, 1989.

Hagen, Gottfried. "German Heralds of Holy War: Orientalists and Applied Oriental Studies." *Comparative Studies of South Asia, Africa and the Middle East* 24, no. 2 (2004): 145–162.

Haqqani, Husain. *Pakistan: Between Mosque and Military.* Washington, D.C.: Carnegie Endowment for International Peace, 2005.

Harris, Christina P. *Nationalism and Revolution in Egypt: The Role of the Muslim Brotherhood*. The Hague: Mouton, 1964.

Haswell, Jock. *British Military Intelligence*. London: Weidenfeld & Nicolson, 1973.

Heikal, Mohammed H. *Cutting the Lion's Tail: Suez Through Egyptian Eyes*. New York: Arbor House, 1987.

Heller, Joseph. *British Policy Towards the Ottoman Empire, 1900–1914*. London: Frank Cass, 1983.

Helms, Richard. *A Look over My Shoulder: A Life in the Central Intelligence Agency*. New York: Ballantine, 2003.

Herring, George C. *From Colony to Superpower: US Foreign Relations Since 1776*. Oxford: Oxford University Press, 2008.

Hersh, Burton. *The Old Boys: The American Elite and the Origins of the CIA*. New York: Scribner's, 1992.

Hillenbrand, Carole. *The Crusades: Islamic Perspectives*. Edinburgh: Edinburgh University Press, 1999.

Hinsley, F. H., and others. *British Intelligence in the Second World War: Its Influence on Strategy and Operations*. Vol. 1. London: HMSO, 1979.

Hiro, Dilip. *The Iranian Labyrinth: Journeys Through Theocratic Iran and Its Furies*. New York: Nation, 2005.

Hohnen, Peter. "Cawthorn, Sir Walter Joseph (1896–1970)," *Australian Dictionary of Biography*. Vol. 13. Melbourne: Melbourne University Press, 1993.

Holland, Matthew F. *America and Egypt: From Roosevelt to Eisenhower*. London: Praeger, 1996.

Holzman, Michael. *James Jesus Angleton, the CIA and the Craft of Counterintelligence*. Amhest: University of Massachusetts Press, 2008.

Homer. *The Odyssey*. Translated by Robert Fagles. New York: Penguin, 1996.

Hood, William. "Angleton's World." In *Myths Surrounding James Angleton: Lessons for American Counterintelligence*. Edited by William Hood et al. Washington, D.C.: Consortium for the Study of Intelligence, 1994.

Hopkirk, Peter. *The Great Game: The Struggle for Empire in Central Asia*. New York: Kodansha International, 1992.

——. *On Secret Service East of Constantinople: The Great Game and the Great War*. London: John Murray, 1994.

Hourani, Albert. *Arabic Thought in the Liberal Age, 1798–1939*. London: Oxford University Press, 1962.

———. *A History of the Arab Peoples*. New York: Warner, 1991.

Howell, Georgina. *Gertrude Bell: Queen of the Desert, Shaper of Nations*. New York: Farrar, Straus & Giroux, 2006.

Hupchick, Dennis P. *The Balkans: From Constantinople to Communism*. New York: Palgrave, 2002.

Hurewitz, J. C. *Diplomacy in the Near and Middle East: A Documentary Record*. 2 vols. Princeton: Van Nostrand, 1956.

Hussain, Rizwan. *Pakistan and the Emergence of Islamic Militancy in Afghanistan*. Farnham: Ashgate, 2005.

Infield, Glenn B. *Skorzeny: Hitler's Commando*. New York: Military Heritage Press, 1981.

Irwin, Robert. "Is This the Man Who Inspired Bin Laden?" *The Guardian*, 1 November 2001.

Jamal, Arif. *Shadow War: The Untold Story of Jihad in Kashmir*. Brooklyn, NY: Melville House, 2009.

Jarvis, C. S. *Three Deserts*. London: John Murray, 1941.

Jeffrey-Jones, Rhodri. *The CIA and American Diplomacy*. New Haven: Yale University Press, 1989.

Johnson, Robert. *Spying for Empire: The Great Game in Central and South Asia, 1757–1947*. London: Greenhill, 2006.

Jones, Matthew. "The 'Preferred Plan': The Anglo-American Working Group Report on Covert Action in Syria, 1957." *Intelligence and National Security* 19, no. 3 (Autumn 2004): 401–15.

Joshi, Pooja. *Jamaat-i-Islami: The Catalyst of Islamization in Pakistan*. New Delhi: Kalinga, 2003.

Karabell, Zachary. *Parting the Desert: The Creation of the Suez Canal*. New York: Knopf, 2003.

Karpat, Kemal H. *The Politicization of Islam: Reconstructing Identity, State, Faith and Community in the Late Ottoman State*. Oxford: Oxford University Press, 2001.

Karsh, Efraim. *Islamic Imperialism: A History*. New Haven: Yale University Press, 2006.

Karsh, Efraim, and Inari Karsh. *Empires of the Sand: The Struggle for Mastery in the Middle East, 1789–1923*. Cambridge: Harvard University Press, 1999.

Katz, Samuel. *Israel Elite Units Since 1948*. Oxford: Osprey, 1988.

Keay, John. *Sowing the Wind: The Seeds of Conflict in the Middle East*. New York: Norton, 2003.

Kedourie, Elie. *Afghani and 'Abduh: An Essay on Religious Unbelief and Political Activism in Modern Islam*. London: Frank Cass, 1966.

———. *The Chatham House Version and Other Middle Eastern Studies*. London: Weidenfeld & Nicolson, 1970.

———. *In the Anglo-Arab Labyrinth: The McMahon-Husayn Correspondence and Its Interpretations*. Cambridge: Cambridge University Press, 1976.

Keegan, John. *The Price of Admiralty: The Evolution of Naval Warfare*. New York: Viking Penguin, 1988.

Kelly, James, and William Stewart. "Syria: The Proud Lion and His Den." *Time*, 5 September 1983.

Kennedy, Paul. *The Realities Behind Diplomacy: Background Influences on British External Policy, 1865–1980*. Glasgow: Collins, 1981.

Kepel, Gilles. *Jihad: The Trail of Political Islam*. Translated by Anthony F. Roberts. Cambridge: Harvard University Press, 2002.

———. *Muslim Extremism in Egypt: The Prophet and the Pharaoh*. Translated by Jon Rothschild. Los Angeles: University of California Press, 1984.

———. *The War for Muslim Minds: Islam and the West*. Cambridge: Harvard University Press, 2004.

Khalidi, Rashid. *The Iron Cage: The Story of the Palestinian Struggle for Statehood*. Boston: Beacon, 2006.

Kimche, Jon, and David Kimche. *The Secret Roads: The "Illegal" Migration of a People, 1938–1948*. London: Secker & Warburg, 1954.

Kinzer, Stephen. *All the Shah's Men: An American Coup and the Roots of Middle East Terror*. Hoboken, NJ: John Wiley, 2003.

Kissinger, Henry. *Years of Renewal*. Vol. 3. New York: Simon & Schuster, 1999.

Knightley, Philip. *The Master Spy: The Story of Kim Philby*. New York: Knopf, 1989.

————. *The Second Oldest Profession: The Spy as Bureaucrat, Patriot, Fantasist and Whore*. London: Andre Deutsch, 1986.

Koestler, Arthur. *Promise and Fulfilment: Palestine, 1917–1949*. London: Macmillan, 1949.

Kramer, Gudrun. *A History of Palestine: From the Ottoman Conquest to the Founding of the State of Israel*. Princeton: Princeton University Press, 2002.

Kumamoto, Robert. *International Terrorism and American Foreign Relations, 1945–1976*. Boston: Northeastern University Press, 1999.

Kyle, Keith. *Suez*. London: Weidenfeld & Nicolson, 1991.

Lawrence, Arnold W., ed. *Secret Despatches from Arabia*. London: Golden Cockerel, 1939.

Lawrence, T. E. *Seven Pillars of Wisdom: A Triumph*. New York: Penguin, 1962.

le Carré, John. "On Kim Philby." In Kim Philby, *My Silent War: The Autobiography of a Spy*. New York: Modern Library, 2002.

Lee, Martin. A. *The Beast Reawakens*. New York: Routledge, 2000.

Lewis, Bernard. *The Assassins: A Radical Sect in Islam*. London: Weidenfeld & Nicolson, 2001.

————. *What Went Wrong?: Western Impact and Middle Eastern Response*. Oxford: Oxford University Press, 2002.

Lia, Brynjar. *The Society of the Muslim Brothers in Egypt: The Rise of an Islamic Mass Movement, 1928–1942*. Reading: Ithaca, 1998.

Lindsay, Franklin. *Beacons in the Night: With the OSS and Tito's Partisans in Wartime Yugoslavia*. Stanford: Stanford University Press, 1993.

Little, Douglas. "Cold War and Covert Action: The United States and Syria, 1945–1958." *Middle East Journal* 44, no. 1 (Winter 1990).

Lucas, Scott, and Alistair Morey. "The Hidden 'Alliance': The CIA and MI6 Before and After Suez." In *American-British-Canadian Intelligence Relations, 1939–2000*. Edited by Maurizio Ferrera and Martin Rhodes. London: Frank Cass, 2000.

Lüdke, Tilman. *Jihad Made in Germany: Ottoman and German Propaganda and Intelligence Operations in the First World War*. Münster: LIT, 2005.

Maalouf, Amin. *The Crusades Through Arab Eyes*. Translated by Jon Rothschild. London: Al Saqi, 1984.

MacDonald, Callum. *The Killing of SS Obergruppenführer Reinhard Heydrich*. New York: Free Press, 1989.

MacMillan, Margaret. *Paris 1919: Six Months That Changed the World*. New York: Random House, 2003.

"Major Roy Farran (Obituary)." *The Times*, 6 June 2006.

"The Man Behind Bin Laden." *The New Yorker*, 16 September 2002.

Mango, Andrew. *Ataturk: The Biography of the Founder of Modern Turkey*. New York: Overlook, 2000.

Mansel, Philip. *Constantinople: City of the World's Desire, 1453–1924*. London: John Murray, 1995.

Masters, John. *The Road Past Mandalay*. New York: Bantam, 1979.

Mattar, Philip. *The Mufti of Jerusalem: Al-Hajj Amin al-Husayni and the Palestinian National Movement*. New York: Columbia University Press, 1988.

Mayer, Karl E., and Shareen B. Brysac. *Tournament of Shadows: The Great Game and the Race for Empire in Central Asia*. Washington, D.C.: Counterpoint, 1999.

Melman, Yossi, and Dan Raviv. *Friends in Deed: Inside the U.S.-Israeli Alliance*. New York: Hyperion, 1994.

Michaud, Joseph F. *History of the Crusades*. Translated by W. Robson. 3 vols. London: Routledge, 1852; repr., New York: AMS, 1973.

Minault, Gail. *The Khilafat Movement: Religious Symbolism and Political Mobilization in India*. New York: Columbia University Press, 1982.

Mitchell, Richard P. *The Society of Muslim Brothers*. Oxford: Oxford University Press, 1969.

Modin, Yuri. "On Kim Philby." In Kim Philby, *My Silent War: the Autobiography of a Spy*. New York: Modern Library, 2002.

Mohs, Polly A. *Military Intelligence and the Arab Revolt: The First Modern Intelligence War*. New York: Routledge, 2008.

Monroe, Elizabeth. *Philby of Arabia*. Reading: Ithaca, 1973.

Morris, Benny. *1948: A History of the First Arab-Israeli War*. New Haven: Yale University Press, 2008.

———. *Righteous Victims: A History of the Zionist-Arab Conflict, 1881–2001*. New York: Vintage, 1999.

Mortimer, Edward. *Faith and Power: The Politics of Islam*. New York: Vintage, 1982.

Moubayed, Sami. "Keeping an Eye on Syria: March 29, 1949." *Mideastviews: Middle East Analysis by Sami Moubayed*, 29 May 2009. http://www.mideastviews.com/articleview.php?art=387.

"Mumbai Terror Attacks: Nightmare in the Lap of Luxury." *The Observer*, 30 November 2008.

Naftali, Timothy. "Reinhard Gehlen and the United States." In *U.S. Intelligence and the Nazis*. Edited by Richard Breitman et al. Cambridge: Cambridge University Press, 2005.

Naor, Mordecai. *Lexicon of the Haganah Defence Force.* Tel Aviv: Ministry of Defence, 1992.

Nasr, Vali. *The Shia Revival: How Conflicts Within Islam Will Shape the Future.* New York: Norton, 2006.

Nawaz, Shuja. *Crossed Swords: Pakistan, Its Army, and the Wars Within.* Oxford: Oxford University Press, 2008.

Nesbit, Roy C. *Eyes of the RAF: A History of Photo-Reconnaissance.* Kettering: Sutton, 1996.

Nutting, Anthony. *No End of a Lesson: The Story of Suez.* London: Constable, 1967.

Oren, Michael B. *Power, Faith, and Fantasy: America in the Middle East, 1776 to the Present.* New York: Norton, 2007.

Painter, Sidney. "The Third Crusade: Richard the Lionhearted and Philip Augustus." In *A History of the Crusades*. Edited by Robert Lee Wolf and Harry W. Hazard. Vol. 2, *The Later Crusades 1189–1311*. Madison. University of Wisconsin Press, 1969.

Pakenham, Thomas. *The Boer War.* New York: Avon, 1979.

———. *The Scramble for Africa: The White Man's Conquest of the Dark Continent from 1876 to 1912.* New York: Random House, 1991.

"Pakistan: Karachi's Madrasas and Violent Extremism." *ICG Asia Report*, no. 130 (29 March 2007).

"Pakistan: Madrasas, Extremism and the Military." *ICG Asia Report*, no. 36 (29 July 2002).

Palmer, Alan. *The Decline and Fall of the Ottoman Empire.* New York: Barnes & Noble, 1992.

Parritt, B. A. H. *The Intelligencers: The Story of British Military Intelligence up to 1914.* Ashford: Intelligence Corps Association, 1971.

Paul, Jim. "Insurrection at Mecca." *MERIP Reports*, no. 91, "Saudi Arabia on the Brink" (October 1980).

Peters, Edward, ed. *The First Crusade: The Chronicle of Fulcher of Chartres and Other Source Materials*. 2nd ed. Philadelphia: University of Pennsylvania Press, 1998.

Peters, Rudolph. *Islam and Colonialism: The Doctrine of Jihad in Modern History*. The Hague: Mouton, 1979.

Philby, Kim. *My Silent War: The Autobiography of a Spy*. New York: Modern Library, 2002.

Pipes, Daniel. "The Alawi Capture of Power in Syria." *Middle Eastern Studies* 25, no. 4 (October 1989): 429–50.

———. *The Hidden Hand: Middle East Fears of Conspiracy*. New York: St. Martin's Press, 1996.

Pollack, Kenneth M. *The Persian Puzzle: The Conflict Between Iran and America*. New York: Random House, 2004.

Powers, Thomas. *The Man Who Kept the Secrets*. New York: Knopf, 1979.

Prados, John. *Safe for Democracy: The Secret Wars of the CIA*. Chicago: Ivan R. Dee, 2006.

Rahnema, Ali. *Pioneers of Islamic Revival*. London: Zed, 2005.

Rais, Rasul Bakhsh. *Recovering the Frontier State: War, Ethnicity, and State in Afghanistan*. New York: Lexington, 2008.

Ranelagh, John. *The Agency: The Rise and Decline of the CIA*. New York: Simon & Schuster, 1978.

Ranfurly, Hermione. *To War with Whitaker: Wartime Diaries of Countess Ranfurly, 1939–1945*. London: Heinemann, 1994.

Rashid, Ahmed. *Descent into Chaos*. New York: Viking, 2008.

Rathmell, Andrew. *Secret War in the Middle East: The Covert Struggle for Syria, 1949–1961*. London: I. B. Tauris, 1995.

Raviv, Dan, and Yossi Melman. *Every Spy a Prince*. Boston: Houghton Mifflin, 1990.

Riedel, Bruce. "Pakistan and Terror: The Eye of the Storm." *The ANNALS of the American Academy of Political and Social Science* 618, no. 1 (2008).

Roberts, Frederick Sleigh. *Forty-one Years in India: From Subaltern to Commander-in-Chief*. Vol. 2. London: Bentley, 1897.

Roosevelt, Kermit. *Countercoup: The Struggle for the Control of Iran.* New York: McGraw-Hill, 1979.

Rosen, Stephen P. *Societies and Military Power: India and Its Armies.* Ithaca: Cornell University Press, 1996.

Rositzke, Harry. *The CIA's Secret Operations: Espionage, Counterespionage, and Covert Action.* Boulder, CO: Westview, 1988.

"Roy Farran (Obituary)." *Daily Telegraph*, 5 June 2006.

Royle, Charles. *The Egyptian Campaigns, 1882–1885: And the Events Which Led to Them.* 2 vols. London: Hurst & Blackett, 1886.

Royle, Trevor. *Orde Wingate: Irregular Soldier.* London: Weidenfeld & Nicolson, 1995.

Runciman, Steven. *The First Crusade and the Foundation of the Kingdom of Jerusalem.* Vol. 1 of *A History of the Crusades.* Cambridge: Cambridge University Press, 1989.

Russell, Tom. "A Lebanon Primer." *MERIP Reports*, no. 133 (June 1985).

Sachar, Howard M. *A History of Israel: From the Rise of Zionism to Our Time.* New York: Knopf, 2007.

"Sacrilege in Mecca." *Time*, 3 December 1979.

Sansom, A. W. *I Spied Spies.* London: Harrap, 1965.

Saunders, Bonnie F. *The United States and Arab Nationalism.* Wesport, CT: Praeger, 1996.

Schofield, Victoria. *Kashmir in Conflict: India, Pakistan and the Unfinished War.* London: I. B. Tauris, 2000.

———. *Wavell: Soldier and Statesman.* London: John Murray, 2007.

Schwartz, Stephen. "Is Saudi Arabia Holy Soil?" *Think Israel* (September–October 2004), http://www.think-israel.org/schwartz.saudiarabia.html.

Seale, Patrick. *The Struggle for Syria.* London: I. B. Tauris, 1985.

Segev, Samuel. *The Iranian Triangle.* New York: Free Press, 1988.

Segev, Tom. *One Palestine Complete: Jews and Arabs Under the British Mandate.* New York: Henry Holt, 1999.

Seymour, William. *British Special Forces: The Story of Britain's Undercover Soldiers.* Toronto: Grafton, 1985.

Shaul Shay. *The A&B of Evil: Iran, Hizballah and the Palestinian terror* New Brunswick NJ: Transaction, 2005.

Simpson, Christopher. *Blowback: The First Full Account of America's Recruitment of Nazis and Its Disastrous Effect on the Cold War, Our Domestic and Foreign Policy.* New York: Macmillan, 1988.

Slatin, Rudolf C. *Fire and Sword in the Sudan: A Personal Narrative of Fighting and Serving the Dervishes, 1879–1895.* Translated by F. R. Wingate. London: Arnold, 1896.

Smith, R. Harris. *OSS: The Secret History of America's First Central Intelligence Agency.* Guilford, CT: Lyons, 2005.

St. John, Robert. *The Boss: The Story of Gamel Abdel Nasser.* New York: McGraw-Hill, 1960.

Stern, Jessica. "Pakistan's Jihad Culture." *Foreign Affairs* 79, no. 6 (November–December 2000).

Storrs, Ronald. *Orientations.* London: Nicholson & Watson, 1943.

Strachan, Hew. *To Arms.* Vol. 1 of *The First World War.* Oxford: Oxford University Press, 2001.

Sykes, Christopher. *Crossroads to Israel.* Cleveland: World, 1965.

"Syria Army Takes Over Government: Leaders Ousted in Bloodless Coup d'etat." *Evening Independent,* 30 March 1949.

Szulc, Tad. *The Secret Alliance: The Extraordinary Story of the Rescue of the Jews Since World War II.* London: Macmillan, 1991.

Tanner, Stephen. *Afghanistan: A Military History from Alexander the Great to the Fall of the Taliban.* Cambridge: Da Capo, 2002.

Tauber, Eliezer. *The Arab Movements in World War I.* London: Frank Cass, 1993.

———. *The Formation of Modern Syria and Iraq.* London: Frank Cass, 1995.

Taylor, A. J. P. *The Struggle for Mastery in Europe, 1848–1918.* Oxford: Clarendon Press, 1965.

Taylor, Peter. *Provos: The IRA and Sinn Fein.* London: Bloomsbury, 1997.

Teitelbaum, Joshua. *The Rise and Fall of the Hashimite Kingdom of Arabia.* London: Hurst, 2001.

Tenet, George. *At the Center of the Storm: My Years at the CIA.* New York: Harper-Collins, 2007.

Thomas, Evan. *The Very Best Men: The Darling Early Years of the CIA.* New York: Simon & Schuster, 1995.

Thomas, Gordon. *Gideon's Spies: The Secret History of the Mossad.* New York: St. Martin's Press, 2007.

Thomas, Lowell. *With Lawrence in Arabia*. New York: Century, 1924.

Thomas, Martine. *Empires of Intelligence: Security Services and Colonial Disorder After 1914*. Berkeley: University of California Press, 2008.

Trento, Joseph J. *The Secret History of the CIA*. New York: Prima, 2001.

Tripp, Charles. "Sayyid Qutb: The Political Vision." In *Pioneers of Islamic Revival*. Edited by Ali Rahnema. London: Zed, 2005.

Trofimov, Yaroslav. *The Siege of Mecca: The Forgotten Uprising in Islam's Holiest Shrine and the Birth of Al-Qaeda*. New York: Doubleday, 2007.

Trumpener, Ulrich. *Germany and the Ottoman Empire, 1914–1918*. Princeton: Princeton University Press, 1968.

Tsafrir, Eliezer. *Big Satan, Small Satan: Revolution and Escape in Iran*. Tel Aviv: Maariv 2002.

Turner, Barry. *Suez 1956: The Inside Story of the First Oil War*. London: Hodder & Stoughton, 2006.

Twain, Mark. *The Innocents Abroad*. Mineola, NY: Dover, 2003.

Tyerman, Christopher. *God's War: A New History of the Crusades*. Cambridge: Harvard University Press, 2006.

"U.S. Accused of Syrian Coup Attempt." *The Age*, 14 August 1957.

U.S. Congress. Congressional Record. 25 April 1950. Washington, D.C.

Usher, Graham. "Taliban v. Taliban." *London Review of Books* 31, no. 7 (9 April 2009).

Vaglieri, Laura Veccia. "The Patriarchal and Umayyad Caliphates." In *The Cambridge History of Islam*. Edited by Ann K. S. Lambton, P. M. Holt, and Bernard Lewis. Vol. 1, *The Central Islamic Lands*. Cambridge: Cambridge University Press, 1970.

Vagts, Alfred. *The Military Attaché*. Princeton: Princeton University Press, 1967.

Vielain, Heinz. *Waffenschmuggel im Staatsauftrag: Was lange in Bonn geheim bleiben musste*. Herford: Busse Seewald, 1986.

Weiner, Tim. *Legacy of Ashes: The History of the CIA*. New York: Doubleday, 2007.

West, Nigel. *MI5: British Security Service Operations, 1909–1945*. London: Triad Granada, 1983.

———. *MI6: British Intelligence Service Operations, 1909–1945*. London: Weidenfeld & Nicolson, 1983.

Westrate, Bruce. *The Arab Bureau: British Policy in the Middle East, 1916–1920.* University Park: Pennsylvania State University Press, 1992.

Whiting, Charles. *Skorzeny: The Most Dangerous Man in Europe.* Conshohocken, PA: Combined, 1972.

Wilber, Donald. *Overthrow of Premier Mossadeq of Iran, November 1952–August 1953.* Nottingham: Spokesman, 2006.

Wildt, Michael. *Generation des Unbedingten: Das Führungskorps des Reichssicherheitshauptamtes.* Hamburg: Hamburger Editon, 2003.

Wilson, Charles McMoran. *Churchill: Taken from the Diaries of Lord Moran.* Boston: Houghton Mifflin, 1966).

Wilson, Jeremy. *Lawrence of Arabia: The Authorised Biography of T. E. Lawrence.* New York: Atheneum, 1990.

Wilson, Peter W., and Douglas F. Graham. *Saudi Arabia: The Coming Storm.* New York: M. E. Sharpe, 1994.

Winstone, H. V. F. *Gertrude Bell.* London: Jonathan Cape, 1978.

———. *The Illicit Adventure: The Story of Political and Military Intelligence in the Middle East from 1898 to 1926.* London: Jonathan Cape, 1982.

Woodhouse, C. M. *Something Ventured: The Autobiography of C. M. Woodhouse.* London: Granada, 1982.

Wright, Lawrence. *The Looming Tower: Al-Qaeda and the Road to 9/11.* New York: Vintage, 2006.

Wright, Peter. *Spy Catcher: The Candid Autobiography of a Senior Intelligence Officer.* Toronto: Stoddart, 1987.

Yasamee, F. A. K. *Ottoman Diplomacy: Abdulhamid II and the Great Powers.* Istanbul: Isis, 1996.

Yergin, Daniel. *The Prize: The Epic Quest for Oil, Money, and Power.* New York: Free Press, 1991.

Ziring, Lawrence. *Pakistan at the Crosscurrent of History.* Oxford: Oneworld, 2003.

Zubok, Vladislav, and Constantine Pleshakov. *Inside the Kremlin's Cold War: From Stalin to Khrushchev.* Cambridge: Harvard University Press, 1996.

Zweig, Ronald W. *Britain and Palestine During the Second World War.* London: Royal Historical Society, 1986.

ABBREVIATIONS AND ACRONYMS

ADC	Aide-de-camp
AIS	Allied Information Services
AMAL	Harakat Amal (Lebanese Resistance Detachments)
ANA	Arab News Agency
APOC	Anglo-Persian Oil Company
ARAMCO	Arabian-American Oil Company
ASCI	Assistant Chief-of-Staff for Intelligence
BAD	Base Ammunition Depot
BBC	British Broadcasting Corporation
BDO	Bund deutscher Offiziere (Federation of German Officers)
BEF	British Expeditionary Force
BL	British Library
BND	Bundesnachrichtendienst (Federal Intelligence Service)
BTE	British Troops Egypt
CENTO	Central Treaty Organization
CIA	Central Intelligence Agency
CIC	Counter Intelligence Corps
CID	Criminal Investigation Department
CIGS	Chief of the Imperial General Staff
C-in-C	Commander-in-Chief
Comintern	Information Bureau of the Communist and Workers' Parties
CP	Communist Party
CPSU	Communist Party of the Soviet Union
CRC	Council of the Revolutionary Command
CUP	Committee of Union and Progress
DAK	Deutsches Afrikakorps (German Africa Corps)
DCI	Department of Central Intelligence
DMI	Director(ate) of Military Intelligence

DP	displaced person(s)
DSO	Distinguished Service Order
EEC	European Economic Community
EG	Einsatzgruppe (Operational Task Force)
EK	Einsatzkommando (Operational Task Squad)
FBI	Federal Bureau of Investigation
FEA	Foreign Economic Administration
FFI	Freedom Fighters of Israel (Stern Gang)
FHO	Fremde Heere Ost (Foreign Armies East)
FO	Foreign Office
FOSH	Plugot Sadeh (Field Companies)
G2	Divisional Staff Intelligence Officer
GCHQ	Government Communications Headquarters
Gestapo	Geheime Staatspolizei (Secret State Police)
GIGN	Group d'Intervention de la Gendarmerie Nationale
GRU	Glavnoje Razvedyvatel'noje Upravlenije (Main Intelligence Directorate)
HMG	His/Her Majesty's Government
HQ	headquarters
HQBTE	Headquarters, British Troops Egypt
IA	Indian Army
IB	Intelligence Bureau
IEM	Ikhwan el Muslimeen (Muslim Brotherhood)
ICG	International Crisis Group
IDF	Israeli Defence Force
INA	Indian National Army
IOR	India Office Records
IRA	Irish Republican Army
ISI	Inter-Services Intelligence
ISLD	Inter-Services Liaison Department
IZL	Irgun Zvai Leumi (National Military Organization)
JAE	Jewish Agency Executive
JI	Jamaat-e-Islami
JIC	Joint Intelligence Committee

JUI	Jamaat-Ulema-e-Islam
KGB	Komityet Gosudarstvennoy Bezopasnosty (Committee for State Security)
KSA	Kingdom of Saudi Arabia
MB	Muslim Brotherhood
MC	Military Cross
MEC	Middle East Command
MEDO	Middle East Defense Organization
MERIP	Middle East Research and Information Project
MI5	Military Intelligence Dept. 5 (Colloquial designation for the Security Service)
MI6	Military Intelligence Dept. 6 (Colloquial designation for the Secret Intelligence Service)
MI9	Military Intelligence Dept 9 (Colloquial designation for POW Escape and Evasion Department)
MP	Member of Parliament
NARA	National Archives and Records Administration
NATO	North Atlantic Treaty Organization
NCO	Non-commissioned officer
NCRC	National Council of the Revolutionary Command
NKVD	Narodnyy Komissariat Vnutrennikh Del (People's Commissariat for Internal Affairs)
NSA	National Security Agency
NSC	National Security Council
ODESSA	Organisation der ehemaligen SS-Angehörigen (Organization of Former Members of the SS)
OPC	Office of Policy Coordination
OSO	Office of Special Operations
OSS	Office of Strategic Services
PFLP	Popular Front for the Liberation of Palestine
PFLP-EO	Popular Front for the Liberation of Palestine—External Operations
PLO	Palestine Liberation Organization
PPS	Parti Populaire Syrien

PS	Palestine Scheme
PSNS	Parti Social Nationaliste Syrien
RAF	Royal Air Force
RAOC	Royal Army Ordnance Corps
RCC	Revolutionary Command Council
RCMP	Royal Canadian Mounted Police
RSHA	Reichssicherheitshauptamt (SS Headquarters)
RZ	Revolutionäre Zellen (Revolutionary Cells)
SANACC	State, Army, Navy, Air Force Coordinating Committee
SAS	Special Air Service
SAVAK	Sazeman-e Ettela'at va Amniyat-e Keshvar (National Intelligence and Security Organization)
SAVAMA	Sazman-e Ettela'at va Amniat-e Melli-e Iran (Ministry of Intelligence and National Security of Iran)
SEATO	Southeast Asia Treaty Organization
SD	Sicherheitsdienst (SS Security Service)
SHAEF	Supreme Headquarters Allied Expeditionary Force
SHAI	Sherut Yediot (Information Service)
SIGINT	signals intelligence
SIS	Secret Intelligence Service (MI6)
SNS	Special Night Squads
SOCAL	Standard Oil of California
SOE	Special Operations Executive
SS	Schutzstaffel
SSNP	Syrian Social Nationalist Party
SSU	Strategic Services Unit
SVR	Sluzhba Vneshney Razvedki (Foreign Intelligence Service)
Tapline	Trans-Arabian Pipeline Company
TNA	The National Archives
TNSS	Turkish National Security Service
TSOPE	Tsentralnogo Obedineniia Politicheskikh Emigrantov iz SSSR (Central Association of Political Emigrants from the Soviet Union)
UK	United Kingdom

UN	United Nations
US	United States
USSR	Union of Soviet Socialist Republics
VEVAK	Vezarat-e Ettela'at va Amniat-e Keshvar (Iranian Ministry of Intelligence and Security)
WIN	Wolnosc i niezawislosc (Freedom and Independence)
WP	Warsaw Pact

CHRONOLOGY

THE WEST		THE EAST
	1090	Hashshashin established by Hasan-I Sabbah
	1095	First Crusade begins
	1098	Massacre of Ma'arra
	1099	Jerusalem falls; First Crusade ends
	1147	Second Crusade begins
	1149	Second Crusade ends
	1187	Third Crusade begins
	1192	Third Crusade ends; Conrad of Montferrat assassinated
	1202	Fourth Crusade begins
	1204	Fourth Crusade ends; Constantinople sacked
Magna Carta is signed	1215	
	1217	Fifth Crusade begins
	1221	Fifth Crusade ends
Birth of Saint Thomas Aquinas	1225	
	1228	Sixth Crusade begins
	1229	Sixth Crusade ends
Inquisition is established	1232	
	1244	Siege of Jerusalem
	1245	Fall of Jerusalem
	1248	Seventh Crusade begins
	1254	Seventh Crusade ends
	1261	Constantinople reclaimed by the Byzantines
	1270	Eighth Crusade

THE WEST		THE EAST
	1271	Ninth Crusade begins
	1272	Ninth Crusade ends
Papacy begins residency at Avignon	1309	
Hundred Years War begins	1337	
The Black Death spreads across Europe	1347	
Start of the Great Schism in the Roman Catholic Church	1378	
Council of Constance ends the Great Schism	1417	
Habsburg Dynasty begins	1438	
Hundred Years' War ends	1453	Fall of Constantinople to the Ottomans under Mehmed II; end of the Byzantine Empire
Gutenberg Bible printed	1455	
Columbus lands in the New World; Catholics conquer Granada and establish Spanish nation; Spanish Moors begin to abandon Islam	1492	
Moors expelled from Portugal	1496	
Moors expelled from Spain	1502	
Martin Luther posts his 95 Theses in Wittenberg	1517	
	1540	Sheikulislam named spiritual leader of all Ottoman Muslims
Defeat of the Spanish Armada	1588	
Last remaining Moriscos expelled from Spain	1616	

THE WEST		THE EAST
Thirty Years' War begins	**1618**	
Thirty Years' War ends	**1648**	
American Declaration of Independence	**1776**	
Treaty of Paris	**1783**	
French Revolution begins	**1789**	
Napoleon Bonaparte seizes power	**1799**	
Habsburg Dynasty ends	**1806**	
War of 1812	**1812**	
	1813	Russo-Persian Treaty; Great Game begins
Congress of Vienna convenes; Treaty of Ghent	**1814**	Congress of Vienna
Battle of Waterloo	**1815**	
	1819	Sadler crosses Arabia
Napoleon Bonaparte dies	**1821**	
Queen Victoria crowned	**1838**	
	1841	Straits Convention becomes effective
	1842	Stoddart and Conolly executed by Nasrullah Khan
	1843	Wolff released by Nasrullah Khan
Year of Revolution in Europe	**1848**	
Crimean War begins	**1853**	
Crimean War ends	**1856**	
	1857	Indian Mutiny begins; Indian Army formed
	1858	East India Company dissolved; Government of India Act enters into force

THE WEST		THE EAST
American Civil War begins	1861	
American Civil War ends	1865	
	1869	Suez Canal opens
France loses Franco-Prussian War	1871	
Congress of Berlin	1878	
	1879	Ismail Pasha abdicates
	1882	Alexandria riots
	1883	Battle of Tel-el-Kebir
	1885	Fall of Khartoum, Gordon killed; Intelligence Bureau established in India by Sir Charles MacGregor
	1889	Committee of Union and Progress founded in the Ottoman Empire
	1896	Menelik II defeats Italians at Adowa
Boer War begins	1899	Kitchener takes Khartoum
Queen Victoria dies	1901	
Boer War ends	1902	
Directorate of Military Intelligence abolished	1904	
	1907	Anglo-Russian Convention; Great Game ends
	1908	CUP takes power in the Ottoman Empire
Secret Service Bureau established	1909	
Assassination of Franz Ferdinand leads to First World War	1914	Sultan-Caliph proclaims *jihad*
	1915	McMahon-Hussein correspondence begins; Armenian Genocide

THE WEST		THE EAST
	1916	Arab Revolt begins; Sykes-Picot Agreement; British surrender at Kut and are defeated at Gallipoli; Arab Bureau created
Balfour Declaration; Bolshevik Revolution begins	**1917**	St. John Philby crosses Arabia
First World War ends	**1918**	Arab Revolt ends
Treaty of Versailles; Irish War of Independence begins	**1919**	
	1920	Haganah created
Ireland partitioned	**1921**	
Mussolini achieves power in Italy; Irish Civil War begins; Irish Free State established	**1922**	Transjordan created as Hashemite kingdom; Ottoman sultanate abolished
Irish Civil War ends	**1923**	Turkey becomes a republic; Ottoman Empire ends; Britain assumes control of Palestine mandate
	1924	Ataturk abolishes caliphate
	1928	Al-Banna founds Muslim Brotherhood
Wall Street Crash; Great Depression begins in United States	**1929**	
	1931	Irgun established
	1932	Iraq gains independence; Ibn Saud proclaims Kingdom of Saudi Arabia
Adolf Hitler becomes German chancellor	**1933**	SOCAL signs oil agreement with Saudi Arabia
Spanish Civil War begins	**1936**	Mufti-incited Arab Revolt begins in Palestine
	1937	Peel Commission proposes Palestinian partition

THE WEST		THE EAST
Germany annexes Austria	**1938**	Oil struck in Saudi Arabia
Spanish Civil War ends;	**1939**	Arab Revolt ends
Germany invades Poland;		
Second World War begins		
Battle of Britain	**1940**	Stern founds Freedom Fighters of Israel (Stern Gang)
Germany invades Soviet Union; United States enters war after Japanese attack on Pearl Harbor	**1941**	Rashid Ali coup fails in Iraq; Allies occupy Iran; Ali and the Grand Mufti flee to Germany; Haganah creates Palmach
Heydrich assassinated	**1942**	Germans defeated at El Alamein
German surrender at Stalingrad; Red Army wins battle of Kursk; Allies invade Sicily and Italian mainland	**1943**	Afrika Korps and Italians surrender to Allies
Allies invade Normandy	**1944**	Lord Moyne assassinated
Nazi death camps liberated; Second World War ends; Special Operations Executive disbanded; FDR dies; Truman becomes president; Churchill loses election	**1945**	Atom bombs dropped on Japan
Greek Civil War begins; Kennan's "Long Telegram."	**1946**	King David Hotel bombing
Truman Doctrine proclaimed; CIA formed; Gehlen establishes Pullach HQ	**1947**	Jerusalem riots; Farran trial; end of British Palestine Mandate; Pakistan gains independence
Apartheid becomes law in South Africa	**1948**	State of Israel created; Arab-Israeli War begins; Bernadotte assassinated; Irgun, Stern Gang, and all other paramilitaries disbanded; Jinnah dies; ISI created

THE WEST		THE EAST
Greek Civil War ends; NATO established; Soviet Union tests A-bomb	**1949**	Liaqat Ali Khan assassinated; Mao proclaims People's Republic of China; Stern Gang granted amnesty
	1950	Korean War begins
Acheson convenes ad hoc Egypt committee	**1951**	
Britain tests Atom bomb; United States tests Hydrogen bomb and launches first nuclear sub	**1952**	Free Officers overthrow Farouk; Revolutionary Command Council governs Egypt
Eisenhower becomes president; Stalin dies; Khrushchev succeeds him; Beria executed	**1953**	Korean War ends; France withdraws from Indo-China; Mossadeq ousted in Iran (Operation Ajax); MI6 recruits Khalil
	1954	Nasser becomes Egyptian president; first attempt on Nasser's life; Algerian war of independence begins; SEATO is established
Warsaw Pact and non-aligned movement established; Pentagon announces plan to develop ICBMs; Eden becomes prime minister	**1955**	St. John Philby leaves Saudi Arabia; Baghdad Pact among anticommunist states; Soviet aid to Syria begins
Khrushchev attacks Stalin in CPSU speech and de-Stalinization begins; Hungarian Revolution crushed by Red Army	**1956**	Hussein of Jordan dismisses Glubb Pasha; Arab News Agency raided; Nasser vows to reconquer Palestine; Suez crisis begins; Britain and France invade Egypt; Israel takes Sinai; Pakistan becomes an Islamic republic

THE WEST		THE EAST
Eden resigns; Macmillan becomes primne minister; Gromyko becomes Soviet foreign minister; Treaty of Rome signed; Soviet Union launches *Sputnik*	**1957**	Suez crisis ends with Israeli withdrawal from Sinai; Suez Canal reopened; Vietnam insurgency begins
EEC founded	**1958**	United Arab Republic created with Nasser as president; Iraq and Jordan unite; Qassim assumes power in Iraq; Soviet aid to Iraq begins; Ayub Khan takes over Pakistan
Castro takes over Cuba; CENTO established; Khrushchev meets Mao	**1959**	Vietnam War begins
Mau Mau uprising ends in Kenya; U2 spy plane shot down; Eichmann abducted in Argentina by Israel; Khrushchev pounds shoe on UN podium; JFK wins election over Nixon	**1960**	Malayan insurgency ends; OPEC formed
JFK becomes president; Bay of Pigs invasion fails; Berlin Wall constructed; Vietnam War begins; Eichmann sentenced to death in Israel	**1961**	United Arab Republic collapses
Eichmann hanged; Cuban missile crisis	**1962**	Algeria gains independence; civil war begins in Yemen
JFK assassinated; LBJ becomes president; Kim Philby given asylum in Moscow; the Profumo affair scandalizes Britain	**1963**	Baathists come to power in Syria and Iraq

THE WEST		THE EAST
Brezhnev succeeds Khrushchev; China tests A-bomb; Wilson defeats Hume at the British polls and forms a Labour government	**1964**	Founding of the Palestinian Liberation Organization in Cairo
Churchill dies; Heath becomes Tory leader	**1965**	US airborne troops and marines deployed in Vietnam; Pakistani troops enter Indian Kashmir
Prime Minister Verwoerd of South Africa assassinated; British Soviet spy George Blake escapes from prison and reaches Moscow; Ronald Reagan elected governor of California	**1966**	Kosygin invites Indian and Pakistani prime ministers to Moscow, and peace is achieved; Indira Ghandi becomes prime minister of India.; Sayyid Qutb executed; Baath Party takes over Syria; China's Cultural Revolution begins
Che Guevara executed in Bolivia	**1967**	Moshe Dayan becomes Israeli minister of defence; Six Day War; Israel captures the Golan Heights and the West Bank; War of Attrition begins
Prague Spring crushed by Warsaw Pact forces; Robert Kennedy and Martin Luther King assassinated; Pierre Trudeau becomes Canadian prime minister; beginning of The Troubles in Northern Ireland	**1968**	Saddam Hussein becomes vice president of Iraq; My Lai massacre in Vietnam
Nixon becomes president; Apollo 11 moon landing	**1969**	Arafat becomes head of Palestinian Liberation

(Continued)

THE WEST		THE EAST
		Organization; Gaddafi takes over Libya, seeks Soviet aid
Nuclear Non-Proliferation Treaty signed; Heath replaces Wilson as British prime minister	**1970**	War of Attrition ends; Nasser dies; Sadat takes over Egypt; Black September in Jordan
Construction of the World Trade Center completed; Australia and New Zealand withdraw their forces from Vietnam	**1971**	Assad becomes Syrian president; Aswan Dam completed with Soviet aid; United Arab Emirates established in the Persian Gulf; East Pakistan gains independence from Pakistan and becomes Bangladesh
The Watergate burglaries; Black September terrorists murder eleven Israeli athletes at Munich Olympics	**1972**	Lod Airport massacre; Nixon visits China; Ali Bhutto becomes president of Pakistan; Pakistan and India sign Simla Agreement
Allende ousted by Pinochet in Chile	**1973**	Yom Kippur War
Nixon resigns in disgrace	**1974**	PLO represents Palestine at United Nations; Turkish invasion of Cyprus
Helsinki Final Act signed	**1975**	Fall of Saigon; Vietnam War ends; Cambodian genocide begins; Lebanese Civil War begins
Harold Wilson finally resigns; James Callaghan takes over No. 10 Downing Street; Soweto riots in South Africa; United States' bicentennial celebrations	**1976**	Hijacking of AF139; Israeli counterterrorist rescue mission at Entebbe, Uganda; Mao dies; Pol Pot becomes prime minister of Kampuchea; North and South Vietnam unite

THE WEST		THE EAST
Jimmy Carter becomes president; mid-air collision over Tenerife kills 583 people; Trans-Alaska pipeline opened; *Concorde* begins regular supersonic transatlantic flights	**1977**	Zia-ul-Haq ousts Bhutto and takes over Pakistan; Likud, led by Menachem Begin, win Israeli election; Sadat visits Israel; SEATO dissolved
Mass suicide by cultists at Jonestown, Guyana	**1978**	Operation Litani, successful Israeli intervention in Lebanon; Begin and Sadat sign Camp David Accords; 2 million demonstrate in Tehran against the Shah; communists take over Afghanistan
USA and China open diplomatic relations; Margaret Thatcher becomes British prime minister; Mountbatten assassinated by IRA Provos; Pope John Paul II visits his native Poland; Sandanistas assume power in Nicaragua	**1979**	Sinai treaty; Egypt recognizes Israel; Soviet Union invades Afghanistan; Shah leaves Iran, Khomeini assumes power, and Tehran hostage crisis begins; Islamic fundamentalists attack and occupy Mecca Grand Mosque; Saddam Hussein takes over Iraq; Zia-ul-Haq has Bhutto executed; Pol Pot regime collapses in Cambodia; 200,000 Chinese troops invade northern Vietnam but are forced to withdraw with severe losses
Marshal Tito dies; Pierre Trudeau returns as Canadian leader; Special Air Service squad successfully storms the Iranian Embassy in London, after its occupation by	**1980**	Iran-Iraq War begins; Israel and Egypt establish diplomatic relations; Muslim Brotherhood assassination attempt on Assad fails; Shah dies in Cairo; Canadian diplomats facilitate escape of American diplomats from

(Continued)

THE WEST		THE EAST
Iranian-born terrorists; Polish Solidarity union is established		Tehran; commando mission to rescue the 52 hostages fails
Reagan becomes president; Poland's last communist ruler, General Jaruzelski, assumes power; both Reagan and the Pope wounded by gunmen in separate incidents; Mitterand becomes French president	**1981**	Sadat assassinated; Mubarak becomes Egyptian president; Tehran hostages released; Israel bombs Beirut
Falklands War between Britain and Argentina; Andropov succeeds Brezhnev	**1982**	Israel invades Lebanon; Hama Massacre; Sabra and Shatila Massacres
Reagan proposes "Star Wars"; Thatcher wins huge landslide victory in aftermath of Falklands War; Soviet fighter downs South Korean airliner in Soviet air space; military rule ends in Argentina	**1983**	United States embassy and marine barracks bombings in Beirut
Chernenko succeeds Andropov; Reagan calls for ban on chemical weapons; over the next two years Palestinian terrorist attacks on Western targets by Abu Nidal and others reach their height	**1984**	US marines withdraw from Lebanon; CIA Beirut station chief William Buckley kidnapped by Islamic Jihad and murdered; Iran accuses Iraq of using chemical weapons

THE WEST		THE EAST
Reagan sworn in for second term; Gorbachev becomes Soviet leader	**1985**	Israel withdraws troops from Lebanon and bombs PLO headquarters near Tunis
Iran-Contra affair causes scandal in Washington; Air India 182 blown up over the Atlantic; Swedish prime minister Olaf Palme assassinated; disco bombed in West Berlin by Libyan terrorists; Chernobyl nuclear disaster	**1986**	United States bombs Libya
	1987	First Intifada begins
Gorbachev initiates *perestroika* (restructuring) in Soviet Union; Libyan terrorists destroy PanAm jumbo jet over Lockerbie, Scotland	**1988**	Zia-ul-Haq dies in air crash; Benazir Bhutto becomes prime minister of Pakistan; Iran Air Flight 655 shot down by U.S. Navy accidentally
Bush Sr. becomes president; Hungarian border opened; Solidarity wins Polish elections; Berlin Wall falls; Velvet Revolution in Czechoslovakia; Ceauşescu toppled and executed in Romania; United States invades Panama	**1989**	Iran-Iraq War ends; *fatwa* issued by Ayatollah Khomeini concerning Salman Rushdie's British publication of *The Satanic Verses* in 1989; Khomeini dies; Soviet Union withdraws from Afghanistan; *mujahideen* factions start fighting; Tiananmen Square demonstrations in Beijing
Germany re-unified; Mandela released; Major succeeds Thatcher as British prime minister	**1990**	First Intifada ends; Lebanese Civil War ends; Iraq invades Kuwait; launch of Operation Desert Shield; North and South Yemen unite. Benazir Bhutto dismissed in Pakistan; Nawaz Sharif takes over and Shariah law is incorporated into legal code

THE WEST		THE EAST
Yeltsin becomes Russian president; USSR and Yugoslavia collapse; former Soviet republics and satellite states gain independence; Warsaw Pact dissolved; KGB is transmuted into SVR	**1991**	The first Gulf War; sanctions imposed on Iraq; former Soviet republics in central Asia gain independence
Apartheid ends, and the United States lifts sanctions against South Africa	**1993**	Oslo Accords signed; Sharif is replaced by Benazir Bhutto in Pakistan
Bill Clinton becomes president	**1993**	
Nelson Mandela becomes president of South Africa; Rwandan Genocide takes place; First Chechen War begins	**1994**	Jordan recognizes Israel
Sarin gas attack on Tokyo subway injures over 5,000; massive bomb destroys Oklahoma City federal building; over 8,000 Bosniaks massacred by Serbs at Srebrenica	**1995**	Yitzhak Rabin assassinated in Tel Aviv
First Chechen War ends; massive Irish Republican Army bomb devastates Manchester city centre	**1996**	Taliban seize power in Afghanistan; Benazir Bhutto dismissed for a second time in Pakistan; Khobar Towers bombing in Saudi Arabia
Tony Blair becomes British prime minister; Princess Diana dies in Paris car crash	**1997**	Nawaz Sharif returns to power in Pakistan

THE WEST		THE EAST
Clinton-Lewinsky scandal breaks in Washington; Clinton is later impeached and cleared; United States embassy bombings in Tanzania and Kenya	**1998**	Pakistan becomes a nuclear power; Osama bin Laden issues *fatwa* declaring holy war on all Jews and "crusaders."
Kosovo conflict culminates in NATO bombing of Serbia; Second Chechen War begins; Putin succeeds Yeltsin	**1999**	Hussein of Jordan dies; Musharraf seizes power in Pakistan
Russian submarine *Kursk* sinks in Barents Sea; Serb president Milosevic ousted; Hillary Clinton elected senator; "dot.com bubble" bursts	**2000**	Second Intifada begins; Assad Sr. dies and is succeeded by his son; Al Qaeda bombs USS *Cole* in Aden
Bush succeeds Clinton as president; 9/11 Al Qaeda attack on World Trade Center and the Pentagon; Al Qaeda shoe bomber fails to detonate device on flight from Paris to Miami	**2001**	Sharon becomes Israeli prime minister; NATO invades Afghanistan; Taliban ousted from power; Pakistani gunmen attack Indian parliament
Britain celebrates Queen's Golden Jubilee; Bush creates Department of Homeland Security	**2002**	Daniel Pearl kidnapped, tortured, and murdered in Karachi; Bali nightclub bombing

THE WEST		THE EAST
Space shuttle disintegrates during reentry; last flight of *Concorde*; Libyan Lockerbie bomber sentenced to a minimum term of 27 years	**2003**	United States invades Iraq, withdraws troops from Saudi Arabia; Saddam Hussein captured; Riyadh compound bombings trigger harsh Saudi response involving mass arrests; Libya admits to building a nuclear bomb; Musharraf escapes two assassination attempts within two weeks
Jihadis bomb Madrid commuter railways; Blair visits Libya in recognition of Qaddafi's dismantling of Libyan WMD program; George Tenet resigns as CIA head and Colin Powell as Secretary of State; Reagan dies; Chechen terrorists take hostages at North Ossetian school with bloody outcome	**2004**	Abu Ghraib prisoner abuse shocks West and East; Singh becomes Indian prime minister; Karzai wins Afghan elections; United States consulate in Jeddah attacked; tsunami hits southeast Asia
Bush inaugurated for second term; John Paul II dies; Cardinal Ratzinger elected pope; *jihadis* bomb London underground and bus; Provisional IRA formally ends terror campaign; Danish newspaper publishes controversial caricatures of Mohammed	**2005**	King Fahd of Saudi Arabia dies; Ahmadinejad elected president of Iran; Saddam Hussein goes on trial; bombings in Amman; Iranian Hercules crashes into 10-storey Tehran apartment block; Shakidor Dam bursts

THE WEST		THE EAST
Aircraft terrorist plot discovered in UK leads to greatly increased preflight security measures; Pope criticizes Islam, provoking mass protests; global housing bubble peaks and bursts; subprime lending triggers beginning of global financial crisis	**2006**	Israel-Lebanon conflict; Sharon suffers massive stroke; Olmert becomes Israeli prime minister; Saddam Hussein executed; Al Qaeda's Iraq leader Zarqawi killed in air raid; "Islamic State of Iraq" set up by insurgents; Mecca stampede kills 362 *Hajjis*; Ahmadinejad affirms Iranian enriched-uranium production and hosts "International Conference to Review the Global Vision of the Holocaust"
Wildfires break out through-out Greece; Putin announces resumption of Russian strategic bomber patrols	**2007**	Musharraf proclaims state of emergency in Pakistan; Benazir Bhutto assassinated
Fidel Castro resigns; brother Raul is elected Cuban president; Medvedev becomes Russian president; Putin is nominally his prime minister; alleged war criminal Karadzic arrested in Belgrade; South Ossetia War breaks out; Somalian piracy intensifies; global financial crisis pushes Iceland to the brink	**2008**	Taliban attempt on Karzai's life; Musharraf resigns from presidency of Pakistan and is succeeded by Asif Ali Zardari, Benazir Bhutto's widower; Israeli attacks against Gaza; Terorists attack Mumbai
Barack Obama succeeds George W. Bush as president;	**2009**	Israel invades Gaza, then withdraws; financial crisis

(Continued)

THE WEST	THE EAST
Russia in energy dispute with Ukraine; Icelandic economy collapses; devastating bush fires in Australia; H1N1 ("swine flu") virus reaches pandemic proportions; Britain releases Lockerbie bomber to Libya on compassionate grounds	threatens apparently solvent Dubai; widespread protests in Iran after Ahmadinejad rigs re-election; Sri Lankan civil war ends; Uyghurs and Han Chinese clash in western China

DRAMATIS PERSONAE

ABDUL AZIZ IBN SAUD - (1876–1953) ruler and first monarch of Saudi Arabia, who founded the Kingdom of Saudi Arabia as a unified nation in 1932. When oil was struck in 1938, his closest advisor and chief negotiator was **Harry St. John Philby**, father of **Kim Philby**.

ABDULHAMID II - (1842–1918) 34th Sultan of the Ottoman Empire from 1876 until deposed in 1909; the last sultan to rule with absolute power.

ABDULLAH I - (1882–1951) Emir and King of Transjordan (1921–1949) and of Jordan (1949–1951), second son of **Hussein bin Ali**. Abdullah worked closely with **T. E. Lawrence** during the Arab Revolt (1916–1918). Shot dead by a Palestinian gunman in Jerusalem while attending prayers with his grandson, who succeeded him as king.

ABDULMECIT II - (1868–1944) last Caliph of the Ottoman dynasty (1922–1924). Nominally crown prince when the sultanate was abolished in 1922, he was elected Caliph by the Turkish National Assembly.

DEAN ACHESON - (1893–1971) secretary of state under President Truman (1949–1953).

WESLEY ADAMS - (n.d.) Second secretary of the U.S. embassy in Cairo.

KONRAD ADENAUER - (1876–1967) German statesman, conservative politician, and first chancellor of the Federal Republic of Germany (West Germany) (1949–1963).

AGRIPPINA THE YOUNGER - (15–59) fourth wife of Emperor **Claudius** and mother of **Nero**; a beautiful woman with political ambitions and a ruthless streak. Executed by her son, although the various historical accounts of how and why she died differ significantly.

MAHMOOD AHMED - Pakistan Army officer and Director General of the Pakistani ISI who helped bring **Pervez Musharraf** to power.

HAFEZ AL-ASAD - (1930–2000) Former Syrian Air Force fighter pilot who was President of Syria for three decades from 1971.

RIFAAT AL-ASAD - (1937–) Younger brother of **Hafez al-Asad** and former commander of the Syrian Defense Brigades, who played a key role in his brother's takeover of executive power in 1970.

HASSAN AL-BANNA - (1906–1949) Egyptian social and political reformer, founded the Muslim Brotherhood, one of the largest and most influential twentieth-century Muslim revivalist organizations.

SALAH AL-BIZRI - (n.d) Chief of the Syrian General Staff.

ALEXANDER I - (1777–1825) favorite grandson of **Catherine the Great**, ruled Russia during the Napoleonic Wars. An interesting man during his lifetime, his possibly staged death from typhoid fever remains shrouded in mystery, and the location of his body unknown. Godfather to Queen **Victoria,** who was christened "Alexandrina Victoria" in his honor.

ALEXANDER II - (?–1073) born Anselmo da Baggio, known mainly for his tolerant attitude toward unrepentant Jews and for endorsing William the Conqueror's invasion of England in 1066, which helped the Normans pacify the English clergy.

HAROLD ALEXANDER - (1891–1969) British Army officer, commander of British forces in the Middle East (1942–1943); later became the last British governor general of Canada (1946–1952).

MUHAMMAD SHARIF AL-FARUQI - (1891–1920) Arab staff officer in the Ottoman army who played a pivotal role in events leading up to the Arab Revolt by either unintentionally or deliberately misinforming the British as to the extent of Arab preparedness to rise against the Turks.

RASHID ALI AL-GAYLANI - (1892–1965) pro-Nazi politician and former prime minister who mounted an abortive anti-British coup in Iraq in 1941, with support from the Mufti, **Hajj Amin al-Husseini**. After escaping to Tehran, he finally reached Berlin, where he spent the remaining war years under Hitler's protection.

HASSAN AL-HUDAIBI - (n.d.) Judge and supreme guide of the Muslim Brotherhood.

HAJJ AMIN AL-HUSSEINI - (1895–1974) Mufti of Jerusalem and militant leader of Palestinian nationalism during the British mandate and one of the modern Arab world's most controversial figures, who at times cooperated with the British, but who was pro-Nazi and spent most of the Second World War in Berlin.

ALI BIN HUSSEIN - (1879–1935) King of Hejaz and Grand Sharif of Mecca (1924–1925), and later regent of Iraq; eldest son of **Hussein bin Ali**.

MAHMUD ABD AL-LATIF - (n.d.) Muslim Brother who made an attempt on **Nasser**'s life in 1954, for which he was condemned to death and hanged.

HASHIM IBN ABD AL-MANAF - (n.d.) Great-grandfather of the Prophet **Mohammed**

RAGHIB AL-NASHASHIBI - (1881–1951) Palestinian politician, mayor of Jerusalem, and the Mufti's chief rival.

ABDULLAH AL-QAHTANI - (?–1979) co-leader of the 1979 seizure of the Grand Mosque of Mecca, proclaimed by his brother-in-law, **Juhaiman al-Utaibi**, to be the Mahdi, and killed during the two-week battle that ensued.

SHUKRI AL-QUWATLI - (1891–1967) President of Syria from 1943–1949 and 1955–1958.

MUHAMMAD ANWAR AL-SADAT - (1918–1981) 3rd president of Egypt, closely associated with **Nasser,** whose policies he initially embraced but later abandoned by reintroducing a multiparty system. In 1978, together with Menachem Begin of Israel, received the Nobel Peace Prize for negotiating peace between their countries, a move that was to prove hugely unpopular in the Islamic world.

JUHAIMAN AL-UTAIBI - (1936–1980) former Saudi National Guard soldier and militant Wahhabi Islamist who led over 1,000 men in the takeover of the Grand Mosque of Mecca in 1979, after which he was beheaded, along with 66 other insurgents. Justified his action by claiming that the Saudi leadership had lost its legitimacy through corruption and imitation of the West. He was married to the sister of fellow insurgent **Abdullah al-Qahtani**, whom Utaibi had claimed was the Mahdi before seizing the mosque.

MUHAMMAD IBN ABD-AL-WAHHAB - (1703–1792) influential Sunni scholar from Nejd (central Saudi Arabia). Although he never specifically called for a separate school of Islamic thought, it is from al-Wahhab that the term Wahhabism was coined to designate the ultraconservative form of Islam observed predominantly in Saudi Arabia.

HELMUT ALLARDT - (1907–1987) West German career diplomat and jurist, who investigated the situation with German advisors in Egypt in 1953 and submitted a whitewash report.

YIGAL ALLON - (1918–1980) Israeli politician, Palmach commander, and general in the IDF.

JULIAN AMERY - (1919–1996) British army officer and politician, militantly anticommunist and strongly supportive of Eden's policy over Suez. Son of **Leo Amery**, he was married to **Harold Macmillan**'s daughter and was a close friend of **Billy MacLean**.

LEO AMERY - (1873–1955) politician, journalist, and mountaineer, a school acquaintance of **Winston Churchill**, with whom he was associated throughout his career, although they frequently disagreed. Father of **Julian Amery**.

ROBERT AMORY - (1915–1989) Harvard University law professor who became CIA Deputy Director of Intelligence in 1952.

WLADYSLAW ANDERS - (1892–1970) Free Polish army officer who in 1941 led an army of Polish and Jewish soldiers (and many civilians) out of the Soviet Union into the Middle East, where they were retrained and formed the 2nd Polish Corps in the Italian campaign under Anders's command. Later C-in-C of all Free Polish forces.

L. Y. ANDREWS - (n.d.) District commissioner of Galilee killed by Arab extremists in 1937.

CECILIA ANGLETON - (n.d.) Wife of **James Jesus Angleton.**

JAMES JESUS ANGLETON - (1917–1987) career intelligence officer and head of CIA counterintelligence operations for over two decades (1954–1975).

AHMAD ARABI (URABI) - (1841–1911) Egyptian army officer who led the Urabi Revolt of 1879 against the Khedive and Turkish influence in the Egyptian military. Finally defeated by the British at the battle of Tel el-Kebir in 1882, after which he spent many years in exile in Ceylon (Sri Lanka).

TUVYA ARAZI - (n.d.) Yishuv intelligence officer in Syria and Lebanon.

SHLOMO ARGOV - (1929–2003) Israeli ambassador to the UK whose assassination was ordered by **Saddam Hussein**.

MUSTAPHA KEMAL ATATURK - (1881–1938) Turkish army officer, revolutionary statesman, and founder and 1st president of the Republic of Turkey from 1923 until his death. Subscribed to the ideals of the Enlightenment and sought to transform the remnants of Ottoman Turkey into a modern, secular democracy.

ZE'EV AVNI - (1920–2007) Israeli diplomat who operated in the 1950s as a KGB mole in Mossad. He was caught in 1956 and imprisoned.

GUS AVRAKOTOS - (1938–2005) Greek-American CIA case officer who was principally involved in organizing and arming the Afghan mujahidin in their struggle against the Soviet Union.

ABDULLAH YUSUF AZZAM - (1941–1989) highly influential Islamic scholar and theologian; taught and mentored **Osama bin Laden;** assassinated in Pakistan.

BERNHARD BAATZ - (1910–1978) SS officer indicted for war crimes in Poland, together with **Joachim Deumling** and others, in the so-called RSHA Trial in 1967–1968.

NASEERULLAH BABAR - (1928–). Pakistani Army officer who served as **Benazir Bhutto**'s interior minister 1993–1996. and who is thought by some to have been the mastermind behind the Taliban.

ROBERT "BOB" BAER - (1952–) American author and former CIA field officer in the MiddleEast.

KHALID BAKDASH - (1912–1995) Syrian Communist Party leader from 1936 until his death.

TAIMOUR BAKHTIAR - (1914–1970) Iranian general and ruthless founding head of SAVAK 1958–1961, assassinated by a SAVAK agent while hunting in Iraq.

ARTHUR BALFOUR - (1848–1930) prime minister of the U.K. (1902–1905); later as foreign secretary authored the Balfour Declaration of 1917, which supported the establishment of a Jewish homeland in Palestine.

EVELYN BARKER - (1894–1983) British Army officer and commander of British forces in the Palestine mandate from 1946 to 1947; miraculously survived many attempts on his life by the Irgun and the Stern Gang, even after he left Palestine.

WALTER BEDELL SMITH - (1895–1961) U.S. Army officer, chief of staff during **Eisenhower**'s tenure at SHAEF, ambassador to the Soviet Union (1946–1948), and director of the CIA (1950–1953).

YISRAEL BEER (BAR) - (1912–1966) Israeli army officer and professor of Military History at Tel Aviv University who was a close friend of **Shimon Peres** but also a Soviet agent. He was convicted of espionage in 1961 and died in prison.

MENACHEM BEGIN - (1913–1995) Israeli politician and head of the Irgun (1943–1948); later prime minister (1977–1983).

ELIAHU BEIT-ZURI - (1922–1945) member of the Stern Gang, hanged in Cairo for the assassination of **Lord Moyne**.

GERTRUDE BELL - (1868–1926) archaeologist, linguist, writer, photographer, traveler, political analyst, and colonial administrator; as Arab Bureau liaison officer she became a friend of **T. E. Lawrence**, an associate of **Percy Cox**, and field controller of **Harry St. John Philby**. Bell was partly if not largely responsible for the birth of the Iraqi nation.

DAVID BEN-GURION - (1886–1973) a passionate Russian Zionist who emigrated to Palestine in 1906; was the first prime minister of Israel 1948–1953 and 1955–1963. After retirement from politics, he lived the rest of his life on a kibbutz in the Negev desert.

ELYASHIV BEN-HORIN - (n.d.) Israeli diplomat who tried to recruit Arabs in the United States as Israeli espionage agents.

FOLKE BERNADOTTE - (1895–1948) Swedish diplomat assassinated by the Stern Gang while on a U.N. assignment in Jerusalem.

EMIL BERNDORFF - (1892–1968) SS officer indicted for war crimes in Poland, together with **Joachim Deumling** and others, in the so-called RSHA Trial in 1967–1968.

ERNEST BEVIN - (1881–1951) British Labour leader, politician, and statesman best known as Britain's wartime minister of labour and postwar foreign secretary. Bitterly opposed to violent Zionist dissidents, like the Irgun and the Stern Gang, and advocated for an independent Arab Palestinian state.

BENAZIR BHUTTO - (1953–2007) Harvard and Oxford-educated prime minister of Pakistan for two terms (1988–1990 and 1993–1996) and eldest daughter of **Zulfikar Ali Bhutto.** Al-Qaeda claimed responsibility for her assassination.

ZULFIKAR ALI BHUTTO - (1928–1979) Berkeley and Oxford-educated foreign minister, president, and prime minister of Pakistan between 1963 and 1977 and father of **Benazir Bhutto**. Sentenced to death and executed under the regime of his successor, military dictator **Muhammad Zia-ul-Haq.**

SAYYID HUSSEIN BIN ALI - (1854–1931) Sharif and Emir of Mecca (1908–1917); King of Hejaz (1917–1924, abdicated).

OSAMA BIN LADEN - (1957–) Saudi-born founder of the jihadist organization al-Qaeda, generally considered responsible for worldwide terrorist activities including the destruction of the World Trade Center in New York on September 11, 2001.

OTTO VON BISMARCK - (1815–1898) Prussian and German statesman known as the "Iron Chancellor" who succeeded in unifying Germany, which had hitherto consisted of hundreds of autonomous principalities and free cities; after unification, Germany became one of Europe's Great Powers and began seeking its "place in the sun," which had the ultimate effect of uniting the other Great Powers (with the exception of Austria-Hungary) against it.

BOHEMOND I - (1058–1111) led the First Crusade (1095–1099), capturing Antioch in 1098 and establishing a Frankish (Norman) monarchy there, which outlasted Norman rule in Europe.

CHARLES "CHIP" BOHLEN - (1904–1974) career diplomat and Soviet expert, served as U.S. ambassador to the Soviet Union (1953–1957). Did not get along well with **John Foster Dulles**.

JOHN BOKER - (n.d.) CIC (Counter Intelligence Corps) officer to whom **Reinhard Gehlen** surrendered in 1945.

SUBHA CHANDRA BOSE - (1897–1945) Indian politician and leader of the pro-Nazi Indian National Army (INA).

WILFRIED BÖSE - (1949–1976) Member of the West German left-wing terrorist group Revolutionäre Zellen (RZ), killed in 1976 in the famous Israeli raid on Entebbe airport,

Uganda. Along with **Brigitte Kuhlmann**, one of two German and six Palestinian hijackers of an Air France flight from Tel Aviv via Athens to Paris.

REGINALD J. BOWKER - (n.d.) British diplomat.

NORMAN N. E. BRAY - (1885–1962) Indian Army and RAF officer, intelligence officer, historian, and biographer.

JOHN BUCHAN - (1875–1940) colonial administrator, intelligence officer, politician, and novelist; as Lord Tweedsmuir became 15th governor-general of Canada in 1935.

WILLIAM FRANCIS BUCKLEY - (1928–1985) U.S. Army officer and CIA station chief in Beirut, kidnapped by Hezbollah in 1984 and later executed by Islamic Jihad.

WILLIAM C. BULLITT - (1891–1961) brilliant, wealthy U.S. diplomat, journalist, writer, and outspoken anticommunist and antifascist. FDR made him the first U.S. ambassador to the Soviet Union in 1933.

FRANZ BÜNSCH - (n.d.) Anti-Semitic Nazi propagandist and expert on "Jewish affairs"; worked as part of **Nasser**'s anti-Zionist propaganda apparatus.

GEORGE H. W. BUSH - (1924–) 41st president of the United States (1989–1993).

GEORGE W. BUSH - (1946–) 43rd president of the United States (2001–2009).

JEFFERSON CAFFERY - (1886–1974) U.S. career diplomat, ambassador to Egypt (1949–1955).

CARLOS THE JACKAL - Alias of **Ilich Remírez Sánchez** (1949–), convicted Venezuelan Marxist terrorist and murderer, in 1997 jailed for life in France. He is since said to have converted to Islam.

CARMEL OFFIE - (n.d.) Confidential secretary to and close associate of William C. Bullitt. Left State Department in disgrace in 1947 and joined the OPC (Office of Policy Coordination), where he became a close friend of Frank Wisner and ran Operations Paperclip and Bloodstone.

LORD CARODON - See **Hugh Mackintosh Foot.**

JIMMY CARTER - (1924–) 39th president of the United States (1977–1981).

CATHERINE THE GREAT - (1729–1796) minor Prussian princess who ruled Russia as Catherine II for 34 years during a period of significant growth in Russian influence, culture, and territory. Subscribed to the ideals of the Enlightenment and had a reputation as a patron of the arts, literature, and education. Is also reputed to have had many lovers.

WALTER J. CAWTHORN - (1896–1970) Deputy Chief of Staff of the Pakistan Army, as well as Secretary of the Pakistan Joint Services Commanders' Committee, who established the ISI.

AUSTEN CHAMBERLAIN - (1863–1937) statesman, politician, and recipient of the Nobel Peace Prize for his part in the negotiations over the Locarno Pact of 1925.

WINSTON CHURCHILL - (1874–1965), prime minister of U.K. during the Second World War, held many political offices between 1910 and 1955, always retaining enormous influence even when out of office.

CLAUDIUS I - (10 B.C.–54) **Nero**'s stepfather, he ruled the Roman Empire from A.D. 41 until his death, which may have been natural or by assassination. An able administrator who endowed Rome and the provinces with many fine public works; a prolific author of histories and other books, regrettably none of which has survived.

ILTYD NICHOLL CLAYTON - (1886–1965) British Army officer and head of British military intelligence in Cairo early in the Second World War. Subsequently served as advisor on Arab affairs to the British government.

GILBERT CLAYTON - (1875–1929) British Army officer, Arab Bureau officer, and colonial administrator. While colleagues and subordinates such as **T. E. Lawrence** achieved worldwide fame, the confidential nature of Clayton's successive offices necessarily obscured the importance of his achievements. Clayton's premature death during a polo match cut short a distinguished career of great promise.

CLEOPATRA VII PHILOPATOR - (69–30 B.C.) Hellenistic pharaoh who ruled Egypt from 51 B.C. until her death. Famous for her political skill, great beauty, and disingenuous liaisons with two famous Romans: Julius Caesar and Mark Antony.

CHARLES CLEVELAND - (1866–1929) Legendary head of the Indian secret service, with a brilliant mind, a larger-than-life physique, and a matching personality. Recruited **Norman N. E. Bray.**

WILLIAM JEFFERSON "BILL" CLINTON - (1946–) 42nd President of the United States from 1993 to 2001.

WILLIAM COLBY - (1920–1996) career intelligence officer and director of the CIA (1973–1976).

MICHAEL COLLINS - (1890–1922) Irish revolutionary leader, politician, and IRA director of intelligence, shot and killed during the Irish Civil War.

ARTHUR CONOLLY - (1807–1842) Indian Army officer, intelligence officer, explorer, and writer who completed many reconnaissance missions in Central Asia during the Great Game (he probably invented the term) and who, like **Charles Stoddart**, was captured and executed by **Nasrullah Khan**.

CONRAD OF MONTFERRAT - (ca.1145–1192) one of the leaders of the Third Crusade (1189–1192); became king of Jerusalem and was famously assassinated by the Hashshashin. Married **Isabella I of Jerusalem** after her scheming mother had forced her to separate from her loving but unambitious husband, **Humphrey of Toron**.

CONSTANTINE THE GREAT - (272–337) first Christian Roman emperor; proclaimed religious tolerance throughout the empire and made Constantinople the capital of Byzantium.

CARLTON S. COON - (1904–1981) U.S. anthropologist and OSS officer involved in North African espionage and the smuggling of arms to French resistance groups in German-occupied Morocco under the guise of anthropological fieldwork.

MILES COPELAND - (1916–1991) musician, businessman, and career intelligence officer; one of the original OSS (Office of Strategic Services) counterintelligence officers in the Second World War; later participated in major CIA political operations from the 1950s through to the 1980s.

PERCY COX - (1864–1937) Indian Army officer and diplomatist; closely associated with **Gertrude Bell**; replaced **Sir Arnold Wilson** as administrator of Iraq.

RICHARD CROSSMAN - (1907–1974) socialist politician, author, and editor of the *New Statesman*; a leading Zionist and anticommunist.

EFRAIM DAFNY - (n.d.) First Jewish volunteer from Palestine to parachute into Yugoslavia in March 1943.

ALBERT D'ÁIX - (n.d.) Chronicler of the First Crusade (1095–1099) on whose writings **William of Tyre** based much of his Crusade history.

MOSHE DAYAN - (1915–1981) Israeli general and Palmach commander, who became defense minister and foreign minister of Israel.

VALÉRY GISCARD D'ÉSTAING - (1926–) 20th president of France (1974–1981).

JOACHIM DEUMLING - (1910–2007) SS (SD) and Police lieutenant colonel and indicted war criminal; the foremost intelligence and security expert in **Nasser**'s Egypt.

XHAFER DEVA - (1904–1978) Albanian interior minister during the Nazi occupation.

BENJAMIN DISRAELI - (1804–1881) Tory statesman and literary figure, served twice as

British prime minister between 1868 and 1880, known for his rivalry with **William Gladstone** and warm friendship with Queen Victoria.

WILLIAM DONOVAN - (1883–1959) U.S. Army officer, establishment lawyer, and intelligence officer, nicknamed "Wild Bill," who headed the Office of Strategic Services (OSS), forerunner of the CIA, during the Second World War.

HASSAN DOSTI - (1894–1991) Albanian justice minister during the Italian occupation.

LARISSA DUBANOVA - (n.d.) Alias of KGB agent who ensnared Royal Canadian Mounted Police officer **Roy Guidon** in a honey trap.

ALLEN DULLES - (1893–1969) lawyer, diplomat, and career intelligence officer; rose to become the first civilian director of the CIA (1953–1961). Younger brother of **John Foster Dulles**.

JOHN FOSTER DULLES - (1888–1959) secretary of state under Eisenhower (1953–1959). Older brother of **Allen Dulles**.

ABBA (AUBREY) EBAN - (1915–2002) Israeli diplomat and politician, and former South African Army officer who served in Palestine as liaison officer between the Special Operations Executive (SOE) and the Haganah.

ANTHONY EDEN - (1897–1977) controversial British prime minister (1955–1957) whose reputation rests largely on his highly skilled performance as **Churchill**'s foreign secretary before and during the Second World War and was severely damaged by his conduct of the Suez campaign in 1956.

HERMANN EILTS - (1922–2006) U.S. ambassador to Saudi Arabia and Egypt; worked with **Sadat** throughout the Camp David Accords.

DWIGHT EISENHOWER - (1890–1969) U.S. Army officer (Supreme Allied Commander [Europe] in the Second World War) and 34th president of the United States (1953–1961).

ROLF ENGEL - (1912–1993) celebrated German rocket scientist who worked at Skoda with **Wilhelm Voss** during the war on liquid and solid fuel rockets and later developed missiles for **Nasser**.

ENVER PASHA - (1881–1922) also known as Ismail Enver, the most famous of the "Three Pashas" who ruled the Ottoman Empire during the Balkan Wars and the First World War (the others were Talat Pasha and Cemal Pasha).

JOHN EWART - (1861–1930) War Office director of military operations and intelligence; a keen supporter of establishing a Secret Service Bureau before the First World War.

WILHELM FAHRMBACHER - (1888–1970) German army officer and one of **Rommel**'s top generals; headed the first contingent of German military advisors to Egypt (1950–1959).

JOHN FARMER - (n.d.) Wartime SOE (Special Operations Executive) officer and career SIS (Secret Intelligence Service) officer.

FAROUK I - (1920–1965) penultimate king of Egypt and Sudan, succeeding his father, Fuad I, in 1936; deposed by the Free Officers revolt and exiled in 1952.

ROY FARRAN - (1921–2006) British army officer, politician, farmer, and author who served in the SAS (Special Air Service) during the Second World War and in Palestine after the war, where he encountered major difficulties with the Stern Gang, ultimately emigrating to Alberta, Canada, where he became a prominent provincial cabinet minister (1971–1979).

FAYSAL BIN ABDUL AZIZ - (1903–1975) king of Saudi Arabia from 1964 until his death; third son of **Abdul Aziz ibn Saud**. Assassinated by his half-brother's son, who was deemed insane but was nevertheless found guilty of regicide and beheaded.

FEISAL I - (1883–1933), king of Iraq from 1921 until his death; third son of Sharif **Hussein bin Ali**. During the Arab Revolt in the First World War, closely supported by **T. E. Lawrence**, and subsequently by **Gertrude Bell**.

BERNARD FERGUSSON - (1911–1980) British army officer who was assistant inspector-general of the Palestine police force (1946–1947). Later governor-general of New Zealand (1962–1967), like his father and both his grandfathers before him.

J. B. FLUX - (n.d.) First secretary for commercial affairs at the British embassy in Cairo, where he began service in 1919. One of two British diplomats (the other was **J. G. Gove**) expelled from Egypt by **Nasser** for their alleged involvement in espionage at the time of the ANA raid and arrests in 1956.

HUGH MACKINTOSH FOOT - (1907–1990) **Lord Carodon,** Britain's last governor of Cyprus.

FREDERICK II - (1194–1250) unlike the militaristic German emperor Frederick I Barbarossa, Frederick II was an enlightened Sicilian who ruled as emperor for thirty years until his death, living mostly with his mother in Palermo as an avid patron of the arts. Despite papal opposition, he led the Sixth Crusade (1228–1229) to the Holy Land, which ended in a bloodless victory, ten years of peace, and considerable Muslim discontent.

GRAHAM E. FULLER - (n.d.) U.S. State Department and CIA officer for 27 years, including a term as CIA station chief in Kabul, Afghanistan, now affiliated with Simon Fraser University as an adjunct history professor.

MAHATMA GANDHI - (1869–1948) political and spiritual leader of India, who pioneered the concept of nonviolent civil disobedience, which ultimately led India to independence.

ROBERT GASCOYNE-CECIL - (1830–1903), Marquess of Salisbury, foreign secretary under **Benjamin Disraeli,** and prime minister of the U.K. for over thirteen years between 1885 and 1902.

DHARMINDRA GAUR - (n.d.) Indian Special Operations Executive (SOE) officer during the Second World War.

NAWAF GHAZALEH - (n.d.) Syrian Druze who assassinated **Adib Shishkali** in 1964.

REINHARD GEHLEN - (1902–1979) German army officer and military intelligence chief on the Russian Front during the Second World War, after which he became head of West German intelligence until 1968.

WILLIAM GLADSTONE - (1809–1898) four times Liberal prime minister of U.K. between 1868 and 1894, nicknamed the GOM (Grand Old Man); famous for his political and personal rivalry with the Tory **Benjamin Disraeli** and his tense relationship with Queen Victoria.

LEOPOLD GLEIM - (n.d.) Former SS colonel who worked in Egypt as **Joachim Deumling**'s assistant and security expert.

SIR JOHN GLUBB - (1897–1986) British Army officer who commanded the Transjordanian Arab Legion (1939–1956). Better known as Glubb Pasha.

CHARLES GORDON - (1833–1885) British Army officer and colonial administrator, known variously as "Chinese Gordon" (he commanded a Chinese army brilliantly in the 1860s), "Gordon Pasha" (he was governor of Sudan), and "Gordon of Khartoum," where he was killed in close combat with the Mahdi's warriors.

J. G. GOVE - (n.d.) Head of the visa section at the British embassy in Cairo. One of two British diplomats (the other was **J. B. Flux**) expelled from Egypt by Nasser at the time of the ANA raid and arrests in 1956.

BILLY GRAHAM - (1918–) U.S. Christian (Baptist) evangelist with universal charismatic appeal.

VICTOR GRAYEVSKI - (n.d.) Polish Zionist journalist who covertly supplied Israel with a copy of **Nikita Khruschev**'s anti-Stalin speech in 1956.

GREGORY VII - (1020–1085) born Hildebrand of Soana, canonized in 1728 as Saint Gregory, one of the great reformers of the papacy.

EDWARD GREY - (1862–1933) statesman, diplomat, and ornithologist; foreign secretary for eleven continuous years (1905–1916): an unbroken record.

ANDREI GROMYKO - (1909–1989) Soviet foreign minister (1957–1985) and Chairman of the Supreme Soviet until 1988, when he was succeeded by Mikhail Gorbachev.

COLIN GUBBINS - (1896–1976) British Army officer and SOE (Special Operations Executive) director of operations and training, the prime mover of SOE during the Second World War; described as one of the war's unsung heroes.

ROY GUIDON - (n.d.) Soviet mole in the RCMP unmasked by Israeli intelligence.

WALTER GUINNESS - (1880–1944) Anglo-Irish politician and businessman who, as **Lord Moyne**, was assassinated in Cairo by the Stern Gang.

HAMID GUL - (1936–) Pakistan Army officer and Director General of the Pakistani ISI under **Benazir Bhutto,** Gul was a devout Muslim from the Punjab with close ties to the Saudis.

GABRIEL HADDAD - (n.d.) Christian Arab advisor to **Ronald Storrs**.

JOHN HADDEN - (n.d.) CIA station chief in Tel Aviv.

ELIAHU HAKIM - (1925–1945) member of the Stern Gang, hanged in Cairo for the assassination of **Lord Moyne**.

SAIYID S. HAMID - (n.d.) Former Indian Military Secretary and Director of the Pakistan National Guard, who became the first director of the Pakistani ISI.

NICK HAMMOND - (1907–2001) Special Operations Executive (SOE) liaison officer with the Arab Platoon in Palestine.

MAURICE HANKEY - (1877–1963) Royal Marines officer and civil servant, cabinet secretary for twenty-six years (1912–1938); highly respected official, Hankey also undertook, as a very young subaltern, unofficial and unpaid intelligence work, an activity he maintained to the end of his public life and beyond.

ISSER HAREL - (1912–2003) Mossad officer who later became director 1952–1963.

BASIL LIDDELL HART - (1895–1970) British soldier, journalist, and military historian. Hart was knighted in 1966.

HASAN-AS-SABAH - (1056–1124) Persian Nizari-Ismaili (Shia) missionary who founded the quasi-religious political cult of the Hashshashin (Hashishiyan), who were trained to assassinate Sunnis.

URGUPLU HAYRI BEY - (n.d.) Sheikulislam (Muslim Patriarch) of the Ottoman Empire and minister of religious affairs under the Committee of Union and Progress (or Young Turk) regime of 1913–1918. Father of Ali Suat Hayri Urguplu, who served briefly as Turkish prime minister in 1965.

MOHAMED HEIKAL - (1923–) leading Egyptian journalist, former editor of the Cairo newspaper *Al-Ahram*; longtime friend of **Nasser** and **Sadat**.

RICHARD HELMS - (1913–2002) naval officer and director of the CIA (1966–1973) who served in the OSS (Office of Strategic Services) during the Second World War and ran OSO (Office of Special Operations) operations in Austria, Germany, and Switzerland immediately after the war.

HENRY II OF CHAMPAGNE - (1166–1197) one of the leaders of the Third Crusade (1189–1192); succeeded **Conrad of Montferrat** as King of Jerusalem and married **Conrad**'s widow, **Isabella I of Jerusalem**, only eight days after the Hashashshin assassination.

OTTO VON HENTIG - (1886–1984) German diplomat who achieved fame during the First World War for his mission to Afghanistan in 1915 and who functioned as a Middle East expert in Ribbentrop's Foreign Office during the Second World War.

HERACLIUS - (575–641) Byzantine emperor of the Roman Empire, thought to be the first to engage the Muslims.

AUBREY HERBERT - (1880–1923) diplomat, traveler, and intelligence officer who worked for the Arab Bureau and was a friend of **T. E. Lawrence**, **Sir Mark Sykes,** and **John Buchan**. An extremely adventurous man, despite being nearly blind from birth.

CHAIM HERZOG - (1918–1997) Israeli military attaché in Washington, who was twice head of Israeli military intelligence (Aman) 1948–1950 and 1959–1962. Herzog later served as president of Israel for ten years (1983–1993).

REINHARD HEYDRICH - (1904–1942) German SS officer who from 1941 governed what remained of Czechoslovakia (Reich Protectorate of Bohemia and Moravia) while remaining in charge of the Berlin HQ of the SS (Reich Security Main Office). He was attacked by Czech partisans on May 27, 1942, and fatally wounded. The Nazis avenged Heydrich's death by annihilating the Bohemian villages of Lidice and Lezaky.

HEINRICH HIMMLER - (1900–1945) immensely powerful Nazi politician and Reichsführer-SS, C-in-C of the SS, who oversaw all Nazi police and security forces (1929–1945) and coordinated the Nazi genocide, presiding over concentration camps, extermination camps, death squads, and a vast business empire.

SAMI HINNAWI - (1898–1950) Syrian Army colonel who seized power in Syria in 1949 only to be displaced by **Adib Shishakli** and murdered in Lebanese exile.

ADOLF HITLER - (1889–1945) Austrian-born politician and genocidal fascist dictator of Germany from 1933 until his suicide who plunged the world into the conflagration of the Second World War.

J. C. HOLLAND - (1897–1956) British Army officer and expert on irregular warfare who is credited with inventing the concept of the commando and who helped **Colin Gubbins** organize and operate the Special Operations Executive SOE during the Second World War.

WILLIAM HOOD - (1920–) journalist, novelist, and former OSS counterintelligence officer with **Allen Dulles** in Switzerland, who later became a close friend of and deputy to **James Jesus Angleton** at the CIA.

ENVER HOXHA - (1908–1985) Marxist-Leninist-Maoist ruler of Albania from 1944 until his death who for forty years effectively sealed his country off from the rest of Europe.

HUMPHREY OF TORON - (1166–1197) first husband of **Isabella I of Jerusalem** with whom he grew up as a child and whom he married when she was eleven years old.

SADDAM HUSSEIN - (1937–2006) notoriously brutal Ba'athist ruler of Iraq who aggressively resisted foreign intervention in the Middle East and advocated for Palestinian independence. Tried, convicted, and hanged for ordering the mass killing of Shiites in 1982.

HUSSEIN BIN TALAL - (1935–1999) became king of Jordan in 1952 and succeeded in guiding his country through four decades of Arab-Israeli conflict, mostly in the context of the Cold War.

HUSSEIN BIN ALI - (1854–1931) Hashemite Grand Sharif of Mecca, ruled Hejaz as part of the Ottoman Empire until 1924, when he was defeated by **Abdul Aziz ibn Saud** and abdicated all his titles in favor of his eldest son, Ali.

MUHAMMAD AHMAD IBN ABD ALLAH - (1844–1885), otherwise known as the Mahdi, Ahmad proclaimed himself the prophesied redeemer of Islam and in 1881 led a bloody and victorious jihad against the Egyptians (and British) in Sudan. Thirteen years after his death, what was left of his army was annihilated by the British at the battle of Omdurman.

KHALID IBN MANSUR IBN LUWAY - (n.d.) Fiercely independent Wahhabi Sharif of Khurma (Hejaz), an important Saudi trade center, who generally supported **Abdul Aziz ibn Saud** in his struggles with the Hashemites, but on his own terms.

ABDULLAHI IBN MUHAMMAD - (1846–1899), otherwise known as the Khalifa, an able general who succeeded Muhammad Ahmad ibn Abd Allah (the Mahdi) in 1885. After his defeat by the British at the battle of Omdurman, he was pursued and killed by Wingate's troops at Umm Diwaikarat.

IBN RASHID - (1900–1920) Saud bin Abdul Aziz was Emir of Hail from age ten and constantly in conflict with **Abdul Aziz ibn Saud**, whom he never succeeded in defeating militarily. After Rashid's assassination by a cousin, **Abdul Aziz ibn Saud** married two of his wives, one of whom gave birth to the future King Abdullah of Saudi Arabia.

ISMET INÖNÜ - (1884–1973) Turkish army officer, prime minister, and 2nd president of the Turkish Republic, also known as Milli Sef (National Chief).

ISABELLA I OF JERUSALEM - (1172–1205) described as "exceedingly fair and lovely," she married four times, her second, third, and fourth husbands, all kings of Jerusalem, were **Conrad of Montferrat**, **Henry II of Champagne**, and Amalric II.

ISMAIL PASHA - (1830–1895), also known as Ismail the Magnificent; Khedive of Egypt and Sudan from 1863 to 1879, when he was removed by the British and the French.

IVAN THE TERRIBLE - (1530–1584) first czar of Russia was intelligent and devout but mentally unstable. Despite the mistranslated epithet associated with his name ("Fearsome" would be more accurate), he was not a particularly cruel ruler but tended to bully his subjects and was given to terrifying outbursts of apoplectic rage. His death is mysterious; it is possible that he was poisoned by Boris Godunov, who became czar fourteen years later.

SALAH JADID - (1926–1993) Syrian general and Baathist politician who became de facto head of the Syrian government for four years until deposed in 1970.

CLAUDE JARVIS - (1879–1953) British Army officer, colonial administrator, and orientalist who served in Egypt and Palestine during the First World War, later becoming a legendary governor in Libya and Sinai with an intimate knowledge of Bedouin customs and law. He was also a prolific author and gifted painter.

MOHAMMED ALI JINNAH - (1976–1948), politician and statesman, leader of the Muslim League and founder of the state of Pakistan.

ABOL-GASHEM KASHANI - (1882–1962) Iranian Shiite ayatollah and populist politician.

JOHN KAYE - (1814–1876) Indian Army officer, colonial administrator, novelist, and military historian who was partly responsible (as well as **Rudyard Kipling**) for popularizing **Arthur Conolly**'s term the "Great Game."

GEORGE F. KENNAN - (1904–2005) U.S. diplomat, political scientist, and historian who dispatched his "Long Telegram" from Moscow to Washington in 1946 highlighting the expansionist nature of Soviet foreign policy and the need for its strategic containment.

KHALID BIN ABDUL AZIZ - (1912–1982) king of Saudi Arabia from 1975 until his death, he was easygoing and apolitical, and willingly allowed his ultimate successor, Fahd, to govern the country. Died of a heart attack.

MAHMUD KHALIL - (n.d.) Head of Egyptian air force intelligence recruited by the SIS (Secret Intelligence Service) as a double agent in an attempt to topple **Nasser** and restore the Egyptian monarchy.

AYUB KHAN - (1907–1974) Pakistan Army commander and first military ruler of the country (1958–1969).

LIAQUAT ALI KHAN - (1896–1951) lawyer, politician, and right-hand man of **Mohammed Ali Jinnah**, who become the first prime minister of Pakistan from 1947 until his assassination.

HUSSEIN KHAYRI - (n.d.) King **Farouk**'s deputy head of Egyptian military intelligence.

RUHOLLAH MUSAVI KHOMEINI - (1902–1989) Iranian politician, scholar, religious leader, and political leader of the 1979 revolution that overthrew the Shah.

DAVID KIMCHE - (1928–) British-born Israeli diplomat and writer who was a Mossad intelligence officer and became DG of the Israeli foreign ministry under **Menachem Begin.**

NIKITA KHRUSHCHEV - (1894–1971) first secretary of the Soviet Communist Party and Soviet premier (1953–1964) at the height of the Cold War. A reformer who, despite his abrasive, pugnacious personality and international saber rattling, effectively de-Stalinized the Soviet Union and introduced a more liberal agricultural, industrial, and foreign policy regime.

RUDYARD KIPLING - (1865–1936) author, poet, and Nobel laureate, one of the most popular writers of late-nineteenth/early-twentieth century English literature, whose principal subject was the British Empire in all its aspects.

HORATIO KITCHENER - (1850–1916) soldier, diplomat, and statesman, famous for his decisive victory over the Mahdi at the battle of Omdurman in 1896, but later notorious for his brutality during the Boer War.

ABRAHAM MARCUS KLINGBERG - (1918–) Epidemiologist who was a Soviet agent in Israel sentenced in 1983 to twenty years' imprisonment for espionage.

ARTHUR KOESTLER - (1905–1983) prolific Hungarian-British author of political commentary and fiction, whose life was controversial and troubled, and whose various causes included communism, anticommunism, and Zionism.

THEODOR "TEDDY" KOLLEK - (1911–2007) Austrian-born, pro-British Israeli agent who worked for the British Security Service (MI5) and knew **Kim Philby**. He became a successful politician and was mayor of Jerusalem for twenty-eight years.

BRIGITTE KUHLMANN - (1947–1976) Member of the West German left-wing terrorist group Revolutionäre Zellen (RZ), killed in 1976 in the famous Israeli raid on Entebbe airport, Uganda. Along with **Wilfried Böse**, she was one of two German and six Palestinian hijackers of an Air France flight flying from Tel Aviv via Athens to Paris.

ABAS KUPI - (n.d.) British choice to be head of the Albanian government-in-exile; Nazi collaborator during the Second World War.

ESHREF KUSHCHUBASHI - (1873–1964) Leading member of **Enver Pasha**'s secret service.

MILES LAMPSON - (1880–1964) British career diplomat who served for many years in Egypt and the Sudan (1934–1946), ultimately as high commissioner and ambassador.

HERMANN LAUTERBACHER - (1909–1988) Nazi gauleiter and deputy head of the Hitler Youth who later became **Reinhard Gehlen**'s liaison officer with the Nazi diaspora in **Nasser**'s Egypt.

HENRY MONTGOMERY LAWRENCE - (1806–1857) British artillery officer and political agent to the Governor-General for the North West Frontier. Killed at the Siege of Lucknow during the Indian Mutiny.

T. E. LAWRENCE - (1888–1935) British army officer and Arab Bureau intelligence officer, famous as Lawrence of Arabia for his liaison role during the Arab Revolt of 1916–1818.

AUSTEN LAYARD - (1817–1894) archaeologist, diplomatist, and politician. Layard was British ambassador to the Ottoman Empire (1877–1880).

MARGUERITE "MISSY" LEHAND - (1898–1944) private secretary to Franklin D. Roosevelt and his close companion for many years.

TOM LITTLE - (1911–1975) head of the Arab News Agency (ANA), correspondent for *The Economist* and *The Times,* and senior SIS (Secret Intelligence Service) officer in Cairo.

JOHN BRUCE LOCKHART - (1914–1995) intelligence officer, educator, and rugby player, who succeeded **Kim Philby** as liaison officer in Washington, where he successfully repaired much of the damage done to the "special relationship" by Philby; later he was responsible for SIS operations in the Middle East at the time of the Suez Crisis.

FRANCIS B. LOOMIS - (1861–1948) U.S. newspaperman, diplomat, and public servant who served as foreign trade advisor to Standard Oil.

JOSEPH MCCARTHY - (1908–1957) U.S. politician who achieved notoriety as an obsessive investigator of suspected communists during the 1950s. His career was ultimately ruined after being formally censured by the U.S. Senate, and he died of alcoholism, aged only forty-eight.

FITZROY MACLEAN - (1911–1996) SAS (Special Air Service) officer, diplomatist, politician, adventurer, and writer, whose possible covert work as a British agent is to this day fiercely denied by those who knew him well. Not to be confused with **Billy McLean**.

HAROLD MACMILLAN - (1894–1986) British prime minister (1957–1963) whose warm friendship with **Eisenhower** helped him repair Anglo-American relations after the Suez Crisis. "Supermac," as he was known, was **Julian Amery**'s father-in-law.

TERENCE MACSWINEY - (1879–1920) Irish politician, writer, and lord mayor of Cork, who died on hunger strike while serving a two-year term for sedition in Brixton Prison, thus becoming an IRA martyr.

MAKARIOS III - (1913–1977) Archbishop and Primate of the Cypriot Orthodox Church and 1st/4th president of the Republic of Cyprus.

ADNAN MALKI - (1918–1955) Deputy Chief-of-Staff of the Syrian Army who led a coup in Syria in 1954 and was assassinated the following year.

FADLALLAH ABU MANSUR - (n.d.) Junior officer involved in the **Hannawi** coup in Syria.

MAO ZEDONG - (1893–1976) military and political leader of People's Republic of China from its establishment in 1949 until his death.

VICTOR MARCHETTI - (1930–) U.S. soldier who joined the CIA in 1955 and became a Soviet expert, rising to the position of chief Soviet analyst and assistant to **Richard Helms**, before resigning in 1969, after which he became one of the agency's fiercest and most outspoken critics.

CHARLES MARTEL - (688–741) Frankish ruler and brilliant general, known as "The Hammer," whose victory at the battle of Tours in 732 arguably prevented the spread of Islam north from Spain.

MAWLANA MAWDUDI - (1903–1979) influential Sunni Pakistani journalist, theologian, and political philosopher.

NEIL "BILLY" McLEAN - (1918–1986) British Army officer, intelligence officer, and politician who became a close personal and political friend of **Julian Amery,** fellow SOE officer in wartime Albania. His main interest was in international affairs; after the war he roamed the globe on many trips as a semiofficial or unofficial power broker, negotiator, and representative of British interests. Not to be confused with **Fitzroy Maclean**.

HENRY McMAHON - (1862–1949) diplomat who served as the high commissioner in Egypt from 1915 to 1917 and is best known for the McMahon-Hussein correspondence concerning the future political status of the Arab lands under the Ottoman Empire.

STEPHEN MEADE - (n.d.) CIA agent in Syria.

MEHMED II - (1432–1481) Sultan of the Ottoman Empire for a short time from 1444 to 1446, and later from 1451 to 1481.

MEHMED V RESHAT - (1844–1918) 35th Sultan of the Ottoman Empire from 1909 until his death shortly before the Ottoman downfall. Had no real power, but did declare jihad against the Allies in 1914.

MEHMED VI VAHDETTIN - (1861–1926) 36th and last Sultan of the Ottoman Empire, reigning from 1918 to 1922.

MENELIK II - (1844–1913) emperor of Ethiopia from 1889 until his death.

YAAKOV MERIDOR - (1913–1995) Israeli politician and head of the Irgun (1941–1943).

GERHARD MERTINS - (1919–1993) Former Luftwaffe Special Forces officer and sabotage expert who trained guerrilla squads for the Muslim Brotherhood in Egypt and later became one of the world's biggest arms dealers.

KLEMENS VON METTERNICH - (1773–1859) Austrian diplomat, politician, and statesman, Prince Metternich became a major figure of his era, associated primarily with the Congress of Vienna (1814–1815), which he chaired and which effectively redrew the European map after the defeat of **Napoleon Bonaparte**.

VASILI MITROKHIN - (1922–2004) Former KGB officer and archivist who, after the fall of the Soviet Union, brought to the West an extensive body of secret archival material covering clandestine Soviet activities dating back to before the Second World War.

YURI MODIN - (1922–) KGB case officer who controlled the "Cambridge Five," including **Kim Philby**, from 1944 to 1955.

BERNARD "MONTY" MONTGOMERY - (1887–1976) British army officer, brilliant but abrasive Anglo-Irish general who aggressively reversed German fortunes at the battle of El Alamein in 1942 and expelled the Axis forces from North Africa.

MOHAMMED MOSSADEQ - (1882–1967) Iranian statesman and prime minister who was forcibly removed from office in 1953 by a CIA-backed coup.

LORD MOYNE - See **Walter Guinness**.

OSKAR MUNZEL - (1899–1992) Former German Afrika Korps panzer general who served as **Wilhelm Fahrmbacher**'s deputy in postwar Egypt.

PERVEZ MUSHARRAF - (1943–) Pakistani general who was Chief of Army Staff 1998–2007 and 10th President of Pakistan 2001–2008.

NAPOLEON BONAPARTE - (1769–1821) Corsican artillery officer during the French

Revolution who rose to become one of history's greatest military commanders, ruling over most of Europe, and establishing the Napoleonic Code, which formed the foundation of the modern French state. Ironically, he is said to have spoken French with a heavy Italian accent and never learned French spelling.

NAPOLEON III - (1808–1873) colorful nephew of **Napoleon Bonaparte**, educated in Switzerland and Germany, Louis-Napoleon, as he was known, led until middle age the lascivious life of a footloose, unmarried political adventurer, living in many places (including the United States and Britain) until he was finally elected president of France in 1848 and became emperor four years later. After his humiliating defeat in the Franco-Prussian War of 1870, he was exiled to Britain where he died, in severly reduced circumstances.

NASRULLAH KHAN - (n.d.) Emir of Bukhara from 1826 to 1860, notorious for cruelly executing British envoys **Charles Stoddart** and **Arthur Conolly** in 1842.

GAMAL ABDEL NASSER - (1918–1970) 2nd president of Egypt (1956–1970) led the Free Officers' coup of 1952, which overthrew King **Farouk I** and ushered in a period of nationalization, industrialization, pan-Arab nationalism, and Cold War brinkmanship.

MOHAMED NEGUIB - (1901–1984) Egyptian army officer and leader of the Free Officers, became 1st President of Egypt (1953–1954) when the republic was constituted after the revolution of 1952 had deposed King **Farouk I**. **Nasser** ultimately forced Neguib's resignation and placed him under house arrest for eighteen years.

NERO - (37–68) given name Lucius, he ruled the Roman Empire from A.D. 54 until his suicide in the face of execution at the hands of a military coup. While there is clear evidence that he persecuted the Christians and had his own mother, **Agrippina**, executed, some modern historians consider depictions of him as a cruel, insane despot to be exaggerated.

WILLIAM NICHOLSON - (1845–1918) British Army officer who, before being appointed chief of the Imperial General Staff (1908) and promoted to field marshal (1911), served for a while as an intelligence officer, becoming director general of mobilization and military intelligence in 1901.

ARTHUR NICOLSON - (1849–1928) diplomat and politician, whose overseas postings included Tehran, Constantinople, and Tangiers. Father of the diplomat Harold Nicolson.

PAUL H. NITZE - (1907–2004) ranking Washington official who helped shape U.S. Cold War defense policy during several presidencies.

ANTHONY NUTTING - (1920–1999) diplomat, politician, and writer who resigned from the **Eden** government in 1956 over British policy on Suez, thereby terminating his political career.

EDWARD OCHAB - (1906–1989) Head of the Polish Communist Party.

MAURICE OLDFIELD - (1915–1981) British counterintelligence officer who had close ties with **James Jesus Angleton** and ultimately became "C" (head of the British Secret Intelligence Service [MI6]) in 1973.

OMAR THE GREAT - (581–644) second Sunni Caliph, regarded as one of the four *Rashidun* (righteously guided Caliphs).

AMICHAI PAGLIN - (1922–1978) Chief of operations of the Irgun who helped plan the bombing of the King David Hotel in 1946.

ANTHONY PALMER - (n.d.) British Special Operations Executive (SOE) officer who commanded Haganah special forces during the Second World War in Palestine.

REZA PARVARESH - (n.d.) Iranian SAVAK officer.

DANIEL PEARL - (1963–2002) American-Jewish journalist kidnapped, tortured, and beheaded by al-Qaeda terrorists in Pakistan.

ROBERT PEEL - Headed the Peel Commission of 1936–1937, formally known as the Palestine Royal Commission, formed to investigate the causes of unrest among Palestinian Arabs and Jews and to propose changes to the mandate for Palestine following the outbreak of the 1936–1939 Arab Revolt.

SHIMON PERES - (1923–) Polish-born Israeli leftist politician and former senior Haganah officer, who has served Israel as cabinet minister, prime minister, and president (with interruptions) for over forty years.

DORA PHILBY - (n.d.) Wife of **Harry St. John Philby**, after whom he named a species of owl.

H.A.R. "KIM" PHILBY - (1912–1988) British intelligence officer and NKVD/KGB mole, the Third Man of the Cambridge Five (Maclean, Burgess, Philby, Blunt, and Cairncross). Son of **Harry St. John Philby**.

HARRY ST. JOHN PHILBY - (1885–1960) Arabist, explorer, and British colonial office intelligence operative who became famous as an international writer and explorer and who acted as advisor to **Abdul Aziz ibn Saud**, playing a dominant role in the Saudi oil negotiations with the Americans that ultimately brought wealth to the kingdom … and to Philby. He converted to Islam in 1930 and became known as Sheikh Abdullah. Father of notorious KGB mole **Kim Philby**.

PHILIP OF DREUX - (1156–1217) warlike Bishop of Beauvais; cousin of **Philip Augustus** and second cousin of **Conrad of Montferrat**; lifelong enemy of **Richard the Lionheart(ed)**, and a leading French participant in the Third Crusade (1189–1192).

PHILIP AUGUSTUS - (1165–1223), also known as Philip II of France; co-led the Third Crusade (1189–1192) with **Richard the Lionheart(ed)** and the elderly Frederick (Friedrich I) Barbarossa.

FRANÇOIS GEORGES-PICOT - (1870–1951) Co-signatory of the Sykes-Picot Agreement of 1916 with **Sir Mark Sykes**, which provided for the annexation of Ottoman Arab lands and their incorporation into the British and French empires.

JOHN POLLOCK - (n.d.) Cairo Special Operations Executive (SOE) chief.

ABDUL KARIM QASSEM - (1914–1963) nationalist Iraqi Army officer who seized power in 1958 and ruled as prime minister until his assassination.

MUHAMMAD QUTB - (1919–) Islamic author, scholar, and teacher resident in Mecca and best known as the younger brother of the Egyptian Islamist thinker **Sayyid Qutb**, and a supporter and promoter of his older brother's ideas after his brother was executed by the **Nasser** government.

SAYYID QUTB - (1906–1966) Egyptian author, Islamist, and the leading intellectual of the Muslim Brotherhood in the 1950s and 1960s. Older brother of **Muhammad Qutb**.

BURHANUDDIN RABBANI - (1940–) Afghan Islamic theologian and mujahidin commander (former president of the Afghan Northern Alliance), now head of the Afghan Jamaat-e Islami party.

MUNIR RADFA - (1934–1998) Iraqi Air Force pilot who defected to Israel in his MIG-21 fighter in 1966.

AKHTAR ABDUR RAHMAN - (1928–1988) powerful Director General of the Pakistani ISI who established the ISI Afghan Bureau. Rahman was a Pashtun from Peshawar on the Afghan frontier and also a close friend of CIA director William Casey.

SAID RAMADAN - (?–1995) Influential son-in-law of **Hassan al-Banna**, who left Egypt to live in Saudi Arabia and Switzerland, where he founded an Islamic think tank in Geneva known as the Islamic Center.

RASHID-AD-DIN SINAN - (?–1194) one of the leaders of the Syrian wing of the Hashshashin sect, known as "The Old Man of the Mountain" (Sheikh-al-Jabal); arranged the assassination of **Conrad of Montferrat** in 1192, possibly at the behest of either **Saladin** or **Richard the Lionheart(ed)**.

DAVID RAZIEL - (1910–1941) head of the Irgun (1938–1941) and one of its first members.

ALEXANDER REYNOLDS - a (n.d.) British former resident of Egypt, tried in absentia by Nasser for espionage in 1957, together with **George Rose**, **John Stanley**, and **George Sweet**.

RICHARD THE LIONHEART(ED) - (1157–1199), also known as Coeur de Lion, Richard I of England; one of the leaders of the Third Crusade (1189–1192) took over virtually sole command after the departure of **Philip Augustus**, scoring major victories against Saladin. Essentially French, the third son of Henry II of England, Normandy, and Anjou, and Eleanor of Aquitaine, who had earlier launched the disastrous Second Crusade (1147–1149), he spent only six months of his entire reign in England, yet enjoyed immense popularity there.

ERNEST T. RICHMOND - (1874–1974) Rabidly anti-Semitic, pro-Mufti member of the British High Commissioner for Palestine's Secretariat, rumored to have been the homosexual partner of **Ronald Storrs** and sometimes described as the "godfather of Palestinian terrorism."

YAAKOV RIFTIN - (1907–1978) Israeli Marxist Knesset member who passed information to the Soviet Union.

FREDERICK SLEIGH ROBERTS - (1832–1914) distinguished Anglo-Irish general, he won the Victoria Cross as a young subaltern during the Indian rebellion of 1857 and later rose to command the Indian Army.

JOHN D. ROCKEFELLER - (1839–1937) U.S. industrialist and philanthropist; founded Standard Oil in 1870.

ERWIN ROMMEL - (1891–1944) German army officer, also known as the "Desert Fox," commanded the German Afrika Korps in the Western Desert and subsequently German forces in occupied France. Forced to commit suicide after the July 20, 1944, bombing attempt on Hitler's life.

ARCHIE ROOSEVELT - (1918–1990) Cousin of **Kermit Roosevelt**

CORNELIUS ROOSEVELT - (1915–1991) Cousin of **Kermit Roosevelt**

FRANKLIN D. ROOSEVELT - (1882–1945) 32nd president of the United States (1933–1945).

KERMIT ROOSEVELT - (1916–2000) CIA political intelligence officer and Middle East specialist; best known for his leading part in the overthrow of Mossadeq in Iran (1953). Grandson of **Theodore Roosevelt**.

SELWA ROOSEVELT - (n.d.) **Archie Roosevelt**'s Lebanese-born wife.

THEODORE ROOSEVELT - (1858–1919) 26th president of the United States (1901–1909). Grandfather of **Kermit Roosevelt**.

GEORGE ROSE - (n.d.) British former resident of Egypt, tried in absentia by Nasser for espionage in 1957, together with **Alexander Reynolds**, **John Stanley**, and **George Sweet**.

HARRY ROSITZKE - (1911–2002) Head of CIA secret operations inside the USSR.

FORSTER SADLER - (n.d.) British Army officer who in the nineteenth century was the first explorer to cross the central Arabian Peninsula.

NURI SAID - (1888–1958) Iraqi politician who served seven terms as prime minister. He attempted to flee the country after the republican revolution, disguised as a woman, but he was captured and killed.

SALADIN - (1138–1193) Kurdish Muslim Sultan of Egypt and Syria who opposed the Third Crusade (1189–1192).

LORD SALISBURY - See **Robert Gascoyne-Cecil**.

HERBERT SAMUEL - (1870–1963) British diplomat, politician, and Zionist, high commissioner for Palestine (1920–1925).

ILICH RAMÍREZ SÁNCHEZ - See **Carlos the Jackal.**

A. W. SANSOM - (n.d.) British army security intelligence officer and chief of field security in Cairo during the Second World War.

ABD AL-HAMID SARRAJ - (1925–) pro-**Nasser** Syrian Army officer, politician, and head of Syrian military intelligence.

SAUD IBN ABDUL AZIZ - (1902–1969) eldest surviving son of **Abdul Aziz ibn Saud**, ruled Saudi Arabia from 1953 until l964.

HJALMAR SCHACHT - (1877–1970) aristocratic German banker and economist; served briefly as a Nazi minister and president of the Reichsbank, although he never joined the Nazi Party. Both during and after the war, he was always closely associated with his son-in-law, **Otto Skorzeny**.

PATRICK SEALE - (n.d.) Sometimes controversial British journalist, author, and Middle East expert.

SELIM I - (1465–1520) also known as "the Grim" or "the Brave," Sultan of the Ottoman Empire from 1512 to 1520.

WILLIAM H. SHAKESPEAR - (1871–1915) Indian army officer, explorer, photographer, and diplomatist, the first Westerner to meet **Abdul Aziz ibn Saud**, with whom he formed an enduring friendship, dying with Ibn Saud's forces at the battle of Jarab.

MEMI DE SHALIT - (1921–2007) Washington-based Israeli liaison officer to the CIA and friend of **James Jesus Angleton**.

REUVEN SHILOAH - (1909–1959) Close friend of **Ben-Gurion** and mastermind of the

Israeli intelligence community, he was the first director of Mossad (1949–1952). He was born Zaslanski, which he later shortened to Zaslani and often substituted with the codename Shiloah.

ZEEV SHIND - (n.d.) Senior commander of Mossad LeAliyah Bet.

ADIB SHISHAKLI - (1909–1964) Syrian military leader and president 1953–1954, assassinated in Brazilian exile.

SALAH SHISHAKLI - (n.d.) Co-conspirator and brother of Syrian dictator **Adib Shishakli**.

PRITAM SINGH - (?–1942) Prominent anti-British Indian expatriate nationalist who led the Indian community in Indonesia and participated in both the Indian and the Indonesian struggle for independence. Killed in an air crash.

MOHAN SINGH - (1909–1989) Anti-British founder and commander, with Axis sanction and support, of the First Indian National Army (First INA), consisting largely of Sikh volunteers captured by the Japanese in Malaya. Later worked with Nazi sympathizer and fellow nationalist **Subhas Chandra Bose** to establish the Indian National Army (INA), which fought fiercely against Allied forces in Burma in 1944–1945.

WALTER BEDELL SMITH - (1895–1961) U.S. general and diplomat, "Beetle" Smith served successively as **Eisenhower**'s chief of staff, ambassador to the Soviet Union, and CIA director.

MOSHE SNEH - (1909–1972) Polish-born Israeli physician and Marxist politician who passed information to the Soviet Union.

ANTHONY SIMMONDS - (n.d.) Head of MI9 for Southern Europe who served with **Orde Wingate**.

GJERGJ KASTRIOTI SKANDERBEG - (1405–1466) the "Dragon of Albania," an Albanian national hero after whom a Waffen-SS division was named.

OTTO SKORZENY - (1908–1975) Viennese engineer and Waffen-SS Special Forces commander in the Second World War; later became an international arms dealer and facilitator for fugitive war criminals. Married to **Hjalmar Schacht**'s daughter.

SAINT SOPHRONIUS - (560–638) Orthodox Patriarch of Jerusalem.

JOSEF STALIN - (1878–1953) Communist Party leader and dictator of the Soviet Union from 1922 until his death. Ethnic Georgian known for his courageous, steadfast leadership of Russia in the Second World War, yet also for his unpredictability and dispassionate cruelty on a massive scale.

JOHN STANLEY - (n.d.) Cairo representative of the Prudential Assurance Company, tried in absentia by Nasser for espionage in 1957, together with **Alexander Reynolds**, **George Rose**, and **George Sweet**.

ABRAHAM STERN - (1907–1942) founder and leader of the Stern Gang, which he organized when the Irgun, of which he was a member, combined with the Haganah to fight the Nazis, a move he could not support.

CHARLES STODDART - (1806–1842) British Army officer, diplomat, and agent in Central Asia during the Great Game who, like **Arthur Conolly**, was captured and executed by **Nasrullah Khan**.

ROCKY STONE - (n.d.) CIA station chief in Damascus, publicly denounced as a spy.

RONALD STORRS - (1881–1955) British army officer and official in the British Foreign and Colonial Office who held several important posts, including governor of Jerusalem. Described by **T. E. Lawrence** as "the most brilliant Englishman in the Near East."

SULEYMAN I - (1494–1566) also known as "Suleiman the Magnificent"; 10th and longest-reigning Sultan of the Ottoman Empire (1520–1566). It was his armies that were checked at the Siege of Vienna in 1529, thus preventing the Ottomans from advancing into northern Europe.

GEORGE SWEET - (n.d.) a British Briton former resident of Egypt, tried in absentia by Nasser for espionage in 1957, together with **Alexander Reynolds**, **George Rose**, and **John Stanley**.

JAMES SWINBURN - (n.d.) Business manager of the Arab News Agency (ANA), which was an SIS (Secret Intelligence Service) cover operation, convicted of espionage and imprisoned by **Nasser**, together with **James Zarb,** in 1957.

MARK SYKES - (1879–1919) British military intelligence officer, traveler, and political advisor, whose name will always be associated with the Sykes-Picot Agreement of 1916, co-signed with French diplomat **François Georges-Picot**, which apportioned postwar spheres of interest in the Ottoman Empire to Britain, France, and Russia.

TAWFIK (TEVFIK) PASHA - (1852–1892) son of **Ismail Pasha**; Khedive of Egypt and Sudan from 1879.

GEORGE TENET - (1953–) CIA director for seven years (1997–2004), whose role in the WMD controversy and the lead-up to the 2003 U.S. invasion of Iraq remains unclear.

LORD TERRINGTON - See **C. M. "Monty" Woodhouse.**

LOWELL THOMAS - (1892–1981) U.S. writer, broadcaster, and traveler best known as the man who made **T. E Lawrence** famous as "Lawrence of Arabia."

JOSEF "SEPP" TIEFENBACHER - (n.d.) SS officer who was **Himmler**'s personal chief of security and served as personal assistant to **Wilhelm Voss** in Egypt.

JOSIP BROZ TITO - (1892–1980) Marxist ruler of federal Yugoslavia (1943–1980). Originally led the communist partisans in the Second World War, after which he resisted Stalin, maintained Yugoslav nonalignment, and kept the lid on ethnic tensions.

CHARLES TOWNSHEND - (1861–1924) British Army officer who led and lost the crack 6th Indian Division on the disastrous first British expedition against Baghdad during World War I, culminating in the siege of Kut. After his return to England, he died in poverty and disgrace.

HARRY TRUMAN - (1884–1972) 33rd President of the United States (1945–1953).

ELIZIER TSAFRIR - (n.d.) Chief of Mossad's Iran station.

MARK TWAIN - (1835–1910) Nom-de-plume of Samuel Langhorne Clemens, famous American author and humorist.

YAAKOV TZUR - (1937–) Israeli ambassador to France who negotiated with Iranian General **Bakhtiar** in 1957.

URBAN II - (1042–1099) born Otto de Lagery, a protegé of **Gregory VII**, he initiated the First Crusade (1095–1099) to wrest the Holy City from the occupying Seljuk Turks. Died two weeks after the fall of Jerusalem, but before hearing the news.

MANUCHER VAJDI - (n.d.) Iranian SAVAK officer.

VICTORIA - (1819–1901) ruled the British Empire as constitutional monarch for 63 years and became the most important symbolic figure of her time.

WILHELM VOSS - (n.d.) SS lieutenant general, economist, and close intimate of **Himmler** and **Heydrich**; administrative leader of the Nazi diaspora in **Farouk**'s and **Nasser**'s Egypt (1951–1956).

ARCHIBALD WAVELL - (1883–1950) British Army officer, commander of British forces in the Middle East (1939–1941).

ERWIN WEINMANN - (n.d.) SS officer and nonpracticing physician; Joachim Deumling's immediate superior at SS headquarters in Berlin. Supposedly killed in action near Prague in 1945, but actually fled to Egypt and became advisor to the police in Alexandria, where he became a permanent resident.

CHAIM WEIZMANN - (1874–1952) Zionist leader and 1st president of Israel from 1949.

SUMNER WELLES - (1892–1961) career diplomat and key official in the FDR administration. Forced out of public life in 1943 by a sex scandal. Said to have played a key role in conceiving the U.N.

KAISER WILHELM II - (1859–1941) grandson of Queen **Victoria** and last German emperor and king of Prussia, who ruled from 1888 until his abdication in 1918, when he was exiled to Doorn, Netherlands. Never formally relinquished his titles and always hoped to return to Germany.

WILLIAM OF TYRE - (1130–1185) Archbishop of Tyre and chronicler of the Crusades and medieval history.

ARNOLD WILSON - (1884–1940) Indian army officer, served in Persia; publicly known for his role as colonial administrator of Mesopotamia during and after the First World War, after which he joined the management of the Anglo-Persian Oil Company (APOC). Killed in action as an RAF air gunner over Dunkirk.

WOODROW WILSON - (1856–1924) 28th president of the United States (1913–1921).

REGINALD WINGATE - (1861–1953) British general and colonial administrator, right-wing, anti-Zionist, pro-Arab brother of **Orde Wingate**.

ORDE WINGATE - (1903–1944) Brilliant but eccentric British pro-Zionist commander of the Israeli Special Night Squads (SNS). He also distinguished himself as a special-forces commander in East Africa and Burma. Much younger brother of Sir **Reginald Wingate**. Killed in an aircraft crash aged only 41.

FRANK WISNER - (1909–1965) U.S. Navy officer, lawyer, and intelligence officer; served in the OSS during the Second World War, became CIA director of plans (head of Office of Policy Coordination) during the 1950s. A manic-depressive, he committed suicide three years after being forced to retire from the CIA.

POLLY WISNER - (n.d.) Wife of **Frank Wisner**.

JOSEPH WOLFF - (1795–1862) German Jewish-Christian missionary and orientalist; journeyed to Bukhara in 1843 in search of the British officers **Charles Stoddart** and **Arthur Conolly**, narrowly escaping death himself at the hands of **Nasrullah Khan**.

GARNET WOLSELEY - (1833–1913) British army officer who, toward the end of his distinguished military career, was given command of the British forces in Egypt and led them to defeat **Ahmad Arabi** at the battle of Tel el-Kebir in 1882.

C. M. "MONTY" WOODHOUSE - (1917–2001) aristocratic British artillery officer, brilliant scholar, diplomat, and politician who served with the Special Operations Executive

(SOE) during the Second World War in Greece. In 1998 he inherited the family title, becoming **Lord Terrington** for the last three years of his life.

PETER MAURICE WRIGHT - (1916–1995) British scientist and Security Service (MI5) counterintelligence officer, who befriended **James Jesus Angleton,** and who fiercely argued that former MI5 director general Sir Roger Hollis was a Soviet mole.

GEORGE KENNEDY "GK" YOUNG - (1911–1990) British journalist, diplomat, and merchant banker who studied at various foreign universities, served with the British Secret Intelligence Service (MI6) during the Second World War, and ultimately became deputy director general in 1959. After retirement in 1961, Young was involved in extreme right-wing British politics.

HUSNI ZAIM - (1897–1949) Commander-in-Chief of the Syrian Army who became military president of the country in 1949 after a bloodless coup. His moderate rule only lasted a few months, after which he was overthrown by **Adib Shishakli** and Sami Hinnawi and was executed.

JAMES ZARB - (n.d.) Maltese owner of a porcelain factory, convicted of espionage and imprisoned by **Nasser**, together with **James Swinburn**, in 1957.

MEHMED ZIA BEY - (n.d.) Ottoman army major in command of Ottoman forces in Mecca during the 1916 attack by Bedouin tribesmen.

MUHAMMAD ZIA-UL-HAQ - (1924–1988) Pakistani army officer, president, and military ruler of Pakistan (1977–1988); killed in a mysterious aircraft crash, along with the U.S. ambassador and several generals.

INDEX